Subversion

Subversion

From Covert Operations to Cyber Conflict

LENNART MASCHMEYER

Oxford University Press is a department of the University of Oxford. It furthers
the University's objective of excellence in research, scholarship, and education
by publishing worldwide. Oxford is a registered trade mark of Oxford University
Press in the UK and certain other countries.

Published in the United States of America by Oxford University Press
198 Madison Avenue, New York, NY 10016, United States of America.

© Oxford University Press 2024

All rights reserved. No part of this publication may be reproduced, stored in
a retrieval system, or transmitted, in any form or by any means, without the
prior permission in writing of Oxford University Press, or as expressly permitted
by law, by license, or under terms agreed with the appropriate reproduction
rights organization. Inquiries concerning reproduction outside the scope of the
above should be sent to the Rights Department, Oxford University Press, at the
address above.

You must not circulate this work in any other form
and you must impose this same condition on any acquirer.

Library of Congress Cataloging-in-Publication Data
Names: Maschmeyer, Lennart, 1984- author.
Title: Subversion : from covert operations to cyber conflict / Lennart Maschmeyer.
Other titles: From covert operations to cyber conflict
Description: New York, NY : Oxford University Press, [2024] |
Includes bibliographical references and index.
Identifiers: LCCN 2023040828 (print) | LCCN 2023040829 (ebook) |
ISBN 9780197745854 (hb) | ISBN 9780197745861 (pb) |
ISBN 9780197745885 (epub) | ISBN 9780197745892
Subjects: LCSH: Hybrid warfare—Russia (Federation) | Cyberspace operations
(Military science)—Russia (Federation) | Subversive activities—Russia
(Federation) | Disinformation—Russia (Federation) | Psychological
warfare—Russia (Federation) | Russia (Federation)—Foreign
relations—Ukraine. | Ukraine—Foreign relations—Russia (Federation)
Classification: LCC UA770 .M38845 2024 (print) | LCC UA770 (ebook) |
DDC 355.020947—dc23/eng/20231201
LC record available at https://lccn.loc.gov/2023040828
LC ebook record available at https://lccn.loc.gov/2023040829

DOI: 10.1093/oso/9780197745854.001.0001

Contents

List of Figures	vii
Preface	ix
Introduction	1
1. Subversion and Power	17
2. Information Technology and Subversion	42
3. Traditional Subversion: Crushing the Prague Spring, 1968–1973	60
4. Cyber-Enabled Subversion: Russia's "Hybrid War" against Ukraine, 2013–2022	117
5. Subversion in War: Russia's full-scale Invasion of Ukraine since February 2022	174
Conclusion: New Possibilities and New Perils	207
Notes	229
Bibliography	291
Index	329

List of Figures

I.1.	The subversive trilemma	13
3.1.	Ukrainian KGB records on activities in Czechoslovakia in 1968	83
4.1.	Comments by Sandworm included in a configuration file deployed to targeted systems in 2014	148
4.2.	Public trust in the government of Ukraine 2015–2020	171

Preface

I started this project expecting information technology to revolutionize conflict and competition. Yet the deeper I delved into this topic, the more I was taken aback by how little has changed—and, conversely, how much we do not know about the role and relevance of conflict short of war. Getting from this vague expectation about information technology and conflict to a dissertation on cyber conflict and escalation and finally to this book took seven years. If I have done my job right, the theory and evidence it presents will be interesting for both researchers and practitioners in intelligence, subversion, and cyber conflict. In an ideal world, it may even make some reconsider their assumptions—just as I have in the process of writing it and hope to continue to do as time passes.

More importantly, getting to this stage would not have been possible without the help and support of many. First, I am indebted to my PhD committee at the University of Toronto, composed of Ronald Deibert, Louis Pauly, and Jon Lindsay, for making that process both enjoyable and inspiring—and helping me through the weeds when I got lost. I am also thankful to the team at Citizen Lab for welcoming me into their midst and challenging my assumptions and ignorance concerning how cyber operations work. I am grateful to Nadiya Kostyuk for generously sharing some of her contacts in Ukraine when I was preparing the field study. In Ukraine, I am indebted to the people who agreed to talk to me and provided me with invaluable insights into not only the facts (or lack thereof) concerning Russian-sponsored cyber attacks but also the perspective and perception on the ground. In conducting these interviews, I would not have made it far without my excellent translator, Olga Paschuk. For gathering and translating local media reporting, government statements, social media posts, and other Ukrainian or Russian language sources, I am indebted to the work of Lesia Bidochko, Oksana Grechko, Daria Goriacheva, Roman Kolodii, and Mariya Green.

In turning these initially disjointed ideas and extensive evidence into a reasonably coherent argument, the constructive feedback from the following people was essential as well: Lucan Way, Jesse Driscoll, Andreas Wenger, Myriam Dunn-Cavelty, Max Smeets, Miguel Gomez, Alexander

Bollfrass, Mauro Gilli, Enzo Nussio, Irene Poetranto, Gabrielle Lim, Adam Casey, Maika Sondarjee, and Michael Poznansky, as well as the editors and anonymous reviewers at *International Security*, the *European Journal of International Relations*, and the *Journal of Strategic Studies* (where I published related articles). David McBride at Oxford University Press provided critical input throughout the process of turning a meandering thesis into a book.

Last but not least, I am indebted to my parents, Ulrike and Andreas, who made it possible for me to get this far in my studies, for their support, together with my sister, Lisa, despite me being far away for so long. Finally, and most importantly, I could not have done this without the love and support of my incredible wife, Marjan, who endured me and helped me hold it together while passing through all the different valleys and peaks this project involved, and our beautiful daughter, Lillian, who teaches me every day again what life is about.

Introduction

In 2014, Russia launched a "hybrid war" against Ukraine that, according to some, ushered in a revolution in conflict. The term is notoriously vague, referring to all measures short of war that states use to attain strategic aims.[1] States, of course, have long used measures in the "gray zone" between war and peace. Yet they did not always have the Internet. By leveraging cyber operations,[2] hybrid war theorists argue, states can achieve "growing intensity"[3] in such conflict, which "dramatically changes the picture" because it enables outcomes that were previously unattainable.[4] Victory thus becomes possible "without the need to engage with an adversary's forces."[5] Russia's aggression against Ukraine has remained the paradigmatic case of hybrid war, and cyber operations have been an essential element.[6] As Andy Greenberg put it, in 2014 Russia launched "a digital blitzkrieg that has pummeled Ukraine . . . a sustained cyberassault unlike any the world has ever seen."[7] And yet, following eight years of intense efforts to subdue Ukraine short of war, in 2022 Russia invaded in full force. This outcome is the opposite of what one would expect if hybrid war was as effective as its proponents assert.

This example is emblematic of a larger issue: a recurring mismatch between expectations and evidence regarding the strategic value of conflict short of war. International relations traditionally studies "the causes of war and the conditions of peace,"[8] yet states have long used means in the gray zone between the two. The concept of hybrid war has many flaws, foremost its lack of clarity and historical perspective.[9] It is useful, however, because the debate surrounding it casts a light on this notoriously understudied area of security competition and the question of how new technologies—and specifically cyber operations—enhance it. Moreover, while it never made much headway in the academic literature, the concept has been highly influential on policy, strategy, and public perception.[10]

Apart from covert warfare, the types of activities hybrid war theorists are concerned about, namely infiltration, sabotage, and influence operations, share a key characteristic: they are means of subversion.[11] It is a shadowy, often evoked and yet notoriously understudied instrument of power.

Drawing on intelligence studies, I define it by its indirect and secret mechanism of exploitation and manipulation that allows projecting power and shifting its balance short of war. This mechanism distinguishes subversion from warfare and diplomacy, the classic instruments of power in international relations. In war, states use force to compel an enemy to one's will. Diplomacy in turn relies on persuasion, threats, and bargaining to get an adversary to do what one wants. These activities happen on the front stage of world politics. Subversion, on the other hand, is a menace that spreads in the shadows, belonging to the world of covert operations. Like a virus infecting the cells of its host, it secretly infiltrates an adversary's society and institutions, manipulating, weakening, and disintegrating them from within. If successful, it subdues an adversary before the latter even realizes it is under threat.

Accordingly, expectations concerning its strategic promise have been vast. In 1972, Lawrence Beilenson warned of the Soviet Union relying on "subversion rather than war as the chief tool to bring about the world-wide triumph of an ideology."[12] Predicting it had "the capability of capturing sufficient additional governments to tip the balance of power against the United States," Beilenson feared "the extension of Communism all over the world."[13] The parallels to current fears of hybrid war are clear. There are also striking overlaps with a forming consensus in cybersecurity scholarship, however. By leveraging the speed, anonymity, and scale of today's ubiquitous information communications technologies (ICTs), a prominent trio of scholars argues, state-sponsored cyber operations can "advance strategic-level cumulative effects without direct exchange, without coercive shaping of behavior, and without war."[14] The result, Ben Buchanan predicts, is "a new form of statecraft, more subtle than policymakers imagined, yet with impacts that are world-changing."[15] To be clear, these theorists do not suggest the end of conventional war is nigh, as some hybrid war proponents have. If they are right, the implication would nonetheless be a revolution in international security because states could achieve outcomes short of war that were previously out of reach.

This congruence in expectations between historic scholars of subversion and current literature in cybersecurity is no coincidence. Rather, I argue, cyber operations are new tools of subversion, distinguished by their reliance on exploitation and manipulation. As such, however, they share not only subversion's promise but also its pitfalls. Contrary to the vast strategic potential Beilenson alluded to, subversion's track record throughout the Cold

War has been less than stellar. Classified records from the KGB stolen by its former archivist Vasili Mitrokhin, who defected to the United Kingdom in 1992, for example, revealed a string of sometimes embarrassing failures.[16] Indeed, subversion scholar Paul Blackstock noted as early as 1964 that its effectiveness "as a means of control or conquest has been overrated."[17] Not only the Ukraine example hints at a similar situation concerning cyber operations. Tangible evidence of their strategic value remains remarkably thin. Even Ben Buchanan, after examining the strategic value of two spectacular cyber operations that sabotaged Ukraine's power grid, ultimately concludes that "it remained unclear how short blackouts in parts of Ukraine far from the front lines served Russian interests."[18] Considering that cybersecurity scholars increasingly agree that cyber operations are new incarnations of covert operations, disagreeing only whether new technologies enhance their strategic value, it is striking that scholarship has not yet systematically explored what types of covert operations cyber operations can reproduce, and how the availability of ICTs alters their strategic role and value.[19] This book does so, developing new theory and contributing rich new empirical evidence in the process. To explain why subversion and cyber operations tend to fall short, I first establish what subversion is and how it works, and then examine how information technology changes it.

In a nutshell, I argue that in theory, subversion is a perfect weapon. It enables a cheap, easy, and effective means of interference in adversary affairs that can produce similar outcomes to war at lower costs and risks. In practice, however, it rarely delivers. In most circumstances, subversion is too slow, too weak, or too volatile to achieve, or measurably contribute toward the attainment of, strategic goals. Ironically, I show that subversion falls short because the very mechanism that enables its promise often prevents its fulfillment.

Subversion holds its promise because the mechanisms of exploitation and manipulation it relies upon are both indirect and secret. It produces outcomes by secretly exploiting flaws in adversary systems and their constituent parts to manipulate the latter to behave in ways neither their designers nor participants expected, producing effects that contribute to the subverter's aims to the detriment of the adversary. Traditional subversion targets social systems, namely groups, organizations, and institutions, as well as entire societies and political systems. Cyber operations, on the other hand, target computer systems embedded in modern societies, organizations, and institutions. The systems differ, but as I explain in more detail below, cyber operations also rely on secret exploitation and manipulation to make systems do things they are not supposed to. They subvert technology and the way it is used. Importantly, the secret and indirect nature of subversion promises both lower risks and costs compared to overt means of intervention. In covert warfare, secrecy lowers escalation risks by avoiding domestic and international pressures to retaliate.[20] Hiding one's identity also decreases reputational costs from violating the nonintervention principle.[21] On top of these known advantages, I argue that subversion's indirect reliance on adversary systems adds a third advantage: it lowers resource costs.

Yet secrecy and indirect action are not given; they must be acquired through significant efforts. These efforts, I show, produce a set of trade-offs that pose a trilemma. To produce strategic value, a subversive operation must manipulate a targeted system to produce desired effects of sufficient intensity to make a mark within a given timeframe. In other words, it requires sufficient speed, intensity, and control over effects. Yet secret exploitation and manipulation pose a distinct set of challenges that constrain precisely these three variables. Moreover, efforts to improve one of them tend to produce corresponding losses for the remaining ones. The faster one proceeds, for example, the lower the intensity of effects tends to be, and the higher the risk of control loss—and vice versa. These trade-offs mean subversive actors can maximize at most two of these variables, at the sacrifice of the remaining one. Fast *and* intense operations, for instance, have doubly increased risks of control loss compared to operations that prioritize either speed or intensity. Subversive actors thus face a trilemma. Because of its trade-offs, in most circumstances, subversion is either too slow, too weak, or too volatile to produce strategic value.

I test this theory through an in-depth comparison of two important cases: the Soviet Union's campaign to crush the Prague Spring in Czechoslovakia from 1968 to 1973 and Russia's campaign to neutralize Ukraine's Euromaidan movement and reverse its pro-Western foreign policy realignment from 2013 to 2018. Furthermore, in a separate chapter, I examine Russia's use of subversion to complement its 2022 invasion of Ukraine. These cases are similar in most aspects but differ in at least one, namely the subversion "technology" involved. In Czechoslovakia, Moscow experimented with the use of "illegal" undercover agents within the Soviet Union, while Ukraine has been Russia's testing ground for disruptive cyber operations. The similarities between these cases allow me to isolate how new technology has altered the operational mechanisms and strategic value of traditional subversion vis-à-vis cyber-enabled subversion. This analysis contributes extensive original data gathered through interviews with cybersecurity experts, policymakers, and (former) intelligence operatives; new archival sources; and recently declassified documents from the former Ukrainian KGB. It builds further on open-source intelligence and forensic reporting, leaked Kremlin documents and emails, leaked emails from separatist leaders, and local media reporting. In both conflicts, I offer the first systematic analysis of the role of subversion.

In developing this argument, this book makes four main contributions. First, it develops a general theory of subversion as an instrument of power. This is important since states regularly use subversion, yet how it matters in world politics remains ill-understood. In the absence of systematic theory and evidence, fear and speculation about possible threats tend to pervade both scholarship and policy. The theory this book develops explains both why subversion holds this promise and why not everything that is possible is also feasible. In clarifying the strategic role and value of subversion, it makes an important contribution to the fields of political science and intelligence studies that is also directly relevant for policymakers aiming to counter subversive threats.

Second, it systematically examines how technological change changes subversion—and, by extension, conflict short of war. Political science, and social science in general, tends to conceptualize technologies as an independent factor determining strategic dynamics and political outcomes.[22] Yet, as Stephen Biddle has shown concerning conventional conflict, *how* actors deploy forces at the operational level is a far more important predictor of victory than the technology they use.[23] I argue that the same applies to subversion and its operational mechanisms. By isolating these mechanisms, identifying both the challenges and opportunities they pose for power projection and then tracing how information technologies alter the latter, this book makes a key contribution to scholarship in political science, intelligence studies, and cybersecurity.

Third, based on this examination, it provides a sound theoretical and empirical foundation for systematic and accurate assessments of the strategic potential of subversion, both in scholarship and in strategy. Prevailing expectations assess cyber threats based more on the possibilities they offer in theory rather than what is feasible in practice. Consequently, they overestimate their strategic potential. Getting this right is important not just to fill gaps in the literature, but because policy that builds on these expectations risks misallocating resources. After a decade of efforts to counter hybrid war, for example, European NATO members have recently found themselves short of the tanks needed to fight an actual war.[24] Meanwhile, the US Department of Defense has now developed an entire strategic framework to fend off the perceived threat of cyber operations and campaigns presumed to be capable of shifting the balance of power short of war.[25] Through "persistent engagement"—the name of this strategy—it strives to prevent adversaries from shifting the balance of power through cyber campaigns pursuing cumulative effects.[26] This goal is clearly aligned with the type of threat posed by subversion. Importantly, however, the strategic value of cumulative effects that cyber campaigns can achieve is far from proven—and, as this book will show, likely pales in comparison to the threat of traditional subversion. Treating cyber operations as a novel, primarily technological phenomenon not only risks missing their constraints but also carries an additional risk: missing historical lessons and counterstrategies against them.

Finally, the book contributes rich empirical evidence on two important cases. Owing to the secrecy pursued by its sponsors, empirical data—and thus case research—on covert operations and cyber operations remains scarce. This situation is particularly dire in the field of cybersecurity, where the great majority of writing remains theoretical and hypothetical, with only a fraction of scholarship conducting empirical work.[27] Rather, most data comes from public reports by the private sector—which suffers from a set of known biases.[28] Both cases involve innovation and experimentation in the use of subversive means in an active conflict, and in the Ukrainian case the evolution of subversion from an independent instrument to a complement to force. The case studies will thus be of interest not only to intelligence and cybersecurity scholars but also to security scholars at large. The findings will also be directly relevant for policymakers and defense planners aiming to develop counterstrategies.

The Topic

This book aims to answer two main questions. First, how does subversion work and what is its strategic value? Strategic value in this context is defined as the capacity to measurably contribute toward the attainment of political goals and/or shifts in the balance of power, including both the impact of individual operations and the cumulative impacts of multiple operations and campaigns over time.[29] Second, how does technological change alter the quality of subversion?

International relations theory falls short of capturing the mechanism subversion relies upon. As discussed, its reliance on exploitation and manipulation distinguishes subversion from force and warfare, the key instruments of power in classical international relations theory. More recent scholarship has identified several other forms of power.[30] Yet, as I have shown elsewhere, none of these capture the indirect way subversion works to undermine and turn adversary systems against the adversary itself.[31] Meanwhile, after long neglect, recently there has been a surge of work on specific subversive covert operations: regime change,[32] election interference,[33] and external support of insurgents.[34] While illuminating these specific activities, however, a general theory of subversion is still lacking. William Wohlforth has pushed in the latter direction, yet this "blunt theory" of subversion in great power competition overshoots the target in the other direction.[35] It defines the goals and location of subversion, namely to weaken an adversary and influence policy internally. It does not specify the mechanisms involved, however, or the strategic scope of effects.

Intelligence scholarship does so—yet fails to integrate its insights into a theory of subversion as an instrument of power. Rather, this literature is mostly historic and narrative. Consequently, the building blocks of a theory are scattered across it like erratic glacial rocks on the northern plains. Cold War scholarship defined subversion mainly based on its goal(s). Frank Kitson, for example, conceives of subversion as "all measures short of the use of armed force taken by one section of the people of a country to overthrow those governing the country at the time."[36] This concept is as vague as hybrid war—it does not specify the instruments used and seemingly excludes any measures aimed at less than overthrow. Among Cold War scholars, Paul W. Blackstock formed an exception, however. He provided both the first and clearest foundation for a general theory by identifying subversion's distinct mechanism of action, which works via the "exploitation not only of political tensions but also of psychological and sociological vulnerabilities."[37]

Homing in on this mechanism in turn helps clarify subversion's strategic relevance, namely as a tool in nonmilitary covert operations. These are intelligence operations involving active interference in adversary affairs. Intelligence in general concerns "secret state activity to understand or influence foreign entities."[38] There are two modes of secrecy in such operations: covert and clandestine. Covertness refers to a mode of operation that aims to obscure the identity of its sponsor.[39] It is distinguished from a clandestine mode of operation, which aims to hide the activity taking place itself.[40] Intelligence operations, meanwhile, encompass both passive information gathering and active influence on an adversary. The former activity is called espionage,[41] while covert operations refer to the latter.[42] They involve a wide range of means to achieve a similarly broad set of ends. Loch K. Johnson has distinguished thirty-eight distinct types of covert operations, placed on an escalation ladder with increasing intensity. It ranges from relatively harmless activity such as low-level funding of political groups, to high-risk options such as embassy break-ins, to extreme options culminating in major secret wars and the use of chemical agents.[43]

A range of nonmilitary options count among these activities, yet not all of these are subversive. Since I argue its distinguishing feature is exploitation and manipulation, operations that primarily rely on coercion and force do not fall within this scope. While there are some borderline cases, as the next chapter will illuminate, the following types of operations Johnson identifies can be clearly excluded: pinpointed retaliation against noncombatants, use of chemical and biological agents, embassy break-ins, training of military forces, hostage taking, hostage rescue attempts, theft of sophisticated weapons or materiel, and all types of arms supplies.[44] Subversive operations as I define them include infiltration, exploitation, and manipulation of groups, institutions, and societies in the pursuit of three distinct goals: first, to manipulate policy and public opinion; second, to sabotage infrastructure, institutions, and other facilities; and third, to effect regime change from within.

Strategically, subversion fulfills a dual role. Cold War scholarship suggests both an independent role as an alternative to force and a complement to the latter. Blackstock, for example, notes that covert operations are independent tools of statecraft but can also support diplomacy and complement the use of force during war.[45] The conditions under which it fulfills what role remain unclear, however. Moreover, Beilenson argued that the Soviet revolutionary founding father Vladimir Lenin had adapted subversion to an independent instrument of power with unprecedented strategic potential compared to "traditional subversion."[46] The expectation that subversion offers significant strategic value, capable of altering the balance of power at less cost and risk than war, pervades Cold War scholarship.[47] In sum, its strategic promise is significant.

Current expectations around cyber operations as instruments of power short of war not only echo these historic perceptions but also posit that new technologies further expand this promise. Specifically, current expectations hold that cyber operations offer superior scale of effects and ease of anonymity over traditional (subversive) covert operations. ICTs form globally interconnected networks with billions of users; hence, operations that exploit them offer potentially global reach. Meanwhile, a design emphasis of convenience over security facilitates anonymity.[48] Accordingly, Michael Warner speculates, information technology may have "fixed covert action's problem of scale."[49] Similarly, Richard Harknett and Max Smeets propose that "an expansion in scope of [covert] operations has been accompanied by an expansion in scale and, when taken together, is resulting in a difference in kind and not merely degree."[50] Consequently, like Beilenson fifty years earlier, current scholarship sees an expansion in the strategic value of covert operations. While Beilenson saw a refinement in Soviet strategy enabling the same means to achieve greater ends, these current expectations go a step further, positing that new means (cyber operations) make possible new ends. This is a plausible argument, yet there is a puzzling absence of supporting evidence as the next section shows.

The Puzzle

Subversion scholarship involves a central puzzle that is increasingly evident in current cybersecurity debates as well. Scholars and policymakers alike have focused primarily on subversion's strategic promise and resulting threats. Yet in practice subversion has regularly fallen short, sometimes spectacularly so. A joint operation by the CIA and MI6 known under the codename "BGFIEND" between 1949 and 1953 offers a case in point. BGFIEND attempted to topple the Communist regime of Albania by mobilizing opposition groups and infiltrating commando units.[51] Yet, as intelligence scholar James Callanan notes, "a tendency of the Western intelligence services [namely the CIA and MI6] to overestimate their own abilities" combined with basic security lapses allowed the Communist regime to discover the operation, leading to failure and the capture and execution of most individuals involved.[52] As mentioned at the very start of this book, such overestimation has been a pervasive tendency throughout the Cold War. In short, there is a persistent mismatch between expectations and evidence regarding the efficacy of subversion. This situation presents a puzzle: why does subversion tend to fall short of its promise?

The situation around cyber operations is similar. To be sure, current arguments about why the properties of information technology expand the effectiveness of covert operations are clearly plausible. However, there is little empirical evidence proving this significant, potentially revolutionary impact in practice. To be sure, there is ample evidence of large-scale cyber espionage operations—which also constitute the most plausible case of cyber operations providing significant strategic value that this strand of theorizing offers.[53] The amount of information and data that cyber operations can exfiltrate unquestionably dwarfs anything traditional espionage could achieve. Of course, the challenges of analyzing these massive troughs of data and turning them into tangible outcomes likely limit the actual value compared to the potential value.[54] Nonetheless, the argument that cyber operations expand the strategic value of espionage operations remains plausible. Yet espionage does not actively "shape" adversary affairs as Ben Buchanan emphasizes cyber operations do.[55] Active interference in adversary affairs requires active effects, namely manipulating systems to cause disruption and confusion, possibly even damage. And yet, few studies have systematically examined the strategic value of cyber operations of this kind—and those that do indicate significant limitations.

The Stuxnet operation sabotaging Iran's nuclear program provides a key example. It marked the first time a cyber operation caused physical damage—some have thus labeled it the first "cyber weapon."[56] Richard Langner suggested this was a "cyber missile" that had "likely already wrecked" a nuclear power plant in Iran.[57] In practice, however, Stuxnet caused neither a nuclear meltdown nor deaths, but rather carefully calibrated sabotage. It degraded and ultimately damaged the spinning mechanisms of centrifuges at the Natanz nuclear enrichment plant through carefully calibrated speed changes.[58] In fact, the key motivation behind Stuxnet turned out to be avoiding military escalation.[59] Both the US and Israel, which were almost certainly behind the attack, shared the objective of preventing Iran from attaining nuclear capabilities.[60] Undoubtedly, Stuxnet was a remarkable tactical success in producing physical effects through cyber means. Its strategic value was at best limited, however, temporarily delaying rather than derailing Iran's nuclear program.[61] Moreover, implementing the operation likely cost more than the damage it produced.[62]

The contrast between the hyperbolic language used to describe Stuxnet and its relatively modest impact is emblematic of the mismatch between expectations and evidence on the strategic relevance of cyber conflict at large. It applies not only to long-held fears of cyber war (doomsday) scenarios that Stuxnet seemed to confirm at the time.[63] On the contrary, as mentioned at the very start, the Russo-Ukrainian conflict reveals that the same mismatch persists concerning the strategic value of cyber operations short of war. This mismatch presents a puzzle: given their significant strategic promise, why do subversion and cyber operations continue to fall short in practice?

The Argument

I argue that the same mechanism that enables the strategic promise of subversion also limits its strategic value—and cyber operations share these limitations. Subversion's reliance on exploitation and manipulation promises a way to gain strategic advantages at lower costs and risks than war. It holds this promise because it is indirect and secret. These two characteristics are not given, however. Rather, they require significant efforts to establish and maintain. These efforts, I show, produce a trilemma that renders subversion too slow, too weak, or too volatile to produce strategic value in most circumstances—and the same applies to cyber operations. While the latter offer some advantages in delivering large-scale effects, they are relatively more constrained in delivering a more intense scope of effects against individual targets. Consequently, technological change does not fundamentally change the quality of subversion.

Subversion is indirect because it produces effects through adversary systems and secret because it hides the exploitation and manipulation involved from victims. Traditional subversion uses spies to target social systems. Humans are fallible; thus, any system designed by humans inevitably contains flaws. Subversive actors exploit these flaws to produce outcomes neither intended nor foreseen by the designers and participants of the system. The next chapter provides a detailed typology of the systems targeted, vulnerabilities exploited, and mechanisms used. Cyber operations target different types of systems, namely networked computer systems. They exploit not only the social vulnerabilities traditional subversion goes after but also flaws in the technology itself—this mechanism is known as hacking.[64] The main means used are social engineering techniques and computer viruses. Despite these differences, the mechanisms of exploitation and manipulation involved follow the same functional principle and pursue the same goal as in traditional subversion: making systems do things they are not supposed to.[65] The second chapter explores these mechanisms and parallels in detail.

As already discussed, its indirect and secret nature endows subversion with significant strategic promise as a cheap, easy, and yet effective instrument of power. Rather than deploying one's own material capabilities, through exploitation and manipulation it secretly turns adversary systems into instruments of one's own power, and therefore sources of harm for the adversary.[66] However, I show that the mechanisms that make this promise possible involve significant challenges. Foremost, secrecy is not only a feature but also a requirement since victims have multiple ways to neutralize subversion once they discover it. Consequently, actors must strive to stay hidden. Similarly, subversion's indirect nature reflects its dependence on adversary systems. Exploiting and manipulating adversary systems while staying secret is difficult by itself. Doing so *and* producing strategically significant effects is exceptionally challenging. Meeting these challenges requires significant efforts.

Crucially, these efforts constrain speed, intensity, and control in subversion. Identifying vulnerabilities and developing means of exploitation and then manipulation all require reconnaissance and learning, which takes time. Dependence on adversary systems, meanwhile, constrains intensity because what effects are possible depends on target system properties, and manipulating the latter without detection requires one to proceed carefully. Moreover, the more capable systems are, the more well protected they tend to be. Finally, control is always temporary and incomplete. Discovery is a constant risk, and systems may behave differently than expected when manipulated.

These challenges not only pose individual constraints but also interact in a way that confronts subversive actors with a set of trade-offs that produce a trilemma—and cyber operations face the same. Holding all else equal, as Figure I.1 illustrates, the more one improves one of these variables, the more one tends to lose out across the remaining ones. For example, the faster one proceeds, the less intense the effects one can produce tend to be, and the higher the risk of being discovered or producing unexpected effects becomes. Conversely, increasing intensity tends to require more time and yet carries greater risk of control loss because it usually means infiltrating

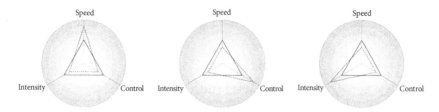

Figure I.1 The subversive trilemma.
From Lennart Maschmeyer, "The Subversive Trilemma: Why Cyber Operations Fall Short of Expectations," *International Security* 46, no. 2 (October 2021): 65, doi:10.1162/isec_a_00418.

more deeply into more sensitive systems. Finally, maximizing control tends to slow speed and lowers the intensity of effects because of the extra care one has to take. Furthermore, increasing effectiveness across two variables tends to "doubly" decrease the effectiveness of the remaining variable. For example, moving fast while also pursuing very intense effects makes the risks of discovery, failure to produce effects, or unintended effects even more likely. Accordingly, aiming to maximize two of these variables at once will tend to produce "double" the losses on the remaining one. Maximizing both speed and intensity, for example, will doubly increase the risk of control loss. Consequently, actors can have at best two out of these three variables. This trilemma—whose causes and permutations I discuss in much more detail in the first chapter—significantly limits the strategic value subversion can achieve in practice.

Since cyber operations involve new technology, it is plausible they may overcome the trilemma. Yet that is not the case. In fact, as I show in the second chapter, the same characteristics of ICTs that make it possible to achieve large-scale, global effects further exacerbate the trilemma. Greater scalability also brings greater risks of control loss. Ironically, considering that the very word "cyber" means "control,"[67] it is the key characteristic that cyber operations lack. Finally, contrary to expectations that cyber operations expand the scope of covert operations, I argue that they further narrow it. They can only produce effects target systems are capable of, while traditional subversion can rely on the action potential of human agents to influence people, manipulate physical machinery, and cause damage. Consequently, I show, cyber operations not only produce a narrower range of effects but also are less effective at producing more intense effects within this narrower strategic bracket. Therefore, cyber operations struggle to produce similar strategic value to traditional subversion, both individually and cumulatively.

The use of new technology thus does not fundamentally alter the quality of subversion.

Case Studies

To test this theory, I compare two important cases: the Soviet campaign to crush the Prague Spring from 1968 to 1973 and the Russian campaign to crush the Euromaidan in Ukraine from 2013 to 2018, as well as preliminary analysis of the use of subversion in Russia's full-scale invasion since 2022. These case studies constitute the first systematic examinations of subversion in these conflicts and its strategic role alongside military force. Overall, I examine over thirty individual subversive operations—in the Ukrainian case, both traditional and cyber enabled. This internal variation allows me to compare the mechanisms and strategic value of subversion not only across these two cases but also within them.

To build these case studies, I leverage rich original data. In 2018, I traveled to Ukraine to conduct field interviews with leading cybersecurity experts, (former) intelligence officers, and government officials. Meanwhile, archival data from five sources helped me piece together the details of subversive operations whose sponsors took significant efforts to hide: 1,135 recently declassified field reports by the former Ukrainian KGB,[68] the archive of the German Stasi Records Agency (known in German as the "Der Bundesbeauftragte für die Unterlagen des Staatssicherheitsdienstes der ehemaligen Deutschen Demokratischen Republik," abbreviated as BStU),[69] dissertations by Eastern German intelligence officers, the archive of the West German intelligence service (Bundesnachrichtendienst, BND), the CIA's Freedom of Information Act Electronic Reading Room archive, and the US National Security Archive. Furthermore, I gathered extensive open-source intelligence from reporting by private threat intelligence vendors and independent researchers. In addition, I analyzed caches of leaked emails by the separatist leader Kirill Frolov and his Kremlin handler Vladislav Surkov. Finally, I gathered local media reporting and social media posts.

I selected cases based on a "most similar" design,[70] meaning they are similar across key variables except one: the technology involved. Consequently, I can isolate and examine how the availability of new technology shapes the quality of subversion. The most important similarity concerns the strategic goals and the novelty of the means of subversion used. In both cases, the subverting actor feared "losing" the target country from its sphere of influence and deployed an innovative new instrument of subversion to prevent this outcome. In Czechoslovakia, the Soviet Union aimed to stop and roll back a domestic and foreign policy shift toward the West started by its new leader Dubcek. To achieve this, the KGB pursued a broad campaign to infiltrate, influence, and weaken Czechoslovakian society and government with an innovative new instrument: "illegal" agents operating undercover. Similarly, in Ukraine, Russia aimed to neutralize a foreign policy realignment toward the West started in earnest in 2013. In response, Russia commenced a campaign to infiltrate, influence, and weaken Ukrainian society and government. Again, an innovative new instrument of subversion assumed center stage: cyber operations. Accordingly, just as Czechoslovakia was perceived as a "testing ground" for the use of subversion,[71] many now see Ukraine as a "test lab" for cyber conflict.[72] These cases not only are similar but also offer conditions under which subversion would be most likely to provide strategic value, namely a powerful actor targeting far less powerful victims in close proximity not only geographically but also culturally and ethnically, and doing so over an extended amount of time. Finally, both cases involve armed force, allowing a close examination of the strategic role of subversion alongside the former.

Findings strongly support the theory, illustrating the persistently constraining role of the trilemma limiting the strategic value of subversion. The theory better explains observable outcomes and the forensic evidence that is available than existing or potential alternate explanations, which I consider and evaluate in detail throughout the case studies. The result is a string of failures, sometimes spectacular, other times downright embarrassing. In Czechoslovakia, for example, the KGB abandoned a devilish false-flag operation to assassinate the spouses of Russians because it was discovered. Meanwhile, its illegals who were tasked with kidnapping civil society leaders failed because they did not speak their language. Similarly, in Ukraine the "world's most dangerous hacking group"[73] failed to blow up a power substation because they sent their commands to the wrong address—despite two and a half years of preparation. At times, subversive operations end just like in spy movies: such as a high-level Ukrainian intelligencer officer escaping the country just after landing his biggest coup, only to get caught months later at the Serbian border in a BMW loaded with cash and precious gems. However, a few exceptional subversive successes also underline its strategic potential—foremost the taking of Crimea in 2014—and the importance of enabling conditions that make it attainable despite the trilemma. Subversion is thus not universally doomed to failure, and identifying the circumstances under which it can succeed is key.

Structure of the Book

Chapter 1 establishes what subversion is, how it works, and its strategic role and value. It starts by identifying the defining characteristics of subversion as an instrument of power, laying out its strategic heritage, mechanism of power, the associated trilemma, and the resulting strategic value. Chapter 2 then examines how the availability of information technology changes this quality. After establishing the subversive nature of cyber operations—long common wisdom among technical experts—I examine how the use of information technology may or may not alleviate the operational trilemma. This discussion reveals that rather than a difference in kind, technological change only brings about differences in degree in the quality of subversion. Traditional subversion is better at more intense effects, while cyber operations have an edge in large-scale effects—yet with increasing risk of control loss. Based on this discussion, I conclude that cyber operations likely provide relatively less strategic value than traditional counterparts. Chapter 3 develops the case study of Czechoslovakia. It commences by establishing the strategic context and Soviet goals in this conflict and then offers an in-depth analysis of the role of subversion in attaining these goals. Chapter 4 examines the "hybrid war" phase of the Russo-Ukrainian conflict from 2013 to 2022. It first establishes the strategic context and goals before examining the use of subversion in the pursuit of the latter. It examines three major traditional subversive operations and seven major cyber-enabled subversion operations. Chapter 5 adds a preliminary analysis of the strategic role and value of subversion in Russia's full-scale invasion of Ukraine since February 2022. Again, it examines and compares traditional and cyber-enabled subversive operations—revealing the shortcomings of the "cyber onslaught" while cementing the relative superiority of traditional means in enabling key strategic gains. The conclusion provides a short summary of the theory and findings before focusing on the implications for world politics. It identifies six important consequences for the evolution of conflict, strategy, and stability. Finally, it evaluates alternative explanations for the findings and discusses the limitations of this study as well as potential future research. It outlines the limitations of this study and lays out an according research program to refine the theory and expand the universe of cases.

1
Subversion and Power

This chapter establishes what subversion is, how it works, and its strategic role and value. It proceeds in several steps. First, it defines the concept of power and identifies established instruments in world politics, namely diplomacy and warfare. Consequently, it shows how and why subversion differs through its reliance on a mechanism of exploitation and manipulation. Drawing on intelligence studies, the analysis establishes that spies are the main "tools" of subversion and identifies through which techniques they exploit which types of vulnerabilities in what types of systems. It shows that subversion can target a range of social systems at the national, supranational, and subnational levels. Building on this analysis, the next section establishes the strategic role of subversion by determining the types of effects it can achieve. In theory, this discussion shows, its versatility and stealthy nature render subversion a highly attractive instrument of power, especially if the alternative is war. Building on historical case studies and theorizing, the chapter then proceeds to identify three distinct strategies of subversion and discusses corresponding possible strategic outcomes. As part of this discussion, it also examines the interaction between subversion and the use of force—and the paradoxical way in which the use of subversion to avoid force can render its use more likely. The reason is that subversion often falls short of achieving strategic goals, and the subsequent section explains why. Ironically, the same mechanism of secret manipulation and exploitation that makes subversion so promising in theory often precludes it from fulfilling this promise in practice. The reason is that secretly manipulating adversary systems presents a set of significant challenges, and the efforts required to overcome them present subversive actors with a corresponding set of trade-offs that pose a trilemma. Holding all else equal, actors can maximize either speed, the intensity of effects, or the control they have over these effects—but they cannot maximize all three at once. Rather, as the analysis shows, the more actors improve one of these variables, the more they tend to lose out across the remaining ones. The faster they go, the less intense the effects become, and the greater the risk of control loss becomes, for example. Overall, actors can maximize at most two out of these three variables, at the cost of the remaining one. Due to this trilemma, under most circumstances subversion is either too slow, too weak, or too volatile to produce strategic value. Finally, the chapter defines the quality of subversion based on these characteristics and formulates expectations for the empirical analysis.

Power in World Politics

To determine what instrument of power subversion constitutes, first an operational definition of power is required. The concept of power is central to the study of international relations, yet its meaning remains hotly contested, and consequently, there exist a variety of rival definitions.[1] Steven Lukes accordingly concludes that power is an "essential contested concept" marked by endless disputes over its proper use where, moreover, "to engage in such disputes is itself to engage in politics."[2] Rather than develop and defend a philosophical position about the concept of power in general, however, this book has a more narrow aim: identifying the distinguishing qualities of a specific instrument of power and its use. Hence, an operational definition is sufficient. Fortunately, despite foundational debates on the concept of power, there is broad consensus over operational definitions concerning its use in practice.[3] Robert Dahl provides an intuitive and highly influential definition of power as a relationship where "A has power over B to the extent that he can get B to do something that B would not otherwise do."[4] This definition provides a useful foundation for analysis, identifying three key characteristics of power "in action": actors linked in a relationship, the intent of the actor exerting power, and an observable outcome.

How A manages to produce the outcome in the scenario above is left open by Dahl's definition, however. Here Max Weber's definition adds a further dimension, namely the victim's capacity to resist this influence. According to Weber, power concerns "the probability that one actor within a social relationship will be in a position to carry out his own will despite resistance, regardless of the basis on which this probability rests."[5] This probability is shaped by the relative power of both actors—the stronger the aggressor and the weaker the victim, the more likely the aggressor is to get what they want. In international relations theory, the established measure of relative power is material capabilities. In both realist and liberal theories of international relations, material capabilities are the main determinant of relative power, including not only military might but also the size of the economy and the population.[6] States and other actors then leverage the power potentials of these capabilities against their adversaries through the application of different instruments of power.

As already touched upon, classical international relations theory distinguishes two key instruments: warfare and diplomacy. There are many ways states can get their way in world politics, but war has remained the "supreme arbiter" of conflict.[7] When diplomacy fails, it offers the last resort to project power or resist it. Consequently, "realists" in international relations argue, at heart the field concerns the study of war. As John Mearsheimer put it, "International relations is not a constant state of war, but it is a state of relentless security competition, with the possibility of war always in the background."[8] Studying world politics accordingly means studying "the causes of war and the conditions of peace."[9] Classical international relations theory accordingly distinguishes two key instruments of power: force and diplomacy. Instruments of power constitute means to "make others do what they would not otherwise do," following Dahl's simple and seminal definition of power.[10] War involves "the use of physical force to compel an enemy to one's will."[11] While the means of war have evolved, its defining characteristic remains the use of force in a struggle of organized violence.[12] It involves direct interaction but can be both overt and covert since attackers can obscure their identity to pursue "secret wars."[13] Diplomacy, in contrast, relies primarily on communication and is thus overt by definition.[14] Recipients must be able to identify both the origins and contents of a message. There are different modes of transmitting messages. In an ideal world, actors can persuade others through reasoned discourse,[15] but in practice diplomacy frequently devolves into bargaining over the distribution of gains.[16] Finally, in situations of security competition diplomacy often turns coercive, involving signaling through nonverbal threats and assurances, as Thomas Schelling has so eloquently captured with the concept of "diplomacy of violence."[17]

Material capabilities underpin both. The key instrument of warfare is force, the intent is to compel the adversary to one's will, and the observable outcome is the opponent surrendering. Hence, the ideal outcome in war is a knockout blow that incapacitates the enemy at a minimal loss of one's own forces. Although superiority in materiel does not guarantee victory,[18] and despite their limited fungibility,[19] material capabilities are still fundamental to win. War is about leveraging one's own capabilities against those of the adversary to break their capacity to resist and impose one's will in the most effective way to generate physical force against opponents, shifting the balance of power by destroying adversary material capabilities and killing population. Provided one's own capabilities are destroyed at a lower rate, it erodes the adversary's capacity to resist until their surrender—giving in to demands the actor would not give in to without warfare—or destruction. Importantly, warfare can be both overt and covert. Especially throughout the Cold War, "secret wars," where both sides aim to obscure their involvement, became a key instrument of power.[20]

Diplomacy, in contrast, is overt by definition because its core mechanism is communication.[21] Negotiations can occur in secret, beyond the public eye.[22] Within any diplomatic interaction, however, for it to be effective the origin, content, and intended recipient of a message must be clear. In the ideal case, reason prevails, and actors get others to do what they would otherwise not do through persuasion or dissuasion, resolving disputes peacefully.[23] In practice, however, diplomacy frequently devolves into bargaining, threats, and sanctions.[24] Armed force is the ultimate means of exerting coercive power against an adversary, but the threat of using force can be an effective bargaining chip to compel others to take action or deter them from taking action.[25] Apart from threatening military action—which again builds on military power[26]—actors can also use their economic clout to induce the adversary to do what one wants, threatening economic sanctions.

In both cases, material capabilities are the main power resources. Similar to warfare, diplomatic means can either directly induce the adversary to do something they would otherwise not do or weaken their capacity to resist by shifting the balance of power against the adversary. Hence, the core diplomatic mechanism of shifting the balance of power is the formation of alliances.[27] Diplomacy can also exert power through nonmaterial means, most importantly through attraction and co-optation. Joseph Nye highlighted this hitherto understudied dimension of power with his concept of soft power, where instead of coercing others to do what one wants, "one country gets other countries to want what it wants."[28]

In short, power is defined as the capacity to produce desired outcomes against resistance, and classical international relations theory distinguishes two main instruments:[29] war, which produces outcomes through force, and diplomacy, which relies on threats, bargaining, persuasion, and attraction. Both involve direct interactions. While diplomatic interactions are overt by definition, however, warfare can be both overt and covert. Both share a reliance on material capabilities.

Subversion: Power through Exploitation and Manipulation

Subversion, in contrast, is indirect and covert and relies on an adversary's own capabilities—turning the logic of power resources on its head. The distinguishing characteristic of subversion, I argue, is its reliance on secret exploitation and manipulation. This mechanism involves identifying vulnerabilities in systems of rules and practices as well as among the participants of such systems and developing means to use these vulnerabilities to gain access and manipulate the system. If successful, it enables the subverting actor to make targeted systems produce outcomes neither their designers nor participants expected, benefiting the subverter to the detriment of the victim.[30] In other words, it turns an adversary's own capabilities against the latter.

Paul W. Blackstock provided a crucial insight toward building a theory of subversive power by linking the definition of subversion to its mechanism of action. Blackstock defines subversion as "the undermining or detachment of the loyalties of significant political and social groups within the victimized state, and their transference, under ideal conditions, to the symbols and institutions of the aggressor."[31] This definition decouples subversion from the objective of overthrowing governments prevalent across the literature of the time, instead identifying its reliance on parts of the targeted state's own population as a defining characteristic.[32] Specifically, Blackstock explains, subversion functions through the "exploitation not only of political tensions but also of psychological and sociological vulnerabilities."[33] This mechanism distinguishes subversion from both warfare and diplomacy. Blackstock primarily examines the historical use of subversion in different strategic contexts, however, and does not fully construct the general theory for which his crucial insight has laid the foundation.

To construct such a theory, recent work by institutionalist scholars is instructive. As Blackstock notes, subversion targets "political and social institutions"[34]—commonly defined as systems of rules and practices.[35] Mahoney, Thelen, and Faletti[36] have examined mechanisms of subverting such institutions, where actors are "following institutional expectations and working within the system" yet exploit ambiguities in rules and practices to use "crucial gaps and openings for action" in order to "work against the system from within it."[37] By targeting systems of rules within the fabric of an adversary's society, subversion thus leverages parts of the victim's own social structure[38] against the victim itself. Through the lens of classical international relations theory, subversion thus turns a state's capabilities against itself.[39]

This mechanism sets subversion apart as an instrument of power. It involves neither force and coercion, nor persuasion and bargaining. Rather than an instrument of warfare or diplomacy, it is thus a distinct instrument. Of course, international relations theory has now developed a far broader understanding of power, not only direct, relational forms of power but also indirect, structural forms of power.[40] Since subversion targets social systems and institutions, one could assume it belongs to the latter kind. However, as I have argued in more detail elsewhere, in fact subversion reverses structural power—thus falling into a category of its own.[41]

Subversion can target a broad range of systems. While most literature focuses on operations targeting entire governments, in principle any organization, institution, or group based on a set of shared rules and practices is vulnerable. Specifically, the targets of subversion are broad: from loose political groups, including activist networks and civil society, to highly structured political organizations and government institutions, the media, private corporations, and state-owned enterprises. Finally, subversion targets not only flaws in the rules and practices that constitute these groups, organizations, and institutions—or social structures, in the parlance of constructivist scholars in international relations—but also its constituent parts, namely the people who participate in them.[42] Functionally, subversion thus exploits flaws in systems of rules and practices and their constituent parts to manipulate the system toward producing effects neither its designers nor participants expected or intended, to the benefit of the subverter and to the detriment of the victim (state). Because it uses these systems to produce effects, it applies power indirectly (compared to the generation of force through one's own capabilities). In other words, subversion turns adversary systems against the adversary.

Importantly, this mechanism of exploitation not only enables a secret mode of operation but also requires it. In contrast to military covert operations where the activity typically occurs in plain sight but the sponsorship is obscured, subversive operations typically proceed both covertly and clandestinely. Military force can be applied against resistance even when the cover has been blown; hence, secrecy is seldom absolute and instead many covert operations fall within a spectrum of increasing implausibly deniable activity.[43] In contrast, subversion requires secrecy due to its reliance on control over adversary systems, which the victim can typically neutralize upon discovery. A spy discovered typically is a spy lost as the target state's law enforcement agencies can simply arrest them—thereby neutralizing the entire operation.[44]

As the previous point suggests, spies have been the key "tools" of subversion,[45] deployed to infiltrate and exploit targeted groups, organizations, or societies under cover identities. The KGB's "illegals" infiltrating Western societies under carefully constructed false identifies are the most infamous examples.[46] Spies can exploit different types of vulnerabilities to gain influence and control. First, they can target a vulnerable group member, thus exploiting individual-level vulnerabilities provided by human fallibility. For example, an agent aiming to infiltrate a political group might identify a lonely and naïve group member, gain their trust and support, and use it to assume an influential position within the group. Or a spy may exploit greed, bribing individuals at a targeted organization to help the spy achieve a position of influence. Once this influence is established, the agent can start their work to manipulate the organization, for example, to mobilize it against the target government or produce another desired effect. Second, spies can exploit flawed security rules and practices. For example, an agent aiming to infiltrate an industrial facility, say an oil pipeline operations center, could exploit a lapse in security protocols to enter the facility and sabotage it, causing destruction and economic damage against the victim state. Or the spy may exploit lax background checks for new employees at an organization to gain employment at a targeted facility under a false identity. In 1959, a KGB agent succeeded in doing just that at a power substation in Germany operating cables crossing the Rhine River, where the agent promptly started gathering intelligence to develop plans to sabotage the latter.[47]

Third, spies can use limited force and coercion to exploit vulnerabilities at the individual or systemic level. Instead of bribing an individual, they can blackmail the individual through threats of disclosing compromising information or of using force.[48] Moreover, spies can use physical force to gain access to sensitive areas, such as breaking a lock. Importantly, in this context the (limited) use of force is a means to facilitate exploitation, rather than the primary means of producing the desired outcome. This primary reliance on exploitation distinguishes subversion from secret warfare. A spy operating under a cover identity at a targeted organization who uses force to gain entry to a sensitive area to place forged documents or sabotage machinery secretly exploits the flaws in the organization that allow the spy to get this far. In contrast, a commando team that instead shoots their way into the facility and then destroys it by placing a bomb conducts clandestine warfare. In short, the reliance on exploitation as the primary means of producing desired outcomes distinguishes subversion from other instruments of power.

The same applies to the provision of material support to opposition groups and movements that subversive operations aiming to overthrow governments often involve.[49] While the material support increases the capabilities of the benefiting group or organization, this group or organization rather than the sponsoring actor uses these capabilities to produce detrimental effects against the targeted government. Hence, the mechanism remains indirect while both the provision of support and the identity of the sponsor remain obscured to the victim. Moreover, such operations exploit the susceptibility of the co-opted proxy organizations to external influence without which the operation would not be possible—underlining the central role of secret exploitation in subversion.

Accordingly, traditional subversion encompasses covert operations carried out by undercover agents who infiltrate, exploit, and manipulate systems for the range of effects just laid out. However, not all nonmilitary covert operations are subversive. As discussed, the distinguishing factor of subversion is exploitation and manipulation, and consequently operations where force is the primary mechanism of action are of a different kind. Looking back at Johnson's list, apart from major secret war, relatively clear exclusion cases are assassinations, crop destruction, pinpointed retaliation against noncombatants, use of chemical and biological agents, embassy break-ins, training of military forces, hostage taking, hostage rescue attempts, theft of sophisticated weapons or materiel, and all types of arms supplies.[50] Yet there are borderline cases that blur the lines. Assassination is one of them. Assassinating a politician with a sniper from afar is clearly not subversion but the simple application of force. If, on the other hand, an undercover agent who has gained the trust of that politician after serving as his close advisor for years puts a few drops of poison into that politician's coffee because the latter has found out the real identity of this agent, it would fall within the definition of subversion outlined here. The agent has infiltrated the office of the politician by exploiting vulnerabilities under false pretenses and uses the position acquired within the targeted organization (i.e., the ministry in question) as well as the trust established with the politician to get the latter to drink the poison—the goal of which is to maintain secrecy, namely preventing others from learning the agent's true identity.

Regime change operations also blur the lines. At face value, overthrowing and replacing a government by secretly infiltrating and mobilizing an opposition group would seem like a clear case of subversion. Yet the lines blur if this overthrow involves the use of force. If the opposition group succeeds in the coup d'état primarily because it uses force or threatens its use, especially if this ability is the result of covert arms deliveries by their external sponsor, the regime change ceases to be subversive and is rather armed revolution. That is the reason I excluded arms deliveries of any kind above. This mechanism-based conception of subversion is narrower but also clearer than existing theories.

Wohlforth, for example, defines subversion based on its goals and location as "statecraft designed to directly influence domestic politics in a target in a manner prejudicial to its foreign policy interests. It falls into two categories: weakening the target; and altering the target's policy from the path the target's government initially intends to follow."[51] This definition captures all different types of subversive operations outlined above—yet without clarifying a mechanism, there is no reason one would not include clandestine or covert military operations, say targeted assassinations of politicians who take positions in conflict with the sponsor's interests, or just simply a military coup. Clearly that is not what Wohlforth has in mind, yet if the goal and location are the defining characteristics, such activities would fall within its scope. Focusing on the mechanism of action as its defining characteristics not only provides conceptual clarity, however, but also helps explain its strategic role and value based on the distinct set of opportunities and challenges this mechanism provides—as the next two sections will explore.

The Strategic Role and Promise of Subversion

Subversion promises a means to produce similar outcomes as using force when diplomacy fails, yet at less cost and risk. By exploiting systems, it can stealthily manipulate or weaken an adversary, even independently shift the balance of power. I identify five types of effects, the tools and resources required to produce them, and their potential strategic value. Meanwhile, the indirect and secret nature of exploitation promises even lower costs and risks than the covert use of force. These properties render subversion a highly attractive, even irresistible, strategic option.

Subversion can manipulate and weaken adversaries through five main types of active effects. First, it can manipulate public opinion, undermining confidence in a target government and/or creating public pressure to influence government policy. The key instrument of doing so is covert propaganda, preparing content and messages to be fed to, and disseminated by, the target country's own media via undercover spies or collaborators within these organizations.[52] One preferred method employed by the KGB has been forged documents.[53]

Second, subversive operations can manipulate government policy, either through blackmail and bribery of officials or through undercover spies assuming appropriate positions of influence within administrations. Such operations thus exploit vulnerable individuals within administrations to turn them into "instruments" of influence, and also exploit insufficient security rules and vetting practices to get undercover spies in positions where they can access such vulnerable individuals themselves. Placing an undercover spy into a position of influence uses the same techniques but also builds relationships of trust within administration that the spy then exploits to exert influence. Former German chancellor Willy Brandt's close advisor and friend Günther Guillaume provides an infamous example of this technique, as he was discovered to be an East German spy in 1973.[54]

Third, subversion can erode a target state's material capabilities. The main means is sabotage of industrial capacity, infrastructure, and military assets. Undercover spies are again a key instrument of achieving access to targeted organizations and facilities. Once spies have achieved access to target facilities or organizations by means of the different techniques of exploitation discussed in the previous sections, they can disrupt the operation of machinery, manipulate machinery to cause damage, or apply force to cause damage—including the use of explosives.[55] Apart from the direct effects against the targeted assets themselves, such sabotage can also pursue economic disruptions resulting from the former.[56]

Fourth, subversion can undermine institutional effectiveness and efficiency through undercover spies in appropriate positions of influence. Gaining access again involves the same techniques of exploitation already discussed. The OSS "Simple Sabotage Field Manual," listing techniques on how agents and collaborators can undermine organizational efficiency, provides a key example.[57] Such subversion may also target military command structures directly, undermining effectiveness in case armed conflict breaks out.

Fifth, subversion can replace a targeted government through regime change.[58] Undercover spies are crucial assets in such operations as well, but success depends on co-optation of proxy actors with sufficient influence and capabilities to replace an existing regime. There are two pathways toward regime change. The first is internal, meaning a coup from within a government. A key technique is expanding covert control over a government, established through the effect type two discussed above by increasing the number of officials under one's thumb and/or the number of undercover spies in positions of influence.[59] With enough powerful individuals (where powerful means influential within the administration) under one's direct or indirect control, it is possible to replace a target government from within, via an internal coup. This approach is extremely challenging since each step toward expansion of control within an administration by "turning" more individuals to one's side carries the risk of discovery and failure.[60] What if the official enticed with bribery instead contacts law enforcement, for example? Accordingly, there are few examples where this succeeded in practice.

The second path toward regime change focuses on external challenges to a regime, using spies to establish contact with opposition groups, either under a cover identity or revealing their actual status, to mobilize these groups, coordinate their activity, and typically facilitate the provision of material support to empower these groups toward the ability of overthrowing a targeted regime. If executed flawlessly, such operations can also succeed without the use of violence, achieving a peaceful transfer of power under the pretense of legitimate elections, for example, although the winning party has become an instrument of the subverting state's power. The other techniques of subversion just outlined can also be used to weaken the target government and influence public opinion to improve chances of success, for example, by undermining public trust in a government. For example, in 1968 the KGB planned[61] a regime change operation in Greece to topple a military dictatorship using the following instruments: (1) providing financial support to the local Communist Party, (2) sending undercover spies to recruit and coordinate local groups to conduct intelligence and sabotage operations, and (3) prepare local Communist allies for guerrilla warfare.[62] In most cases, however, regime change operations have ultimately involved the use of force, either in the form of internal armed revolution or through external intervention, that is, through the subverting state sending covert troops to help the challenging group take control.[63] Hence, regime change operations just sit right at the threshold between purely subversive (i.e., nonmilitary operations) and covert wars.

Given these effect types, as I have argued elsewhere, three distinct strategies of subversion emerge: manipulation, erosion, and overthrow.[64] Manipulation aims to manipulate government policy toward specific outcomes, either through direct infiltration of the government itself or via manipulating public opinion.[65] Erosion, on the other hand, does not pursue specific outcomes but rather strives to weaken an adversary over the long term by undermining social cohesion and public support for a government, as well as sabotaging infrastructure and institutions.[66] As such, it corresponds to what J. C. Wylie and John B. Hattendorf call a "cumulative strategy," where individual operations are not linked in any causal or sequential way but rather are independent elements in a campaign whose cumulative impact over time counts.[67] Overthrow, finally, aims to replace a government.[68]

In the pursuit of these strategies, actors may conduct subversive campaigns consisting of multiple operations over time. Meanwhile, these strategies are not mutually exclusive but can be used in parallel, complementarily, and cumulatively. To give an example of the latter case, a subverter running an erosion campaign may perceive it to have weakened an adversary enough to then escalate goals, transitioning toward the overthrow strategy.

In short, subversion can produce a range of political outcomes that manipulate or weaken an adversary. In doing so, prevailing expectations hold that subversion can produce similar outcomes as going to war, including achieving significant shifts in the balance of power. As mentioned in the introduction, in the Cold War Lawrence Beilenson feared subversion's potential to make possible the expansion of Communism around the world.[69] Senator Joseph McCarthy's infamous crusade against what he feared was widespread Communist subversion in the United States during the 1950s further attests to this prevailing threat perception.[70] Moreover, subversion not only allows similar effects to the use of force but also enables outcomes beyond the reach of coercive instruments of foreign policy. As Lindsey O'Rourke underlines, while coercive strategies aim to change behavior, "regime change offers the possibility of altering the underlying preferences of a foreign government."[71]

Subversion can produce value not only as an independent instrument, however, but also as a complement to force. Blackstock accordingly saw it "as an ally of diplomacy in peacetime, and as a valuable auxiliary to military force in time of war."[72] The conditions under which this role may shift, however, and how the use of subversion could contribute to such a change in strategic context remain unclear in the literature. Beilenson similarly argues that subversion can be used as an auxiliary tool not only to "help the subverting nation in a present or future war"[73] but also to avert war.[74] Importantly, as mentioned at the outset of this book, Beilenson argued that the Soviet Union had elevated subversion strategically from a primarily auxiliary to a primarily standalone tool in the Cold War's bipolar power struggle.[75] Rather than the strategic genius of Soviet leader Lenin who adapted subversion toward this role, according to Beilenson, there is a systemic explanation for this shifting role: the increasing destructiveness, and thus costliness, of war. Accordingly, Blackstock underlines how during the Cold War the "condition of strategic thermonuclear deterrence . . . provided an element of stability under which both sides have pursued an alternative and complementary policy of keeping the opponent off balance by means of political warfare, i.e., essentially non-military tactics."[76] Since weapons have continued to increase in destructiveness, this attractiveness of subversion can be expected to persist. Hence, subversion is likely to continue to fulfill a primarily independent strategic role.

Subversion offers significant strategic potential. First, it promises significantly lower resource investments and potential losses compared to force. As discussed, war is a clash of materiel and personnel where each side tries to subdue the other by generating superior force. Consequently, it involves significant investments in resources and manpower, as well as corresponding potential losses. The more force is generated, the more resources are required—and the higher the potential losses are. These costs generally render war an inefficient means to solve disputes compared to a diplomatic bargain since "under very broad conditions bargains will exist that genuinely rational states would prefer to a risky and costly war."[77] Importantly, this applies to warfare whether done overtly or covertly. Covert warfare lowers the relative risks of unintended or accidental escalation, that is, intensification of conflict beyond a set threshold. By limiting the intensity of engagement, covertness lowers resource costs and potential losses compared to overt wars. Yet covert warfare will still accrue greater material costs compared to subversion due to the latter's reliance on an adversary's own systems to produce effects.

Second, subversion's lower intensity of effects (compared to the death and destruction that war entails) further reduces the potential costs and risks of escalation compared to the use of force. Using armed force can lead to repercussions and reputational costs from the international community if the intervention pursued violates the nonintervention principle, but operating covertly avoids these risks.[78] Yet the victim may discover the sponsorship of the operation, "blowing" the cover and revealing the sponsorship to the international community. In the latter case reputational costs are still accrued, despite added efforts to obscure sponsorship. Because subversive operations do not involve the deployment of armed forces but rely on local proxies, the risk of reputational losses is further reduced—even if discovered.

Third, the typically clandestine and covert approach of subversive operations further reduces the risks of discovery and associated follow-on costs. In the ideal case, if a subversive operation manages to obscure both the activity itself and the identity of the sponsor until the desired effect is produced, it thus not only avoids any repercussions but also obscures the very existence of a power relationship. In other words, if successful, the victim remains unaware that another actor has exerted power over them.

To sum up, subversion promises an alternative to the use of force that promises influence over an adversary at lower risks and costs due to its secret and indirect mechanism of exploitation.[79] These properties render subversion a highly attractive option for leaders. Moreover, the higher the potential costs and risks of going to war are, the more attractive subversion as an alternative becomes. Accordingly, the condition of strategic nuclear deterrence elevated subversion to a central instrument of great power competition during the Cold War.[80] Successful subversion can thus render the use of force unnecessary if it provides the subverter with a sufficient degree of control over the relevant institutions of an adversary to fulfill given strategic ends[81]—in the extreme case by installing a new government. If control remains insufficient to produce the desired end, subversion can still produce independent strategic effects, however. Through its erosive effects, namely degrading material capabilities, institutional capacity, and societal cohesion, in theory subversion can independently shift the balance of power.

Yet in practice subversion has often required the use of force, either to help it succeed or to salvage failed operations. Blackstock, for example, notes that at the conclusion of a subversive campaign, "the intervening power may openly seize power."[82] This seizure, he observes, "frequently involves the use or threat of military force."[83] Similarly, as discussed, despite conceiving of subversion as an alternative to warfare, Beilenson highlights how subversion usually culminates in a "final blow by force."[84] Considering the Cold

War context both wrote in, that makes sense as they conceived of subversion primarily as the pursuit of regime change—which often involved an armed revolution. Yet for less ambitious goals and associated effect types of manipulation and erosion, the costs and risks involved in the use of force would in most cases render obsolete the strategic advantages of using subversion in the first place. Hence, it is unlikely that leaders would choose such a course of action, especially considering the increasing destructiveness of war, and the risk of nuclear escalation if nuclear powers are involved. Consequently, rather than as a planned support to subversion, in such cases the use of force is more likely as a contingency in case of subversive failure—especially if the perceived stakes of failure have increased in the meantime. Blackstock accordingly notes that "when covert operations end in . . . spectacular failure or are clearly inadequate, the two most likely alternatives open to the aggressor are to call them off or to intervene directly with military action."[85] The constraints and trade-offs forming the subversive trilemma laid out in the next section explain such cases of failure.

An Operational Trilemma Limits Strategic Value

Subversion thus holds great strategic promise, yet the same mechanism of secret exploitation that enables this promise also poses a trilemma that limits its strategic value in practice. To produce any effects, subversion requires three basic conditions: (1) an available target with suitable vulnerabilities and (2) a subversive agent (i.e., spy) with suitable abilities to (3) exploit this vulnerability without being discovered. Fulfilling these conditions poses three corresponding challenges.

First, subversion is limited in speed because exploitation requires adaptation to the target and its vulnerabilities, a learning process that takes time. Identifying targets with suitable vulnerabilities requires reconnaissance, that is, obtaining information about its properties either through an agent in the field or from a collaborator in the target society. Placing an agent or finding a collaborator in turn requires additional preparation time. Once a target is chosen and a suitable vulnerability identified, the subverter must develop a means of exploitation. Because subversion depends on adversary systems, means of exploitation must be adapted to the properties of these systems. This may necessitate additional reconnaissance and intelligence collection. It is also likely to require (further) training of the field agent(s). All of this takes time. For example, take a subversive operation targeting an industrial facility in a given state to conduct sabotage. The subversive agent needs to be highly trained in tradecraft to avoid detection and be fluent in the national language—ideally without an accent. Such basic training typically takes years.[86] Acquiring the specific skills to exploit a chosen target requires further adaptation, hence further time. In the example, the spy may attempt to gain employment at the plant under a false identity, which requires building a suitable cover story and obtaining the skills that are needed for the role. This may take months or years. The more complex the target is, the more demanding the adaptation process will be—take a nuclear enrichment facility, for example. Meanwhile, the more valuable the target, the better its protection is likely to be. In the above example, the facility may have strong background checks of prospective employees; hence, it may be necessary to identify an official involved who is susceptible to bribery or blackmail. The more demanding the adaption process, the longer it is likely to take. In short, the need to adapt thus slows the operational speed of subversion, and the more so the more sensitive the target is.

Second, the intensity of effects is limited because they depend on manipulation of targeted systems *and* maintenance of secrecy. As a starting point, the capabilities of the subverting agent (i.e., the spy) and the properties of the targeted system provide a hard ceiling on the maximum intensity of effects possible in theory. For example, subverting an organization of professional accountants is unlikely to enable the production of some physical damage because such organizations do not typically operate physical machinery with the potential to create such effects. Rather, it is likely to provide access to financial transactions and the ability to manipulate them in order to create economic disruptions. The reach of a target system into societal processes thus determines the type of effects that are possible and their maximum possible intensity. Within this hard limit posed by target system properties, the intensity of effects that subversion can produce in practice is determined by the scope and scale[87] of access and the degree of adaptation to a target system. To give a concrete example, producing physical effects is only possible if the subverting actor has found a way to access the physical machinery required to create these effects and developed a means of exploiting and manipulating that machinery to produce that effect—without being discovered before doing so. Hence, sabotaging a complex machine requires a spy who understands enough about the machine to manipulate it in a way that causes damage, and without getting caught.

Expanding and deepening access to a system, meanwhile, increases the intensity of effects that can be achieved yet also tends to increase the risk of discovery. Avoiding discovery is necessary because once it becomes aware of the subversive operation, the victim can simply arrest the spies involved, allowing the victim not only to neutralize the operation itself[88] but also often to capture the subversive agent—providing a counterintelligence "win."[89] There may be strategic contexts under which subversive actors aim to reveal the fact as a means of strategic signaling, as will be examined further below, but typically subversion requires "full" secrecy (i.e., both covert and clandestine) at least until the moment it manipulates systems to produce the desired effect, because premature discovery generally allows the victim to neutralize it. Hence, the subverting actor must balance the potential benefits of deepening and widening subversion of a target system with the increasing failure risk and associated costs resulting from premature discovery. The result is a secrecy-size dilemma identified by O'Rourke, as operations with sufficient scale to produce a desired effect are unlikely to remain secret, while those small enough to avoid discovery are unlikely capable of producing the effect.[90] As previously mentioned, spies can also produce effects through their own ability to apply force, including placing explosives on targeted machinery or other assets. Similar constraints apply in these circumstances though: the greater the scale of effects, the likelier the operation is to be discovered. Imagine a spy attempting to smuggle enough bombs into a military facility to blow up a tank regiment, for example. Doing so is unlikely to remain unnoticed. The same applies to less reckless activities, such as the recruitment of individuals within a target government to facilitate internal regime change, as already mentioned. The more individuals the spy approaches, the likelier one of them is to raise the alarm and cause the operation to be discovered.

Furthermore, the more sensitive the targeted organization or facility, the less likely it is to have easily exploitable vulnerabilities. For example, a nuclear missile silo can be expected to have more robust security practices and more scrutiny over who works there than a simple car factory. Similarly, the activities required by subversive agents to achieve more intense effects are also more likely to raise suspicions, further increasing the risk of discovery. For example, an agent in an organization taking home a few documents is less likely to raise suspicions than an agent tampering with industrial machinery—particularly if the machinery subsequently fails.

Third, subversive actors by definition have incomplete control over target systems and thus limited control over effects. In general, control over targets is limited because it depends on the veil of secrecy—discovery, as discussed, allows the victim to neutralize control. Hence, control tends to be temporary. Furthermore, subverting actors have only partial familiarity with target systems and their design. For example, spies may be unable to gain access to parts of a targeted organization to carry out reconnaissance or may lack the language skills required for infiltration.[91] Moreover, sabotage always involves the risks of "unknown unknowns"[92] that only become apparent at the moment the attempt is made to produce a desired effect. Consequently, the target system may react differently than expected to manipulation. For example, it may have additional security measures the infiltrating spies missed, preventing the manipulation attempted by the spies. Accordingly, Melissa Lee highlights that relying on proxy groups not only keeps resource costs low but also introduces the risk of control loss.[93] The results can be blowback, especially when an operation's cover is blown or it produces collateral damage.[94] Gregory Treverton thus concluded that "not only are covert actions unlikely to stay secret, their results are especially likely to differ from policy-maker's intentions."[95] Importantly, subversive actors only know for certain whether they achieved a sufficient level of adaptation to produce a desired effect when it is too late to do something about it—further limiting control over effects.

For the reasons laid out above, the greater the scope or scale of effects pursued, the more complex exploitation tends to be and thus the higher the risk becomes that something goes wrong. More importantly, the greater the scope and scale of effects, the greater the potential costs resulting from control loss become as well. Effects may produce collateral damage that runs counter to the strategic ends of the subverter, for example. Say a regime change operation succeeds in toppling a government but the new regime turns out to become a predatory one, causing sufficient grievances among the population to target a popular revolt that installs a revolutionary leader, who declares the original subverting state the main enemy. Precisely this happened in the CIA-sponsored operation to topple Mossadegh in Iran, laying the foundations for the Islamic Revolution in 1979 that produced the regime still challenging the United States today. Finally, the subversive agents themselves may behave unexpectedly. A common risk in subversive operations involving undercover agents has been agents going off the rails or turning rogue under the pressures involved.[96] Not only the challenges of secretly exploiting unfamiliar systems thus plague subversion and raise the risk of control loss, but also the pathologies of principal-agent[97] relationships.

Importantly, these three variables of speed, intensity, and control not only pose individual constraints but also interact in a way that confronts subversive actors with a set of trade-offs that limit the strategic value of subversion. These trade-offs present subversive actors with a trilemma because, holding all else equal, efforts to increase the effectiveness of one or more variables tends to produce corresponding losses across the remaining variables. Ideally, subversive operations will be fast and intense and reliably produce effects. Yet actors cannot achieve all three characteristics at once. Rather, at a given level of resource investment, subversive actors face a choice of prioritizing either speed, intensity, or control at the cost of other variables. Moreover, they can maximize at most two of these variables at the cost of the remaining one.

Consider, for example, an actor aiming to maximize speed. Increasing speed reduces the time available for reconnaissance and development of means of exploitation. The actor and its operatives will thus be relatively less familiar with the target system than if they had spent more time and will have relatively less scope and scale of access to that system. In practical terms, an undercover spy who has infiltrated an organization will tend to have access to fewer parts of that organization and have a less influential position after six months than a spy who spent two years there. Consequently, the intensity of effects that spy can produce will tend to be lower as well. Meanwhile, less familiarity tends to bring a higher risk of discovery, as well as a higher risk of unexpected reactions by the target system to manipulation. Moreover, agents in a rush are more likely to miss things or mess up. Therefore, the faster an operation proceeds, the lower the intensity of effects and control tend to be. The faster subversive operations thus tend to be, the weaker and more volatile the effects they can produce tend to be, just as their risk of discovery tends to increase.

Conversely, increasing effect intensity tends to lower speed and control. Producing more intense effects requires more familiarity with the target system, as well as deeper and wider access to the latter. Both require extra time for reconnaissance and development—reducing speed. A spy who has just recently infiltrated a research facility as a new security guard will be less likely to have access to a sensitive experiment than one who has been in place for months or years, having gained the trust of staff, for example. Meanwhile, expanding the scope and scale of access increases the risks of discovery, lowering control. The longer the subversion lasts, and the deeper and wider subversive agents burrow into targeted systems, the more likely someone is to notice. The more sensitive the targeted system and its specific parts are, the more likely they are to be closely guarded. Moreover, the deeper agents have to penetrate target systems, and the more capable such systems are of producing detrimental effects against the victim (state), the more demanding and complex the exploitation and manipulation process tends to be—and correspondingly, the higher the chance becomes that something goes wrong and one gets discovered, that the manipulation fails, or that it produces unexpected effects. Therefore, actors tend to have less control over effects pursued the more intense the latter are. As a result, the more capable subversive operations are of producing intense, strategically significant effects, the slower and more volatile they tend to be.

Finally, increasing control tends to lower speed and intensity. In general, it means proceeding carefully, spending extra time to learn how target systems work and consider eventual contingencies, and avoiding any actions likely to raise suspicions. The better one's spies know their environment, and the better trained they are, the less likely they are to make mistakes and/or get discovered. Yet increasing their familiarity and training both require extra time investment, slowing speed. Alternatively, lowering the scope or scale of effects attempted at a given level of familiarity also tends to lower the risk of producing unintended effects, thus increasing control—yet at the expense of intensity. A spy who starts a relationship with a lonely local politician will require less time to do so than on trying to rise to a position within the inner circle of the prime minister of a country. Yet the former is also far less likely to influence policy than the latter. Overall, the more actors prioritize control over effects, the slower an operation tends to be, and the weaker the effect tends to be.

Speed, intensity, and control are key determinants of strategic value, enabling the production of desired effects when and where they are needed to contribute to strategic goals without compromising secrecy. And yet each of these variables can prevent a subversive operation from fulfilling these requirements, while the trade-offs of the trilemma mean no more than two can be maximized at once. Increasing effectiveness of two variables tends to "doubly" decrease the effectiveness of the remaining variable. Maximizing both speed and control over effects severely restricts the possible scope and scale of effects that can be produced because of limited reconnaissance time and corresponding level of familiarity of the target system. The less time there is to get to know a target system and establish access and influence within it, and the more there is a need to control effects, the less sensitive targets that can be infiltrated will tend to be, and the less risks actors can take in doing so will tend to be as well. Consequently, the effects of such types of operations are highly unlikely to be strategically significant, that is, to make a difference in the pursuit of strategic goals.

Similarly, simultaneously increasing speed and intensity in turn tends to doubly increase the risk of losing control, either through discovery and failure to produce effects or through producing unexpected effects with unintended outcomes. With little time to get to know targets, manipulating sensitive, well-protected parts of systems is likely to be both extremely challenging and complex. Spies involved must likely take daring risks, leading to a very high chance of being discovered, as well as high risks that the manipulation produces undesired or unexpected effects. Operations of this kind are thus highly likely to fail entirely or to produce unintended effects that are counterproductive in the pursuit of strategic goals. In other words, if they succeed to produce effects, such operations are thus likely to produce strategically significant ones—yet with a high risk that the latter run counter to the subverter's strategic ends.

Finally, maximizing both intensity and control tends to slow speed to a glacial pace due to the added needs for reconnaissance and development of means of exploitations that ensure a high degree of familiarity *as well as* significant scope and scale of effects. Such operations are most likely to produce strategically significant and useful effects, yet the more urgently these effects are needed in the pursuit of strategic goals, the less likely such operations are to produce them in time. If goals are important yet not urgent, one could conclude that such slow-moving operations are the ideal use of subversion, guaranteeing strategic value despite the trade-offs of the trilemma. However, there is a problem: the longer spies linger in place, the higher the probability becomes that they make a mistake out of human fallibility or that victims discover them by simple chance. In other words, the very time investment actors make to improve their control over targets and effects starts to work against them as time passes—adding a further trade-off. Where the threshold lies between "sufficient" and "excessive" time investment is the more difficult to predict the less familiar one is with target systems, and yet the efforts to get familiar with these systems may alert victims to one's presence. Just biding one's time thus does not offer a reliable way out of the trilemma.

To conclude, subversive operations involve significant challenges that constrain their speed, intensity, and control. In meeting these challenges, subversive actors face a set of trade-offs that confronts them with a trilemma. This trilemma and its trade-offs limit the strategic value subversion can achieve in practice because in most circumstances it will be either too slow, too weak, or too volatile to contribute to strategic goals. These shortcomings in turn help explain why subversion has rarely offered a viable standalone alternative to force, as discussed in the preceding section—as well as the escalation to force many subversive campaigns have resulted in.

Defining the Quality of Subversion

This chapter has developed a theory of subversion as an instrument of power and identified three distinguishing characteristics. First, subversion primarily relies on a mechanism of secret exploitation and manipulation that indirectly undermines adversary systems and their constituent parts or manipulates them against the latter. It exerts power by exploiting flaws in systems of rules and practices, the institutions and organizations that make up the adversary's social fabric. Exploitation means using existing rules and practices to manipulate systems to produce unexpected outcomes (from the victim's perspective), such as assuming control over parts or the whole of a targeted institution and using it to produce effects detrimental to the adversary. In doing so, if successful, subversion turns targeted institutions into instruments of power that allow the subverting actor to get the adversary to do what they would otherwise not do or erode the latter's capacity to resist other means of influence.

Second, subversion promises significant strategic value, both as an independent instrument and as a complement to force, by manipulating policy and public opinion, eroding institutions and capabilities, or overthrowing an adversary's regime. Because it is secret and indirect, using the adversary's own institutions and population, subversion provides a way to interfere in adversary affairs at lower risks of escalation and reprisals as well as lower material and human costs compared to the use of force. And yet, it is still capable of producing strategically significant effects. Subversive campaigns can get an adversary to do what they would otherwise not do by manipulating public opinion, by infiltrating and manipulating government, or by eroding an adversary's capacity to resist by degrading its material capabilities, disrupting its economy, undermining institutional effectiveness and efficiency, and disintegrating social cohesion. Finally, subversion can replace entire regimes by mobilizing and coordinating opposition groups to assume power from within and overthrow them.

Third, the same mechanism that enables subversion's strategic promise poses an operational trilemma whose trade-offs limit its strategic value in practice. The faster operations are, the less intense their effects will tend to be, and the less control actors will have over them. The more intense effects an operation pursues, the slower it will tend to be, and the higher the risk of failure and control loss will be. Conversely, the more actors try to maximize control in subversive operations, the slower the latter and the less intense their effects will tend to be. Finally, operations that maximize two of these variables will tend to involve a near-total loss of the remaining variable. Accordingly, the majority of subversive operations will be either too slow, too weak, or too volatile to contribute to strategic goals. Due to these shortcomings, in most circumstances subversion will also fall short of providing a viable alternative to the use of force. The more vital the interests at stake, and the more ambitious the strategic goals subversion is aimed to fulfill, the likelier the eventual use of force becomes—either to help subversion succeed despite its limitations or as a contingency response to its failure.

To clarify, this theory does not mean that subversion is universally doomed to failure. Given the right circumstances, it is possible that subversive operations, or campaigns consisting of multiple operations over time, produce significant strategic value. However, the theory predicts that these circumstances are hard to meet because they usually require exceptionally capable actors who are exceptionally lucky in exploiting targeted systems that are exceptionally vulnerable and yet exceptionally capable of causing harm to victims. In less exceptional circumstances, the trilemma makes it very difficult to produce effects that significantly, or at least measurably, contribute toward the achievement of strategic goals within reasonable timeframes and at reasonable chances of success. One way actors can meet this difficulty is to increase resource investments into an operation, such as by hiring more personnel, improving training and infrastructure, or simply allocating existing resources over a longer timeframe. Yet the more one increases resource investments, the more subversion loses its cost advantage compared to alternatives. In other words, the more harm one wants to cause an adversary, the less cost-effective subversion will likely tend to be compared to alternative instruments of power (including force).

Finally, as the preceding point already suggests, when measuring strategic value, it is important to distinguish between operations, campaigns, and strategies. Individual operations may fail to make a measurable contribution to strategic goals, yet multiple such operations that form a campaign may cumulatively achieve a measurable contribution. Individual campaigns may in turn fall short of making a contribution, but multiple campaigns in the pursuit of manipulation, erosion, or overthrow strategies may fulfill a goal. The wider one zooms out, the likelier measurable contributions become—but the harder isolating the causal impact of subversion toward the achievement of strategic goals vis-à-vis other variables becomes. This challenge is even more pronounced when assessing erosion strategies that do not pursue a specific goal but rather have the general aim of weakening adversaries. To meet these challenges, in the empirical analysis I start by establishing the subverter's strategic goals as clearly as possible and proceed by evaluating each subversive operation's individual contribution toward these goals and, finally, the cumulative contribution of larger campaigns. Because evidence is often incomplete, even where there is a lack of tangible impact, I consider at least a plausible causal pathway toward making a contribution. Finally, to assess the cumulative and diffuse impact of erosion strategies, I consider not only such plausible pathways but also more general indicators where correlation with subversive activity may indicate a possible impact, namely economic data and survey data on public support for a government.

When testing this theory of how subversion works and its strategic value against the case studies, the strongest type of evidence supporting it would document the constraints and trade-offs it predicts across multiple operations. The concept of the trilemma and its trade-offs form the core of the theory. Evidence of the challenges in the process of exploitation and manipulation that produce these trade-offs supports the foundations of that theory. Absence of such evidence poses a problem on the other hand, especially if the constraints and trade-offs the theory predicts are evidence regardless—suggesting other causal mechanisms must be at play. Because decision-making processes happen behind closed doors and little evidence is typically available, trade-offs usually only become apparent in the shifting prioritization of speed, intensity, and control across multiple operations by the same actor. Evidence showing that such shifting prioritization of individual variables produces corresponding losses across the other variables supports the theory. Evidence showing these trade-offs to be consistent across multiple operations pursuing different kinds of effects strongly supports the theory. Meanwhile, absence of evidence of these trade-offs—in other words, operations that evade the trilemma despite stable external conditions—challenges the theory. Individual instances of such evasion suggest a need to refine the theory to integrate the additional variables that might explain their diverging outcomes. Consistent evidence of such evasion means the theory must be rejected since it is clearly wrong.

The theory would be further supported by evidence confirming the hypothesized strategic role of subversion as a primarily independent instrument of power as well as its use as a complement. Evidence challenging these assumptions indicates the need for refinement of the theory but does not threaten its core. Evidence showing subversive operations producing significant strategic value occasionally is in line with the theory, but evidence showing this regularly, or even consistently, indicate a more fundamental problem with the theory—and would likely go hand in hand with evidence disconfirming the trade-offs of the trilemma discussed above. It would indicate the theory to be invalid.

Finally, change in the quality of subversion would mean a significant departure from at least one of the defining characteristics. If technological change makes it possible, for example, to introduce vulnerabilities in adversary systems that were not previously there, this fundamentally changes the nature of subversion as it no longer depends on existing vulnerabilities. Similarly, if new technologies make it possible to overcome one or more of the constraints and resulting trade-offs posed by the trilemma, for example, both the strategic role and value of subversion are likely to change significantly. Current expectations around cyber operations see precisely this kind of change occurring, as the next chapter will show.

2
Information Technology and Subversion

Information technology offers new opportunities for subversion, but it does not overcome the trilemma. Rather, as this chapter will show, in cyber operations this trilemma is further exacerbated. To show why, the chapter first establishes how cyber operations work: they subvert information communications systems by exploiting vulnerabilities and manipulating systems to do things they are not supposed to. This analysis identifies the different types of vulnerabilities cyber operations exploit, the kinds of systems they can target, and the means they employ. The nature of these means finally explains why cyber operations struggle to achieve some effects that are relatively easy to achieve with traditional subversion.

Rather than human agents, cyber operations rely on immaterial subversive "agents"—namely computer programs and algorithms—to produce effects. Since the agents are immaterial, any material effects an operation aims to produce depend entirely on the properties of the systems it targets. In practice, this means that any societal process that is not partially or fully computerized remains beyond the reach of cyber operations.

Consequently, the subsequent section explains, cyber operations occupy a narrower strategic role than traditional subversion. They are unable to implement manipulation and overthrow strategies on their own. However, and conversely, due to their reliance on immaterial agents, cyber operations have an advantage in producing large-scale effects. Computer viruses can multiply and spread in ways human agents cannot. With these properties, cyber operations are most suited for the third type of subversive campaigns, namely erosion. Within this narrower strategic scope, meanwhile, cyber operations face the same types of constraints as traditional subversion. The third and main section thus argues that the trilemma persists and examines its permutations in cyber operations. Examining the specific challenges and trade-offs involved reveals that the scale advantage of cyber operations also comes with a heightened risk of control loss. The greater the capacity of a computer virus to spread automatically across a wide range of systems, the harder it becomes to control or even predict its spread—and thus ensure that the effects this virus produces align with strategic goals. This challenge of control thus limits or forfeits practical strategic gains in many circumstances. Meanwhile, due to their reliance on immaterial agents, cyber operations face steeper hurdles to produce physical effects compared to traditional subversion. A spy can exert physical force on their own, while a computer virus can only cause physical effects if the system it compromises is capable to do so. Consequently, both the range of effects and the ease of achieving them are reduced in cyber operations compared to their traditional counterparts.

The final section thus concludes that the quality of subversion does not fundamentally change. Rather than revolutionizing conflict, cyber operations constitute an evolution in techniques of subversion, with their own distinct advantages and disadvantages. Finally, it discusses the strategic limitations and formulates expectations for empirical analysis.

The Subversive Nature of Cyber Power

Early theorizing conceived of cyber operations as means of warfare; hence, theories of cyber power from that era conceived of them primarily as military capabilities—sometimes expressed in the idea of "cyber weapons."[1] Yet as Max Smeets has shown, rather than stockpiling weapons, even military cyber commands act more like service providers, developing the capacity to meet the challenges posed by exploitation.[2] As this example underlines, like traditional subversion, cyber operations produce outcomes through secret exploitation of flaws in systems of rules and practices. They target a new type of system, however, namely information technologies embedded in modern societies. These are best conceptualized as complex sociotechnical systems, composed of both technical artifacts and their users.[3] Just as the targeted systems differ, so do the types of vulnerability involved. Cyber operations exploit not only social but also technical flaws. Despite these differences, this section shows, the mechanism of exploitation involved functions the same fundamental way. Cyber power thus involves the capacity to subvert adversary computer systems and the way they are used to produce outcomes that benefit the subverter.

The central mechanism employed by cyber operations is hacking, most commonly defined as the exploitation of vulnerabilities in information communications and technologies (ICTs) to gain unauthorized access and control.[4] ICTs do not exist separately from society but are increasingly embedded in it, forming complex sociotechnical systems composed of the technical artifacts involved, the interactions they enable, and the rules and practices surrounding their use.[5] Accordingly, hackers can target two types of vulnerabilities: social and technical. Social vulnerabilities consist of flaws in the security rules and practices regulating the use of computer systems as well as the fallibilities of the human users of the systems. The parallels to traditional subversion are obvious, and the earliest practitioners of such techniques recognized them accordingly. Susan Headley, a member of the notorious "Cyberpunk" hacker group that became infamous for their various exploits during the 1980s, is among the pioneers of such techniques, which she called "psychotechnical subversion."[6] Headley would combine her technical knowledge with skills in deception and persuasion to get users to unwittingly disclose access credentials for sensitive systems.[7]

There are many means to trick users into giving out access credentials or to simply steal them, commonly known today as "social engineering." A classic, widely used means of social engineering is "phishing" emails. Phishing exploits human emotions and behavioral characteristics (such as evoking fear, leveraging loss aversion, inducing curiosity, and exploiting trust[8]) to induce the targeted individual to unwittingly provide access to a target system or service to the perpetrator. A key example is an email targeting Gmail users suggesting their email account has been compromised, and a fake Google password recovery page that looks like the real thing yet sends the password to a server in Russia—as happened to John Podesta, chairman of Hillary Clinton's 2016 presidential campaign.[9] As this example illustrates, social engineering involves the exploitation of weaknesses in security rules or human behavior to gain access and control over targeted systems.

Apart from social vulnerabilities, the architecture of ICTs provides a second type of vulnerability in the technology itself. What ICTs do is determined by a set of logical instructions and routines, commonly known as computer code.[10] Such code creates the applications and services that run on computer systems and enable us to interact with, and via, them.[11] They also exist at a deeper level, hard-wired into the computer components themselves, known as firmware.[12] Hacking targets flaws in this code in order to make computer systems do things not intended by their designers and owners. Programming code consists of logical instructions to machines but is written by humans. Because we are fallible, code inevitably contains vulnerabilities that enable exploitation. As Jon Erickson explains:

Exploiting a program is simply a clever way of getting the computer to do what you want it to do, even if the currently running program was designed to prevent that action. Since a program can really only do what it's designed to do, the security holes are actually flaws or oversights in the design of the program or the environment the program is running in.[13]

Although this type of vulnerability is novel, and so is the technology targeted, the primary reliance on exploitation underlines the subversive nature of cyber operations.

The need for secrecy required to succeed with this exploitation further underlines these parallels. Hence, Erickson stresses, "stealth is one of the hacker's most valuable assets" because "the sooner an intrusion is detected, the sooner it can be dealt with and the more likely it can be contained."[14] As in traditional subversion, discovery thus allows the victim to neutralize the compromise, leading to a loss of access and control over the target system. Accordingly, cyber operations also usually proceed both covertly and clandestinely.

Considering these parallels, it is unsurprising that the subversive nature of hacking, especially of the politically motivated kind, has long been recognized in technical circles. Already in 1972, a "Computer Security Technology Planning Study" by James P. Anderson for the Electronic Systems Division of the US Air Force warned that "the nature of shared use multi-level computer systems present to a malicious user a unique opportunity for attempting to subvert through programming the mechanism upon which security depends (i.e., the control of the computer)."[15] In 1980, when the Internet consisted only of a handful of universities, Alan Myers, then a master's student in computer science at the Naval Postgraduate School, posited that "the subversion of a computer system is the covert and methodical undermining of internal and external controls over a system's lifetime to allow unauthorized and undetected access to system resources and/or information."[16]

Today, technical analysis of cyber operations routinely refers to their subversive nature. For example, the *Hacker's Handbook* by Susan Young and Dave Aitel labels a description of a fictional hacking operation a "case study of subversion."[17] Meanwhile, a recent paper in computer science discusses a new type of virus that "subverts the self-protection features of several antivirus software solutions."[18] Similarly, a report by information security vendor RSA described how "a software application used by system administrators to analyze Windows logs had been subverted at its distribution point with malicious, signed code."[19]

Some political scientists have highlighted the use of cyber operations for subversion. Thomas Rid's 2013 classic *Cyber War Will Not Take Place* argued that rather than warfare, cyber operations are best suited for espionage, sabotage, and subversion.[20] Yet, drawing on Kitson's work, he conceived of subversion in the narrower Cold War sense as the undermining or overthrowing of authority—and thus separated cyber operations that pursued this goal from sabotage and espionage.[21] In contrast, I argue that all these operations share a reliance on the same mechanism, namely exploitation and manipulation of computer systems. In other words, they depend on the subversion of technology. Jon Lindsay highlighted this subversive nature of hacking in a 2017 paper as well, but without linking this crucial insight to a theory of cyber power and examining its differences compared to traditional subversion.[22] The remainder of this section commences this work.

In short, I argue that cyber operations subvert ICTs and the way they are used to produce a range of outcomes. As instruments of subversion, they also share its indirect production of effects—using adversary systems against the adversary. This indirect approach is further pronounced in cyber operations, however, since they typically rely exclusively on immaterial means of exploitation. Whereas traditional subversion involves the deployment of spies to adversary territory, and possibly even material resources to support opposition groups, cyber operations can be carried out entirely remotely.[23] Only information passes borders, be it phishing messages to conduct social engineering or malicious code to exploit software vulnerabilities. Hence, it requires far less resources, infrastructure, and organizational capacity in the target country compared to traditional subversion.

The ability to access systems remotely is not only an advantage, however. Their reliance on immaterial means of exploitation also limits the scope of effects. The previous chapter discussed how the capacity of spies to exert force and threaten people can help them in some cases to gain access to systems without suitable vulnerabilities, or if they lack the skills or time to exploit the latter. That option does not exist in cyber operations. Computers cannot be swayed through force or threats thereof. They always and only do exactly what their programming logic prescribes, and this logic cannot be overridden by force. As Martin Libicki notes, there is "no forced entry in cyberspace. Whoever gets in enters through pathways produced by the system itself."[24] Computers can be destroyed, but in contrast to humans, they cannot be compelled or coerced to take action that violates their internal logic. In this light, cyber operations could be considered a "purer" form of subversion, entirely dependent on target systems.

Importantly, this limitation applies even to cyber operations that involve human agents in the field who establish physical access to target systems, such as the USB key example mentioned above. Such agents can, of course, damage or destroy equipment, but in that case the operation in question would be simple traditional sabotage. Beyond generating access to systems, the human potential for physical action becomes irrelevant in cyber operations, however, because only the exploitation of flaws in the logical rules and routines at the software level allows manipulation of the system's actions. For example, the infamous "Stuxnet" cyber operation that degraded Iran's nuclear enrichment program in 2010 by damaging centrifuges most likely started with a human agent who connected a USB stick or engineering diagnosis device to the Natanz nuclear enrichment facility.[25] But with that action the human involvement already reached its zenith as the connected device installed the US- and Israeli-designed Stuxnet malware on the Natanz systems, which then proceeded to manipulate the rotation speed of these centrifuges at the software level while displaying deceptive information to the human operators of the system showing all worked as normal.[26]

The effects cyber operations can produce thus depend exclusively on the capacities of the computer systems they target. Operators may interact directly with people through computer systems, for example, sending phishing emails through an email provider that the victim opens on their workstation. The interaction is mediated through the system, however. The person getting fooled only opens a way in, just as with the USB stick in Stuxnet. Any effects such exploitation enables depend entirely on the properties of that targeted system. The means of manipulating what computer systems do are immaterial, as are their immediate effects, namely entering logical instructions that produce unexpected and unintended outcomes (from the victim's perspective). Yet in some computer systems such manipulation enables social and physical effects because they are embedded in such processes.[27] The more deeply systems are embedded in social, economic, and physical processes, the greater the scope of effects. The more devices and/or people are affected, meanwhile, the greater the scale of effects that becomes possible. For example, hacking someone's personal laptop will not allow producing physical effects because the laptop does not regulate any physical processes.

Producing physical effects thus requires control over a computer system that operates physical machinery, such as industrial control systems.

On a strategic level, the scope and scale of effects cyber operations can produce in theory is thus limited by the availability of suitable target systems and the scope and scale of their embeddedness in adversary society. As computerization grows, so does the range of possible effects cyber operations can produce. For example, the more military hardware involves computer systems, and the more such computer systems are networked, the greater the potential becomes that cyber operations can produce militarily relevant effects. Crucially, however, even in such cyber operations targeting military equipment the mechanism of action is subversive. They still involve the exploitation of vulnerabilities and cannot substitute the latter with force. If cyber operations fail to successfully exploit a vulnerability or fail to manipulate the computer system in a military asset, the sponsor of the operation can, of course, choose to destroy the targets with conventional weapons. Yet this is simple use of force, rather than a cyber operation.

To conclude, cyber operations rely on a subversive mechanism that produces effects through the secret exploitation of flaws in computer systems and the way they are used. Moreover, cyber operations are both more dependent on exploitation and more indirect in their effects compared to traditional subversion. In other words, cyber operations may in fact be considered more "purely" subversive. The next section will show why these characteristics narrow the strategic role of cyber operations compared to traditional subversion.

The Strategic Role and Promise of Cyber Operations

Since cyber operations rely on a subversive mechanism of action, they share the latter's perceived strategic promise. The preceding chapter discussed why subversion promises a lower-risk and lower-cost alternative to force. Current expectations hold that information technology further enhances its strategic value, enhancing both its scope and scale. Yet this section shows their strategic role is actually narrower.

Current scholarship suggests information technology increases the speed of conflict, the scale of effects, and the ease of anonymity. Lucas Kello emphasizes the advantages of "the technology's sheer speed of action . . . released from the restrictions of the physical laws of motion."[28]

Michael Warner argues that "the technology of cyberspace seems to be producing something unexpected: operations and effects that resemble covert actions but are much larger in their scale and reach."[29] Ben Buchanan similarly stresses that "because of cyber operations' possibility for automation and rapid propagation, disruption can scale."[30] Despite these advantages, cyber operations offer a relative ease of anonymity, such as Harknett and Fischerkeller's notion of actors' ability to "manage attribution."[31] Combined, Harknett and Smeets argue, these advantages expand both the scope and scale of cyber operations, "resulting in a difference in kind" to traditional covert operations.[32]

There are clear indications that cyber operations can produce superior scale effects over traditional subversion. The global Internet is growing in both scope and scale. Both the number of devices and the scope of their embeddedness in societies are increasing. ICTs are involved in more and more social, economic, and physical processes. The "attack surface" for cyber operations, to use a military-inspired term popular with technical analysts, is thus vast and growing. On top of this, cyber operations have another advantage: the ability to leverage self-proliferating programs, meaning programs that independently create copies of themselves and spread them to vulnerable systems within a targeted network.[33] Such programs are commonly known as viruses or worms. This is an obvious advantage compared to traditional subversion, which typically requires sending additional personnel or material resources to the field to expand scale. In general, the scale of effects that cyber operations can produce in theory is likely greater than traditional subversion, and scaling up effects is likely easier and cheaper compared to traditional subversion. In this regard, prevailing wisdom is correct.

However, the scope of effects cyber operations can produce is significantly more limited compared to traditional subversion. The reason is their dependence on the capacities of target systems touched upon in the previous section. Not only the scale but also the scope of computerization is increasing—yet key areas of social and political life remain out of reach. Most importantly, and contrary to prevailing cyberwar fears, cyber operations cannot (currently) reproduce military covert operations. There are (still) no computer systems that can fully autonomously project force; hence, there are currently no suitable targets to exploit and manipulate. Cyber operations can, on the other hand, disrupt the operation of computer systems used in military applications. That way, they can provide advantages in conflict as "force multipliers," for example, by disabling enemy weapons or disrupting communications lines.[34] Yet this is a complement to the use of force, increasing the latter's effectiveness. As long as there are no autonomous computer-controlled weapons systems deployed at scale—ideally, never—cyber operations will not be able to generate force analogous to military operations.

Even compared to nonmilitary, subversive covert operations, however, cyber operations offer an inferior scope of effects. As discussed in the previous chapter, subversion is capable of five types of effects:

(1) manipulating public opinion
(2) manipulating government policy
(3) degrading material capabilities and disrupting the economy
(4) undermining institutional effectiveness and efficiency
(5) regime change

Because of the limited reach of computerization, cyber operations can currently reproduce only three out of these types of effects, namely 1, 3, and 4. The most consequential subversive operations, namely manipulation of policy and all-out regime change, are beyond their reach. Rather, cyber operations are primarily suited for long-term "erosion" strategies combining one or more of the three effect types above.[35] The current strand of theorizing in cybersecurity that emphasizes that cyber operations produce strategic value primarily through cumulative effects, which also informs the US emerging strategy of "persistent engagement" designed to counter it, reflects this situation—although it does not draw the connection to historic uses of this strategy and limits.[36]

Manipulating public opinion (effect type 1) is clearly within the purview of cyber operations, even in the narrower conception I use in this comparison. Hack-and-leak operations, which involve the targeted public release of sensitive information obtained through hacking, are a key instrument of manipulating public opinion. The staggered release of Hilary Clinton's emails, obtained through exploitation of her email server, as part of the Russian-sponsored 2016 election interference campaign constitutes a key example of this technique.[37] The global reach of online news platforms, and especially social media, also provides cyber-enabled subversion with a plausible advantage in scale compared to traditional means. Although in this analysis I had to exclude dedicated social media disinformation campaigns for simple reasons of space, some emerging evidence challenges this expected scale advantage, as I highlight in the conclusion.

Government manipulation (effect type 2), on the other hand, is beyond the reach of cyber operations. Although government officials use digital means of communication, the actual business of government and policy formulation is carried out by people rather than computers. Hence, direct influence on government policy in the way subversive agents in high government positions enable is out of the reach of cyber operations alone.[38]

In contrast, most modern societies have computerized a significant and growing proportion of physical and economic processes. The rise of the "Internet of Things" (small sensor devices connected to the Internet, such as fitness trackers),[39] the computerization of industry (dubbed "industry 4.0"),[40] and the growing digitalization of financial transactions[41] are key examples. This increasing computerization enables cyber operations to produce a growing range of physical or economic effects, thus allowing the use of cyber operations to affect a targeted state's material resources and economic capacity (effect type 3). Similarly, the growing computerization of internal processes in public and private institutions, such as communication, accounting, and supply chain management, enables cyber operations to manipulate or disrupt these processes. In doing so, cyber operations can thus undermine the effectiveness and efficiency of targeted institutions (effect type 4). Consider the example of shutting down government communication systems, especially in times of crisis.

Overthrowing governments is beyond the scope of cyber operations for the same reason as government manipulation: it requires mobilization of opposition groups and continued control, and often also material support to the latter—typically through subversive agents placed in positions of influence.[42] To be sure, ICTs may help in communication with opposition groups, but they cannot replace the material resources and personnel required for such types of operations. To put it bluntly, as long as government is carried out by people rather than computers,[43] cyber operations alone will be incapable of overthrowing them (effect type 5).

In short, with the mechanism of exploitation and manipulation, cyber operations share the same strategic role as traditional subversion. Contrary to prevailing expectations that cyber operations offer superior scope and scale of effects over traditional covert operations, the discussion showed that their scope of effects is more limited—and with it their strategic role.

This limitation indicates overall more limited strategic value. Of course, new revolutionary theories suggest, and the discussion confirmed, that cyber operations have clear scale advantages. Hence, even within their narrower scope of effects, the new technology utilized by cyber operations may enable such vast scale of effects that it fundamentally changes the strategic role and value of subversion—thus altering its quality. Yet examining its operational constraints, as the next section does, reveals the opposite is the case.

The Subversive Trilemma Persists

The use of information technology does not overcome the subversive trilemma. Cyber operations do promise superior scale of effects, yet as this section shows, at the cost of increased risk of control loss. Meanwhile, cyber operations' dependence on remote systems further constrains the intensity of effects they can reliably achieve. Combined with their narrower scope of effects, cyber operations thus likely provide more limited strategic value than traditional subversion.

Electrons move at the speed of light, but cyber operations do not. For the data packets carried by streams of electrons across the global network to produce effects, their contents must be designed to exploit a given vulnerability in targeted systems. As in traditional subversion, this takes time. Target systems must be identified, their properties and vulnerabilities must be reconnoitered, and means of exploitation must be developed. Operatives must familiarize themselves with target systems so well that they discover things the system's designers themselves missed, then use their creativity and skill to come up with a way of exploiting them. Once exploits are developed, the speed of electronic transmission means effects can be produced almost instantaneously. Yet getting means of exploitation ready requires human learning and ingenuity, which moves at a different pace. Identifying vulnerabilities in software and developing exploits often takes months.[44] Because cyber operations depend on both social and technical vulnerabilities, and because computer systems are increasingly complex, they tend to be more demanding than traditional subversion. More complexity means more effort, and thus more time. Combined with reconnaissance and familiarization with the target system's operation, sophisticated cyber operations like Stuxnet can require years of lead time before they reach the stage where active effects can be attempted.[45] Add to this the years, or possibly decades, of training and experience required for operatives to succeed at this high level. In short, communication is fast, yet exploitation remains slow.

Meanwhile, dependence on target systems limits the intensity of effects. As explained, the maximum possible scope and scale of effects cyber operations can produce is determined by the reach of target systems (i.e., the social and physical processes they regulate). The actual scope and scale of effects, in turn, is further limited by the extent of control an actor has over the target system at a given moment in time. Compared to the use of spies, physical effects are generally only within reach if an actor has gained control over the specific computer systems within an organization's networks that operate attached machinery. Even when control is established, however, there remains a risk of discovery. The more capable a targeted system is of producing significant effects, the more complex and the more likely it is to be protected and monitored—increasing both the efforts needed to exploit it and the risk of discovery.[46] The TRITON malware, one of the most advanced malicious programs targeting industrial control systems, illustrates that risk. This highly advanced malware was, in theory, capable of physically damaging target systems with the potential of causing fatalities.[47] The hackers also succeeded in gaining access to and control over relevant industrial control systems at Middle Eastern energy providers.[48] Yet in the process of establishing and expanding this control, they inadvertently triggered a built-in safety measure of these systems. It caused an automated shutdown and prompted an investigation by the victim that led to discovery of the operation before the destructive effects it was capable of could be produced.[49]

Cyber operations can achieve greater scale than traditional subversion because computer programs can multiply and spread on their own. However, this advantage is a double-edged sword since greater scale of effects impacts risks of discovery and control loss. In principle, the design of the Internet, where security was initially not a primary concern, makes it easy for actors to hide their identity.[50] However, obscuring an ongoing compromise in a system requires constant efforts, and the greater its scale, the greater the risk of being found out tends to become. Consequently, the secrecy-size dilemma still likely applies to cyber-enhanced subversion. More critically, automated proliferation may spread beyond targeted networks, further increasing discovery risks. Stuxnet, for example, was discovered only because it spread far beyond its intended target in Iran. Eventually, a hitherto little-known antivirus firm in Belarus detected and identified the virus.[51]

Similarly, the more sensitive the target system, the more vigilant its operators tend to be, further raising discovery risks. Each discovery in turn not only "blows" the cover of the current operation but also reveals tactics, techniques, and procedures (TTPs) used by a set of public and private sector analysts. These TTPs can then be used to identify the actor behind future operations, now a routine procedure carried out by both private sector "threat intelligence" providers and governments.[52] Combined, these risks pose significant challenges to the maintenance of anonymity online. The decreasing "dwell time" of intruders on systems, meaning increasing speed of discovery, and the growing set of cyber operations publicly attributed to state actors attest to this risk.[53]

Finally, cyber operations also face comparable limits to control as traditional subversion. Importantly, the ability of computer viruses to self-reproduce further increases the likelihood and risks of control loss. In general, the control of an actor pursuing a cyber operation against an adversary is limited in several ways. First, control is always incomplete because discovery allows the victim to initiate countermeasures and neutralize the compromise. Second, hackers will have incomplete familiarity with target systems. Knowledge goes only as far as reconnaissance has reached, and there is always a chance operatives missed characteristics of those systems that have been reconnoitered (see the TRITON example earlier). Third, because of this limited familiarity, there is a risk of the target system reacting differently to manipulation than expected. It may not produce the intended effect, or it may produce an unintended effect. Fourth, both subversive agents and proxy groups may act differently than expected or become entirely uncontrollable. Both state-sponsored and independent hacking groups may act independently, producing unintended consequences.[54] Moreover, just like spies have tended to go off the rails under the pressure of undercover life,[55] malicious programs can proliferate out of control and wreak unintended havoc. A classic example is the "Morris worm," named after its creator Robert Tappan Morris and one of the first computer viruses released into the wild in 1988.[56] Intended as a network-mapping tool for the early Internet, the program's ability to spread independently and carry out resource-intensive measurements at affected systems caused widespread disruption.[57] None of this was intended by its creator, yet once released, the creator had lost all control over the virus—at one stage even considering releasing a second virus to the network to delete the first one.[58] In short, cyber operations face the same types of limits to control as traditional subversion. The dependence on adversary systems constrains the extent of control over the target system as well as over the effects produced through that system. In case of the use of self-proliferating malware, cyber operations also face limited control over the subversive agent.

With their reliance on exploitation and manipulation, need for secrecy, and dependence on adversary systems, cyber operations thus share the same types of constraints as traditional subversion. Accordingly, actors implementing cyber operations also face the same types of trade-offs. Just like in traditional subversion, the faster an operation is, the less intense its effects tend to be and the higher the risk of control loss. Increasing speed decreases the time available for reconnaissance of target systems and their vulnerabilities and development of means of exploitation. Consequently, hackers will be less familiar with the target system and its users, and the risk of missing something or losing control increases. A virus developed to spread in a network from administrative systems to industrial control systems may thus fail to do so because the network is configured differently than the hackers anticipated. Or it might be discovered before it spreads to the industrial control systems themselves. Even if it reaches these systems, it may fail to produce the intended effect—as illustrated by TRITON.

Similarly, increasing intensity tends to decrease speed and control. More intensity requires greater scope and scale of access to targets, which requires more reconnaissance and development time. In cyber operations, this generally means reaching systems that reach into social, economic, and physical processes in the real world. Burrowing into such systems itself takes time because they tend to be more complex and closely guarded than "standard" systems; furthermore, it requires learning not only how the computer system functions but also the processes it controls.[59] With that added complexity come added risks of discovery as well as of something going wrong when proceeding with the manipulation to produce some unexpected and unintended outcome for the victim using the system—and thus the risk of control loss.

Finally, as in traditional subversion, increasing control tends to decrease both speed and intensity. It requires increasing familiarity with the target and refining means of exploitation—both of which take time. Increasing control also requires extra care when proceeding, which in practice means limiting the scope and scale of subversion of a targeted system to avoid premature detection as well as the risk of making mistakes when spreading toward the "edges" of systems reaching into social, economic, or physical processes.

As in traditional subversion, this negative correlation also extends to increases in two variables at once, which tends to "doubly" decrease the effectiveness of the remaining variable. Operations pursuing intense effects at high speed are very likely to fail or run out of control. Maximizing control and intensity meanwhile tends to reduce speed to a glacial pace, requiring at least multiple years of preparation. Consider Stuxnet, which took five years of preparation and painstaking efforts to limit its spread to the highly specialized systems at the nuclear enrichment facility it targeted—and still went out of control, leading to its eventual discovery in Belarus. This example also illustrates the associated risk of chance discoveries as time proceeds, leading to diminishing returns for operations that sacrifice speed at the cost of intensity and control.

Consequently, just like their traditional counterparts, cyber operations will mostly be too slow, too weak, or too volatile to reliably contribute to strategic goals when and where needed. Technological change does not overcome the trilemma. On the contrary, the properties identified above indicate that they face *further* limitations in strategic value. Since producing physical effects involves greater complexity and demands, cyber operations are likely relatively less efficient and effective at producing effects of a given level of intensity (say sabotage of industrial machinery). Furthermore, greater complexity also raises the risk of control loss. Conversely, cyber operations have a clear advantage in scale, and the resulting ability to produce mass disruptions is of potential strategic significance. Again, however, the greater complexity and sheer scale involved raise the risk of control loss. Hence, while mass effects may be strategically significant, there is a considerable risk they do not contribute to strategic goals. If control is lost through one of the mechanisms described above, effects may fail to produce the subverter's objective or run counter to it—possibly even resulting in a net strategic loss.

To sum up, cyber operations not only exhibit the same types of constraints in speed, intensity, and control as traditional subversion but also are subject to the same operational trilemma produced by the interaction between these constraining variables. Hence, both the characteristics of the operational mechanism and its constraints are marked by continuity rather than change.

However, the differences in the relative ease of maximizing the scope and scale of effects have important strategic implications concerning the interplay with the use of force and associated escalation potentials. Cyber-only campaigns are less likely to involve a final blow by force than traditional subversive campaigns or mixed campaigns because their scope of effects is more modest. Cyber operations and campaigns, on the other hand, may have a higher failure risk due to limits of control. Whether this characteristic increases the chance of sponsors of cyber operations opting for force to avoid their impending failure is an open question, however. Considering cyber operations are primarily suited for long-term erosion campaigns pursuing the diffuse and difficult-to-measure goal of weakening adversaries, such critical failures perceived to necessitate the use of force are probably rather unlikely.

Continuity over Change in the Quality of Subversion

Information technologies provide new opportunities for exploitation but also new challenges in implementing it. Overall, and contrary to the assumptions of new cyber revolution theorists, similarities outweigh differences to traditional subversion. Technological change has produced differences in degree rather than in kind, this chapter has shown, primarily concerning the scope and scale of effects. Consequently, the quality of subversion has remained stable across its three dimensions.

First, like traditional subversion, cyber operations rely on secret exploitation and manipulation of adversary systems to produce unexpected and unintended outcomes, from the victim's perspective, that benefit the sponsor of the operation to the detriment of the victim.

Second, like traditional subversion, cyber operations can fulfill both an independent strategic role and a complement to other instruments of power. Contrary to prevailing expectations, however, their strategic role is likely more limited than traditional subversion. While they can reproduce some of the effects of traditional subversion, namely erosion strategies manipulating public opinion and sabotaging institutions and infrastructure, the manipulation of government policy and regime change are beyond their reach. The superior scale of effects cyber operations can produce in theory is weighed down in practice by the complexity involved and the risk of control loss limiting the strategic value of scale-maximizing operations.

Third, and accordingly, the subversive trilemma persists, limiting the strategic value of cyber operations. Consequently, actors in cyber conflict still have to make trade-offs between speed, intensity, and control, although each of these variables is essential to implement operations capable of producing effects when and where they are needed that reliably contribute to strategic goals. Moreover, each of these variables can individually lead to failure if actors sacrifice too much of one for the sake of maximizing the others. Overall, like traditional subversion, cyber operations can thus be expected to be either too slow, too weak, or too volatile to produce significant strategic value in most circumstances. Consequently, and combined with their more limited strategic scope, cyber operations do not expand the range of outcomes states can achieve, short of war, compared to traditional subversion. On the contrary, these characteristics indicate they further narrow it.

These characteristics also cast doubt on the assertion that cyber operations can produce greater strategic value than traditional means through cumulative effects. Given that cyber operations can produce a narrower range of less intense effect types than traditional subversion and face greater challenges in controlling effects especially at scale, it is hard to see why the cumulative effects of cyber campaigns would be expected to be superior to traditional subversion.

When testing this theory against the case studies, evidence of the continuing relevance of the trilemma's constraints and trade-offs across multiple cyber operations would provide the strongest empirical support for the theory. Specifically, evidence showing that cyber operations pursuing similar effect types under similar circumstances face similar types of constraints as traditional subversion supports the theory. Trade-offs only become clear in the comparison of multiple operations since variation in actors' prioritization of speed, intensity, and control is expected to produce corresponding shifts in effectiveness across these variables. Consistent evidence of these trade-offs, and the different permutations of the trilemma laid out in the previous section, across multiple operations with such variation strongly supports the theory. Evidence of operations "escaping" from these constraints and trade-offs challenges the theory and must be considered for further refinements, especially considering the potential missing variables explaining these anomalies. In general, the theory expects cyber operations to provide significant strategic value mostly in exceptional circumstances involving "unicorn" scenarios where actors are both exceptionally capable and exceptionally lucky in exploiting target systems that are exceptionally vulnerable and yet have the capacity to cause significant harm to victims. Evidence of success in such unicorn scenarios does thus not necessarily challenge the theory. However, evidence of operations evading these constraints and trade-offs beyond such scenarios, especially if consistently, would challenge the theory.

Concerning the differences in the strategic role and value between cyber operations and traditional subversion—or lack thereof, as the theory predicts—evidence of both types of operations producing the same effect types overall supports the theory. Evidence of cyber operations producing types of effects that enable entirely new subversive strategies, as well as evidence of cyber operations producing effects of significantly greater strategic value than traditional subversion, challenge the theory. The less evidence there is of cyber operations producing such effects being hampered by the constraints and trade-offs of the trilemma, the more fatal such disconfirming findings would be.

3

Traditional Subversion

Crushing the Prague Spring, 1968–1973

On January 5, 1968, the Czechoslovakian Communist Party (KSC) voted in a young and idealistic leader named Alexander Dubcek as its first secretary, who promptly commenced an ambitious reform program later known under the slogan "Socialism with a Human Face."[1] It involved liberalizing domestic politics and implied a foreign policy shift away from the strict Soviet line. As a CIA memorandum from January 12, 1968, succinctly put it, "A European Communist state is becoming less Communist and more European, and neither the pace nor the goals of the transition are likely to please Moscow."[2] This liberalization push became known as the "Prague Spring," and from Moscow's perspective it posed a threat not only to the military balance of power in Europe but also to regime stability. Czechoslovakia was a key member of the Warsaw Pact with significant industrial capacity and a strategically important location in the center of Europe. The liberalization movement of the Prague Spring raised the possibility of Czechoslovakia drifting from its sphere of influence. Moreover, from the Kremlin's perspective, it threatened the stability of the Communist regime itself. It challenged the legitimacy of Communist ideology and raised the risk of surrounding countries jumping on the bandwagon. Consequently, the Kremlin pursued two key strategic goals: first, to reverse Czechoslovakia's reform course, and second, to undermine and neutralize domestic support for this course.

The Kremlin thus went into crisis mode. For several months, from March to July 1968, the Soviets exerted diplomatic pressure that turned increasingly coercive, attempting to get the Czechoslovaks to change course. These efforts were fruitless, and Dubcek's government continued its reforms. In August 1968, the Soviets finally sent in their tanks, crushing the Prague Spring with the military might of the Red Army. Images of Soviet tanks rolling through the streets of Prague have since become iconic symbols of Soviet repression. Accordingly, most existing historiography focuses on the invasion as the ultimate means to stop Czechoslovakia from liberalizing.

This case study challenges this established story. I argue that while the military invasion was the most visible means of intervention, it was in fact part of a contingency plan to salvage a botched subversive campaign. Recently declassified documents and evidence from biographies show that the Soviets deployed subversion as an independent instrument from early in the crisis, seeking an alternative to force. To that end, the KGB innovated in using one of its most sophisticated agents, "illegals" with carefully constructed cover identities. Illegals were trained to infiltrate Western societies, but in Czechoslovakia the KGB used them for the first time within the Soviet Union in two distinct campaigns codenamed PROGRESS and KHODOKI. PROGRESS aimed to infiltrate civil society to collect intelligence and identify its leaders and infiltrate the KSC to influence government policy and identify pro-Soviet cadres. KHODOKI operations, meanwhile, aimed to weaken and discredit the liberal movement through daring "active measures." Illegals attempted to kidnap opposition leaders, mount disinformation operations, assassinate Russian spouses of liberalization leaders, and deploy false arms caches as "evidence" of counterrevolutionary forces.

Stringing together evidence from primary sources, established historiography, and intelligence scholarship, this chapter reconstructs the KGB's illegals' efforts to infiltrate and manipulate Czechoslovakian society and institutions. Relying on a large cache of recently declassified field reports by the Ukrainian KGB, biographies, and revelations by former intelligence agents, it identifies how illegals infiltrated and exploited Czechoslovakia, the challenges they faced, and the strategic impact of these two campaigns. KHODOKI moved fast and pursued daringly high-intensity effects; as expected, these operations failed due to a loss of control—either through premature discovery or a failure to produce effects. By and large, KHODOKI operations thus failed to produce desired effects and showed no measurable contribution toward strategic goals. Speed and intensity came at the cost of control and, consequently, strategic value. The PROGRESS campaign, on the other hand, succeeded in infiltrating both civil society and the government while its agents remained undiscovered. However, these agents only collected intelligence without attempting active measures of the kind pursued by KHODOKI. Evidently, the high level of speed and control in PROGRESS operations came at the cost of intensity. Consequently, it failed to measurably influence the Dubcek administration. Subversion thus failed to achieve the Soviets' two core goals; Czechoslovakia continued its reform course, and public support for these reforms even increased over the course of 1968.

Faced with strategic failure, the Kremlin implemented contingency plans. A pro-Soviet group within the KSC identified and mobilized by the KGB's illegals was to mount an internal coup, replacing Dubcek's government and reversing course back toward the Soviet line. The situation was increasingly dire and urgent, as these cadres and the KGB's agents warned of an impending "armed counterrevolution." To protect the internal coup and preempt the counterrevolution, Moscow ultimately opted for the use of force and launched the invasion that has since become infamous. The invasion itself proceeded near flawlessly, overwhelming Czechoslovakian forces and taking control with minimal casualties. The coup failed miserably though, as the KGB's puppets missed their moment to challenge Dubcek—whose government persisted against all odds. This failure further illustrates the limitations of subversion. Like its predecessors, this operation proceeded fast and pursued a high intensity of effects—overthrowing a government—but the agents and collaborators involved did not have sufficient influence and capabilities to produce the effect desired. Instead, the result was a loss of control as the KGB's collaborators lost any remaining cover they had at the time and were sidelined in the KSC's leadership. This outcome provides further evidence of the constraining role of the trilemma, but it also highlights an additional danger: falling prey to one's own deception and disinformation. Not only did the KGB's agents and collaborators overstate their own capabilities and influence in their reports to the Kremlin, but also the impending counterrevolution was a figment of the KGB's imagination fed by the false evidence planted in its KHODOKI operations.

Ironically, the failure of PROGRESS and KHODOKI thus ultimately contributed to precisely the armed escalation they were intended to avoid, while the limits and pathologies of subversion doomed the contingency plan to salvage these campaigns as well. The Soviets now had a costly armed occupation and were facing a hostile population, while Dubcek's government resisted the continued pressure to step down. The botched overthrow combined with the experience of armed invasion further galvanized public resistance to the Soviets and support for Dubcek. Accordingly, despite being in full control of the military and, increasingly, the security apparatuses, it took the Soviets several months to bring down Dubcek. Importantly, as the analysis will show, subversion played a key role in his eventual downfall. With less time pressure in this phase of the conflict subversive operations achieved greater intensity of effects and control, thus producing superior strategic value. Yet Soviet control over Czechoslovakia remained precarious.

Despite the best efforts of the conformist regime under Gustav Husak that replaced Dubcek in 1969, the opposition movement regrouped and continued to organize resistance to Communist rule until the end of the Soviet Union. Reflecting these limits of control, the military occupation that the Kremlin had intended to be temporary until "normalization" was complete became permanent as well. Subversion alone failed to subdue the liberalization movement; hence, force was necessary to maintain control. And yet while "normalizing" the situation in the short term, the occupation indirectly undermined the Soviets' goals, galvanizing domestic unity and resistance over the long term.

Kremlin Perception and Strategic Goals

The Kremlin's primary goal in this conflict has been to stop and reverse the liberalization reforms of Dubcek's government to prevent a "loss" of Czechoslovakia from its sphere of influence. A secondary, related goal has been to undermine domestic support for these reforms. While there is considerable disagreement among historians about most aspects of this case, there is broad consensus concerning both the Soviet leadership's threat perception and corresponding strategic goals. Kieran Williams highlights that "Soviet leaders indeed feared that, unchecked, Czechoslovakia might quit the socialist bloc, fall under West German influence, disrupt the post-war balance of power, and possibly endanger European security."[3] Similarly, according to Jiri Valenta, "given the requirements of his office, Brezhnev could not tolerate the 'loss' of Czechoslovakia."[4] In fact, this strategic aim was subsequently turned into doctrine, as the Soviet intervention in Czechoslovakia in August 1968 "spawned the 'Brezhnev Doctrine' and Soviet claims for the right of intervention in its own sphere of influence if its 'sovereignty' was threatened."[5]

Domestically, the prospect of liberalization also posed a threat to the stability of the Communist regime itself. According to Valenta, "from the Soviet point of view . . . the situation had the potential for affecting neighboring East European countries as well as the Soviet Union itself. The Czechoslovak slogan of 'socialism with a human face' implied that the face of Soviet socialism was less than human."[6]

Former Czechoslovak intelligence officer Ladislav Bittman confirms this assessment, noting the Kremlin feared the "negative impact on the domestic situation in the Soviet Union and other bloc countries by spreading the disease of democracy."[7] This assessment is confirmed by established historiography as well.[8] Bittman also confirms, however, that the primary Kremlin fear was a shift in the balance of power as the "new Czechoslovak foreign policy could undermine the military status quo in Europe."[9] Avoiding this outcome thus required stopping the liberalization movement.

To achieve these goals, the Kremlin relied on diplomacy, force, and subversion. Existing histories of this conflict have focused on the invasion, yet subversion played an important role in Kremlin strategy from the start. Below I piece together how Kremlin perception and preferences evolved as tensions rose following Dubcek's election.

Initially, the Kremlin welcomed Dubcek's ascent due to his predecessor Antonin Novotny's perceived failures. In 1967, Novotny had failed to curb a rising reformist movement in Czechoslovakia, using heavy-handed tactics and violence that further intensified protests.[10] Losing his grip on power, Novotny invited Soviet leader Leonid Brezhnev for support to a meeting of the KSC Central Committee in December 1967. Yet, after convening with the KSC leadership, Brezhnev concluded that "Novotny was in the wrong,"[11] instead expressing his support for Dubcek.[12] While Brezhnev urged KSC leaders to avoid "public quarreling," he nonetheless requested that the KSC plenum consider Dubcek's proposal for Novotny to surrender one of his two leadership positions (he was the president as well as first secretary of the KSC).[13] Although the KSC did erupt into public quarreling subsequently, with open calls for Novotny's resignation, Dubcek's consequent ascent to power as KSC first secretary appeared to stabilize the situation and was in line with Brezhnev's request as Novotny retained his presidency.

Accordingly, there is general consensus among historians that Moscow perceived the situation in Czechoslovakia with calm between January and February 1968.[14] As Prozumenshchikov's study of recently declassified internal documents of the Soviet Politburo reveals, "At the beginning of 1968, the KSC leadership is perceived in the Soviet documents as a monolithic force engaged in the struggle against the class enemy's 'hostile' and 'antisocialist' intrigues."[15] At the first official meeting between Dubcek, Brezhnev, and other senior Soviet leaders in Moscow on January 29–30, Dubcek made an effort to assure Brezhnev his reform plans did not post a threat to stability. In fact, as Dubcek notes in his memoirs, he "carefully avoided all terms that would trigger hostility from these dogmatic Marxist-Leninists—such as reform, reformist, or revision."[16] Although Dubcek faced some skepticism for his reform plans, there was no official pushback at this stage. As he recounts, "They did not say much, but I could sense that what I had told them was not what they would have liked to hear. Yet, there was no sign of open disagreement."[17] On the contrary, "during the meeting Brezhnev assured Dubcek that the new leadership could count on full Soviet support in resolving internal problems, and apparently made no mention of Novotny's removal."[18]

The next meeting of the two leaders on February 21 at a ceremony in Dresden to commemorate the Communist takeover of Czechoslovakia followed the same pattern. Significantly, at this event Dubcek outlined his reform plans in a speech, and Brezhnev signaled limited approval. According to Dubcek, "Brezhnev sent my draft back a few hours later with objections to only two paragraphs, which . . . would not weaken any of my substantive ideas, and I cut them without pain."[19] Consequently, Dubcek claims, the ceremony "ran its normal, boring course."[20] However, this exchange may not have gone as smoothly. The secretary of the Slovak Communist Party, Vasil Bilak, who was also present, recounts significant tensions preceding the meeting as "in a telephone conversation with Dubcek, Brezhnev protested that there would be a scandal if that speech were delivered and implied that the Soviet delegation would certainly have to walk out."[21] Regardless of the tone of the exchange, however, Dubcek was evidently allowed to hold his speech without overt signs of alarm by the Kremlin. Therefore, based on overt activity, there were indeed no signs of rising tensions in this period.

Intelligence collection activity, however, does show signs of increasing tensions even in the early crisis period. First, the Soviets increased intelligence collection efforts almost immediately after the leadership change, with the Politburo ordering regular reports from Czechoslovakia in January.[22] This change in itself does not indicate increased tension, but it does document an increase in attention—reflecting increased uncertainty and possible suspicions about Dubcek. Accordingly, in a meeting between Brezhnev and Dubcek in Moscow at the end of January, the Soviets "did reveal just how closely they were monitoring events, citing specific articles and television appearances that disturbed them and inquiring in minute detail about personnel changes."[23]

Although available evidence is insufficient to determine what occurred with full confidence, some of this intelligence reporting was likely provided by subversive agents within the KSC—in particular concerning personnel changes. This conclusion is corroborated by Dubcek's mention of Soviet efforts to exert subversive influence on government policy starting in early

February. As Dubcek recalls, "The Soviets launched their lobbying sometime at the beginning of February 1968. In the next weeks and months, their meddling became more obvious and more aggressive. Soon I was able to recognize when Kolder or Bilak was simply repeating Brezhnev's arguments, sometimes word for word."[24]

At this stage, it is not clear to what extent this meddling was coordinated from Moscow, and how. Available evidence indicates that the first KGB agents tasked with identifying and coordinating "healthy forces" arrived only in March (see further below); hence, it is conceivable that Kolder and Bilak repeated Brezhnev's arguments out of their own account to improve their standing with Kremlin leaders. Regardless of the means of coordination, however, these attempts at influencing policy reflect an increasing split between Moscow and Prague.

Kieran Williams's analysis of new available archive materials provides further support for this conclusion, with one former Soviet official indicating that concerns about Dubcek arose in Moscow as early as January.[25] The evidence that is available indicates that tensions had been quietly rising in Moscow and finally boiled over in a Politburo meeting on March 15, where KGB director Yuri Andropov called for military intervention.[26] The same meeting also revised a letter to be sent to the KSC leadership condemning the changes and highlighting the influence of "anticommunist forces" to establish capitalism and Western countries attempting to "drive a wedge" between Czechoslovakia and its Soviet allies.[27] Finally, Andropov repeated this push for the use of military force at another Politburo meeting on March 21, drawing an analogy to Hungary and urging members to "ready the military if necessary."[28] He did not succeed with this request, yet the KGB assumed central importance in Soviet efforts to quash the Prague Spring.

The resignation of Novotny violated a guarantee Dubcek had given to Brezhnev just two months earlier and meant the loss of the last pro-Soviet figure in a leadership position.[29] Reflecting the urgency of this matter, Moscow called an emergency conference in Dresden for the following day to discuss the issue and the course of reforms under Dubcek. Hence, there is "universal agreement among both Soviets and Czechoslovaks that the decision to call the Dresden meeting marked the real beginning of the crisis."[30] Rather than averting a deepening of the crisis, however, the conference exacerbated it. Dubcek's memoirs illustrate the breakdown of official diplomacy at the conference. Having mounted a passionate defense of his government's reform program, Dubcek notes, "the conference ended in a cool mood. There were no conclusions, no joint declaration, only a very formal final communiqué. We disagreed completely."[31] Diplomacy had broken down.

As diplomacy failed, the Kremlin commenced contingency planning to prevent a "loss" of Czechoslovakia. These contingency plans involved two instruments of power: subversion and military force. As the situation was turning into crisis, Moscow's diplomatic approach became increasingly coercive, involving more and more thinly veiled threats. At the Dresden meeting, Moscow had already signaled its resolve in an explicit reference to armed force. As William recounts, "Upon arrival they [the Czechoslovak leaders] had been struck by the heavy presence of Soviet and East German generals and, when Cernik inquired about their presence, Brezhnev responded jovially, 'So that in case we need help in solving Czechoslovak matters it can be rendered immediately.'"[32] Moscow not only threatened but also commenced actively planning a military invasion, taking three key steps. First, following the Dresden conference, Soviet and East German military units were relocated to the southern German Democratic Republic (GDR).[33] Second, on April 8, 1968, a special strike force was created in the Warsaw Pact forces.[34] Finally, on April 12, detailed invasion plans were presented to the future commander of the invading force, General Mayorov.[35] Two weeks after Dresden, the Soviets were thus ready to invade. Consequently, it is tempting to conclude that Soviet intervention was now no longer a question of if, but when. Accordingly, both Andrew and Mitrokhin as well as Russian historian Nikita Petrov suggest that military action was all but certain at this stage.[36] Matthew Ouimet, then a foreign policy analyst at the US Department of State, however, criticizes an "artificial sense of inevitability"[37] pervading existing historiography.

And in fact, efforts to crush the liberalization movement without invasion were already in full swing. While Andropov called on the Politburo to use armed force against Czechoslovakia in March, he was also overseeing preparations for ambitious subversive campaigns with the innovative use of a key tool in the KGB's arsenal: illegal agents. Such illegals were highly trained, elite agents with carefully constructed cover identities that allowed them to blend into foreign societies. They were called illegals because they operated separately from the spies under official cover employed at KGB residencies at Soviet embassies, and hence conducted "illegal" spying activities. Hitherto, such agents had been deployed only outside the Iron Curtain, however—using them within the Soviet Union itself was a new idea, and Czechoslovakia provided the "testing ground" for this experiment.[38]

The exact start date of these operations is not recorded, but Andrew and Mitrokhin indicate that Andropov ordered the dispatch of illegal agents "no later than March," aiming for at least fifteen illegals in place by May 12.[39] These agents played a central role in Soviet strategy, as Andrew and Mitrokhin argue: "In Czechoslovakia in 1968, as in Hungary in 1956, Andropov's strategy was based on a mixture of deception and military might."[40] The Czechoslovakian case was the first time the KGB used its precious illegal agents for such purposes,[41] whereas in Hungary the KGB had focused mostly on violent suppression of the opposition to the pro-Soviet government.[42] Yet the role of subversion vis-à-vis force remains unclear: did the deployment of these illegal agents facilitate or forestall the use of force?

Unfortunately, existing case studies offer few insights since most entirely bracket covert operations, focusing exclusively on the military dimension.[43] Valenta forms an exception, but only briefly touches upon one possible KGB operation later in the crisis.[44] Fortunately, however, more evidence has become available, allowing a systematic analysis. This evidence indicates that the Soviets opted for subversion as an alternative to force early in the developing crisis. At the Central Committee of the Communist Party of the Soviet Union's (CC CPSU) plenum on April 9, Brezhnev highlighted his preference to avoid the use of force, noting that in Czechoslovakia "one has to strengthen discipline in all areas of society and must not be reduced to a situation where one has to resort to extreme measures."[45] In a subsequent meeting on April 12 where invasion plans were finalized, Brezhnev explicitly forbade sharing the plans with the rest of the party, suggesting that planning is necessary, "but perhaps we may not have to."[46] Prozumenshchikov's analysis of temporarily declassified Kremlin documents (now unavailable again) revealed multiple additional instances where these preferences are explicitly expressed; hence, he underlines that during the crisis months, "leading Soviet figures ... were working hard to avoid a solution that involved the use of force."[47] This assessment is echoed by the defector Bittman, who as an intelligence officer in Prague had access to classified information during the time of the crisis itself. Bittman notes that "Moscow's reactions between March and August 1968 indicated that the Soviet plan to suppress the democratization process presupposed a military invasion only if the attempts to split the movement and accomplish a 'silent invasion' with official sanction of Czechoslovak authorities proved unsuccessful."[48]

The decision to intervene was taken much later, possibly only days before the actual invasion. Accordingly, after the threat of invasion at the Dresden conference in March, the Soviets made no further references to the use of force, instead signaling restraint or possible acquiescence. A CIA memorandum from April 23, 1968, on the situation in Czechoslovakia echoes this conclusion, stating that "the leaders of the Soviet Union appear to have conceded, though grudgingly, the Czechoslovak party's right to reform itself and to attempt Communist 'democratization.'"[49]

Force was an unattractive option due to the potential reputational damage to the cause of socialism. As Prozumenshchikov highlights, "Moscow realized that . . . 'reestablishing order' in the Eastern Bloc through the use of military means was only going to give the world at large one more reason to doubt the viability and the progressive character of socialism."[50] Similarly, Eidlin concludes that "there was strong and stable consensus within the Soviet decision-making system that a political solution with an appearance of legitimacy was to be sought, rather than subjugation by force."[51] While the motivation behind the Soviet leadership's preference to avoid the use of force is relatively clear, evidence on the reasons for the choice in favor of subversion remains scarce. Nonetheless, the strategic promise of subversion to exert influence without revealing it is directly congruent with the stated motivation to maintain an appearance of legitimacy. In line with this conclusion, the Kremlin saw the need for a post facto justification of the invasion couched in the language of rights and obligations in what was later to become known as the "Brezhnev doctrine": "The weakening of any of the links in the world system of socialism directly affects all the socialist countries, and they cannot look indifferently upon this. . . . To fulfill their internationalist duties to the fraternal nations of Czechoslovakia and to defend their own socialist gains, the Soviet Union and the other socialist states were forced to act and did act in decisive opposition to the anti-socialist forces in Czechoslovakia."[52]

However, there is another possible explanation for this decision: deterrence. It is plausible to assume the Soviets feared Western intervention in case of using force. However, there are reasons to doubt this fear. Most importantly, Czechoslovakia was behind the Iron Curtain, and NATO later explicitly gave Moscow its acquiescence when invasion was imminent. Accordingly, in the preparations of the military operation, deterrence was evidently not a relevant constraint. Williams documents that throughout the decision-making process leading up to the invasion, there is simply "no evidence of any leading official ruling out the use of force as too risky."[53] This conclusion is further supported by the fact that the US subsequently—possibly unintentionally—signaled they would not intervene in Czechoslovakia. In a meeting on July 22, 1968, between Secretary of State Dean Rusk and Soviet ambassador Anatoli Dobrynin, Rusk condemned interference in Czechoslovakia yet added that "this is a matter for the Czechs first and foremost. Apart from that, it is a matter for Czechs and other nations of the Warsaw Pact"—a comment perceived as a "green light" by Moscow to take whatever measures deemed necessary to regain control in Czechoslovakia.[54] Hence, deterrence unlikely was a relevant factor in the decision.

In short, the Soviet Union opted for subversion when diplomacy had failed as an alternative to force that promised to get Czechoslovakia to change course at lower risks and costs. And yet the Soviets did ultimately intervene, indicating that subversion fell short of achieving its promise or merely provided a means to "soften up" Czechoslovakia before invasion. To examine what effects subversion achieved and how, where it fell short and why, and in what way its strategic role evolved, the next section examines the subversive operations Russia deployed to attain this end, tracing their mechanisms, effects, and contributions to strategic goals.

Commencing the "Silent Invasion": KHODOKI and PROGRESS

To bring Czechoslovakia back in line, in 1968 the KGB implemented two ambitious subversive campaigns with distinct yet complementary objectives. The first, codenamed KHODOKI, pursued active measures to discredit the liberalization movement, exaggerating the threat they posed to stability and their violent nature and constructing a grand deception by fabricating evidence of a CIA-supported counterrevolutionary coup.[55] Success would help both undermine support for the liberal groups by discrediting them as pawns of the West and provide a justification for later intervention. A second campaign called PROGRESS employed illegal agents to infiltrate both civil society and the Czechoslovak government itself. Civil society subversion aimed to monitor their activity, identify leaders, and directly influence opposition activity "if necessary."[56] At the same time, other illegal agents were sent to infiltrate the KSC to identify and support pro-Soviet cadres.[57] The evident aim was to achieve the "silent invasion" alluded to by Bittman above, changing government policy from within. It failed.

Planning and preparation of PROGRESS and KHODOKI commenced in parallel with the development of invasion plans. Available evidence does not indicate whether covert options were discussed during the meetings planning military steps, but it does show planning commenced no later than April 5. On this day, a Politburo meeting discussed special KGB operations in response to the "action programme" published by the KSC.[58] Because this program proposed to soften the Communist monopoly of power and to limit party control over the Ministry of the Interior, it threatened to compromise the existing network of KGB agents within much of Czechoslovakia's government and security agencies—causing anxiety in Moscow.[59] To alleviate this loss of access, the KGB dispatched its illegals.

Training such agents and developing their cover story to ensure they can successfully adapt to the target society takes time—typically several years.[60] Time was short, however. Facing the loss of most of its agent network in Czechoslovakia, the KGB had to react swiftly. Yet its existing illegal agents were mostly trained for deployment in Western societies; hence, their handlers had to improvise. Leveraging their existing training, agents deployed to Czechoslovakia were to pose as Westerners. As Andrew and Mitrokhin explain, "During the Prague Spring illegals, posing as Western tourists, journalists, businesspeople and students, were for the first time used in significant numbers in a country of the Soviet Bloc for both intelligence collection and active measures."[61] Importantly, these illegals thus likely lacked Czechoslovak language skills and cultural competencies—limiting their capacity to adapt.

The operational timelines further underline the relatively rushed pace of these campaigns. The first illegal agents were deployed only eleven days after the Politburo had first discussed new KGB operations on April 5. A CC CPSU resolution from April 16, 1968, ordered the dispatch of the illegals Georgii Fedyashin and Aleksandr Alekseev to Prague, under cover identities as Soviet journalists.[62] Ten days later, a secret and unofficial KGB residency was established in Prague to coordinate the activity of illegal agents, complementing its existing legal residence.[63] Its head was Vladimir Surzhaninov, and two operatives were in charge of the illegal agents: Gennadi Borzov and V. Umnov.[64] Within only three weeks, the KGB had set up the basic infrastructure for its subversive campaigns.

The overall scale is not clear, but at least thirty illegals were deployed. According to Andrew and Mitrokhin, "Probably in March, Andropov ordered that by May 12 at least fifteen of the illegals should be deployed in

72 SUBVERSION

Czechoslovakia—more than had ever been dispatched to any Western country."[65] KGB defector Gordievsky later reported that altogether over thirty illegal agents were dispatched.[66] This was a relatively large-scale operation by KGB standards, yet considering the ambitious objectives, it meant that only a few dozen agents were tasked with bringing down a government and liberalization movement that enjoyed broad public support: in polling between March 24 and 28 (i.e., at the start of the crisis), 55% of Czechoslovakians expressed their trust in Dubcek.[67] In short, not only were these campaigns limited in scale, but also their rushed timeframe meant agents had little time to prepare and adapt to their targets—and nonetheless, they pursued relatively intense effects. Achieving their ambitious strategic goals under these conditions thus posed significant challenges. Unsurprisingly, failures began to mount.

KHODOKI: Daring Active Measures (and Their Failure)

The KHODOKI campaign involved three major subversive operations. They pursued daring objectives: apart from routine disinformation, they involved kidnapping, assassination, and even the planting of false weapons caches. Given the short timeframe and these highly intense effects, however, things started to go wrong, and two out of these three operations ended in clear failure.

The first KHODOKI operation aimed to weaken the liberalization movement by kidnapping two of its leading intellectuals. The plan was for illegals to deceive targeted individuals by offering help from persecution, gain their trust, and then extradite them to the Soviet Union. Yet these agents only had days to prepare, while pursuing highly intense effects. Loch K. Johnson has developed an "escalation ladder' for covert operations that distinguishes thirty-eight types of effects ranked by their intensity and escalation potential (measured in terms of "intrusiveness").[68] Kidnapping ranks high on this ladder, on rung thirty of thirty-eight, sitting among the "extreme options,"[69] Since they operated undercover, the illegals involved had to gain their victims' trust, then exploit it to lure the latter into a trap. But in the short time they had to prepare for this mission, these illegals lacked even the basic skills required to get to a point where they could attempt to build trust.

The targets were two of the leading intellectuals of the Prague Spring movement: Professor Vaclav Cerny and the writer Jan Prochizka. Cerny and Prochizka had been identified as key threats to stability by the KGB the previous month, as documented in a top-secret cable by Soviet Foreign Minister Gromyko to Communist leaders in Hungary, Bulgaria, the GDR, and Poland. The cable claimed Cerny and Prochizka were leaders of an "illegal, anti-state group" with the aim "to discredit the CPCz [KSC] in the eyes of the Czechoslovak people, to subvert the foundations of socialism in the CSSR and to gradually return the country to the path of bourgeois development."[70] Moreover, the cable asserted, the group had a specific action plan for regime change: first it would undermine the rule of the KSC, and then once the KSC had "lost control," the group around Cerny and Prochizka would "declare itself an independent party and take charge of all forces that oppose the current regime."[71] The cable does not specify its sources; it only states that findings were made "according to our information," but the fact that it contains records of personal meetings in March 1968 between Cerny and Prochizka, as well as from another personal meeting with writers Benes and Havel,[72] indicates that intelligence was provided by an illegal KGB agent(s) who had infiltrated the group.[73]

To neutralize this perceived threat, the KGB's plan was to "behead" the group by kidnapping its leaders, and it tasked two agents with this objective: GROMOV (real name: Vasili Antonovich Gordievsky) and GURYEV (real name: Valentin Aleksandrovich Gutin), who had been in Prague only three weeks. Both were to act as West German sympathizers, and on May 10, 1968, they were to approach Cerny and Prochizka, warning them they were "in danger" and luring them to a "safe" hiding place—if necessary, through the use of drugs.[74] Once Cerny and Prochizka were in the hiding place, they would be picked up by the KGB's "special action" department and exfiltrated to East Germany by car.[75] Available evidence does not document further plans for Cerny and Prochizka after their exfiltration, but in line with common KGB practices and the objectives of PROGRESS operations, the most likely objective was to force them to admit to "counterrevolutionary plans" under duress and blackmail in order to discredit their movement.

Apart from the overall urgency of the crisis, the operation's timing suggests time pressure resulting from the intent to maximize the psychological impact of the kidnapping. On the same day the operation was to be carried out (May 10), Soviet forces conducted large-scale military exercises at the Czechoslovak border that were intended to signal resolve to Czechoslovak leadership.[76] The seizure of two key leaders of the liberalization movement on the same day would have underlined this scarcely veiled threat, while intimidating the population and, ideally, throwing the liberalization movement into disarray.

Insufficient reconnaissance and adaptation precluded exploitation, however, leading to total failure. The first target, Cerny, was used to persecution, and GURYEV could simply not persuade him to move to the supposed safe house.[77] Meanwhile, unbeknownst to GROMOV, Prochizka had been supplied with a bodyguard by the Czechoslovak interior minister. Moreover, GROMOV, posing as a West German, was unable to communicate with Prochizka, who only spoke Czech. After a few weeks, both agents gave up their efforts empty-handedly.[78] They had failed to establish the trust required to deceive their victims and, in doing so, influence and "control" their actions. This failure provides the first practical illustration of the constraints of the trilemma: the operation proceeded fast and pursued highly intense effects, but (or because it did so) did not achieve sufficient control over targets to produce those effects.

While its outcome is thus as one would expect, why the KGB designed the operation this way is puzzling, however. The KGB cable cited earlier indicates it had access to both Cerny and Prochizka's inner circle. If the KGB had information on what was said at personal meetings, it should have at least been aware of the targets' language skills, their vulnerabilities (or lack of them), and the presence of bodyguards. This divergence suggests that the initial KGB information on the targets was instead derived from Czechoslovak intelligence. By April, this source likely had dried up due to the purges of KGB agents and informers in the Czechoslovakian State Security Service (which is called "Státní bezpečnost" in Czech, and abbreviated as "StB")—the key reason the KGB scrambled to dispatch illegal agents, as discussed above.

The second planned KHODOKI operation involved a reckless and immensely cynical assassination plot, constituting a significant increase in the intensity of effects compared to preceding operations. Assassination plots rank among the most intense effects covert operations can pursue, at rung thirty-six out of thirty-eight on Johnson's escalation ladder, only surpassed by secret and chemical warfare.[79] The objective was to assassinate Russian women with Czechoslovak spouses, and the deaths were then to be blamed on "counterrevolutionary forces" in Czechoslovakia in order to discredit them. Recent evidence discovered by Petrov suggests that the Soviet Communist Party Central Committee decided these plans, as recorded in an official transcript from April 16, 1968.[80] The existence of such an operation is also supported by Mitrokhin's notes, although they only "lend some, though not conclusive support" to the claim, apparently first made by an StB defector.[81] However, operational details are scarce—neither the precise timeframe, nor the number of agents, nor the number of targets is clear. The only known details are that the operation was planned for August 1968 and that it was discovered and neutralized by the StB before assassinations could be carried out.[82] Accordingly, it remains unclear whether this was still what I could consider a borderline subversive operation, where illegals would try to get close to victims through some means of exploitation and manipulation, or rather the simple use of force, such as using sniper rifles. Similarly, there is no evidence available clarifying the details of this discovery. Nonetheless, and assuming it was subversive, the fact that this operation was discovered prematurely underlines the increasing risk of control loss when maximizing both speed and intensity. Proceeding with the same high speed but far higher intensity than preceding KHODOKI operations, the operational trilemma would predict a doubly increased risk of control loss and failure in this operation—and this is evidently what happened.

Because evidence is so scarce, analysis of the mechanism of exploitation and causes of discovery must ultimately remain speculation. Importantly, however, considering that the key objective was to blame the assassinations on counterrevolutionaries, it is clear that the illegals involved had to maintain cover and construct some kind of false evidence linking the deaths to counterrevolutionary forces. Perhaps they would have simply used sniper rifles to shoot the victims from a distance, leaving some evidence behind implicating Czechoslovakian "counterrevolutionaries." In this case, the operation would veer closely toward military operations since the main mechanism is force. To get to the point where they could carry out such orders, however, the illegals involved had to successfully infiltrate Czechoslovakian society, exploiting weaknesses in border security checks and identity verification practices, as well as weaknesses of the individuals involved in this process. Without this prior exploitation, the operation would be impossible, underlining its subversive nature, and bringing in soldiers instead to shoot the victims would have made it impossible to blame the shootings on Czechoslovakians. Moreover, in practice, the illegals likely infiltrated the personal circles of victims to get close enough to them to carry out the assassination, assuming identities of presumed "counterrevolutionaries." In short, while we do not know the details of what happened, we do know that this operation required exploitation and the maintenance of cover—which was lost at some stage in the process.

The final KHODOKI operation also involved planting false flag "evidence" of an armed counterrevolution, aiming to link it to the CIA. In July 1968, KGB illegal agents placed weapons caches near the West German border, some of them bearing large stickers stating "Made in USA."[83] One such cache was "discovered" on July 12 near the small town of Sokolovo in Eastern Czechoslovakia.[84] As it turned out, a KGB agent had infiltrated a local newspaper under a cover identity as a journalist, using this cover to plant the evidence and thus manipulate Czechoslovakian media into reporting on the impending counterrevolution. Yet it failed because the agent lost his cover, or at least a suspicious colleague noticed the agent had gone to the very location where the arms caches were "discovered" on the night before. Consequently, Czechoslovakian leaders debunked the story and it failed to stick.

The apparent Soviet plan behind this operation became clear when on July 19 the Soviet newspaper *Pravda* reported that American weapons had been found together with a copy of a "secret plan" by the CIA to overthrow the Communist regime in Czechoslovakia—a report that received wide coverage in the Soviet press.[85] Meanwhile, the KGB provided false intelligence to the Czechoslovak intelligence service StB implicating opposition groups KAN and K-231 in the impending coup.[86] The forging of false evidence is a routine instrument of disinformation, in this case aiming to deceive Czechoslovakians as well as international audiences, which Johnson counts among high-risk options on rung twenty-five of thirty-eight on the escalation ladder.[87] Hence, this operation pursued medium-high-intensity effects. Meanwhile, it proceeded even faster than predecessors—circumstantial evidence suggests merely a few days of preparation. As one would expect, it failed to achieve its objective. Speed and intensity came at the loss of control.

The allegations made in the *Pravda* article were grave, and if the evidence held up to scrutiny, they could have easily proven sufficient grounds to justify military invasion. However, an investigation by the Czechoslovak intelligence service quickly debunked the evidence as false.[88] The KGB had made several errors. First, the weapons used were US World War II models, but they were packed in Soviet-made bags.[89] This detail undermined the claim in the *Pravda* article that the weapons had been brought over the border from West Germany to support Sudeten German activists.[90] Three other pieces of evidence undermined the validity of the story: the weapons found were of mixed origins and apparently included East German models, Soviet press reports were published before the Czechoslovak intelligence service had reported the discovery, and finally, eyewitnesses quoted in the *Pravda* articles could not be found after.[91] The attribution of the arms caches to Sudeten German organizations held up at first glance, as a leader of a Sudeten German organization calling for the return of Sudeten Germans to Czechoslovakia openly admitted the existence of arms caches in the region.[92] However, as he pointed out, the World War II–era weapons found "are quite obvious leftovers from the American occupation of the area during World War II."[93] This conclusion is congruent with the packaging of the weapons in Soviet bags. Without any evidence linking these weapons to their alleged Western intelligence services, Valenta concluded, even long before Mitrokhin's archive revealed the KGB's involvement, that the KGB "almost certainly" had a hand in this "discovery."[94]

Due to these weaknesses, the deception failed—at least in Czechoslovakia. Based on the evidence, in a statement published in *Rude Pravo* (the main Communist newspaper in Czechoslovakia) the interior minister Pavel strongly rejected the claims in the *Pravda* article, instead accusing the KGB of planting the evidence in what he called a "provocation."[95] Additional Czech leaders published further rebuttals in the following days, with multiple newspaper articles debunking the claims.[96] Consequently, the matter was dropped within Czechoslovakia.[97] Accordingly, there is no indication that the fake arms caches influenced public perception of opposition groups within Czechoslovakia, nor of an influence on Soviet leaders involved in decision-making. First, Ukrainian KGB reports from the period in question make no mention of the arms caches and show no detectable change in opinions and perceptions following the publication of the *Pravda* article—neither in Czechoslovakia nor in Ukraine.[98] Second, the arms caches do not come up in any CIA assessments or memoranda around and after the *Pravda* article publication.[99] Although the CIA archive contains multiple reports and assessments per day during this period, these caches or the report on their discovery evidently was not considered to be significant enough to warrant intelligence assessments.

Instead, CIA reports around the publication of the *Pravda* piece on arms caches focus on a range of topics, for example, divisions among European Communist parties. Among them is a detailed fourteen-page assessment of an article by I. Aleksandrov published in *Pravda* on July 11 with intense criticism of the Czechoslovakian reform movement that draws a comparison to Hungary in 1956—bringing in the specter of military invasion.[100] The CIA was clearly paying attention to what was being published in *Pravda*, yet this deception effort was evidently not deemed significant enough to be included in a report. Third, the arms caches did not influence decision-making on the crisis—Kieran Williams's meticulous reconstruction of the Soviet decision-making process leading up to the crisis does not once mention these caches.[101] Hence, all available evidence supports the conclusion that this mission failed in its objective to discredit the opposition—more so since the alleged involvement of opposition groups K-231 and KAN that KGB intelligence suggested was also explicitly rejected by the StB.[102]

The weakness of the evidence it planted was exacerbated by the rushed nature of the operation, undermining the cover of the agents involved. With the little time available, the agents involved could not establish sufficient influence or trust within the organizations they infiltrated to maintain cover and achieve the deception needed for this mission to succeed. The memories of a colleague of one of the illegal agents in the operation who had taken up a cover identity as a journalist illustrate these shortcomings:

> Vladlen Krivosheev, an Izvestiya correspondent, recorded an instance of the activities of the KGB agents that were to serve as proof for the "activation of the counterrevolutionary forces." . . . He was given an assistant, a journalist previously unknown to him, "an expert in international affairs" and, as he did not realize until later, a member of the KGB. When a short time later a "weapons arsenal" was discovered in the western part of Czechoslovakia consisting of a couple of handguns and grenades, Krivosheev remembered that his new assistant had gone there the previous night in Izvestiya's car, a Volga.[103]

Mitrokhin's archive confirms this timeframe, remembering a colleague, KGB Colonel Viktor Ryabov, informing him in mid-July he would be "going away for a few days" and, upon his return, suggesting that there "would be an interesting article in Pravda the following day"—which turned out to be the July 19 article on arms caches.[104] Hence, the lead time[105] in this operation consisted of at worst a few days and at best several weeks.

Evidence on bureaucratic politics in the Kremlin supports the conclusion that mere days of preparation were involved. The operation was almost certainly designed to create evidence to support the July 11 *Pravda* article warning of an imminent counterrevolution in Czechoslovakia. KGB head Yuri Andropov had previously expressed his preference for military action, and this operation would have provided him with hard evidence to push the matter. While the historian Karen Dawisha claims that a shift in favor of intervention among Kremlin leaders was already occurring around the time of the operation,[106] as discussed above Williams has conclusively shown that more recent evidence does not support this presumed split. However, we do know that in the weeks preceding the operation, there had been repeated debates in the Politburo about military intervention, with Brezhnev maintaining a moderate course.[107] When the plenum of the Communist Party on July 17, 1968, aimed to push through a resolution authorizing military intervention—in line with Andropov's preferences—Brezhnev intervened, urging that "before extreme measures are taken, we will exhaust, together with the fraternal parties, all political means at our disposal to assist the Communist Party of Czechoslovakia."[108] Hence, it is reasonable to conclude that he ordered to rush the arms caches operation as he sensed an opportunity to influence decision-making.

This conclusion is further supported by the fact that the publication of the July 19 *Pravda* article revealing the arms caches coincided with another meeting by the Politburo discussing "extreme measures" to be taken in Czechoslovakia—possibly convened in response to the publication of the article.[109] At the meeting, "Andropov emerged as the chief spokesman of those who wanted extreme measures immediately. . . . [I]t was a bad-tempered meeting. Andropov became involved in a furious argument with Kosygin, whom he accused of 'attacking' him, presumably because of his call for immediate military intervention."[110] As discussed above, the rushed operation involved considerable risks, and the failure to move the Politburo toward intervention despite these risks and the efforts involved in the operation would explain Andropov's frustration. Ultimately, the false evidence failed to nudge Soviet decision makers toward intervention, however, as the Politburo instead decided in favor of another meeting with the Czechoslovak leadership to avert escalation—highlighting the persisting preference to avoid escalation.

The historian Jiri Valenta provides an alternative explanation, suggesting the arms caches operation was designed to influence public opinion in the Soviet Union to prepare people for the impending invasion.[111] This motivation is certainly plausible, but if domestic deception was the primary objective, the risks involved in planting weapons were extraordinarily high compared to the marginal effects. Risks included the loss of illegal agents, either by having their cover blown or being arrested, resulting in considerable embarrassment and lost investment (e.g., if the photo of the agent is circulated, limiting the potential for future subversion under cover). These risks were significant, and accordingly Andrew and Mitrokhin highlight that despite these failures, "illegals behind Khodoki ... went undetected."[112]

The high risks involved cast doubt on Valenta's suggested objective—in particular since we now know the intervention was not decided at the time. *Pravda* was a party-controlled newspaper and was routinely used for disinformation and propaganda, often relying on forged evidence to deceive audiences.[113] Hence, the July 19 article alone would have sufficed to influence public opinion in the Soviet Union, perhaps with a forged photo of the evidence. In short, if domestic deception was the only aim, the risks and expenses of placing the actual arms caches were simply not necessary. The fact that these risks and expenses were taken to fabricate evidence, however, indicates that the target of deception was the Czechoslovak and international audience—which is in line with the primary objective of KHODOKI, that is, discrediting the liberalization movement.

In short, available evidence indicates that the operation was intended to deceive the Czechoslovakian public and the international audience into believing that the liberalization movement in Czechoslovakia was in fact a CIA-supported subversive effort aiming to violently overthrow Communist rule. The deception failed due to a lack of preparation and influence within targeted organizations, namely the local newspaper infiltrated by an illegal agent—and a resulting loss of control as colleagues distrusted the agent's identity and Czechoslovakian leaders debunked the claims in *Pravda*.

Interestingly, there were multiple opportunities to develop a more convincing deception. Yet all of them would have required more time. The most elaborate deception could have been achieved by infiltrating the Sudeten German groups to which the weapons were attributed, supplying the latter directly with weapons before catching them "in flagranti." At a less elaborate level, a well-established illegal with sufficient lead time could have easily identified vulnerable individuals (i.e., exploitable through bribery, blackmail) in the target region to act as eyewitnesses, while also making sure weapons were not packaged in Soviet bags. Instead of infiltrating local organizations, however, an illegal working undercover at a newspaper placed the weapons, who had to travel to the target region in an official car that was easily traceable—and a colleague did so, as mentioned above. This approach squandered the relative advantage of illegal agents: infiltrating and subverting a target organization to establish control within the organization to produce intended effects. Using an illegal at a newspaper to plant evidence and requiring him to travel to another region create a dual risk since the task is obviously beyond his remit, immediately raising suspicions if the activity is discovered, and furthermore involved traveling to an unfamiliar location. Considering that suitable illegal agents with Western German cover identities were in place and there was a suitable target organization (Sudeten Germans) for infiltration, time pressure is again the most likely explanation for this missed opportunity.

The failure was not absolute, however. While the false evidence did not sufficiently influence Soviet leaders to decide for intervention, Brezhnev nonetheless used it later to justify the intervention. As Andrew and Mitrokhin recount, in the final meeting between Brezhnev and Dubcek on the eve of the invasion, "Brezhnev stuck to the fabricated KGB story that 'anti-socialist' forces had been preparing a coup," telling Dubcek that "underground command posts and arms caches have now come to light."[114]

To conclude, KHODOKI operations failed to contribute measurably toward Soviet goals or a shift in the balance of power. The constraining influence of the operational trilemma is clearly evident across all operations, as high speed and relative intensity of effects come at the cost of control over targets and effects. In particular, the arms cache operation illustrates the trade-offs involved, as there were several available options to improve upon the deception, yet they were unavailable due to the time constraints. Consequently, all three operations failed to fulfill their objectives and fell short of providing measurable strategic value.

PROGRESS: Subverting Government and Civil Society

In contrast to KHODOKI's failures, the KGB's efforts to infiltrate Czechoslovakia's government and civil society bore more fruit. Illegals succeeded with infiltration within only a few weeks, and none were discovered or captured. However, they did not pursue active effects of the kind in KHODOKI, but rather focused on intelligence collection. Consequently, overall PROGRESS had no measurable impact on the liberalization movement or government policy. In other words, this campaign proceeded fast and maintained control, yet at the cost of intensity.

Illegals deployed for PROGRESS operations had the objective to infiltrate a wide swath of civil society organizations, including the union of writers, radical journals, student bodies at Charles University, the dissident organization K-231, and the activist group KAN.[115] In addition, Andrew and Mitrokhin note the codenames of the first five agents as YEFRAT, GURYEV, YEVDOKIMOV, GROMOV, and SADKO.[116] However, apart from the targeting and deployment details, there is little available evidence on the effects of this operation. As discussed further above, GURYEV and GROMOV were the two agents behind the failed kidnapping attempt. Apart from this operation, however, there is no evidence of further attempts at influencing the liberal movement. Absence of evidence is not evidence of absence, yet the behavior of civil society groups does not show any signs of changes in activity aligned with Soviet goals. On the contrary, the publication of the "2000 Words Manifesto" in June, an intense critique of Communist rule written by Ludvík Vaculík and signed by a long list of Czechoslovak intellectuals and artists, was widely supported by the groups targeted in PROGRESS operations.[117] Hence, the agents deployed either did not attempt to influence the opposition or, if they did, failed at achieving significant effects.

Instead of influence, available evidence indicates that following the kidnapping debacle, their main focus was on intelligence collection. Andrew and Mitrokhin suggest that Andropov used "slanted intelligence" throughout the crisis to influence the Politburo and "strengthen its resolve to intervene"[118] but remain thin on the details of the collection efforts involved. However, the archive of the former Ukrainian KGB, now housed by the Ukrainian security service SBU, does provide detailed evidence of collection efforts through human agents—although limited to those agents in direct contact with the Ukrainian KGB. The archive contains 270 individual reports from Czechoslovakia starting in March 1968 (i.e., coinciding with the start of the crisis). As depicted in Figure 3.1, out of these 270 individual reports, 269 discuss intelligence collection, the majority of which (170 reports, or 62.9% of reporting) is collected from field agents or informers in Ukraine (coded as HUMINT).[1]

The body of the Ukrainian KGB reports indicates two things. First, the large proportion of HUMINT sources indicates that the KGB quickly established a significant network of spies and informers. The reports range from mundane details of meetings between border officials to extensive surveys of opinions on Communism and the Soviet Union expressed by citizens in Czechoslovakia and Ukraine—underlining the scope and scale of the network of spies and informers. This reporting also provides one piece of

---

[1] Signal Intelligence Collection via technical means is coded as SIGINT.

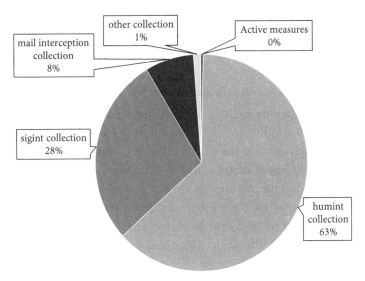

Figure 3.1 Ukrainian KGB records on activities in Czechoslovakia in 1968.

evidence confirming the infiltration of opposition groups, as a report dated October 1968 discusses a meeting between Ukrainian operatives and (illegal?) agents infiltrating the opposition group K-231. Significantly, the report laments the lack of active measures: "State security units that perform the functions of combating internal reaction are developing members of Club 231, who have assumed an illegal role, but no active measures are being taken to curb their hostile activities."[119] This explicit reference to a lack of active measures confirms the conclusion that infiltration of civil society groups was mainly, if not exclusively, used for intelligence collection following the kidnapping failure.

These collection efforts have not led to failures leading to discovery of agents. Evidently, none of the over thirty illegal agents were compromised, indicating that the subversion of the opposition was successful and would have provided a constant flow of intelligence assessments of the opposition to Kremlin leaders. This finding confirms the expected lower failure and discovery risks when pursuing less intense effects. The KGB was able to maintain access to the targeted organizations without being discovered (i.e., a loss of control over its agents and the targeted organization). Interestingly, the apparent shift toward collection may reflect the KGB's recognition of the relative effectiveness of illegal agents in collecting intelligence, rather than active measures—which would be congruent with the dismal track record of the active measures discussed above. After initial experimentation with active measures, it is possible the KGB adjusted operational objectives in PROGRESS to maximize the depth of infiltration and thus the scope of collection efforts.

In contrast to its extensive evidence of HUMINT collection through undercover agents, the sole mention of active measures in the Ukrainian KGB archives involves a rather outlandish plot: writing letters to Czechoslovak schoolchildren to "inform" them about the benevolent Soviet intentions—which was likely never carried out.[120] Of course, the priorities of the Ukrainian KGB are not necessarily the same as Moscow's, yet the overall focus on collection over active measures evident in its reporting supports the conclusion that PROGRESS operations focused on burrowing deeper into the liberal movement rather than risking discovery by aiming to influence or disrupt it.

The infiltration of the KSC, meanwhile, aimed not only to collect intelligence, but also to manipulate government policy. It failed, however, as agents and their collaborators did not wield sufficient influence within the government. The first infiltration operation commenced in May, spearheaded by the high-profile illegal Mikhail Sagatelyan (head of the TASS News Agency Washington bureau), who was sent to Prague under a cover identity as a journalist for *Izvestiya* to meet with Czechoslovak politicians.[121] Sagatelyan worked quickly, confirming in a report to Moscow on June 4 that he had established contact with key pro-Soviet politicians in the KSC and obtained secret party documents.[122] Furthermore, Sagatelyan specified the objective of regime change, as he "recommended that the Czechoslovak Communist Party leadership create a pro-Soviet group to achieve personnel changes, including the removal of the First Secretary of the CPC [the Soviet abbreviation for the KSC] Central Committee, Alexander Dubček."[123] Significantly, Sagatelyan recommended this course of action as "a lesser evil than military force," and KGB director Andropov endorsed the proposal[124]—underlining the Soviets' primary reliance on subversion over force.

The parallel use of overt means of influence confirms the Soviet pursuit of regime change from within. While Sagatelyan (and possible colleagues) commenced the infiltration of the KSC, the Kremlin summoned Czechoslovak leaders to Moscow for bilateral talks on May 4, where they resisted pressure to curb reforms, resulting in a failed meeting.[125] Subsequently, the Kremlin organized a summit meeting among leaders of the Soviet bloc on May 8 without Czechoslovakia, where Brezhnev expressed distrust for the "sly fox"

Dubcek, while emphasizing that only the pro-Soviet group of politicians in the KSC around Josef Smrkovsky, Vasil Bilak, Alois Indra, and Drahomir Kolder could be trusted.[126] Sagatelyan thus focused his efforts to subvert the Czechoslovak government from within on these individuals.[127] At the same meeting, Bulgarian leader Zhivkov supported Brezhnev and called for Soviet forces to move into Czechoslovakia, yet Brezhnev decided against this and emphasized the need to identify the "healthy core" in the KSC to be supported, while ordering Warsaw Pact maneuvers in mid-May as a "show of support" to this healthy core.[128] Accordingly, the Soviets organized a military exercise in Poland near the Czechoslovak border from May 10 to 28, which the CIA assessed as a "show of force."[129] Hence, overtly the Soviets signaled their resolve to use force if necessary, while behind the scenes the subversive operation this show of force was supporting was in full swing.

Accordingly, on June 5 Andropov forwarded a secret action plan to the Politburo based on Sagatelyan's report. It laid out a roadmap for regime change, which involved mobilizing the pro-Soviet faction within the KSC to take control and developing contacts to maintain a steady flow of information. Moreover, it specified that implementation of these measures would require a KGB undercover operation to be active for six weeks, necessary "because existing KGB operatives in Prague were well known to Czechoslovak state security organs and had to be replaced"—underlining the challenges faced by the KGB.[130] The Ukrainian KGB archives illustrate the success of the intelligence collection efforts of this operation in the striking level of access to Czechoslovakian leaders. One report from August 6, 1968, for example, notes how "people close to Dubček notice his high irritability, he doesn't sleep enough."[131]

The operation also succeeded in fostering closer relations between the Kremlin and the "healthy forces." While relations between Moscow and the reformists around Dubcek continued to deteriorate, contacts with the pro-Soviet group worked by Sagatelyan intensified. Valenta notes that contacts between "antireformists" and Soviet leaders started in May and June 1968, and highlights in particular the role of Indra and Bi'lak. While Indra became active in organizing a "People's Militia" meeting that deplored the "irresponsible actions" of the Czechoslovak media, Bi'lak pursued a close relationship with CCP Politburo member Shelest.[132] While even today there is no hard evidence that the KGB was involved, the timing of these intensified contacts and Bi'lak's pursuit of closer relationships to the Kremlin directly correspond to Sagatelyan's key objectives and occurred shortly after he commenced his operation—unlikely to be a coincidence. One of these meetings confirmed that plans for the overthrow of Dubcek from within were now a primary objective. On June 14, in a private meeting in Moscow, Brezhnev offered Smrkovsky to become Dubcek's successor.[133] Smrkovsky refused, for reasons unknown—perhaps reflecting uncertainty about the prospects of the regime change plans.

While the illegals in the KSC helped coordinate with Moscow and collect intelligence, PROGRESS operations failed to exert any noticeable influence on the Dubcek administration. Throughout the six-week period from June 5, there was no detectable change in Czechoslovak government policy toward the Soviet line, even though the subversive operation was complemented by increasingly menacing coercive measures. From June 18 to 30, Warsaw Pact troops commenced a large-scale military exercise (codename "Sumava") on Czechoslovakian territory to signal resolve and intimidate the reformists—moreover, thousands of troops remained in Czechoslovakia after the termination.[134] Rather than intimidating the liberalization movement, however, this show of force catalyzed resistance, manifested in the "2000 Words Manifesto" published on June 27,[135] which called for a radical speedup of liberalization through grassroots action.[136] Dubcek denounced this manifesto, but throughout July he nonetheless quietly continued reform efforts, causing Kremlin leaders to be increasingly wary that they might miss the moment to intervene.[137] If Sagatelyan and his colleagues were trying to coordinate the pro-Soviet faction to influence policy and facilitate a shift in the balance of power against Dubcek, there were no visible signs of success.

In short, while successfully infiltrating the government and keeping this infiltration secret, PROGRESS operations failed to measurably impact policy. High speed and a high level of control evidently came at the cost of intensity, providing further illustration of the trade-offs posed by the trilemma.

Failure and Fallback to Contingency Planning

As the KGB's subversive campaigns fell short, the Soviets refocused their efforts on diplomatic pressure while intensifying preparations for regime change. KHODOKI and PROGRESS had failed to achieve Moscow's key goals. Dubcek's government maintained its reform course, and public support remained strong. In fact, and despite the KGB's efforts to the contrary, public opinion during the crisis period saw a remarkable increase in support for Dubcek, from 55% to over 70% of respondents to polls expressing trust in him.[138] In response, the KGB switched strategy and prepared a more ambitious contingency plan: from attempting to manipulate and undermine Dubcek's government, the goal was to replace it from within, mobilizing the "healthy forces" identified through PROGRESS. Importantly, the invasion was to support this internal coup and protect it from possible armed resistance. As subversion fell short, the Soviet Union thus escalated to the use of force.

KGB assessments and statements by Kremlin leadership indicated confidence in its chance of success. And yet, Warsaw Pact forces conducted a massive military invasion on August 20, posing a key question: did subversion merely prepare the use of force, or did its failure require the fallback option? A close look at the evidence reveals that the purpose of the military invasion was to protect the peaceful regime change from a perceived threat of armed counterrevolutionaries. With the limited number of agents in place and lack of armed proxy groups, the Soviets opted for invasion to protect the regime change operation from this threat. Evidently, the subversive campaign could not be scaled up and intensified within the time available while maintaining secrecy. In other words, the constraints posed by the operational trilemma likely necessitated the use of force to protect the subversive operation from armed resistance.

As the publication of the "2000 Words Manifesto" marked the failure of influence on policy via PROGRESS operations, the Soviet Union refocused on diplomatic efforts. On July 19—exactly within the six weeks Sagatelyan's action plan for regime change had suggested—the Politburo met to discuss the situation in Czechoslovakia. Andropov renewed his push for military intervention.[139] On the same day, in an unlikely coincidence, *Pravda* published an article highlighting the discovery of arms caches—planted through the KHODOKI operation discussed above—as evidence of an imminent CIA-supported counterrevolutionary coup.[140] However, he failed to convince the Politburo members—further underlining the failure of KHODOKI. Instead, the Politburo decided on renewed diplomatic pressure, setting up a bilateral meeting with Dubcek and the KSC leadership.[141]

The meeting, held at Cierna from July 29 to August 1, ended in an unexpected success, momentarily defusing tensions. Although Andrew and Mitrokhin allege that the meeting was a failure as no agreement was reached, rendering it "no more than a necessary preliminary to invasion,"[142] this conclusion is doubtful for several reasons. First, the Soviets had ordered a large-scale military exercise to be held near the Czechoslovak borders in Germany and Poland, starting on the second day of the conference and thus sending an unmistakable signal of resolve to Czechoslovak leaders.[143] If the conference was indeed a failure and merely a steppingstone toward invasion, the reasonable expectation would be for these exercises to transition into actual invasion. Second, although the conference did start contentiously, Williams highlights that overwhelming evidence—including written records by other Warsaw Pact officials—confirms a secret meeting being held between Brezhnev, Kosygin, Podgornyi, and Suslov and Dubcek, Cernik, Svoboda, and Smrkovsky, where the Czechoslovak side made six oral promises that placated Kremlin leaders.[144] The conclusion of Cierna with a joint official declaration and the decision to hold another conference at Bratislava two days after to edit this text confirms that the Soviets at least perceived potential for progress.[145]

The outcome of the Bratislava conference that followed further confirms the apparent diffusion of tension, and a move away from intervention plans. The Bratislava conference concluded with a joint declaration where Czechoslovak leaders pledged allegiance to the Soviet bloc and promised sweeping censorship laws as well as removal of "rightist" (i.e., reformist) forces from power. This declaration helped dissolve tensions and averted intervention for the time. As Prozumenshchikov concludes, "At this stage, at least part of the Politburo of the CC CPSU considered the problem at least partly, if not wholly, solved. This was why the question of a military intervention moved to the background for the time being."[146] This conclusion is confirmed by a CIA memorandum on the conference, assessing that after Bratislava, the "appearance given was that Moscow was willing at least to give the Czechs—presumably chastened by the nearness of their approach to the brink—a respite."[147]

While Bratislava ended in overt signals of agreement and calm, behind the scenes conformist collaborators in the KSC requested military support in fear of counterrevolutionaries. Alongside the official meeting schedule, at Bratislava the KGB had organized a secret rendezvous between high-raking Politburo member Shelest and the pro-Soviet faction in the KSC—in the lavatory. In between the stalls, Bilak handed Shelest a letter signed by himself, Kapek, Indra, Kolder, and Svestka that warned a "counter-revolution was underway, and there was no power in Czechoslovakia that could resist it," and most importantly, the letter directly "asked the Soviet Union to intervene."[148]

This request thus both increased the urgency of the crisis and proposed a solution.

Significantly, the Kremlin not only followed the guidance of its illegals and collaborators but also left much of the planning of the regime change operation in their hands. As Williams highlights, newly released archival sources document "the extent to which the Politburo left them . . . to prepare the coup and took guidance from them on how and when best to intervene."[149] Somewhat paradoxically, despite their fear of counterrevolution, the pro-Soviet coalition inside the government was confident they could take over control. Accordingly, KGB reports from the time assessed that "Dubcek did not have the situation in Czechoslovakia under control and enjoyed support only from a few pressure groups and extremists; he lacked support among the masses, especially among the workers."[150] Importantly, the Kremlin leaders evidently believed these assessments. As Valenta underlines, "new evidence suggests that after Čierna, the Soviet leaders believed that Dubček, Smrkovský, Černík, Kriegel, and Šimon would be in the minority during future meetings of the Czechoslovak Presidium."[151] Consequently, when planning the takeover of the KSC, it was "assumed that the anti-Dubcek coalition could count on six of the eleven full (voting) members of the Presidium, thus putting them in the majority."[152]

The final decision to intervene ultimately fell on August 17, three days before the invasion. It reflected the Kremlin's fear of counterrevolution and confidence in the prospect of regime change. In the Politburo meeting where the final decision to invade was made, Brezhnev quoted two key reasons: first, "a genuine threat that at the upcoming congress the 'rightist' wing would triumph," and second, "that the Czechoslovak 'healthy forces' had worked out a plan" that he concluded was "acceptable on the whole,"[153] since they had "demonstrated unity" and were "ready for a decisive battle with the rightists."[154] The purpose of invasion was thus to protect the subversive regime change operation, ensuring its success by suppressing presumed "counterrevolutionary groups." Accordingly, General Mayorov, who subsequently led the invasion, later recalled in an interview that on August 17, "the decision was made according to which the troops will move into Czechoslovakia . . . in order to suppress, and if necessary, crush and liquidate the counterrevolution."[155]

This decision is significant in two ways. First, it underlined the limits of subversion, whose earlier failures necessitated the pivot to regime change.

Meanwhile, operational constraints evidently precluded the ability to scale up the subversive campaign in time to stave off the counterrevolution alone. Clearly, the thirty-odd illegal agents deployed to Czechoslovakia had no prospect of defeating such a counterrevolution. Furthermore, such an expansion, for example, targeting presumed counterrevolutionary cells while infiltrating and mobilizing pro-Soviet factions, would have required the usual time for reconnaissance and adaptation. This time was not available (at least based on the perception of imminent counterrevolution). Moreover, it was questionable whether the KGB had the required personnel for further expansion since it had already deployed an extraordinarily large number of illegal agents—at least some of whom had been removed from their existing posts, straining operations in other countries.

Second, it underlines the paradox consequences of opting for subversion in the hope of avoiding force, only to be then forced to intervene to avoid strategic failure as subversion fails to deliver due to its inherent constraints. Brezhnev's statement quoted above justifies the decision to intervene with the need to ensure the regime change operation can proceed. Hence, while one initial rationale for the use of subversive campaigns was hope to avoid the use of force—recall Brezhnev's mention of an extreme option that the Soviets could use but "perhaps do not have to"—as that campaign failed to deliver, the Kremlin faced two options: accept failure or escalate. Ironically, the use of subversion as an alternative to force thus led to its ultimate use, as the operational trilemma limited strategic value, precluding the attainment of the Soviet's core goals. One might imagine an alternative history where instead of betting on their subversive efforts, the Soviets had presented the Dubcek government with a simple ultimatum: fall in line or face invasion.

Importantly, while there is considerable disagreement among historians about the details of the causal mechanism that ultimately led to the decision to intervene, there is a consensus regarding the importance of this perception of impending revolution, the confidence in the pro-Soviet faction to topple Dubcek from within, and the need for armed force to protect this internal coup. Importantly, this perception reflected the assessments of the KGB's subversive agents and collaborators within Czechoslovakia, who simultaneously overestimated their own capabilities to succeed with their internal coup while overstating (if not outright inventing) the extent of an external threat to their mission. In other words, subversion contributed to escalation in two ways. The failure of KHODOKI and PROGRESS led to the contingency plan of regime change, while the flawed intelligence assessments provided by PROGRESS agents contributed to the decision to intervene to ensure this plan succeeded.

This interplay is clearly evident across existing historical analyses of the case, where the main point of disagreement rather concerns the relative influence of Andropov in the Kremlin and the extent to which bureaucratic politics influenced Politburo decision-making compared to the deterioration in the personal relationship between Brezhnev and Dubcek. Andrew and Mitrokhin for one suggest that KGB head Andropov's personal preference for intervention was instrumental in shaping the decision to intervene as he "supplied the Politburo throughout the crisis with slanted intelligence designed to strengthen its resolve to intervene."[156] To drive home this point, they cite Andropov's destruction of countervailing evidence by the KGB operative Oleg Kalugin stationed in Washington. Following the July 19 article in *Pravda* warning of counterrevolution, Kalugin sent a letter to Moscow stressing that there was no evidence at all that Western intelligence services were supporting counterrevolutionary groups in Czechoslovakia.[157] Kalugin himself later revealed that he had sent his analysis directly to Andropov himself—who destroyed the letter rather than pass it on to reveal the failure of his operation to the Soviet leaders.[158]

Overall, however, Andropov's capacity to control the information provided to the Politburo was limited. For example, one key source of information was minister-counsellor Udal'tsov at the Soviet embassy in Prague, who provided uniformly alarmist assessments of the situation—yet the Politburo was alerted by the deputy editor of *Pravda* that these assessments were inaccurate.[159] Moreover, instead of passing through Andropov's hands, most intelligence reports were delivered directly to Brezhnev and Suslov at the Politburo—a fact Andropov complained about after the invasion.[160] Finally, reports by the Ukrainian KGB consistently show both positive and negative assessments of the situation in Czechoslovakia. It is thus unlikely that Andropov alone was able to shift Politburo preferences through slanted intelligence, but it is possible that was not necessary.

Rather than one man's influence, Valenta persuasively argues that the Politburo's decision-making process was instead affected by a shifting alliance from anti-intervention to pro-intervention factions—informed by slanted KGB assessments. Hence, pressure exerted by the military leadership as well as other Soviet bloc leaders ultimately led to the decision to intervene.[161] However, Valenta also highlights the relevance of the KGB, whose "assessments of Dubcek's popularity and the balance of the forces between the reformist and antireformist coalitions were distorted."[162] This distorted information, Valenta concludes, combined with pressure exerted by the pro-Soviet faction in the KSC, was "a key consideration in the August 16–17 decision to invade."[163] The bureaucratic politics explanation thus supports the conclusion that overestimates of the prospect of the internal coup attempt shaped the decision to use force.

The importance of these assessments comes out in Kieran Williams's work as well, although he challenges Valenta's bureaucratic politics theory, emphasizing the personal relationship between Dubcek and Brezhnev.[164] Accordingly, Williams concludes that the key turning point in the crisis was a phone call between Brezhnev and Dubcek on August 13 following up on Dubcek's failure to implement the promises made in the Bratislava agreement. After Dubcek had offered different excuses for the lack of progress and offered to resign, Brezhnev accused Dubcek of deception: "Well, what can I say to you, Sasha? Doesn't this mean a new deception? It is another fact showing that you are deceiving us, I can call it nothing else and I will be completely open with you: if you are unable to resolve this question, then it seems to me that your Presidium has lost all power."[165]

Despite this different causal mechanism, however, Williams nonetheless concedes that "new materials [declassified after the publication of the first edition of Valenta's book] do confirm Valenta's supposition that Soviet leaders' perception of Czechoslovakia was influenced by the one-sided, unduly alarmist information they were being fed by the KGB and Prague embassy."[166] Accordingly, at the August 17 Politburo meeting, rather than focus on the untrustworthiness of Dubcek, Brezhnev cited the threat of counterrevolution and the need to support the pro-Soviet faction to conclude the need for a regime change. Things did not play out as the Kremlin hoped, however, as the next section documents.

A Failed Coup and Tanks in Prague

The previous chapter showed how the Soviets' attempts to get Dubcek's administration to change course through diplomacy and subversion failed. Meanwhile, the crisis intensified as the Soviets feared an imminent armed counterrevolution. As the strategic context shifted, so did the Soviets' key objectives. The Kremlin now pursued two complementary objectives: first, replacing Dubcek's government, and second, defeating the counterrevolution. To achieve the first objective, the Soviet Union relied on its subversive agents and collaborators within the government, supported by armed invasion to hold back the counterrevolutionaries. The invasion was timed to coincide with the overthrow of Dubcek by the "healthy forces" within the KSC, providing the Soviet Union with full control over both the political system and the territory of Czechoslovakia.

Since the Soviets had opted for subversion as the primary instrument of power to establish control by changing the government, success was crucial. Yet the regime change failed as the pro-Soviet faction within the Czechoslovak government lacked support and failed to coordinate its attempt at takeover with the invasion. This chapter will provide a brief overview of the military operation, before examining the causes of failure of the regime change operation. It will show why the vulnerabilities the Soviets had identified in Czechoslovakia's government (pro-Soviet leaders) and the means of exploitation they attempted to use (coordinating an internal coup) turned out to be incapable to establish control, revealing a lack of familiarity with the target. This failure provides further evidence of the constraining role of the operational trilemma but also reveals an additional pathology of subversion: falling prey to one's own poison. The operation was fast while pursuing a highly intense effect, but it lost control and failed to produce the effect. Time spent on reconnaissance and development was insufficient to achieve the degree of control needed to produce the desired effect. Meanwhile, claims of counterrevolution turned out to be greatly exaggerated—there was no such thing. Despite the military success, the Soviet Union thus fell short of achieving its key strategic goal of toppling Dubcek.

Since established historiography focuses on the role of the military invasion in crushing the Prague Spring, details about the operation abound and need not be recounted here in detail. Rather, I will highlight an underappreciated contribution of subversion to this success. The invasion began at 11 p.m. on August 20, 1968. The Warsaw Pact forces met no resistance, and within twenty-four hours they had established full military control over Czechoslovakia without major bloodshed. This resounding success reflected the overwhelming might of the invading army, careful planning, and the discipline of the troops.[167]

However, another factor was crucial in ensuring success: the influence of subversive actors in Czechoslovakia's government. The Czechoslovakian leadership around Dubcek did not expect the invasion. As he wrote in his memoirs, "My problem was not having a crystal ball to foresee the Russian invasion. At no point between January and August 20, in fact, did I believe that it would happen."[168] Hence, there was a considerable risk of unintended escalation through miscalculation in the heat of the moment. Yet as it turned out, the Czechoslovakian defense minister had given an order not to resist.[169] The reason, General Mayorov, the commander of the invading Soviet forces, was the influence of one of the "healthy forces" nurtured in the KSC, namely President Svoboda (Novotny's successor). According to Mayorov, "The fact is that President Ludvik Svoboda stood at the head of the Czechoslovak People's Army as commander-in-chief. And he was our man!"[170] This claim is supported by Williams's analysis, showing that Svoboda was successfully deceived by the Kremlin into believing a majority of the KSC presidium had requested the invasion. Svoboda thus agreed to ensure that the invasion would not meet any resistance.[171]

Although doing so was not its primary purpose, the subversive campaign thus significantly contributed to the success of the military operation by manipulating Czechoslovak defense policy. This dynamic illustrates the flexible role of subversive campaigns initially deployed as an independent instrument, then pivoting toward a complementary role to facilitate the use of force as these campaigns fall short.

Under the protection of the armed invasion, the regime change operation proceeded as "healthy forces" were to overthrow Dubcek while, simultaneously, KGB agents were to take over the Czechoslovak security apparatus. Both failed. The plan by the "healthy forces" around Indra that got Brezhnev's approval was to initiate a vote of no confidence in Dubcek at the KSC presidium just before the invasion. As the Soviet armies arrived, the conspirators would form a new government under Indra, which would then officially request "fraternal assistance" by the Soviets, as well as from Czechoslovak state security agencies.[172] Since it involved justifying the invasion, assuming political control, and co-opting the security apparatus, "the entire success of the political aspect of the Soviet invasion plan depended upon the formation of this new government."[173] The evident lack of careful preparations by the conspirators betrayed the central importance in the success of their coup d'état attempt for the Soviet intervention. The coup failed entirely as the conspirators around Indra did not succeed in challenging Dubcek at the presidium meeting in time for the invasion. Embarrassingly, as Williams points out, one reason for the failure was an apparent "mix-up between Moscow time and Central European time" that resulted in the conspirators moving too late to challenge Dubcek.[174] Moreover, when the invasion was announced, the presidium voted seven to four to condemn the Soviet invasion—underlining the lack of political support enjoyed by the pro-Soviet faction. Recognizing this lack of support, the group thus refrained from challenging Dubcek.[175] Consequently, the subversive operations failed to fulfill the three core objectives: Dubcek's government remained in place, the Soviet invasion lacked legitimacy, and Czechoslovak state security agencies had not been co-opted by an official call for assistance.

The causes for this failure are twofold. First, the constraints posed by the trilemma are clearly evident. This operation proceeded very fast while also pursuing very intense effects. It involved only a few weeks of preparation, compared to two years for the CIA's operation PBSUCCESS, which brought down Guatemalan president Jacobo Árbenz in 1954, for example.[176] Meanwhile, "small scale coup d'état" ranges near the top of Johnson's escalation ladder, on rung thirty-five of thirty-eight.[177] High speed and intensity came at the cost of control, as the KGB's agents and collaborators had insufficient influence and capabilities to manipulate Czechoslovakia's government from within. Instead, the collaborators were discovered and sidelined. Interestingly, however, the cause for this failure goes deeper as the ambitious design of the operation reflected overconfidence and delusions fed by the KGB's own reporting and disinformation. As discussed earlier, the KGB's agents and collaborators had assessed their situation overly favorably, reporting that they had the support of a majority within the government when in fact they did not. Meanwhile, the notion of an impending counterrevolution that fed a sense of urgency compressing the operational timeline was itself a KGB disinformation narrative, supported by the false evidence planted through KHODOKI operations. In other words, the KGB's misperception and deception shaped an operational design pursuing both high speed (urgency due to counterrevolution) and high intensity (overconfidence in influence and capability to mount a coup) that increased the risk of control loss, compounding the risk of failure as misperception and disinformation met reality. Herman's notion of subversion "putting a virus into the bloodstream" of an adversary comes to mind here[178]—evidently, just like with biological warfare, subversive actors can fall prey to their own virus.

As the subversive operation had failed, the Soviets again fell back to force. On August 21, Soviet troops surrounded all key Czechoslovak government buildings, and a KGB-led delegation of Czechoslovak police and Soviet officers arrested the KSC leadership in their offices.[179] The pro-Soviet faction was now nominally in control over the government and met in the Soviet embassy to discuss plans of forming a new government with Soviet ambassador Chervonenko. However, at the same time the remaining members of the KSC organized a secret Party Congress where they elected a new presidium that included all the members arrested by the KGB, while excluding the pro-Soviet group around Indra due to their collaboration with the Soviets. Importantly, this meeting was broadcast via Czechoslovak radio—which the KGB had failed to shut down[180]—thus undermining the legitimacy of the Soviet-backed Indra "government."

The continued operation of Czechoslovak radio stations was the result of another failure of the conspirators, reflecting lack of preparation, and part of an overall Soviet propaganda failure—providing further confirmation of misplaced confidence in the success of the coup d'état. As Williams highlights, evidently "the conspirators had overlooked a number of areas in which they ought to have recruited technicians," and several technicians at several different Czechoslovak radio stations revolted against the Indra government, instead continuing broadcasts supporting the Dubcek government.[181] Not only were there continued anti-Soviet broadcasts, but also a failure to prepare their own propaganda measures meant the Soviets had no rival means of influencing public opinion.

At the time of the invasion, there were no propaganda cadres in place and no high-quality propaganda materials available.[182] Moscow did dispatch a high-ranking propaganda expert, Aleksandr Yakovlev, first deputy director of the CC CPSU Propaganda Department, but only on the day of the invasion.[183] Consequently, it took two days until the first propaganda document arrived from Moscow in the form of the "hurriedly edited" text of the "Address to the Citizens of the Czechoslovak Socialist Republic."[184] Pamphlets were dropped in Prague, Bratislava, Kosice, and Plzen justifying the Soviet invasion and asking for collaboration of the public with occupation forces.[185] Yet these last-minute measures largely failed to produce the intended effects on public opinion—even by the Kremlin's own assessment.

A Kremlin evaluation in November 1968 thus concluded that the invasion had occurred in a "propaganda vacuum," which helped the "rightist forces" to gain the sympathy of the population—75% to 90% of which consequently saw the invasion as an "occupation" within the first week.[186] Accordingly, an intelligence assessment by the West German Intelligence Service (known in German as "Bundesnachrichtendienst," abbreviated as BND) dated August 22 noted that "despite overwhelming psychological pressure" through the presence of armed forces, efforts to "intimidate the population failed," concluding that "further resistance and protests are to be expected in the large cities."[187] This near-total, and uncharacteristic, propaganda failure reflected a clear lack of preparation. Evidently, the Soviets had assumed broad popular support for their "military assistance" as promised by Indra and the KGB assessments. In practice, they faced broad public resistance. Despite the failed coup, the KGB still moved ahead and implemented plans to take over the key security agencies in order to institute mass arrests of civil society leaders. However, as Žáček has documented, although pro-Soviet members of the StB were activated on August 20–21 to take control of secret police and paralyze party and state institutions, they failed due to public and institutional resistance, and the operation resulted in the entire StB apparatus falling apart.[188]

The most likely explanation for this failure is a lack of adequate preparation—reflecting a rushed pace, in line with the overall overestimation of public support and overconfidence in success discussed above. The timeline of the decision-making process discussed further above indicates that the intervention was decided only on August 17, 1968—leaving very little time to prepare subversive operations to complement military with political control. Confirming this timeline, the first KGB agents to be deployed in the invasion arrived only on the same day. This rushed operation apparently sacrificed secrecy for scale, taking the unsubtle approach of flying in agents via military planes. According to the *Czech Black Book*, "A story circulated at the Ministry of Interior—and it was not considered a secret—that a special airplane carrying officials of the Soviet KGB had landed as early as August 17, 1968, at Ruzyně Airport."[189] With only three days to prepare the takeover of state security organs, and moreover, having evidently alerted Czechoslovak state security to their arrival, chances of success were slim. Accordingly, while the KGB succeeded to occupy the StB offices, its agents had to withdraw due to unexpected resistance after only five days.[190] This failure significantly hampered the implementation of the planned mass arrests of reformists and opposition groups.[191]

More coordinated and larger-scale efforts may have succeeded in taking over the state security apparatus. Yet the already low public support for both the conspirators and the invading forces was further eroded by the continued broadcasts of Soviet-critical radio programs—and no coordinated pro-Soviet propaganda push to counter it. Lacking technicians, the pro-Soviet actors had no means of taking over radio stations or preventing them from popping up again even after assuming full control of the Ministry of the

Interior's switchboard.[192] Consequently, Dubcek remained in power, liberal civil society remained alive and well, and Dubcek's government enjoyed continued public support.

Rather than "liquidating the reformists leaders physically and politically" as had apparently been the original plan, this lack of political control forced Kremlin leaders to accept Dubcek and his colleagues as negotiating partners.[193] From August 23 to 26, Dubcek and his allies negotiated with the Kremlin leaders in Moscow and forged a deal that allowed them to remain in power in exchange for accepting occupation, giving in to Moscow's demands for censorship.[194] Despite these concessions, considering the primary Soviet aim had been regime change, this outcome was a significant failure. Reflecting this failure, Moscow decreed to leave the invasion forces—initially supposed to be withdrawn swiftly—in place. The resulting agreement was the Moscow Protocol, signed on August 27, which foresaw a temporary occupation until the situation had "normalized."[195]

Finally, the same misperception of popular support that doomed the regime change operation hampered the occupation itself. Public resistance significantly impacted the soldiers, as "an almost immediate collapse of supply lines forced troops to beg for food and water from an uncooperative population."[196] Due to this lack of support, within a week after the invasion Soviet units ran out of food and reportedly started looting local shops and houses.[197]

To conclude, the regime change operation failed due to an ambitious operational design driven by overconfidence and misperception, and a resulting inability to produce the desired outcome. High confidence in their ability to take control of the government combined with fear of an impending counterrevolution led the KGB to proceed at high speed while pursuing intense effects. As predicted by the operational trilemma, high speed and intensity tend to come at the cost of control, manifested here in the failure to manipulate targeted institutions—most importantly, the Czechoslovak government—and the consequent loss of assets and access. Finally, the fact that the Soviets did allow Dubcek to remain in power although they could have used their military control to keep him and his government in prison while imposing martial law on the population is congruent with their expected concern with reputational costs. Evidently, the Soviets deemed the reputational costs to socialism too great to proceed with this latter course of action, although they certainly had the means of doing so. Correspondingly, as soon as the failure of the regime change operation became clear, and despite the failure of the subversive operations thus far, the Kremlin again opted for subversion as a key instrument to bring Czechoslovakia in line during the final phase of the conflict.

Following its failed regime change, the KGB drastically expanded the scale of its subversive operations. On the same day the takeover of the Czechoslovak state security apparatus failed, in an unlikely coincidence, the KGB flew in hundreds of undercover agents. According to the *Black Book*, on August 25, "Czechoslovak Radio reported that approximately eight hundred members of the occupation powers have landed in Prague today in civilian clothes. They are furnished with forged Czechoslovak passports and speak fluent Czech and Slovak. They are said to be members of the Soviet State Security, and they are being assigned to various cities. About forty are already in Bratislava."[198]

The official newscast by the KSC provided more details, stating, "Airplanes from Moscow bring more members of the Soviet State Security. The latter change their clothes at the airport, taking off their civilian clothes and putting on civilian clothes of Czechoslovak manufacture. They have cards identifying them as members of our Public Security as well as other cards identifying them as Czechoslovak citizens, in addition to large amounts of money in new banknotes."[199]

The description of these agents clearly identifies them as undercover agents with fake identities, but likely less robust ones than the elite illegal agents who would cross borders via official customs checks. There are no records of any immediate activity undertaken by these agents; hence, they most likely spread to their assigned regions and cities to start infiltrating civil society groups as well as recalcitrant government agencies. These objectives would be congruent with the Kremlin's recognition at this stage that "normalization" and the neutralization of the opposition would take significant time, in contrast to the expected swift takeover and realignment of Czechoslovakia with the Soviet line.[200] Subversion was to prove of central importance in attaining them.

"Normalization" and Permanent Occupation

In the final phase of the conflict, the stakes remained the same, but the urgency subsided. With military control established and the specter of counterrevolution banned, the Soviet Union faced much less time pressure to "reign in" the liberalization movement. The overall strategic goal to replace

Dubcek and reverse Czechoslovakia's reform course remained unchanged, and so did the central importance of subversion as the means to attain that end. In the aftermath of the invasion, this goal received an official name as a policy of "normalization." With more time at hand, subversion had greater potential to fulfill its strategic promise as a slower operational pace allowed increased intensity of effects and control. Consequently, and in line with the theory, the longer subversive operations ran during this phase, the greater the strategic value they tended to exhibit.

With the invasion complete, the Soviets had full military control, but political control was incomplete. Despite the concessions he was forced to make in the Moscow Protocol, Dubcek and his government remained in power. Moreover, the invasion had united the Czechoslovak population against the occupying force. Consequently, the Soviets renewed their subversive efforts to weaken Dubcek's basis of political and public support. In contrast to the rushed operations during the crisis phase, this subversive campaign was both more subtle and slower. There were no more daring attempts at active measures such as sabotage, kidnapping, or assassinations. Instead, the Soviets aimed to slowly weaken public resistance by both disintegrating the liberalization movement and eroding remaining political support for Dubcek. Furthermore, the KGB expanded the scale of its operations, thus expanding the possible scale of effects. Despite this expansion, with hundreds of additional agents dispatched for PROGRESS, there is little evidence of expanded effects. Instead, these agents seem to have focused mostly on intelligence collection, identifying "liberal elements" and civil society leaders for arrests. Yet these arrests only temporarily set back dissenters. It only took civil society two to three years to regroup and continue its resistance against Soviet policies, necessitating the permanent occupation (from the Kremlin's perspective).

Conversely, the KGB scaled down its KHODOKI operations and abandoned the daring high-risk attempts at producing intense effects that characterized the first phase. Accordingly, there is little evidence indicating that KHODOKI had any impact on opposition activity or public perception of the latter. However, one operation very likely contributed to the attainment of the Kremlin's key goal. Following a violent protest at the Aeroflot office in Prague instigated by KGB undercover agents to discredit the liberalization movement, Dubcek resigned—importantly, citing the operation as a primary cause. This operation thus produced significant strategic value. Proceeding at lower speed while pursuing lower-intensity effects compared to the crisis phase experiments, as expected, the subversive operations in this phase exhibited significantly greater control over targets and effects. There are no indications of failed operations, nor reports of agents blowing their cover. Moreover, there is the qualified success of the Aeroflot operation mentioned above, reflecting its likely extensive preparation time. These findings thus strongly support the theory, providing further evidence of the inverse correlation between speed, intensity, and control predicted by the trilemma.

Although the military was in control of the streets, the Soviet Union faced continued resistance in the Czechoslovak government, law enforcement, and civil society. In line with the preference to avoid using brute force where possible, it relied on subversion to erode that remaining resistance and get Czechoslovakia to abandon its reform course. This strategic goal was officially sanctioned in its postescalation policy of "normalization" first set out in the Moscow Protocol. While allowing Dubcek to stay in power, the Moscow Protocol set thirteen conditions when "normalization" would be achieved, justifying the withdrawal of the Warsaw Pact forces. The document clearly reflects the two core Soviet strategic goals identified at the outset, namely maintaining Czechoslovakia within the Soviet sphere of influence and reversing liberal reforms. The Moscow Protocol accordingly required that "Czechoslovakia would follow the Soviet line on European security, Germany, and the permanence of post-war borders" while obliging Czechoslovak leaders to assist the Soviets to "restore full control over the media, eliminate unacceptable clubs and organizations, cleanse the party and state apparatus of 'compromised individuals.'"[201]

The protocol thus stated the ends, while a piece of evidence from Brezhnev himself specified subversion as the primary means of achieving them. In a note titled "Notes on the Preparation of Politico-Military Action on 21 August 1968" that was found on his desk on the day of the invasion, Brezhnev stressed, "It is imperative for us to add to the military control a political and administrative one. What we are aiming for are massive interferences in the affairs of Czechoslovakia. . . . To achieve this goal an extensive plan involving disinformation measures had to be developed. It is crucially important to discredit the right-wing leaders, to compromise them, to strengthen the contacts to those right-wing elements in order to enable the broad masses to charge the right-wing leaders with collaboration."[202]

To achieve this "massive interference," the Kremlin significantly expanded the scale of its subversive campaigns. It deployed additional agents from the

Soviet bloc to augment the PROGRESS campaign of infiltrating government and civil society to erode resistance and exert influence. This expansion also placed increased focus on law enforcement agencies. Meeting notes of the East German intelligence service MfS from early October 1968 specify the key objective of its operations in Czechoslovakia as "exploiting all political-operative opportunities to penetrate the counterrevolutionary base of the CSSR," while noting it required "constant oversight of influential and/or exploitable, progressive forces in the CSSR, in particular employees of the security services."[203] Law enforcement thus became a third key target sector of the subversive campaign.

On October 17, the Soviet Union (specifically, the Central Committee of the CSPU) created a new KGB department (Osobyi Otgel) to coordinate postinvasion operations in Czechoslovakia and recruited an additional 334 officers.[204] This increase in organizational capacity significantly expanded the potential scale of effects subversive operations could achieve. These efforts bore success, as Žáček notes that "gradually, they [the KGB] managed to blunt the anti-Soviet sting; State Security focused again on monitoring and investigating ideological enemies and forwarded the results of its findings to the KGB."[205] Hence, the KGB illegals could increasingly rely on the support of Czechoslovak state security agencies.

Yet despite this expansion, there was no significant increase in the scale of effects. Rather, key successes involved a deepening of the scope of subversion of opposition groups through illegal agents. Mitrokhin's notes indicate that spies involved in PROGRESS continued to focus on secretly penetrating more deeply into civil society organizations, exploiting vulnerabilities such as the group's affinity to Westerners to establish trust and gain access to leadership. According to Mitrokhin's archive, between October 1968 and 1969, KGB illegals ALLA, ARTYMOVA, and FYODOROV successfully deceived a leader of the prominent opposition group K-231, Leo Lappi, into believing they were Western supporters of the Prague Spring hoping to assist in its restoration[206]—allowing a subversion of the organization from the top down. Lappi introduced FYODOROV not only to K-231 members but also to the (illegal) Christian Democratic and Socialist opposition parties.[207] ALLA and ARTYMOVA were both among the first group of illegals sent to Prague between April and May 1968,[208] and evidently it took them at least five months to penetrate deeply enough into the opposition to gain the trust of one of its leaders. By the time they had achieved this objective, the crisis had long passed—further underlining the ineffectiveness of subversion in crisis response.

In line with the assessment above, over the months that followed the invasion, PROGRESS did not produce a measurable impact on the liberalization movement, or in fact any measurable effects at scale. One way to measure the effectiveness of PROGRESS is via arrest statistics, as individuals identified by KGB illegals could be targeted by law enforcement. Available data does not indicate any massive spike in arrests following the invasion—on the contrary, the Soviets refrained from implementing planned mass arrests due to the perceived lack of control over law enforcement.[209] This conclusion is further supported by Evanson's study of repression patterns in Czechoslovakia, documenting that the first major trial of opposition activists only occurred in 1971.[210] In fact, official statistics by the Czech Ministry of the Interior show that *fewer* people were tried and sentenced for political offenses in the postinvasion phase than in the precrisis years.[211]

Intelligence reports further underline the initial lack of impact from PROGRESS. The East German intelligence service in a report from November 29, 1968, noted the "continued existence of an illegal network of hostile forces, the unleashing of a new wave of nationalism and an increased anti-Soviet smear campaign," concluding that the "forced disintegration process was particularly advanced among students."[212] Similarly, on December 16, 1968, the Ukrainian KGB documented an assessment by a Czechoslovak KGB officer (in the Slovak region) warning that "press and youth organization have anti-Soviet attitudes, K-231 is operating illegally," while the "majority of Slovak intelligentsia believes the USSR . . . embodies an undemocratic and inhumane form of socialism."[213] He concluded that at the current rate, without the use of force, "normalization might take 10 years."[214] The final document in the SBU Archive on the Prague Spring, a report from January 1969, relays an assessment by Czechoslovakian intelligence officers noting that "secret counter-revolutionary organizations continue to operate in Prague."[215]

In short, PROGRESS had no measurable impact at this stage. Spies were slowly penetrating more deeply into civil society, establishing access to and trust of leading figures, and the lack of any known losses of cover of these agents indicates their success at maintaining secrecy while proceeding with exploitation. The most likely explanation for the lack of active effects during these first months is the time needed to establish access and trust. Any mass arrests in turn would have caused alarm in affected organizations, increasing paranoia by members, and thus lowering their susceptibility to infiltrating spies. Since urgency was low, the KGB was able to focus on deepening the subversion of these organizations without risking discovery by intensifying effects (i.e., proceeding with arrests). Meanwhile, it relied on KHODOKI active measures to influence public opinion.

KHODOKI Redux: "The Aeroflot Incident" as Its Crowning Achievement?

The KGB resumed active measures operations under the KHODOKI campaign, but much more cautiously. It pursued lower intensity of effects and decreased operational speed. As predicted by the operational trilemma, this approach increased control over targets and effects, thus increasing effectiveness and strategic value. The primary focus of active measures was on propaganda and disinformation, reflecting Brezhnev's prescriptions. Effects were at best marginal, however. Meanwhile, a single well-executed operation to discredit civil society through deception likely made a significant contribution. This operation, known as the "Aeroflot incident," triggered Dubcek's resignation, thus contributing to a key goal of "normalization." The analysis will trace how it achieved this outcome and show why continued uncertainty about the very existence of the operation indicates the extent of control the KGB had established through extended preparations. Very slow speed thus ensured control despite high-intensity effects, namely the mobilization of opposition groups to commence physical acts of violence.

Rather than spread overt propaganda, in this phase the KGB established two media outlets to covertly spread Soviet disinformation while also implementing more targeted operations. The first outlet was a radio station, called Vltava, established shortly after the invasion and broadcasting from Eastern Germany.[216] Second, KGB agents founded an "underground" magazine called *Zpravy* spreading pro-Soviet messaging, whose first issue was published on August 30, 1968.[217] Meanwhile, available evidence also suggests scattered disinformation campaigns targeting specific individuals. Bittman describes one such campaign a few months after the invasion. It aimed to discredit the Prague Spring leader Smrkovsky with pamphlets describing him as a "power-hungry and corrupted individual" who had been involved in anti-Soviet activities after World War II.[218] Considering the prevailing anti-Soviet mood among the Czechoslovak population, this pamphlet was unlikely to have the desired effect. On the contrary, it may have reminded people why they supported Dubcek and his administration in the first place.

Overall, the intelligence assessments quoted above indicate that these active measures had little measurable impact. Accordingly, survey data analyzed by de Sola Pool indicates overwhelming public support for Dubcek and Svoboda in September 1968, with 95% of respondents expressing support, which only slightly decreased to 90% for Svoboda and to around 82% for Dubcek by December 1968.[219] Hence, if concerted propaganda efforts did contribute to this slight drop in support, their effect was marginal at best.

Letters of the occupying military force intercepted by the Ukrainian KGB, meanwhile, document continued public resistance. One soldier wrote in a letter in October 1968: "I was in Ostrava [a small town near the Polish border], it's better not to go there: they throw stones, rotten eggs, even shoot. There are already many victims on our side.... [A]t first we were forbidden to shoot at Czechs, now they have given orders to shoot when they shoot at you."[220] One of his colleagues reveals the personal costs of this operation in stark terms: "You can hardly see the sun, you live like in prison, you do not see brightness. Sometimes you sit down and start thinking, and quite often I just want to take a gun and put a bullet in my head."[221] Another soldier offers a more reserved analysis, noting that "armed thugs drive through the villages and intimidate the peasants not to give us anything, not to talk and not to contact us at all," concluding with remarkable foresight, "we are gradually teaching them to obey, but we have made enemies for decades."[222] The KGB's meticulously collected excerpts of letters by Soviet soldiers are overwhelmingly negative,[223] attesting to the continuing hostility among the Czechoslovak population.

In contrast to the relative insignificance of the disinformation efforts, the operation that (most likely) produced what became known as the "Aeroflot incident" contributed to a decisive change in the course of the conflict. This operation, whose existence remains contested, involved agitation of violent anti-Soviet protests at the Aeroflot building in Prague. In its aftermath, Dubcek resigned, citing fears of further violence. The operation did not alter the material balance of power but rather achieved a psychological effect by signaling Soviet resolve to incite violent protests to discredit anti-Soviet groups in the eye of the public. Whether this signaling effect was indeed the intended outcome of the operation or rather a welcome byproduct of the agitation efforts aimed to discredit the liberalization movement cannot be conclusively established due to lack of evidence. However, Dubcek's resignation nonetheless marked the collapse of reformist forces in the government, thus paving the way to conclude the regime change and re-establish full political control—the primary Soviet objective. The discussion below will first outline the sequence of events involved and its impact on the conflict, before evaluating the available evidence supporting the conclusion that this was, in fact, a covert operation. The continued uncertainty surrounding the latter question ultimately attests to the effectiveness of the operation, reflecting the degree of control achieved thanks to the long preparation time.

Following the win of the Czechoslovak hockey team against the Soviet team on March 28, protestors threw stones and demolished the building of Soviet state airline Aeroflot in Prague, in response to which the Soviets demanded intervention by the Czechoslovak armed forces. Early suspicions questioned "whether this incident was spontaneous or whether it was a provocation mounted by agents of the political police."[224] Today, widespread consensus among historians holds this protest as a Soviet covert action. Yet as Tuma highlights, "Although the interpretations are presented without a shadow of doubt, they are not supported by explicit evidence or sources."[225] Hence, it is necessary to discuss the chain of events and evaluate available evidence in some detail.

In fact, Dubcek himself is a key source. His memoirs state that the protest was a carefully staged operation run by Soviet agents within Czech State Security. As he describes, "Police agents under cover as city workers had unloaded a heap of paving stones in front of the offices of Aeroflot . . . supervised directly by the Czech minister of the interior, Josef Groesser, as Soviet agent."[226] Importantly, the operation required the Soviet team to lose; "what they then needed, of course, was a victory by our team."[227] Although qualifying it as an "improbable stretch of the imagination," Dubcek suggests the Soviet team may have been "'advised' to lose the game."[228] The Soviets did lose in any case, and huge crowds began to fill the streets of Prague, including Wenceslas Square, in front of the Aeroflot office. Soon after, "State Security agents who were mingling with the crowd began to throw the conveniently placed stones at the Aeroflot office. Few Czechs followed their lead."[229] In Dubcek's perception, "This was the first act in a chain of events that led to decisive moves against us," as shortly after, "the Soviets were asking the Czechoslovak military to intervene in the streets."[230] Although he resisted these demands, fearing further such provocations and the possibility of a bloodbath, Dubcek resigned the following day.[231]

Dubcek's version of events is adopted by Andrew and Mitrokhin, who state the operation as simple fact.[232] However, they do not provide any additional references; hence, it can only be assumed that Mitrokhin's notes confirm the operation.

Similarly, Kieran Williams's study of internal documents by the Czech security service StB found no evidence for this operation, instead concluding that these materials provide an impression of "an organization . . . in such internal disarray throughout the Dubcek period that it was in no position to coerce the public into quiescence."[233] Due to the lack of hard evidence, Tuma et al. doubt the veracity of Dubcek's "conspiracy theory," pointing out four key flaws. First, the presence of "conveniently placed" pavement stones cited by Dubcek provides rather weak evidence since Prague's streets were in disrepair following the Prague Spring and piles of stones were a common sight.[234] Second, neither does the presence of "burly men" among the protestors highlighted by former US diplomat Skoug, who was personally present at the scene, provide strong clues of a subversive covert operation. According to Tuma et al., most of the protestors in 1968 and 1969 were in fact young workers rather than students (whom Western media reports focused on).[235] Third, Tuma et al. question how the operation could have been planned in advance "if favorable conditions for its implementation depended on the outcome of the [hockey] match."[236] Finally, Tuma et al. point out that "comparable incidents occurred in more than twenty places" as evidence of a tense atmosphere in which violence could have broken out spontaneously—unless one "wants to expand the conspiracy theory and admit that the incidents . . . had also been provoked."[237] While these are useful points to consider, none of them decisively refutes the covert action theory—and some miss important evidence.

Tuma et al.'s first two points of criticism effectively suggest that the presence of pavement stones and "burly men" among the protestors are not "smoking gun" pieces of evidence. Yet the fact that both can be plausibly explained by the demographics of protesters in Prague and prevailing conditions on the street does not prove that this was not a covert operation. On the contrary, these details can just as well be seen as evidence of careful planning and adaptation, ensuring cover and plausible deniability. Point three, on the advance planning, appears significant only at first glance. It rests on the premise that Czech victory was the necessary condition for riots—yet there are ample examples of sports fans exploding into violence following a loss of their team.[238] It is thus hardly inconceivable that the operation was planned beforehand despite a lack of certainty about the outcome of the match. In short, protests were planned whether they win or lose.

Accordingly, Williams's research reveals that Groesser had attempted to generate fear of violent groups only a few weeks before the incident, as "in February Czech interior minister Groesser tried to generate hysteria by telling party bosses that the StB had exposed armed groups intending to attack the country's leaders."[239] Moreover, paranoia of violent counterrevolutionary groups had been a key theme across KGB intelligence reports throughout the conflict, just as discrediting opposition movements had been the primary objective of KGB active measures. Therefore, the Aeroflot incident is in line with both the KGB's previous messaging and strategic objectives. The planners of the operation obviously would not have been able control the public reaction to the match itself, but they were able to create the infrastructure necessary to opportunistically exploit public agitation—if not after this match, perhaps in another context. The lack of certainty about the match outcome thus does not preclude the execution of an operation. This point leads to the shortcomings of Tuma et al.'s final criticism.

Point four, the coordination of protests across multiple cities, which Tuma et al. assert requires an "expansion of the conspiracy theory," is in fact confirmed by the key primary source in this case. The memoirs of former StB agent Josef Frolik state, "Josef Grösser [using the German spelling], the Czech Minister of the Interior, following orders by Soviet advisers, instructed Molnar to prepare an assault of a Soviet building in Prague. Similar tasks were given to the regional chiefs in Ústí nad Labem and others [other cities where similar protests did occur]."[240] There is no evidence to the contrary, nor is there an apparent plausible motivation for Frolik to lie about this. Finally, the Soviet services and their network of collaborating agents within the StB were clearly able to conduct such an operation. As discussed, the KGB had dispatched hundreds of agents in addition to the already established network of illegal agents. Moreover, illegal agents had been in place for almost a year, and additional KGB agents dispatched had half a year to establish themselves—providing ample adaptation time to establish the necessary scope of reach, that is, gaining the trust of their colleagues or comrades, to conduct this operation.

In short, Tuma et al.'s criticisms do not decisively refute the conclusion that the Aeroflot incident was an active measure. Apart from the reasons outlined above, the effect of this violent incident—Dubcek's resignation— was the primary objective of Soviet overt and covert measures since the start of the crisis. Importantly, the decisive causal relevance of the Aeroflot incident in Dubcek's ultimate defeat and removal was established long before trickles of statements on its nature as a covert operation were published.[241] Based on the available evidence and clear congruence between prior operational methods and objectives and primary strategic objectives, it is thus reasonable to conclude that the Aeroflot incident was indeed a subversive operation.

However, it is unlikely that Dubcek's resignation was the intended outcome of the operation. Instead, the immediate effects of the operation, and the Soviet response, indicate an objective of increasing political tension, fabricating a crisis. As Dubcek recalls, the Kremlin requested the Czech military to intervene on the same night as protests broke out, and three days later (March 31) Soviet General Marshal Grechko traveled to Czechoslovakia with Deputy Foreign Minister Semyonov demanding new censorship measures and the deployment of Czech armed forces to suppress the alleged "counter-revolution."[242] Hence, the protests were means to justify the use of force—in direct parallel to the arms caches operation prior to the Soviet invasion providing the "proof," however brittle, of counterrevolutionary forces, justifying an armed intervention. It is highly likely that Kremlin leaders perceived the threat of counterrevolution as significant, as had been the case prior to the invasion. Dubcek's response to step down was thus most likely an unintended, if highly welcome, consequence of the operation.

Regardless of intentionality, the protests were a resounding operational success compared to active measures preceding the invasion. While details of this operation remain incomplete and contested, triangulation of the evidence available has indicated an operation with a high intensity of effects as well as a high degree of control that had proceeded at a correspondingly slow speed—in line with the theory. Moreover, the very fact that the existence of this operation continues to be contested attests to its successful maintenance of secrecy—if it did happen, of course.

However, two additional factors that go beyond the variables of the trilemma facilitated success, underlining the importance of enabling conditions. First, this operation leveraged subversive reach into local law enforcement, including the use of local agents, who were much better adapted to the target groups compared to illegal agents posing as Westerners. As locals, these agents would naturally blend in much better, providing superior stealth, and would also have had more time to infiltrate opposition groups involved in the demonstration—making their appearance and activities less suspicious. Of course, the StB's pro-Soviet alignment was also useful as it ensured there would be no compromising intelligence reporting challenging the official accounts, in contrast to the operations placing fabricated arms caches. Second, it could build on a much larger network of subversive agents, enabling the necessary scale of effects. The theory would predict a higher chance of discovery as scale expands, and yet this operation was not discovered. Apart from the greater care the subversive actors could take due to less time pressure, the reliance on local agents who blended in is one likely explanation for this successful maintenance of secrecy.

PROGRESS and a Normalization Incomplete

The final phase of the subversive campaign solidified political control over state security agencies and leveraged this control to intensify persecution of civil society groups. Dubcek's resignation enabled the pro-Soviet leader Gustav Husak to take his position in April 1969, finally concluding the regime change that was the primary objective of subversion. As Husak consolidated his grip on power by purging the Communist Party of "rightists," identified by subversive agents, Husak also prioritized the completion of the takeover of law enforcement and intelligence organizations by pro-Soviet elements.[243] The more time passed, the more the Soviets used these institutions to arrest opposition leaders identified by illegal agents, luring them into carefully laid traps. The extended development time paid off; these operations showed a high success rate and none of the agents were compromised. Slower speed thus ensured control over the targeted institution and successful production of active effects.

One of the earliest victims of arrest was Ludek Pachman. In early 1969, the illegal KRAVCHENKO, under a fake Austrian identity, succeeded in gaining the confidence of Pachman, who had organized illegal Soviet-critical broadcasts after the invasion, leading to Pachman and his friends being arrested and imprisoned in August 1969.[244] Yet despite Soviet control of the state organs following Dubcek's resignation and the continuing subversion of the opposition by illegals, facilitating arrests of its leaders, public resistance remained significant throughout 1969.

The most dramatic display of continued resistance occurred around the one-year anniversary of the invasion, underlining the latter's role as a catalyst of national unity. East German intelligence, in characteristic German pedantry, diligently documented these manifestations of resistance in a report in late 1969:[245]

(1) a coordinated campaign distributing anti-Soviet flyers starting in June 1969, with 880 individual cases;
(2) A widespread "decrease in the political-moral condition of wide swaths of the population" caused by "enemy demagoguery and subversion";
(3) protests involving 160, mostly adolescents, in Prague on August 18;
(4) renewed protests on August 19 in Prague at 1 p.m. involving 150 people, which grew to 2,000 people by 5 p.m., which were "pushed back by security forces using chemical agents," only to reassemble by 7 p.m.;
(5) large-scale protests in Prague on August 20, reaching 5,000 people by 4 p.m., involving some rioting and ultimately an "open attack on the security forces" by 9 p.m., with some protestors firing shots (that curiously lead to the death of two protestors);
(6) the spreading of these protests to multiple cities in Czechoslovakia. While these protests subsided again after the anniversary of the invasion and did not escalate into a wider revolution, they illustrate the remaining degree of public discontent and organizational capacity of opposition forces who coordinated the preceding pamphlet campaigns.

Resistance continued through 1970, as pro-Soviet leaders received anonymous threats, malicious rumors spread, and even some acts of sabotage targeting the railways occurred, which were attributed to opposition groups.[246] However, the efforts to neutralize resistance also had some successes, such as an StB front organization dedicated to "socialism with a human face" that helped identify secret supporters of the Prague Spring.[247] Gradually these efforts bore fruit and resistance weakened sufficiently for Andropov to suggest a withdrawal of operative KGB groups in Czechoslovakia, approved by Brezhnev on March 3, 1970.[248] The official part of the KGB's official role in normalization was thus concluded, marked officially a few months later with medals given to many of the operatives in—for Petrov—the "final act in the Czechoslovakian drama."[249]

Yet illegal operations continued, and in 1972 PROGRESS produced another key success. An illegal succeeded in turning Leo Lappi, founding member of the dissident group K-231, into an unwitting double agent. Since he was first approached by illegals in 1969, Lappi had become a key source of intelligence on the identity of opposition members for their later arrest.[250] Having won his full trust, the illegal FYODOROV convinced Lappi in January 1972 that he was working for the BND to support the opposition and successfully recruited Lappi.[251] Hence, the Soviets now had a leader of the liberal movement working for their own ends, who was unwittingly weakening the very cause he was thought to be fighting for. This case illustrates what the mechanism of exploitation can achieve when sufficient time and skill are available. Note that it took over three years to sufficiently adapt to the target group and gain Lappi's trust in order to produce this outcome.

Despite these high-level successes, public resistance continued. In 1972, Andropov complained to the deputy director of Czechoslovak security that opposition forces "remain too strong," making continued subversion with agents "essential."[252] The effects of this continued subversion are not documented, but Evanson notes that a total of forty-six opposition members were found guilty of subversion and incarcerated in the summer of 1972 alone.[253] It is likely that most of these individuals were identified through illegal agents.

In the short run, PROGRESS operations, now with the backing of Czechoslovak security services, measurably contributed to a weakening of civil society, resulting in a decrease in displays of public resistance. Accordingly, Husak eased repressive laws on the freedom of expression in 1973, marking the end of this normalization period.[254] The Soviets had achieved a key strategic goal. On the surface, it may thus appear as if the subversive campaign was a full success. However, subsequent developments challenge this assessment. Soviet political control remained incomplete and public resistance remained, with civil society reorganizing into a new, coordinated group by 1976. Reflecting this limited control, the Kremlin did not withdraw the occupying troops until the end of the Cold War. The Moscow Protocol had specified withdrawal once normalization was complete. Evidently, this objective was thus never fulfilled.

Moreover, a closer look at the conclusion of the normalization phase shows that the two main causes for the return to stability were external to the subversive campaign. The first cause of greater stability was an economic recovery from 1972 that led to a significant increase in living conditions and facilitated public acceptance of the pro-Soviet regime.[255] Second, Williams suggests normalization was in fact the unintended consequence of a more or less explicit "deal" offered by the Prague Spring leaders, as "reformers signaled very openly that if citizens refrained from exercising their new liberties, rulers in turn would attempt to salvage as much of the reform programme as possible."[256] The failure to deliver on this promise then fostered such pervasive disappointment among the population that it "served unwittingly to demobilize a society that had only just reawakened."[257] Combined, the increase in living conditions and disillusionment with the reformist leaders were a necessary condition for the return to stability. Subversion surely contributed to this outcome, but considering its shortcomings, it is unlikely subversion alone could have produced it in the absence of these external developments.

This conclusion is confirmed by the resurgence and reformation of dissident movements once economic conditions deteriorated in the second half of the 1970s, starting with a severe drought in 1976. In the same year, a new opposition group had formed, called "Charter 77," that rapidly grew in membership and remained active until the collapse of the Soviet Union in 1989, when many of its members formed the leadership of newly independent Czechoslovakia.[258] Significantly, the preceding subversive campaign aiming to weed out reformists from public positions had planted the seed for this regrowth of resistance. As Fawn and Hochman stress, "The expulsion of some leading figures from the party and their marginalization in society inadvertently provided another important dimension to the dissident movement that would coalesce in the 1970s."[259]

Subversion thus did not weaken resistance but rather pushed it back into the underground, where it lingered until the collapse of the Soviet Union. Normalization remained incomplete, and the occupation continued to be perceived as necessary. Despite multiple years of subversive efforts, the campaign was ultimately unable to achieve a lasting change in public support for the Soviets.

Discussion: Subversion and Its Limits

In conclusion, the analysis showed that subversion played a key role in the Soviet campaign to crush the Prague Spring, yet its limitations precluded the attainment of core strategic goals and ultimately contributed to armed escalation. Both the use of subversion and its limitations confirmed key expectations of the theory. First, it documented the reliance on illegal agents who leveraged different means of infiltration and exploitation to produce effects by undermining or manipulating targeted organizations and groups, such as civil society, law enforcement agencies, media, and the Czechoslovakian government itself.

Second, it confirmed the primary use of subversion as an independent instrument but also revealed an instance of subversion complementing and facilitating the use of force—namely the nonresistance order given by the head of Czechoslovakia's armed forces. Evidence from Kremlin decision-making illustrated Soviet leaders perceived its strategic promise as an alternative to war, yet also used force to help subversion succeed in face of its shortcomings.

Meanwhile, and third, findings in the analysis of the individual operations involved produced strong and consistent evidence of the constraints and trade-offs predicted by the trilemma. The daring KHODOKI operations at the outset of the crisis aimed to maximize intensity and speed, at the cost of control—and thus failed to produce intended effects. Conversely, PROGRESS operations maximized speed and control, yet at the cost of intensity. As expected, these shortcomings limited the strategic value of subversion at the campaign level as well, and in this case to such an extent that the combined campaigns failed to achieve the Soviet's key objectives. Ironically, these shortcomings and resulting strategic failure ultimately contributed to the armed escalation that the use of subversion promised to avoid. Paradoxically, the reliance on subversion to avoid escalation may have ultimately increased the latter's likelihood compared to a strategy that relied exclusively on diplomacy. As Dubcek's memoirs reveal, his government never expected invasion—hence, it is worth considering an alternate history where the Kremlin simply posed an ultimatum to stop reforms under the threat of invasion. It is at least possible that Dubcek would have budged, and thus the Soviets could have gotten their way without the costs incurred by implanting the subversive campaigns and invasion. Considering that the subversive campaigns by and large failed to achieve their objectives, even the exclusive reliance on the invasion may have been a less costly and thus more efficient strategic choice.

The mismatch between promise and reality became especially clear in the regime change operation and the overconfidence of the KGB and the Kremlin in the prospect of the regime change operation. Its subsequent failure in turn provided dramatic evidence of the shortcomings and pathologies that prevent fulfillment of this promise. Moreover, it showed that the pathologies of preceding subversive operations shaped the very operational design that, in hindsight, was all but doomed for failure. Finally, the superior value offered by the operations during the final "normalization" phase of the conflict reflects the slower pace made possible by the invasion. As the trilemma predicts, at the cost of speed, these operations improved both intensity and control compared to the preinvasion campaigns. Consequently, they provided more measurable strategic value, contributing to the fulfillment of both of the Soviet's core goals. In lower-urgency situations, subversion thus provided the expected strategic value in attaining high-stakes goals. Nonetheless, the course of the conflict after the regime change had concluded indicated the overall limitations. Control remained incomplete and impermanent, with civil society regrouping shortly after the conclusion of PROGRESS, necessitating a "perennial" occupation of Czechoslovakia.

Overall, the evidence thus confirms key tenets of the theory. However, individual operations also indicated the importance of enabling conditions and external developments that go beyond the theory in explaining key subversive successes in this conflict. The Aeroflot incident was most likely successful because of the availability of local agents who could blend in, ensuring secrecy despite an expansion in the scale of the operation compared to predecessors, while macroeconomic changes and disillusionment with the Prague Spring leadership were key factors in the (temporary) success of "normalization."

These latter points finally lead to the question of cumulative effects of subversion over the long term, gradually weakening Dubcek's regime rather than achieving specific strategic goals. The type of effects the KGB operations discussed pursued could most plausibly have undermined public support for the government—which coincides with the Soviet's second strategic goal—as well as the efficiency of government institutions from within. As already highlighted in the analysis, there is no evidence of any negative trend in public support for Dubcek and his government. On the contrary, public support increased, from 55% at the start of the crisis to 95% at the end of 1968.[260] Similarly, the drop in public support for the Prague Spring leadership throughout the normalization phase in turn reflected their increasing abandonment of liberalizing reforms—which the public evidently still supported. Meanwhile, there are no indications of any friction or dysfunction in Dubcek's government and its institutions that could plausibly be linked to the subversive operations discussed—in contrast to the glaring ineffectiveness and lack of coordination among the "healthy forces" factions that Soviet subversion had fostered. Finally, since there were no attempts at sabotage against the military or critical infrastructure, nor other means of economic warfare, there is no plausible causal impact on military capabilities or economic capacity.

Moving on to the interaction between subversion and military force, this case highlights an additional interesting dimension: the reduction of vulnerabilities subversion can exploit due to the experience of invasion. Subversion depends on vulnerabilities in societies, such as tension, fragmentation, and discontent. The Soviet invasion, however, united the Czechoslovak population against a hostile external force, thus reducing such vulnerabilities. While the Kremlin's assessment ascribed the failure of its disinformation efforts to the initial propaganda vacuum and the effectiveness of the "rightist" goal-oriented activities, Prozumenshchikov highlights a more obvious, and more persuasive, cause for the pervasive rejection of the Soviet invasion and its political measures: the national humiliation the invasion inflicted on the Czechoslovak people.[261] As confirmed by the observations of Warsaw Pact soldiers in their letter discussed above, the use of armed force created the (rather accurate) perception of a hostile force invading the homeland. The unifying effect external aggression has on the victim society, bridging divisions in defense against a common enemy, is a well-established fact.[262] Accordingly, Prozumenshchikov underlines that the "military intervention had a unifying effect on Czechoslovak society, albeit in an antisocialist and anti-Soviet direction."[263] A CIA assessment from November 7, 1968, similarly notes a marked "increase in anti-Soviet nationalism" in Czechoslovakia and Eastern Europe as a whole.[264] Importantly, this unifying effect severely constrained the effectiveness of subversion, possibly explaining the lack of effectiveness despite significant increases in scale.

Ultimately, the Soviet intent to limit reputational costs by opting for subversion to bring Czechoslovakia in line thus resulted in a situation where the Soviets nonetheless suffered the reputational costs without the gain of control over their adversary. As they had refrained from removing Dubcek and neutralized public resistance by force, the military occupation undermined what little public support the Soviets had in Czechoslovakia in the first place, further limiting the effectiveness of subversive operations attempting to shift the balance. This finding indicates that the use of force as a "final blow" to an enemy after using subversion to weaken its capacity to resist in fact risks forfeiting some of the gains made through subversion, while still incurring the costs associated with armed force.

4

Cyber-Enabled Subversion

Russia's "Hybrid War" against Ukraine, 2013–2022

In early 2013, Ukraine set out on a course toward closer alignment with the West, committing to an Association Agreement with the European Union. As in the Czechoslovakian case, Russia feared to "lose" Ukraine from its sphere of influence. To avoid this outcome, Moscow mounted intense efforts in the pursuit of two key goals: first, reversing Ukraine's pro-Western foreign policy, and second, undermining the pro-European and pro-Western movement. To achieve them, it deployed multiple instruments of power: diplomacy, including economic pressure; covert military forces; and subversion—both traditional and cyber enabled. While multiple books and analyses have covered the use of diplomacy and force,[1] the role and impact of subversion remains as murky as the activity itself. This chapter casts light on the latter.

The strategic context and the goals that Moscow strove to achieve through subversion are broadly congruent with the case of Czechoslovakia. Yet Ukraine differs in a crucial aspect: the availability of a new subversive tool, namely cyber operations. If they do indeed enhance the effectiveness of covert operations, as current wisdom has it, this conflict is where we would most expect to see their potential in action—especially considering Russia's being widely held as one of the world's most capable cyber powers.[2] Indeed, news reports have suggested a dire state of affairs with Ukraine being subjected to "massive" and "devastating" cyber-attacks, including the "first major act of cyberwar on a civilian population."[3] Consequently, a 2019 analysis in Politico argued that "there may be no better place to witness cyber conflict in action than Ukraine today."[4] Studying its impact produces surprising findings, however. As the analysis will show, Russian-sponsored subversion produced key strategic gains early in the conflict when it did not rely on cyber operations. In contrast, when Russia later turned to cyber warfare in earnest, tangible gains were far harder to discern.

Initially, Russia focused on diplomatic pressure. It succeeded to get Ukraine's president Viktor Yanukovych to abandon negotiations with the

European Union in November 2013. Ironically, this diplomatic success produced a crisis though. Ukrainians were far less enthusiastic about this change than Moscow expected. Rather, they took to the streets en masse, culminating in the Euromaidan protests in Kyiv that made global headlines and led to Yanukovych's downfall in early 2014. In response, the Kremlin activated a contingency plan: taking Crimea through a subversive overthrow strategy. Local subversive groups, coordinated from Moscow and supported by unmarked Russian forces, took over government buildings under the guise of spontaneous "protests," then organized a supposedly democratic referendum showing majority support for joining Russia. Shortly after, Moscow annexed the territory—producing a significant strategic gain without any major bloodshed. As the analysis shows, extensive preparation time combined with expansive local vulnerabilities enabled this success. Significantly, cyber operations played no role in this gain. Having tasted success, Russia attempted the same playbook in the Donbass region yet failed due to unexpected public resistance that provided Ukraine's armed forces with the opportunity to intervene. This covert military conflict quickly reached a bloody stalemate with mounting losses on both sides yet no significant changes on the frontlines.

Unwilling to bear the costs and risks of escalating its use of force, Russia turned to subversion. In May 2014, it commenced an erosion campaign to weaken Ukraine that bet heavily on cyber operations. Between 2014 and 2017, Russian-sponsored hacking groups mounted seven major cyber operations against Ukraine. These attempted election interference, critical infrastructure sabotage, and economic warfare. Several made global headlines. Yet I show most failed to produce any measurable contribution toward Russia's goals or changes in the balance of power. The analysis shows the constraints and trade-offs of the trilemma running like a golden thread through these operations, explaining their limited strategic value. Indeed, piecing together scattered evidence from forensic reports, field interviews, and local media reporting reveals a string of surprising mistakes and losses of control. In fact, the one operation that forms the exception concerning the significance of its impact, NotPetya, only did so because of a total loss of control over effect. Consequently, it produced collateral damage that hampered its overall strategic value, thus highlighting this risk associated with the scalability of cyber operations. In some cases, pure luck became a crucial variable in enabling hackers to produce effects despite their failures.

Findings underline not only that cyber operations continue to be hampered by the trilemma but also that the comparison with traditional subversion confirms they are even further constrained. Overall, the tangible strategic value cyber operations provided toward the achievement of Moscow's core goals fell far short of traditional subversion—both individually and cumulatively. Specifically, comparing critical infrastructure sabotage through cyber means to traditional means showed the former to be both easier to carry out and yet far more damaging, thus producing superior strategic value. These shortcomings of cyber sabotage likely reduce its effectiveness in broader campaigns, especially when erosion is the aim. Since cyber operations produced less strategic value than traditional subversion individually, unsurprisingly their cumulative effects also paled in comparison to the gains traditional subversion achieved. Their most tangible impact is economic, amounting to a fractional loss of annual gross domestic product (GDP), compared to traditional subversion, achieving both territorial gains and economic losses consuming 75% of annual GDP. Despite the significant gains traditional subversion produced, combined with the marginal economic damage cyber operations contributed, Russia's "hybrid war" strategy overall fell short of achieving its goals, confirming the limitations of subversion. Consequently, as in Czechoslovakia, Russia reverted to the use of force, commencing its full-scale invasion in 2022.

Kremlin Perception and Strategic Goals

Russia's recent aggression against Ukraine is a response to the latter's pro-Western foreign policy shift, triggered by Ukraine's Parliament's vote in favor of starting accession negotiations with the European Union in February 2013. In a close parallel to Czechoslovakia, the Kremlin perceived a risk of "losing" Ukraine from its sphere of influence. Accordingly, its two core strategic goals have been highly similar as well, namely to stop and reverse Ukraine's foreign policy shift and to undermine domestic support for it. Finally, its auxiliary goal has been to weaken Ukraine and erode its capacity to resist further aggression. Ascertaining Russia's strategic goals is a challenge because the Kremlin's strategy involves spreading "rumour, speculation, half-truth, conspiracy, and outright lie, to obscure the realities of Russian activities."[5] Consequently, the drivers of foreign policy continue to be hotly debated, with scholars placing varying emphasis on the role of domestic politics, Putin's personality, or the balance of power.⁶ Yet while Kremlin decision-making remains inaccessible, a leaked document called the "Complex of Measures" lays out two key strategic goals: influence Ukraine's government policy and undermine and discredit pro-European civil society.

The "Complex of Measures" outlines Russia's subversive campaign in remarkable detail. It confirms the goals of influencing Ukrainian foreign policy and neutralizing the Europeanization movement, while also highlighting the prominent role of subversion to attain them. The document lists four main priorities:

1. Prevention of the signing of agreements of Ukraine with the European Union on the Association Agreement
2. Formation of an influential network of pro-Russian social and political forces capable of deterring the Ukrainian authorities from unfavorable actions for Russia, as well as forcing them to enter Ukraine in the Customs Union (CU) and the Common Economic Space (CES)
3. Neutralization and weakening of the political and media influence of European integrators
4. Creating conditions for the accession of Ukraine to the CU and the CES until 2015⁷

Points two and three clearly state the mechanisms and objectives of subversive operations, namely mobilizing political groups to influence the government and weakening anti-Soviet groups and individuals. Accordingly, the document further specifies the objective to create "a concentrated and comprehensive impact on decision centers based on friendly and pragmatic forces in the government, parliament, business circles, the scientific and journalistic community, while activating supporters and neutralizing opponents of Ukraine's participation in the CU and CES."⁸ Furthermore, it also underlines the need to operate secretly: "a program of actions, covering government, business, parliamentary, scientific, cultural, spiritual, regional and shadow channels, should be implemented by the Ukrainian public, not giving reasons to present this activity as the 'hand of Moscow.'"⁹

Russian officials were quick to dispute its authenticity, including pro-Russian politicians in Ukraine such as Oleg Tsarev from the Party of Regions.¹⁰ However, few non-Russian experts doubted its authenticity. Former Ukrainian foreign minister Volodymyr Ohryzko stressed the authenticity of the document, stating that he "had no doubt it reflects

Moscow's intentions."[11] Moscow ultimately confirmed this assessment, as documented in emails by Kirill Frolov, vice director of the Institute for CIS Countries and a key figure of the separatist movement in eastern Ukraine, obtained by the hacktivists around the Ukrainian Cyber Alliance.[12] When Frolov emailed a representative of the Institute for CIS Countries in Moscow, the representative's brief reply was clear: "this is not a leak, this is a real document."[13]

Accordingly, even amid acrimonious academic debates on the specifics of Kremlin decision-making, there is broad consensus around the two core goals identified above. Russian scholarship further supports this assessment. For example, Shtol highlights Moscow's priority to "stop the pro-Western Kiev government,"[14] while Stanislavovich underlines Russia's goal to change Ukraine's foreign policy and prevent its alignment toward the European Union and the North Atlantic Treaty Organization (NATO).[15] Shturba and Makhalkina accordingly explain that "Russia looks at the former USSR states as creating arcs of safety in Eastern Europe."[16] Finally, public statements by Russia's leadership are congruent with both goals as well, warning Ukraine against the "inevitable financial catastrophe"[17] that would result from European Union integration. Russian president Vladimir Putin has repeatedly called the prospect of Ukrainian NATO membership a "direct threat" to Russian national security[18] and has repeatedly emphasized the shared history of Ukraine and Russia and their "sameness"[19] as "one people."[20] The Kremlin also perceived the prospect of Ukrainian European Union membership as a domestic threat, in a second clear parallel to the Czechoslovakian case. A liberal, Western-aligned Ukraine is seen as threatening the Putin regime's stability—the fear being that the revolution is exported to Russia.[21] Moreover, the foreign and domestic policy aims are likely complementary. As Galeotti argues, "As Putin loses his old basis for legitimacy—his capacity to guarantee steadily improving standards of living—he is seeking to shore up his position with a narrative of foreign threats and external triumphs."[22] In short, Russia's goals can be established with reasonable confidence.

To achieve these goals, Russia initially employed a mix of diplomacy and subversion. In response to the Ukrainian parliament's vote in favor of the European Union accession process in February 2013, it commenced a diplomatic charm offensive promising short-term gains from joining Russia's alternative regional framework, the Eurasian Custom Union.[23] However, Ukraine's government maintained course. Hence, Russian foreign policy became increasingly coercive. It imposed an import ban on Ukrainian food products in July 2013, causing an estimated damage of $500 million to $2.5 billion.[24] Finally, on November 9, 2013, President Yanukovych flew to Moscow for a clandestine meeting with Putin.[25] Details are unknown, but Putin evidently made Yanukovych an offer he could not refuse,[26] since two weeks later the latter unexpectedly and unilaterally suspended talks with the European Union.[27] This diplomatic success produced a crisis. The Ukrainian population took to the streets in protest, gathering on Kyiv's Maidan Square in what became known as the Euromaidan movement.[28]

These protests grew, and an increasingly heavy-handed carrot-and-stick tactic by the government over the following months failed to quell them. In December 2013, Yanukovych obtained a generous US$15 billion aid package from Moscow aimed to demonstrate the benefits of integration with Russia.[29] Protests continued. Throughout January and February 2014, police forces used increasing violence against the protestors, producing mounting casualties and culminating in a massacre with thirty-nine protestors killed on February 19.[30] Rather than stopping the protests, this violence further eroded support for Yanukovych.[31] Out of options, Yanukovych fled to Russia on February 22, 2014, leaving the Euromaidan movement in control of the government. In response, the Kremlin fell back to contingency plans and initiated a semicovert invasion of Ukraine's eastern provinces, resulting in a protracted stalemate that lasted until 2022.

This brief summary of diplomatic and coercive instruments, culminating in the use of force, reflects established wisdom on the case. Yet, as the "Complex of Measures" suggests, subversion has been a key instrument in Moscow's efforts to get Ukraine to change course—and below I will start evaluating its strategic value.

"Rock for Russia"—Subversion Falters

To achieve its goals, Russia commenced a two-pronged subversion campaign in 2013 to bolster public support for pro-Russian foreign policy and manipulate Yanukovych's government from within. Both failed because the subversive agents involved had insufficient influence to cause any significant effects.

Over the preceding years, Moscow had nurtured a network of proxy groups in Ukraine—the "friendly network" just discussed. Ukrainians have long suspected Russian meddling in their affairs, and emails by separatist leader Kirill Frolov finally confirmed these suspicions. These emails[32] document a long-running Russian subversion campaign supporting pro-Russian political and religious groups in Ukraine to foster support for Russia as a means of exerting influence over Ukrainian government policy going back to 1997.[33] As the emails show, a key focus of this campaign has been to prevent Ukraine from strategic alignment with the West, through "mass anti-NATO propaganda" and fostering separatist sentiments in Crimea.[34] In 2007, high-ranking Putin advisor Sergey Yuryevich Glazyev started coordinating directly with Frolov,[35] indicating the strategic importance of this campaign.

In 2013, Moscow mobilized this network to run a series of pro-Russian rallies and concerts. The Ukraine Cyber Alliance, a hacktivist collective, obtained firsthand evidence of these efforts by gaining access to the email accounts of Kirill Frolov, vice director of the Institute of the CIS Countries in Moscow. On August 22, 2013, Frolov wrote to Vladimir Granovski, a consultant in the Yanukovych government, proposing that "according to Sergey Yuryevich [referring to Sergey Glazyev, a high-ranking aide of Russian president Vladimir Putin], I coordinate the rally and concert . . . against the Association of Ukraine with the EU. He ordered me to work with you"[36]—confirming that Frolov's orders came directly from Moscow. Frolov continued, "I have now approached all possible Orthodox, pro-Russian groups by regions of Ukraine, which present plans for me by region. I think it is logical to hold the first meeting in Kiev in the second half of October."[37] On September 13, Glazyev asked Frolov to send the invoice for the planned rallies and suggested he work directly under Vladislav Surkov: "send a generalized cost estimate for your participation in the agitation and concert tour across Ukraine. Do you still have a desire to work in the Administration (this time under Surkov alongside my supervision)?"[38] Surkov is another high-ranking Kremlin advisor who had been dismissed earlier in 2013 but was reassigned as a Putin advisor on the Moscow-backed separatist Georgian regions of Abkhazia and South Ossetia.[39] Evidently, his new responsibilities also included covert support of Ukrainian separatists.

These efforts continued throughout 2013 but failed to achieve any measurable effects. Most activity, as evident from Frolov's emails, concentrated on organizing the concert tour. Multiple additional email exchanges discuss funding for events, planning for rallies, and establishment of closer collaboration among the different movements—including financial support by the Russian oligarch Konstantin Malofeev.[40] Yet these proxy groups did not have the necessary influence, nor apparently the skills needed, to cause any shift in public opinion. While the concert tour did happen in October and November, it failed to achieve the unifying effect envisioned by its organizers. On the contrary, media coverage of the tour was largely negative.[41] Accordingly, rather than increasing support for pro-Russian foreign policy, public approval collapsed. In March 2013, 57% of respondents to a survey by the Kyiv International Institute for Sociology stated that joining Russia's customs union is a better choice than joining the European Union.[42] By November 2013, the end of this phase of the conflict, that support had dropped by nearly a third, to 41%.[43]

Efforts at manipulating Yanukovych's government from within fell similarly short. As Sanshiro Hosaka has documented, "A handful of Party of Regions parliamentarians co-opted by the Kremlin began to publicly voice their discontent about the party's line," with Tsarev challenging the constitutionality of the European Union Association Agreement on August 7, and Vadim Kolesnichenko calling on the government to abandon European integration.[44] These efforts failed to shift the Yanukovych government's course, however. Despite increasing diplomatic pressure, Ukraine maintained its pro–European Union foreign policy. Only the secret meeting between Putin and Yanukovych changed this.

Unfortunately, there is insufficient evidence to conclusively evaluate whether constraints posed by the trilemma hampered effectiveness. The preparation time is unknown; however, we do know that in the time available, Moscow's subversive agents did not establish sufficient influence within Ukraine's political system and society to achieve the campaign's goals. The proxy groups run by the Kremlin did not have enough of a public following to measurably shift public opinion—let alone fill concert halls. Similarly, the parliamentarians Russia tried to use to manipulate government policy did not have the necessary clout to effect a policy shift. Moreover, Kremlin co-optation of these parliamentarians was already an open secret, undermining their credibility and ultimately leading to their ousting from the Party of Regions a few months later.[45]

The 'Shadow Forces' Take Crimea

As Yanukovych's position weakened over the Euromaidan protests, the Kremlin shifted its strategy and devised a contingency plan: taking Crimea. Another leaked document called the "Kremlin papers" lays out this shift in remarkable detail. As always, the authenticity of such leaks cannot be confirmed with absolute certainty, yet the content and tone strongly suggest its legitimacy. Moreover, independent experts hired by the publication that first published it, the Ukrainian newspaper *Novaya Gazeta*, confirmed its authenticity.[46] Noting that Yanukovych's power could "end at any moment," the Kremlin papers stressed the need for Russia to intervene and shift strategy as it "should in no way limit its policy toward Ukraine only to attempts to influence the political situation in Kyiv."[47] Instead, it suggested that Russia should focus its efforts on those regions with "positive electoral moods towards Russia" and "initiate the accession of its eastern regions to Russia, in one form or another."[48] It proposed that "to start the process of a 'pro-Russian drift' of Crimea and eastern Ukrainian territories, [certain] events should be created beforehand that can support this process with political legitimacy and moral justification."[49]

The start of the operation involved protests—activating the "shadow forces" the "Complex of Measures" alluded to—where "initially, the protesters should articulate their unwillingness to be 'hostages of the Maidan,' of its attempts to usurp the right of other regions and the majority of the country's population to its own civilizational and political choice."[50] Subsequently, "the political movement for a pro-Russian choice and associative relations between the eastern and southern Ukrainian territories and the Russian Federation needs to be institutionalized and legally registered. To do this, the grounds to hold referendums in Crimea and in the Kharkiv region (and then in other regions) should be created."[51]

Actual events in Crimea closely adhered to this plan, which succeeded despite its improvised and evidently relatively rushed timeframe—posing a potential challenge for the theory of the trilemma.

On February 23 and 24—just hours after Yanukovych's escape—unmarked Russian special forces moved out of their bases in Sevastopol, Crimea, while others were airlifted to the Kerch strait connecting Crimea to Russia.[52] They provided armed support to the subversive takeover of Sevastopol, a major port in Crimea, by a Russian major. Protestors, seemingly from the local population, surrounded its city hall on February 24, chanting, "A Russian mayor for a Russian city."[53] Inside, the city council installed pro-Russian politician Aleksei Chaliy as mayor. The reliance on local protestors exactly adhered to the Kremlin papers. Meanwhile, unmarked Russian naval forces stationed themselves in the town square, providing armed protection.[54] The same pattern of local pro-Russian groups facilitating or enabling the political takeover of key institutions backed by unmarked forces would be repeated multiple times across the region.

Accordingly, on February 27 alleged "pro-Russian demonstrators" seized the Crimean parliament and government buildings.[55] Hours later, the protestor-controlled parliament passed a resolution announcing a referendum on the question of joining Russia for May 25, 2014.[56] Importantly, these "pro-Russian demonstrators" were later identified as fifty members of a Russian special forces unit.[57] Moscow's close coordination of these operations is further corroborated by the fact that Putin advisor Surkov, whose involvement in the takeover attempt of the Donbass is illustrated by another trove of leaked emails,[58] had personally visited Crimea to meet local leaders only days before the start of the operation.[59] Finally, on the same day that "protestors" took over the Crimean parliament, the director of the Institute of CIS Countries, Konstantin Zatulin, discussed the occupation of eastern Ukraine with Putin advisor Glazyev in an intercepted phone call—where Glazyev confirmed he had transferred US$25,000 for "operations" in Kharkiv, Odessa, and Crimea.[60]

Meanwhile, Russian covert forces not only protected the political takeover of key institutions against possible public resistance but also quietly neutralized potential military resistance. The way these operations proceeded, however, shows a primary focus on the avoidance of firefights and bloodshed, further underlining their support role. Accordingly, Kofman et al. document how Russian covert troops "made ad hoc arrangements with trapped Ukrainian troops at bases across the peninsula to maintain the siege without violence."[61] These efforts succeeded; hence, within a few days they had "effectively boxed in Ukraine forces,"[62] ensuring the political takeover could proceed without bloodshed, which would have undermined its legitimacy. On March 1, the Russian parliament authorized the use of force in Ukraine,[63] and on the same day Russia started bringing in reinforcement troops via landing ships.[64]

A leaked email from separatist leader Andrey Novikov to Frolov from March 4, requesting armed assistance for the takeover of the Regional Council of Crimea planned for March 6, explicitly specifies the support role of military force. In the email, Novikov stresses, "activation is possible only with concrete help of the units of the 'Crimean self-defense,' the protection of meetings by it. It is necessary to occupy the regional council on March 6 on the day of the extraordinary session."[65] The reference to "self-defense" units is congruent with Kremlin messaging at the time, with Putin stating on the same day that widely shared images and videos of troops in Crimea were in fact showing "volunteer self-defense" groups—leading to the rise of the infamous term "little green men" for the invading force.[66]

The occupation Novikov proposed worked out as planned, and accordingly on March 6 the now pro-Russian parliament of Crimea voted to secede, requesting Moscow's support for a referendum set for March 16.[67] Significantly, phone intercepts revealed Moscow's direct involvement in this supposed act of self-defense. On the same day, Glazyev told the new self-proclaimed "prime minister" of Crimea, Sergey Aksyonov, "that the wording of the questions of the so-called 'referendum' on seceding from Ukraine to be held ten days later 'were problematic,' and that 'we here are thinking how to formulate them.'"[68] This referendum proceeded as planned, and official results reported 95.7% votes in favor.[69] The Kremlin officially annexed Crimea on March 17.[70] Over the next forty-eight hours, Russian forces claiming to be "local militias" completed the military takeover, occupying Ukrainian military bases and its navy headquarters in Sevastopol.[71] The Ukrainian military was forced to admit defeat, officially withdrawing from Crimea on March 19.[72] This takeover was a resounding success, producing a fait accompli with minimal losses.

And it did so despite being apparently implemented on short notice, as a contingency plan in response to the unexpected Euromaidan crisis. At face value, this success challenges the theory. High operational speed in pursuit of an intense effect—Johson lists a "small-scale coup d'etat" of the kind Russia orchestrated here near the top of the escalation ladder, on rung thirty-five of thirty-eight[73]—did not result in a loss of control. However, looking deeper into the conditions on the ground provides a potential explanation in line with the theory. While the operation itself proceeded swiftly, it built upon years of preceding efforts to cultivate the network of shadow forces that helped the takeover succeed. Leaked emails obtained by Ukrainian hacktivists provide primary evidence of these efforts going back to at least 1997.[74] These seventeen years of cultivating proxy actors ensured that a network of sufficient scale was in place and leaders aligned with Russian interests and loyal to their handlers from Moscow headed this network. Without such a network in place, this operation could not have proceeded the way it did. Consequently, even though they were not part of the operation itself, these preparations were integral to its success.

The apparent lack of resistance to the takeover of government building and military installations in turn likely reflects another outcome of preceding subversive campaigns: the penetration of security services with Russian agents. There is a long history of collaboration between Russian and Ukrainian intelligence services, which survived the collapse of the Soviet regime and provided the Federal Security Service of the Russian Federation (known in Russian as "Federal'naya sluzhba bezopasnosti Rossiyskoy Federatsii", abbreviated as "FSB") with extensive opportunities for infiltration.[75] Accordingly, at the start of the crisis, Russian agents had infiltrated the Ukrainian Security Service (known in Ukrainian as "Sluzhba bezpeky Ukrainy", abbreviated as "SBU") to such an extent that its former director Valentin Nalivaychenko stated that "in the SBU in 2012–2014, and I think in most other law enforcement agencies . . . the leadership in these institutions consisted to 100% of people who now are now being persecuted for 'state treason.'"[76] Similarly, an analyst at the Ukrainian Centre for Economic and Political Studies, a think tank, estimated that nearly a third of SBU agents worked either for the FSB or the Russian military intelligence service (known in Russian as "Glavnoje upravlenije General'nogo shtaba Vooruzhonnykh sil Rossiyskoy Federatsii", abbreviated as "GRU").[77] There are no specific estimates for penetration rates in Ukraine's eastern regions, but it is reasonable to expect at least the same situation, and probable that penetration rates are even higher considering the apparent success of pro-Russian propaganda discussed below.

While the preceding subversive campaign thus helps explain the success of the operation, this situation indicates a potential limitation of the theory's focus on the operational level. The operation itself was fast, but the subversive campaign that made it possible in the first place proceeded very slowly. Accordingly, it makes sense to expand focus beyond the operational to the campaign level to fully assess speed.

Furthermore, available evidence suggests an additional explanation for this operation's success beyond the scope of the theory: public support for closer relations with Russia and the role of propaganda in fomenting the former. According to Dmitry Dubov from the National Institute of Strategic Studies, a long-running propaganda campaign to foster pro-Russian sentiment in Crimea was a key variable explaining success.[78] This assessment is in line with findings of an independent representative survey carried out by market research institute GfK in March 2014, showing majority support among Crimeans for joining Russia over remaining part of Ukraine (71% versus 11%).[79] This propaganda campaign, Dubov speculates, fostered acceptance of the invasion; "because of propaganda people expected that the invasion would happen sooner or later, so when it happened everyone took it as normal."[80] This causal influence cannot be conclusively established without further evidence. However, the observed lack of public resistance is exactly congruent with what one would expect if propaganda was successful. Accordingly, the people behind the propaganda campaign shared this assessment as well. For example, Georgiy Brusov wrote in an email to Surkov on July 16, 2014: "the experience of Crimea clearly demonstrated how greatly influenced by the mood of the population is the factor of the presence of Russian TV channels and the local media sympathies with Russia, converting their influence into political positions, it is possible to achieve mass support."[81]

Independent research showing a clear positive correlation in Ukraine between consuming Russian television—highly popular in Crimea—and electoral support for pro-Russian politicians further supports this conclusion.[82] The high proportion of Russian speakers and people who identify as Russian in Crimea may further explain the success of these propaganda efforts and the subversive takeover that followed in their wake.[83] In short, building on existing, long-term subversive campaigns, combined with the favorable extent of available vulnerabilities as a key enabling condition, best explains the success in Crimea.[84] Finally, cyber operations played no role in this operation—it relied exclusively on traditional means of subversion, whose effectiveness underlines its continued relevance even in the face of technical innovation. On the contrary, the irrelevance of cyber operations is in line with their expected limitations as means of regime change.

Failure in the Donbass and Escalation

Since the Crimean takeover was such a resounding success, it is unsurprising that Russia attempted to repeat this feat in the Donbass region (composed of the Donetsk and Luhansk oblasts, or administrative regions) in eastern Ukraine following the same playbook. Yet this failed, leading to escalation. As in Crimea, the operation commenced with the occupation of key institutions in the region by "protestors" supported by covert military forces. Again, Ukraine's armed forces were (initially) outflanked. In contrast to Crimea, however, the public offered unexpected resistance—providing Ukraine's military the opportunity to intervene. This outcome confounds the theory since the operation could build on similar pre-existing subversive efforts, instead underlining that the extent of available vulnerabilities is a crucial condition for subversive success.

Tensions commenced with protestors occupying government buildings in Luhansk, capital of the synonymous oblast, on March 9.[85] Security forces managed to clear the building the following day. Yet on March 22, protests broke out in the city of Donetsk (capital of Donetsk oblast), with crowds calling for the return of ousted president Yanukovych.[86] These protests intensified and on April 6, protestors occupied government buildings in seven cities across the Donbass, while the city of Donetsk declared itself independent.[87] As in Crimea, the partisan-controlled government set a referendum date to join Russia. "Protestors" also succeeded in occupying the buildings of the security service SBU in Donetsk and Luhansk.[88] Many suspected Russian intelligence services coordinated the takeovers of key administrative buildings,[89] but no hard evidence confirms this.[90,91] However, there is evidence that widespread neglect of duty and defection among security services facilitated this takeover—reflecting the former's permeation with Russian agents.[92]

Until then, the operation had proceeded smoothly. Accordingly, on April 9, Novikov emailed Frolov with the following assessment: "Donetsk and Luhansk: Everything is clear here—by armed means, directly or through disguised special forces, to repel the punitive detachments of the Kiev junta, to support the new proclaimed state in Donetsk."[93] The explicit mention of "disguised special forces" finally confirmed the presence of Russian operatives among "protestors."[94]

However, this takeover lacked public support. Separatists were isolated from the local population[95] and faced continuing resistance by remaining Ukrainian security forces, leading to deadly clashes.[96] This situation provided Kyiv with the opportunity for military intervention, which launched an "anti-terrorism operation" on April 15.[97] Clashes continued, but Russian/Russian-backed forces initially succeeded in pushing back. Hence, two weeks later, Ukrainian interim president Turchynov conceded the loss of control over the Donbass.[98] Finally, on May 11, the separatist administrations in the Donbass carried out the announced referenda, declaring victory after claiming 89% of voters favored joining Russia.[99] At this stage, Russia held factual control over most of the Donbass. Yet in contrast to Crimea, this control remained contested—military clashes continued for years after.

The divergent outcomes of the Crimea and Donbass operations pose a puzzle. Both were relatively fast, both pursued highly intense effects, and yet only one succeeded to establish full control over the target region while the other faltered halfway. What explains this difference? There are several plausible explanations. First, the evidence suggests that the Crimea operation involved several months of preparation, whereas the Donbass operation was more spontaneous—possibly in reaction to the unexpected success in Crimea. The Kremlin papers only mention Crimea and Kharkiv by name, and similarly the leaked emails by Frolov contain multiple references to plans for the takeover of Crimea—but no specific mentions of the Donbass. Plausibly, lack of planning and preparation in the Donbass explains the failure. However, the evidence is thin and far from conclusive.

Moreover, both operations built on long-term subversive efforts spanning years. And yet despite this shared characteristic, both differed in outcome. Preparation time is thus at best an incomplete explanation, especially considering the actual takeover of government buildings seems to have proceeded smoothly in the Donbass. Rather, unexpected public resistance hampered progress and led to escalation, leading to the second explanation: the extent of available vulnerabilities. Whereas in Crimea even independent polling indicated majority support for joining Russia prior to the operation, the opposite was the case in the Donbass region. A survey of Donetsk residents by the Institute of Social Research and Political Analysis in April 2014 showed only 18% support for joining Russia, versus 50% in favor of remaining part of Ukraine.[100] This is the key difference between both operations, supported by tangible evidence, thus providing the strongest explanation for their diverging outcomes—underlining the need for further theorizing on the conditions for subversive success and failure.

Swaying the Vote? Subversive Election Interference, 2014–2015

The military conflict between pro-Russian separatists supported by covert (increasingly less so) Russian forces and Ukraine's armed forces that commenced in April 2014 continued to swelter throughout the following years. Frontlines moved, casualties mounted, ceasefires came and went—yet until 2022 neither side managed to make decisive enough gains to claim victory.[101] Contrary to expectations about a revolution in warfare, cyber operations remained irrelevant to the conflict's military dimension.[102] Russian hackers attempted to use cyber operations to facilitate artillery targeting, yet as discussed further below, its impact likely fell far behind sensationalist reporting. Overall, Russian hacking groups primarily deployed cyber operations as independent instruments. First, they tried to interfere in Ukraine's elections in 2014 and 2015. Yet both operations failed.

Shortly after Euromaidan leaders took over Ukraine's government, they announced presidential elections for May 2014. Russian-sponsored hackers tried to disrupt them by disabling the computers of Ukraine's Central Elections Committee (CEC). Their apparent aim was to undermine public trust in the election and paint the Kyiv government as a fascist regime by publishing false election results showing a Far Right candidate winning. This operation pursued very high-speed and medium-intensity effects: on Johnson's escalation ladder, election interference is on rung eighteen of thirty-eight.[103] Yet it failed to cause any impact. Moving fast, the hackers missed a key characteristic of the target system and lost control before the elections happened.

Rather than supporting military efforts, the operation pursued an independent effect against Ukraine's democracy. On May 21, a hitherto unknown malware started disrupting the CEC's computer systems dedicated to electronic vote counting.[104] Neither the attack vector nor details about the malware used are known. The precise duration of the disruption is also unclear. While Nikolay Koval, former head of Ukraine's Computer Emergency Response Team, indicates it lasted for twenty hours,[105] Victor Zhora, then director of the cybersecurity firm Infosafe IT who was personally involved in the mitigation of the compromise, suggests only "a few hours" of disruption.[106]

On May 23, the hacker group CyberBerkut[107] claimed responsibility, proclaiming on its website that "We, CyberBerkut, have totally destroyed the network and electronic infrastructure of the Ukrainian Central Election Commission as a sign of protest against legitimation of the Kiev junta crimes."[108] CyberBerkut have since been linked to the Russian intelligence service GRU.[109] Furthermore, according to Koval, malware found on CEC servers was attributed to the infamous GRU hacking group APT28.[110] CyberBerkut's stated aims are congruent with Victor Zhora's assessment, who was involved in the mitigation efforts and saw the hackers trying to "make functionality during the elections impossible, expecting that CEC would be unable to recover."[111] Meanwhile, their reference to the "Kiev junta" is congruent with the Russian goal to delegitimize the Ukrainian government laid out in the Kremlin papers.

Yet the operation failed because the CEC had backups, allowing them to fully mitigate the disruption before election day.[112] In an apparent attempt at damage control, Nikolay Koval describes how CyberBerkut instead compromised the CEC website and posted an announcement that right-wing leader Yarosh had won the elections, twelve minutes before polls closed.[113] Zhora specified, however, that the photo was merely uploaded to the server, not posted on the CEC website[114]—thus remaining invisible to any visitors. The hackers concluded the operation with a DDoS attack disrupting access to the CEC website on the morning of May 26, which, however, remained inconsequential.[115] The hackers failed to disrupt the CEC sufficiently long enough to affect vote counting and reporting. Accordingly, the official report by the Organization for Security and Co-Operation in Europe (OSCE) on the elections concluded that "voting and counting process were transparent and largely in line with procedures,"[116] as the cyberattack only "delayed the CEC's announcement of preliminary results."[117] Consequently, Petro Poroshenko's election victory remained unchallenged. The operation provided no measurable strategic value.

The most likely reason for this failure is insufficient reconnaissance. The hackers had to move fast since, as Zhora highlights, the elections were only announced two months in advance.[118] Forensic evidence accordingly showed that CyberBerkut/APT28 had compromised the CEC system shortly after the announcement in March 2014.[119] In this short reconnaissance time, the hackers evidently missed the existence of backups. As predicted by the trilemma, high speed and intensity constrained the degree of control the hackers had over the target—ultimately leading to a failure to produce strategic value.

In October 2015, a second attempt at cyber-enabled election interference followed. This time, the infamous Sandworm group orchestrated it. Rather than the election itself, it aimed to interfere in media reporting, disrupting computer systems at leading media organizations. However, it failed to impact broadcasting and thus had no effect on audiences. This operation moved slower than its predecessor, with five months' development time, and as expected the hackers were able to produce more intense effects: lasting destruction of data. And yet, they did not achieve sufficient control to affect broadcasting. Moreover, in the pursuit of maximum intensity, Sandworm made a crucial mistake that not only led to control loss but also unintentionally left behind all of their toolkit for forensic analysis, hampering future operations. In short, as predicted, maximizing intensity came at the cost of speed as well as a heightened risk of control loss.

Like its predecessor, this operation fulfilled an independent strategic role, aiming to undermine public trust in Ukraine's democratic system. There is no evident correlation with military or diplomatic events. On the diplomatic front, both sides agreed on a ceasefire in August 2015, which held throughout the following months.[120] Accordingly, the military conflict was de-escalating, with significant withdrawals and relative calm persisting throughout October 2015.[121]

Sandworm pursued maximum disruption. Yet, contrary to their reputation as one of the world's most advanced and dangerous hacking groups,[122] they made a relatively basic error that prevented further damage. The operation proceeded as follows. In the runup to the 2015 local elections, Sandworm disrupted the computer systems of several leading TV stations by wiping data, including video materials.[123] While some media reports have suggested that the CEC website was "again taken down,"[124] these claims are not supported by any evidence—and Zhora emphatically rejected them.[125] To get into the computer systems of these TV stations, circumstantial evidence suggests Sandworm used spear phishing in March 2015, thus exploiting a social vulnerability to deliver the malware BlackEnergy (specifically, BlackEnergy 3, an updated modular malware based on a popular malware suite developed mainly for cybercrime).[126,127] They installed it on target systems two months later in May 2015,[128] giving Sandworm five months for reconnaissance and adaptation.

As Aleksey Yasinskiy, former chief strategy officer of Starlight media (one of the affected media firms), describes, in this time Sandworm steadily expanded their reach and by October had established deep reach into Starlight Entertainment's networks via its domain controller servers.[129] Such servers form the link between corporate networks and the wider Internet, thus constituting crucial "choke points." On October 25, 2015, Sandworm wiped the data on these servers, rendering them inoperable. Specifically, the KillDisk module the hackers installed overwrote all data with random data and corrupted the Master Boot Records of hard drives, meaning servers would not start up again after being shut down.[130] Evidently, by focusing on these servers, Sandworm's objective was to achieve maximum disruption as fast as possible—as Yasinskiy put it, "The goal is to destroy the data on the maximum possible amount of PCs."[131] However, by starting with the servers—the "core" of the network—the intruders lost access to the entire network, and all computers within it they had previously infected with malware. As Volodymyr Styran, cofounder of the cybersecurity firm Berezha Security, explained: "The thing is, Domain Controllers serve as DNS servers in Windows networks, and when DNS goes down, everything goes down. Including the malware—so they lost access to their malware, leaving it dead in the water. This is just bad, bad planning."[132]

Consequently, these trails of data left behind allowed Yasinskiy to pick apart the malware used and reverse-engineer the entire KillDisk module.[133] While the operation succeeded in destroying data and disrupting some computer systems, the hackers had not achieved control over broadcasting systems, which remained unaffected.[134] Consequently, there was no effect on media coverage.

Yasinskiy published his findings in February 2016, which allowed other potential victims to take countermeasures against future intrusions using the same techniques and tools. As he highlights, "We got a free penetration test, the invaluable experience of a real APT investigation."[135] Through its mistake, Sandworm had blown its cover and risked neutering its time-triggered protocol (TTP). Accordingly, the group soon abandoned the BlackEnergy malware it had used here. Its last known use was a daring sabotage operation, as the next section will show.

Sabotage: Cyber versus Traditional Subversion

Having failed to sway election results, Sandworm transitioned to critical infrastructure sabotage. In 2015 and 2016, it disrupted Ukraine's power grid, triggering dramatic headlines across the West. By pursuing physical effects, these operations maximized effect intensity. As expected, this came at the cost of speed and control. They required exceptionally long preparation time and yet lost control over target systems quickly as victims simply switched to manual control. Consequently, their strategic impact remained negligible—especially in contrast to two highly destructive traditional sabotage operations carried out at the same time, which I examine in comparison. This comparison indicates that when intense, physical effects are the aim, cyber operations are slower, more challenging, and yet relatively less effective than traditional means. Table 4.1 summarizes key findings.

Table 4.1 Traditional versus Cyber Sabotage

	Traditional		Cyber	
Case Name	Crimea Power Lines	Kalynivka Arms Depot	Sandworm I	Sandworm II
Type of effect	Power outage	Explosion	Power outage	Power outage
Strategic value	Major disruption of public life, significant economic damage	Major degradation of military capabilities, significant disruption of public life, damage to infrastructure	Minor nuisance, negligible economic damage	Minor nuisance
Speed	Several days	Days to weeks	19 months	31 months
Complexity	Very low (attaching a mine to a post)	Low (bribing, lighting a match)	High (mastering power substation operation)	Very high (mastering power substation operation and compromising industrial control system)

Sandworm I: The 2015 Blackout

On December 23, 2015, the lights went out for 230,000 people living in the rural province of Ivano-Frankivsk in western Ukraine. Soon after it became clear this had been a cyber attack, reflecting a long-held threat scenario among Western analysts. Sensationalist reporting about the growing threat of cyberwar followed.[136] In contrast to this hype, however, a closer look reveals the shortcomings of this operation and its resulting lack of strategic value. This operation pursued highly intense effects, namely disrupting physical processes with the potential for causing considerable harm to people affected: a lasting power outage in Ukraine's frigid winter could conceivably result in casualties. As such, this operation would fall squarely within the "extreme options" at the top of Johnson's escalation latter.[137] Since it is impossible to establish whether loss of life was intended, however, actual effect intensity is best captured by the category of "economic disruption without loss of life" on rung nineteen of thirty-eight.[138] Even with this conservative interpretation of intent, effect intensity is greater than the two preceding cyber operations. As expected, very high effect intensity required a very long development time, nineteen months in total. Moreover, as the analysis will show, the targets provided near-ideal conditions for cyber sabotage to succeed. Nonetheless, and despite the extensive time the hackers spent, this operation achieved little measurable strategic value—underlining the limitations of cyber operations due to the constraints of the trilemma.

Strategically, this operation proceeded independently of diplomatic and military efforts. There were no significant diplomatic developments at the time,[139] nor apparent linkages to military action. Pro-Russian and Ukrainian forces had agreed to a truce over the holidays, but clashes continued.[140] The most plausible linkage to other Russian-sponsored efforts is to another potential intelligence operation: sabotage to Crimea's power supply in November 2015.[141] Some have thus interpreted Sandworm's cyber sabotage as retaliation.[142] Whether or not that is the case cannot be conclusively established. In either case, however, it proceeded independently from military and diplomatic efforts, as expected.

The timeline is as follows: at 3.30 p.m. on December 23, 2015, Sandworm remotely triggered the disconnection of around thirty power substations of the utility providers Prykarpattyaoblenergo, Chernovtsoblenergo, and Kievoblenergors, cutting power to 230,000 customers.[143] Meanwhile, they flooded the firms' service centers with calls, overwhelming operators and rendering them unresponsive for customers.[144] Ninety minutes later, the hackers activated a KillDisk module that wiped all data on affected computers, hampering restoration efforts.[145] However, victims had a way out: switching to manual control. Within six hours, power was back.[146]

Yet achieving these six hours of outage took nineteen months of preparation—in other words, over three months of development time spent for each hour of outage. Forensic evidence indicates that Sandworm started development on May 12, 2014—the day after the Donbass referendum. Again, the operation initially exploited a social vulnerability, sending phishing emails with file attachments to employees of targeted firms.[147] Curiously, these "bait documents" involved information related to the Ukrainian railway system—thus not relevant to the work of recipients at the energy firms targeted.[148] Successful exploitation thus required the presence of a careless employee who was either very bored or very excited about trains. Luckily for Sandworm, someone fitting that profile worked at at least one of the targeted utility providers, clicking on the attachment and unwittingly installing malware on their system.[149]

138   SUBVERSION

The hackers had now compromised corporate networks, and hence they needed to expand to systems controlling physical machinery.[150] This took at least five months. In October 2014, security vendor iSight discovered a new zero-day vulnerability[151] in Microsoft Windows being exploited by Sandworm in a campaign targeting unnamed energy firms that had started in September 2014.[152] Such zero-day vulnerabilities in popular software are neither easy nor cheap to come by and require either significant time to discover or significant investments to acquire on the black market.[153] Looking deeper into iSight's findings, TrendMicro detected evidence that Sandworm was targeting SCADA systems (Supervisory Control and Data Acquisition, a type of industrial control systems), and a specific type of SCADA system: GE CIMPLICITY HMI (Human Machine Interface) systems.[154] Human Machine Interface systems, as their name suggests, allow human operators to interact with complex machinery. Sandworm had now identified the specific systems operating physical equipment at power substations. It was still far from the ability to control these systems though.

Getting there required an additional fourteen months. As Dragos's report highlights, compromising HMI systems alone does not enable physical effects.[155] However, it is ideal for reconnaissance to "learn the industrial process and gain the graphical representation of that ICS [industrial control system] through the HMI."[156] In short, the hackers had become familiar with the target system. It took fourteen months for them to be confident enough in their abilities to try and manipulate these systems.

As with the initial compromise, sheer luck again was a key factor enabling Sandworm to proceed further. The longer hackers stay in a target system, the likelier the victim becomes to notice them. As expected, all affected Ukrainian energy firms discovered the compromises months before the actual outage, but—lucky for the hackers—none of them disclosed the breaches nor attempted to mitigate them.[157] Sandworm thus benefited from both luck and its victims' complacency, allowing the operation to succeed despite discovery. In fact, unusually lax security measures were a crucial enabling condition. Sensitive industrial control systems are typically "airgapped" (physically separated from the Internet), but this does not seem to be the case here. Volodymyr Styran recalls a question posed to a representative of Ukrenergo (the national Ukrainian energy provider) at a security conference[158] in February 2016: "We tried to get a direct answer from this Ukrenergo guy, the regulator of the energy sector in Ukraine, on the question: 'do you have a requirement for air-gapping industrial network from general purpose network?' After the third or fourth attempt, we got an answer: 'No'. Energy security is suboptimal. . . . [I]t [the network] should be physically segregated, and I thought it was, until that panel."[159]

Hence, this cyber sabotage attempt faced ideal conditions: "soft" targets lacking security measures and ample time for reconnaissance and development. And yet, even under these ideal conditions, cyber sabotage achieved rather underwhelming effects.

Finally, after nineteen months, Sandworm switched off the power—manually. While reporting suggested that a virus caused the outage,[160] the hackers actually had to manually enter a carefully rehearsed set of commands that triggered an outage by leveraging a safety mechanism of the industrial control system. As SANS highlights, "Neither BlackEnergy 3 nor KillDisk contained the required components to cause the outage. The outages were caused by the use of the control systems and their software through direct interaction by the adversary."[161] Accordingly, operators at the affected substations reported seeing "the cursors on their screens move as if controlled by ghosts," activating circuit breakers one by one that shut down the power supply.[162] Hence, the system operated as designed but with its functionality subverted. As in traditional sabotage, human agents manipulated machinery to produce unintended consequences for the victim. The only difference was that commands were entered remotely.

Developing this capacity for exploitation, meanwhile, required extensive learning. Basically, the hackers had to do a crash course as power substation operators, learn how its systems work, and identify weaknesses to leverage the system against itself. As Dragos puts it, "They learned the operations and used the legitimate functionality of distribution management systems to disconnect substations from the grid."[163] Despite extensive preparations, Sandworm missed a key property of the target system: the capacity to switch to manual control. Hence, even though its KillDisk malware disabled industrial control systems, victims were able to restore power within a few hours by simply flicking a switch. As Sych puts it, technicians "promptly figured out the situation, turning off the compromised and disabled systems, transferred the control of the switches in the power distribution systems to manual mode and restored the power supply."[164] The hackers lost control. As a result, they only achieved a few hours of power disruption.

In short, as expected, the pursuit of very high-intensity effects came at the cost of very long preparation time and increased risks of control loss, illustrated by the premature discovery of the operation and the short duration of the outage due to the switch to manual control. These shortcomings limited strategic value. Both the psychological and economic impact were minimal. Cyberattacks on critical infrastructure, and especially power grids, have long been central to "cyber doom" scenarios and corresponding threat perceptions.[165] Accordingly, this operation received significant attention in Western media, whose coverage reflected fear and foreboding.[166] However, despite the heightened threat perception in the West, with media reports speculating this was "perhaps the first major act of cyberwar on a civilian population,"[167] the event barely made headlines in Ukraine. Only a handful of media reports covered the issue, and they mostly relied on secondary Western sources.[168] Moreover, these reports did not receive front-page coverage and lack any of the heightened threat perception and outright panic evident in Western coverage.[169] Meanwhile, there are no official statements by the Ukrainian government on the case, only a short press release by the intelligence service SBU stating, "Employees of the Security Service of Ukraine found malicious software in the networks of individual regional energy companies. The viral attack was accompanied by continuous calls (telephone 'flood') to the numbers of technical support of oblenergos [energy providers]."[170] Consequently, only a small proportion of the population was aware of the operation, limiting its psychological impact. The lack of media attention reflects its relative strategic insignificance in the wider context of the conflict. It is unsurprising that a temporary power cut captured little attention while military conflict continued in the Donbass where, despite a ceasefire, two people were killed on the day prior to the SBU press release alone.[171] This evidence underlines that it is important to consider cyber operations within the wider context of a conflict to assess their strategic value.

Its economic impact was also barely measurable. A government advisor I interviewed in Kyiv in 2018 underlined that "economic damage was minimal."[172] As Oleg Sych at Zillya calculated, the outage affected only roughly 1% of Ukraine's population, and the power lost over the roughly one to three hours of outage made up only about 0.015% of Ukraine's daily consumption.[173] In short, this was a minor nuisance—yet producing this nuisance required disproportionate efforts.

Since effects on Ukraine itself were negligible, some analysts have suggested that the operation was instead intended to signal capabilities. While possible, however, this alternate explanation does not alter the conclusions above. Moreover, even if it was a signal, it was likely a bad one. Joseph Nye argues that "if the Russian state was connected to the 2015 attack on the Ukrainian power grid, was it reminding Ukraine of its vulnerability in a hybrid war with a different level of plausible deniability . . . ?"[174]

If threatening Ukraine was indeed the aim, however, the operation had little measurable success considering Ukrainian media barely noticed it. Accordingly, others have suggested the intended audience was not Ukraine, but the West, and in particular the United States.[175] That is also possible. Importantly, however, the very existence of multiple plausible interpretations of what the signal was undermines the signaling interpretation. For a signal to be effective, both its content and its recipient must be clear.[176] Neither is the case here. Moreover, the "signaling the West" interpretation neglects an important consequence of this operation. The publicly available detailed forensic evidence presented above has also helped improve resilience of critical infrastructure in the West. As Marcus Sachs, chief security officer of the North American Electric Reliability Corporation, highlighted following the 2015 outage, "American power companies have already learned from Ukraine's victimization."[177]

Sandworm's subsequent activity suggests a possible recognition of these limitations. ESET discovered evidence that shortly afterward, Sandworm split into "at least two" different groups, which they labeled GreyEnergy and TeleBots.[178] The TeleBots have exclusively focused on Ukraine, while GreyEnergy campaigns were observed in other jurisdictions.[179] Since TeleBots have filled the same strategic niche of large-scale espionage and disruptive active measures within Ukraine as Sandworm, I will continue to use the latter name for clarity and continuity. The motivation behind its split is currently unknowable. However, its timing is congruent with the conclusion that the group reoriented its efforts in response to the limited strategic success of the power sabotage operation.

Traditional Sabotage I: The 2015 Crimea Blackout

A month before the operation just discussed, sabotage knocked out power in Crimea by traditional means: explosives. The act itself was carried out by a ragtag group of Tartar "activists."[180] However, it is plausible that Ukrainian intelligence services coordinated their actions. As mentioned, some have speculated that the cyber sabotage operation was retaliation for Ukraine's actions. That is possible, although preparations for the cyber sabotage had started long before. Ultimately, the hackers' intentions remain inaccessible, preventing any final conclusions. However, it is possible to compare the relative effectiveness of these operations, the constraints involved, and strategic value. Doing so reveals decisive relative advantages of traditional subversion in producing intense physical effects. The Crimean power grid sabotage caused significant and lasting disruption to over two million people, producing considerable economic damage. Meanwhile, because it leveraged the ability of human operatives to exert physical force, it required minimal development time or effort. In short, it achieved far more strategic value with far less effort and time.

There is no discernible coordination with diplomatic or military actions. In early November 2015, a ceasefire agreed to in August 2015 started to break down with increasing clashes in the Donbass—but no activity in or near Crimea.[181] Meanwhile, Russia imposed an embargo on Ukrainian food exports, crippling a core part of Ukraine's economy.[182] Ukraine did not take any diplomatic action in response, however. If Ukrainian intelligence services did indeed coordinate this operation, a plausible motivation would be retaliation for this instrument of economic warfare—further underlining the independent strategic role of subversion.

In any case, publicly available evidence on the operation is scarce. What is known is that on November 22, 2015, unknown perpetrators attached explosives to the power pylons connecting Crimea to Ukraine, destroying them.[183] The president of Russia at the time, Dmitry Medvedev, accused Ukraine of being behind the operation, yet no tangible evidence of intelligence involvement has appeared.[184] While attribution remains unclear, the mechanism through which these activists caused the power cut is very clear and helps highlight the differences to the cyber sabotage operation.

There are two key differences to the cyber sabotage operation. First, it required physical access. For well-protected facilities, gaining such access is a challenge. In this case, however, the individuals involved could simply approach the evidently unguarded pylons. Accordingly, they did not need to exploit and manipulate machinery but could instead simply use force to cause damage—making this a borderline case of subversion (the reliance on "Tartar activists" as a group infiltrated and manipulated by Ukrainian intelligence agents would maintain the subversive element). Consequently, reflecting the ease of access, this operation was decidedly low-tech. Investigators suspect anti-tank mines were used to destroy the pylons,[185] and these are readily available in the region. For example, in 2017 the Ukrainian SBU caught military officers roaming the same region attempting to sell "multiple bags full of stolen anti-tank mines."[186] Meanwhile, executing the sabotage would have required no more than a few people and no specialized skill. Accordingly, a *New York Times* reporter who traveled to the scene the day after the explosion encountered "about half a dozen fighters, their boots sinking into a sodden field, [who] were guarding the downed electricity pylons."[187]

Yet despite its simplicity, this operation caused a massive and lasting power outage: power to Crimea was only partially restored after two weeks of repairs.[188] Consequently, it caused significant economic disruption: estimates in January 2016 placed the costs of the outages at US$12 million.[189] By causing a lasting outage in the dead of winter, this operation was much likelier to harm the well-being of people depending on power for heat, risking loss of life and thus placing it among the extreme options of Johnson's escalation ladder where "lives of innocent people may be placed in extreme jeopardy."[190] Moreover, it affected two million people. Hence, both the scope and scale of effects were much higher than in any cyber operations discussed thus far.

To be clear, there is a marked difference between this operation and cyber sabotage that precludes a full comparison of their relative strategic impact, as Ukraine continued to control the energy supply. However, these differences do not preclude the comparison of the mechanism of action or of the immediate effects of the sabotage, which lasted around two weeks. The duration of the outage increased both the economic and societal costs for the victims. Ukrenergo repaired the damage to the pylons, partially restoring the connection severed by the November blast on December 8, 2015.[191] When another blast destroyed the remaining power lines again on December 31, Ukrenergo proceeded with repairs significantly faster than the first time. Within four days, workers fixed the damage.[192] If the cyber sabotage was indeed retaliation for the initial blast cutting off power to Crimea, one could thus speculate that it had been a successful signal to Ukrainian authorities, spurring them to swift action for fear of further cyber attacks.[193]

However, Ukrenergo never actually restored power. A Ukrainian government official explained on January 14 that Russia had refused to sign a contract renewal for the energy supply because the contract specified Crimea as an "occupied territory" of Ukraine.[194] Consequently, Russian officials admitted in January 2016 that outages would last several months.[195] Even after Russia connected Crimea to its national grid in May 2016,[196] shortages and outages continued for two more years.[197] These shortages had a significant strategic impact by disrupting economic activity and undermining public morale, revealing the inability of Russian authorities to implement a reliable power supply.[198] This point raises the question of why Ukrainian intelligence services would sponsor a destructive sabotage operation of this kind when Ukrenergo could simply cut the supply. A possible explanation is that the former provided plausible deniability, that is, denying any involvement in the operation and justifying the delay of restoration efforts. This interpretation is also congruent with the fact that Ukrenergo only cut the power after the Russian cyber sabotage operation, which offered Ukrainian authorities a legitimate justification for such an act.

Importantly, regardless of the intent, this comparison underlines the greater effectiveness of traditional sabotage in producing damage and destruction. Due to the limited evidence and the remaining uncertainty over whether this was in fact an operation sponsored by an intelligence service, the constraining role of the subversive trilemma cannot be assessed conclusively here. However, it is clear this traditional operation was far simpler than the cyber sabotage operation above while producing far greater strategic value. The reason is the ability of human agents to wield physical force, unavailable for cyber operations that rely on immaterial code and commands and thus must find ways to manipulate target systems to produce such effects. This contrast becomes even clearer when examining the limitations of Sandworm's second cyber sabotage operation.

Sandworm II: The 2016 Kyiv Blackout

One year later, on December 17, 2016, Sandworm cut off the power again. This time, they targeted Ukraine's capital city, Kyiv. This cyber operation involved more advanced malware capable of causing physical destruction, leading to significant risks to citizens' health and life. Hence, it pursued by far the most intense effects of all operations examined—Johnson places sabotage of industrial facilities with the potential to cause loss of life near the top of his escalation ladder (rung thirty-four of thirty-eight).[199] Despite its violent potential, however, in practice the 2016 operation was less effective than its predecessor, achieving only a seventy-five-minute disruption. The reason this operation fell short, as the analysis will show, was the failure of the more advanced malware to deploy because the hackers had missed something. In other words, they did not know the target system well enough to produce this effect. Meanwhile, the victims had learned from the 2015 operation, and they shifted to manual control even faster as Sandworm fell back on the same technique used in the previous year. As predicted by the trilemma, this operation's pursuit of more intense effects increased both development time and the risk of control loss. Consequently, it provided even less strategic value.

Like its predecessor, this operation proceeded independently from diplomatic and military efforts. On the military front, the main events were infighting among rebels in the Donbass during the weeks preceding the sabotage and the assassination of a key rebel leader nicknamed "Motorola."[200] There were no diplomatic developments at the time. Hence, the cyber operation fulfilled an independent strategic role, weakening Ukraine through sabotage. A government advisor I interviewed suggested its purpose was psychological harm to Ukraine's population.[201] Yet its operational shortcomings prevented such an effect.

The sabotage unfolded as follows. At 11:53 p.m. on December 17, 2016, the Severyana power substation near Kyiv was de-energized, reporting a loss of 202.9 megawatts of power load.[202] Based on this power loss, it likely affected several hundred thousand households.[203] Soon after, the CEO of Ukrenergo, Ukraine's national energy provider, blamed "external intervention through data networks" for the outage via a Facebook post.[204] Forensic analysis revealed that the malware involved was significantly more advanced than the 2015 toolset, capable of directly controlling physical processes. According to ESET, "The malware is able to directly control switches and circuit breakers at power grid substations using four ICS protocols and contains an activation timestamp for December 17, 2016, the day of the power outage."[205] Developing this additional capacity required significant time: preparations evidently took an entire year[206] and directly built upon the skills and experiences gained in the 2015 operation. As Dragos put it, this operation involved the "codification and scalability in the malware towards what has been learned through past attacks."[207] The malware deployed (dubbed INDUSTROYER) thus constituted a significant advancement, subverting industrial control systems directly.

In total, it took thirty-one months of development. Moreover, it required not only significant learning and development but also possibly investments into test equipment. Considering the "deep knowledge and understanding of industrial control systems," ESET researchers argue, "it seems very unlikely anyone could write and test such malware without access to the specialized equipment used in the specific, targeted industrial environment."[208]

Two experts from a leading cybersecurity firm in Ukraine I interviewed in Kyiv echoed this assessment: "For Industroyer they [Sandworm] either bought the ICS systems before, or they had access for so long they could discover it. . . .[T]his could not be done just like that without preparation. These equipments have special protocols, there are hundreds of them, so you need to know complete which one is used. From a security point of view it is a complicated task, you need time, money and human resources as well as skills . . . basically unlimited money."[209]

Accordingly, the operation pursued the most intense effects of all cyber operations examined. INDUSTROYER was designed to cause significantly more severe disruption than in 2015, even damage to physical equipment. Researchers at ESET discovered an additional module in the malware, which Dragos's analysis revealed to be designed to execute rapid activation and deactivation of power circuits to trigger an automated protective system that would take the targeted substation offline—called "islanding."[210] If multiple substations were attacked at the same time, such "coordinated targeting of multiple electric sites could result in a few days of outages."[211] More alarmingly, a further additional module targeted a vulnerability in Siemens protective relays that would allow deactivating them, allowing overloading circuits to permanently destroy them.[212] Lasting power outages have a realistic potential of causing casualties during Ukraine's frigid winter—placing the operation near the top of Johnson's escalation ladder, on rung thirty-four of thirty-eight, as "major economic dislocation."[213] However, INDUSTROYER fell short of producing this effect.

There was no destruction or damage to the affected substation. Rather, it triggered merely a temporary disruption, and as in 2015, victims were able to restore power by switching to manual operation. Moreover, they did so faster, drawing on lessons learned. According to a Facebook post by Ukrenergo CEO Vsevolod Kovalchuk, "Our specialists quickly transferred the equipment to manual control. . . . [W]ithin an hour and fifteen minutes, power was restored in full."[214] The 2016 operation thus only achieved about a fifth as long of an outage as in 2015. Consequently, psychological and economic impacts were less significant as well. Moreover, when the blackout occurred, most people were asleep. Accordingly, Ukrainian media barely mentioned it.[215] In short, it produced even less strategic value than its predecessor.

The apparent nonuse of more damaging functionality in the malware used again led some to argue that the operation was meant to signal capabilities. For example, cybersecurity researcher Marina Krotofil argued that "the

2016 attack was not intended to have long and serious consequences. It was more like a demonstration of strength."[216] Similar to Krotofil's assessment, cybersecurity firm Dragos's report concludes that "many elements of the attack appear to have been more of a proof of concept than what was fully capable in the malware."[217] Other interpretations see the intended target not only in the Ukrainian government but also across the Atlantic in Washington, DC "to signal the risk of escalation in a crisis and gain a position of advantage in the event of a militarized dispute."[218] Andy Greenberg similarly perceives this operation as a means of deterrence, highlighting that "by turning the lights out in Kiev—and by showing that it's capable of penetrating the American grid—Moscow sends a message warning the US not to try a Stuxnet-style attack on Russia or its allies.... [I]t's all a game of deterrence."[219] Accordingly, several commentators underline how Sandworm has demonstrated abilities it could use to disrupt power systems in other nation-states. Dragos CEO Robert M. Lee stressed that INDUSTROYER could be repurposed to target Western countries, stating the following: "Washington, DC? A nation-state could take it out for two months without much issue."[220] Subsequent media reports have accordingly emphasized the threat INDUSTROYER poses for the US power grid.[221] Finally, the idea that the 2016 power grid operation was a shrewd signaling move fits prevailing perceptions of Russia "winning" in cyber conflict, and particularly perceptions of Putin as a "strategic genius."[222]

There are multiple problems with this interpretation, however. First, for signals to be effective, both their content and recipient must be clear. Neither is the case in this context, however. Second, it is highly unlikely an actor would spend years developing a capability without at least attempting to produce strategic gains. Moreover, doing so risks losing the capability by allowing potential future victims to remove the vulnerabilities it exploits. In the words of Lee himself, whom I followed up with afterward, "it would be extraordinarily weird to stage an entire attack as just a proof of concept."[223] Third, there is no empirical evidence supporting this interpretation. Sandworm has not used INDUSTROYER again, nor has it pursued other critical infrastructure sabotage using similar methods. Significantly, the 2017 intrusions in the US energy grid attributed to Russia that are often quoted in this regard were the work of a different actor and shared no tools or techniques.[224] Fourth, the "proof of concept" interpretation ultimately suggests that cyber operations are instruments of future higher-stakes conflict where actors use more powerful capabilities. That is opposite to how current theories and strategies see them. Finally, and most importantly, a signal meant to convey a threat (deterrent) requires a third characteristic: it must be credible.[225] Instead, however, as the remainder of this section shows, the 2016 operation documents the *limitations* of Russia's capabilities, undermining the credibility of the threat.

Before delving into the details of Sandworm's mistakes, it is worth noting that the strategic restraint that the signaling explanation ascribes to Sandworm is not in line with its past behavior. It is worth considering that the same group thought to have shown exceptional discipline and refinement in executing a shrewd strategic signaling move involves the same people who felt the need to include the message shown in Figure 4.1 in a file involved in a 2014 operation targeting routers.

Contrary to their boastfulness above, here Sandworm revealed the limits of their abilities—illustrating the limits of control. The initial Dragos report already underlines the challenges involved in realizing the full potential of the malware Sandworm had developed, noting that the destructive effect on protective relays it was theoretically capable of "would be very difficult to do

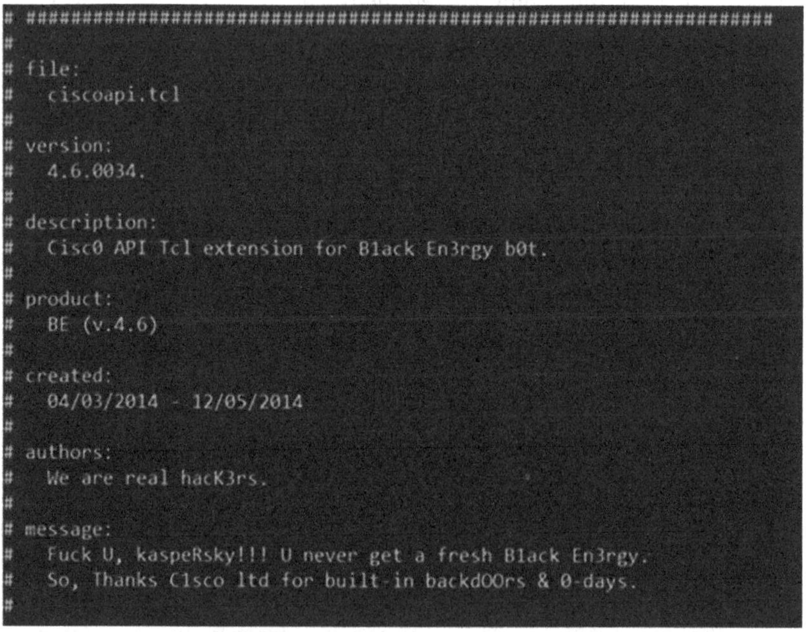

```
# ################################################################
#
# file:
#    ciscoapi.tcl
#
# version:
#    4.6.0034.
#
# description:
#    Cisc0 API Tcl extension for Black En3rgy b0t.
#
# product:
#    BE (v.4.6)
#
# created:
#    04/03/2014 - 12/05/2014
#
# authors:
#    We are real hacK3rs.
#
# message:
#    Fuck U, kaspeRsky!!! U never get a fresh Black En3rgy.
#    So, Thanks C1sco ltd for built-in backd00rs & 0-days.
#
```

Figure 4.1 Comments by Sandworm included in a configuration file deployed to targeted systems in 2014.

From Kaspersky, "BE2 Custom Plugins, Router Abuse, and Target Profiles," November 2014, https://securelist.com/be2-custom-plugins-router-abuse-and-target-profiles/67353/.

at scale properly and would require a significant investment on behalf of the adversary."[226] Considering these challenges, perception of this operation as a means of signaling and a blueprint of what is to come is likely inflated—as Sean Townsend states, "Western researchers are exaggerating this threat."[227] Hence, Ukrainian cybersecurity experts are largely in agreement that the 2016 operation was an example of operational failure. Victor Zhora speculates that the targeting was accidental and that "probably Kyivenergo was not a target, they burned their samples, that was not a smart idea to lose it."[228] Volodymyr Styran, on the other hand, expects operational failure to be the main cause, noting nonchalantly, "I think they are just people. And they just screwed it up at some point, as they did in previous incidents,"[229] referring to the group's botched intrusion at Starlight Media discussed above. Nikolay Koval echoes this assessment, noting that "the malware had to launch a loop of switching off and switching on of a facility—but they failed to make a loop, they just switched it off. Probably they missed something. It happens all the time."[230]

A follow-up analysis by Dragos ultimately confirmed these suspicions. As it turns out, Sandworm made a simple network configuration error that meant commands were sent to the wrong address. According to the report, INDUSTROYER exploited a vulnerability in protective relays aimed at preventing damage from power fluctuations and, by disabling these relays, "aimed to create an unsafe, unstable condition for reconnected transmission lines at the moment of physical restoration."[231] The result would be dangerous overcurrents with the potential to cause physical destruction.[232] Hence, Sandworm aimed to exploit the defense action of substation operators they had observed in 2015, namely the switch to manual control. This devious mechanism highlights the parallels to traditional subversion: here the intruders not only leveraged the functionality of the subverted safety systems to cause unintended outcomes but also aimed to leverage the victim's own recovery efforts against themselves to trigger destruction.

The plan was cunning, but implementation failed due to a basic error. According to the Dragos report, the networking protocol of the industrial control systems Sandworm targeted reversed IP addresses when commands were executed, but the hackers had missed this reversion and thus entered the wrong addresses—resulting in "nonsensical communication."[233] In short, "they failed due to poor understanding or implementation of ICS communication protocols within the victim's environment."[234] This was not the first time Sandworm had made a mistake of this kind. Kurt Baumgartner's analysis of the predecessor of the malware used in this operation revealed two "extraordinary coding fails," which hampered its functionality.[235] While the consequences of this previous error are unknown, in this case the result was not only a failure to activate the destructive payload but also the loss of the malware suite as researchers publicly dissected it, allowing potential future victims to remove the exploited vulnerabilities and detect the malware.

Due to these shortcomings, the operation provided even less strategic value than its predecessor. Dragos itself concludes that "while ambitious in scope and reach," the operation's "actual impact can be judged as a failure."[236] This failure is underlined by Sandworm's subsequent abandonment of INDUSTROYER, and in fact a total abandonment of cyber sabotage. This abandonment poses a further challenge for the assumed signaling value of the operation. If 2016 was intended to show off capabilities, why did the group abandon INDUSTROYER and energy sector sabotage overall? Instead, as discussed further below, Sandworm subsequently pivoted to less ambitious, lower-intensity operations that leveraged the scale rather than the scope of effects.

To conclude, the 2016 cyber sabotage pursued even more intense effects than its predecessor. As expected, developing the means to produce this effect was more challenging, taking even longer to prepare. The greater complexity involved in turn involved a greater risk of control loss. Accordingly, Sandworm failed to produce the physical damage its malware was designed to achieve because they had missed a key characteristic of the target. When they attempted to manipulate the system to cause damage, the system behaved unexpectedly and failed to produce the intended effect. This failure in turn provides further evidence of the relative ineffectiveness of cyber operations when physical effects are the goal compared to traditional subversion—especially in contrast to the devastating operation discussed in the next section.

Traditional Sabotage II: Arms Depot explosion in Kalynivka

On September 26, 2017, a massive explosion ripped through an ammunition storage facility near Kalynivka in central Ukraine. Initial estimates calculated the loss at 68,000 tons of ammunition but were later revised to 188,000 tons—a catastrophic blow to the Ukrainian military.[237] Furthermore, it produced massive collateral damage, devastating infrastructure and a nearby town. Rather than an accident, this turned out to be sabotage. It was deviously effective. By severely degrading Ukraine's warfighting ability, this operation produced significant strategic value—far greater than any cyber sabotage operation discussed. And yet, as the analysis below shows, this was a decidedly low-tech operation. A subsequent Ukrainian investigation revealed that two or three people had "walked straight into the depot," let in by a bribed security guard, and used a set of tools that would make MacGyver proud: "2 lighters, 2 packets of matches, 6 packs of cigarettes and a canister of petroleum products."[238] In short, this operation was far simpler yet far more destructive than any of the cyber sabotage operations.

Again, this operation proceeded independently of diplomatic or military efforts. There were no major developments in the military conflict around the time, and the main diplomatic event was the Ukraine–European Union Association Agreement entering into force on September 1.[239] One could speculate that Russia aimed to punish Ukraine for continuing to pursue European Union integration, but there is no hard supporting evidence.

The Kalynivka operation achieved the most intense effects of all sabotage operations examined. Considering the scale of the explosion, the effect type counts clearly among the "extreme options" at the top of Johnson's escalation ladder, whose distinguishing characteristic is that "lives of innocent people may be placed in extreme danger."[240] While its reliance on sabotage with the risk of causing deaths and its collateral damage correspond to major economic dislocations, on rung thirty-four out of thirty-eight, the targeting of military installations in fact comes close to actual secret warfare, on rung thirty-seven of thirty-eight.[241] Despite its destructiveness, however, it required no special equipment or training; hence, preparation time was likely minimal. The SBU investigation of the incident found evidence of "workers of a privately owned company with prohibited flammable substances entering the compound" shortly before the blast.[242] The court indictment provides further details on these materials, as quoted above.[243] In short, the equipment used could be bought at any convenience store.

Plausibly, these "civilians" may have been Russian intelligence agents—in which case time spent on their training must be included in overall development time. However, more likely Russian intelligence services hired locals, further minimizing development time. There is no hard evidence linking this operation to Russian intelligence, but the targeting, timing, and mode of operation all strongly point toward Russia. The target was highly valuable from a military standpoint not only for the ammunition itself stored there but also due to its close proximity to the Ukrainian Air Force headquarters housed in the nearby town of Vinnytsia—providing the opportunity for collateral damage to its command and control structures.[244] Moreover, the explosion occurred on the birthday of Ukraine's president at the time, Volodymyr Groysman, adding symbolic value.[245] Accordingly, the speaker of Ukraine's parliament at the time, Andriy Parubiy, expressed that he was "nearly certain" this was sabotage carried out by Russia.[246] Former Ukrainian intelligence officer Lieutenant General Vasily Bogdan expressed the same certainty, highlighting furthermore that the operation followed the typical modus operandi of Russian operations in recruiting local agents: "they are looking for people, recruiting and using them to carry out such actions."[247]

Access to the facility did not require any ingenious means of exploitation, but a simple bribe. As the investigation by local law enforcement revealed, a corrupt security guard had simply let in the saboteurs. As the court indictment specified, "A soldier who tolerated these things was fined."[248] Finally, on November 10, 2018, the Kalinovsky district court of Vinnytsia ordered this guard, named as "Senior officer Major B.," to pay a fine for "carelessness on duty."[249] The fine amounted to 2,465 Ukrainian Hryvnias[250] (at February 2023 exchange rates, this amounts to roughly US$67). Considering the amount fined and the low wages for military personnel in Ukraine, the bribe unlikely involved more than a five-figure dollar amount.[251]

The high intensity of effects came with limited control, leading to collateral damage. The explosion caused significant damage to the nearby town, resulting in the evacuation of thirty thousand people whose homes were destroyed or damaged by the blast.[252] In addition, forty-seven trains had to be rerouted and thousands of train tickets refunded.[253] Although this collateral damage was likely intended, once the fire was lit, they would have had little control over the damage. To illustrate this point, it is worth noting that there had been seven fires at the installation shortly before, indicating multiple failed attempts at igniting the ammunition.[254] The eighth time, it finally worked—causing a massive blast. Because of the latter's size, casualties were a likely consequence of this operation. Yet despite the devastation to surrounding areas, it only caused two injuries and no deaths.[255] Luck, however, rather than control over effects, prevented deaths.

This operation provided significant strategic value to Russia. According to the secretary of the Ukrainian Security and Defence Council, Oleksandr Turchynov, as a result (combined with another similar event in March 2017[256]), "the country has suffered the biggest blow to our fighting capacity since the start of the war."[257] On top of the destroyed military capabilities, this was a huge financial loss as well—Russian news agency TASS estimated the ammunition's value at US$800 million.[258] Furthermore, collateral damage to surrounding areas destroyed infrastructure and housing, causing both economic damage and hardship. As such, the operation weakened Ukraine militarily and economically and impacted public morale. And yet, it did all this with minimal development efforts and time.

To conclude, the Kalynivka operation provides further evidence that traditional subversive operations are significantly more effective—and likely also more efficient—in producing physical effects than cyber sabotage. Whereas the 2016 cyber sabotage operation required years of preparation and likely consumed millions of dollars in investment, all it ultimately achieved was a temporary inconvenience to a small fraction of the Ukrainian population. In contrast, Kalynivka required only a fraction of the cost, involved only the most basic equipment, and required no special training. And yet, it produced vastly more intense effects and correspondingly greater strategic value. Curiously, the subsequent evolution of Sandworm's cyber operations indicates a possible recognition of this relative disadvantage of cyber operations: the group abandoned attempts to cause physical effects in favor of lower-intensity but larger-scale effects—more in line with the expected relative advantages of cyber operations.

Economic Warfare: Sandworm's Pivot to Scale

The 2016 power grid sabotage marked Sandworm's last known attempt to cause physical effects through cyber means. Instead, the group switched to operations pursuing lower-intensity effects but at a larger scale, specifically economic dislocations. There were three operations of this kind: first, a mostly unknown yet highly effective disruption of the pension payment systems in 2016 that marks the highwater mark of producing strategic value via cyber means; second, the NotPetya malware that disrupted businesses and public services first across Ukraine and then globally in 2017, producing the greatest scale of effects yet demonstrating the risks of control loss and its perils; and third, the BadRabbit malware that replicated NotPetya's proliferation mechanism but implemented clear efforts to control its spread, leading to strategic irrelevance.

Sandworm III: The 2016 Compromise of the Ministry of Finance

While Sandworm was preparing the power grid sabotage in 2016, it also pursued a side project: disrupting Ukraine's Ministry of Finance. This operation passed by almost unnoticed, receiving little international media attention—likely since it pursued a less intense effect than the power grid sabotage, which fed right into fears of a "cyber Pearl Harbor." The effect type falls within the same category of "economic disruption without loss of life" as the power grid sabotage operation on rung eighteen out of thirty-eight. However, rather than attempting a physical effect, here Sandworm simply deleted data and disrupted computers, using its familiar KillDisk malware. As expected, the operation required far less development time, and yet there are no signs of control loss through premature discovery, failures, or collateral damage causing unintended consequences. While the effect type itself was low in intensity, the importance of the organization targeted led to a massive scale of impact on Ukraine's economy and the lives of its citizens. Consequently, this operation produced significant strategic value—and, in doing so, challenges the theory.

Strategically, as with the other operations examined, there are no apparent linkages to or correlations with Russian or military efforts. How it unfolded is also straightforward. On December 6, 2016, Ukraine's Ministry of Finance published a terse statement that "a cyber-attack was launched on the Treasury Information and Telecommunication System. The Treasury apologizes and assures you that all necessary steps are taken to restore functionality."[259] Restoring functionality, however, ultimately took three days—during which pension and social security payments, as well as the entire Value Added Tax (VAT) tax processing systems, were unavailable. Despite this significant effect, development time was extraordinarily short, taking at most one month.

Subsequent analysis showed that the operation involved minimal efforts, reusing old malware and relying on simple curiosity to infiltrate systems. ESET shortly afterward published a report on a phishing campaign by Sandworm targeting[260] "high-value targets in the Ukrainian financial sector."[261] While the report doesn't name the victim, there is little doubt about the target since the lure document attached to the phishing emails was titled "MoF critical IT needs_eng.xls" (MoF = Ministry of Finance).[262] The Microsoft Excel document used the same macro as in the 2015 power sabotage operation, and the phishing emails were sent from the same mail server, underlining the minimal effort behind this operation.[263] Meanwhile, the phishing email did not attempt any social engineering to trick users into deactivating Excel's content protection system (which prevents execution of the malicious macros included in the file). Instead, it relied on the simple curiosity of users to deactivate this protection themselves.[264] Someone clicked on it, unwittingly installing a slightly modified version of the KillDisk module from the 2015 power grid disruption.[265] This malware was programmed to automatically activate on December 6 at 9:30 a.m.[266]

Reflecting the minimal development and reconnaissance involved, forensic evidence indicates that development took only a few weeks. The last change to the Excel lure document was committed on November 10, 2016—just over three weeks prior to the operation—and an account created to communicate with infected machines and install additional malware was last used on November 11, 2016.[267] While this evidence does not allow establishing the lead time of the operation with absolute confidence, there is no countervailing evidence indicating that efforts took any longer. Moreover, the short timeframe is entirely congruent with the low customization of the methods and tools employed.

And despite these minimal efforts and high speed, the operation produced significant strategic value. The two days of disruption were sufficient to cause significant economic damage due to both the choice of target and the timing. First, as in other countries, the Ministry of Finance is integral to the functioning of Ukraine's financial system. By disrupting its computer systems, Sandworm succeeded in disrupting two core processes of Ukraine's financial system: tax payments and treasury transactions. Businesses could not pay taxes, and the treasury was unable to process transactions for VAT refunds, pensions, social security, and government salaries. The resulting economic damage likely accumulated to around 800 million Hryvnias (about US$22 million at March 2023 exchange rates) per day. Second, the timing of the disruption amplified effects, both economically and psychologically. As Dmitry Dubov at Ukraine's National Institute for Strategic Studies explained, December 6 is when "all pensions and social payments are made, and when they are blocked this might cause some social problems. There are 12m of pensioners, and they will be angry."[268] The ministry admitted as much, stating on its website it was "currently facing some problems with the full implementation of payments."[269] Not only would people have been angry, but also there would have been significant hardship, especially for social security recipients unable to pay bills.

Finally, recovery efforts and data destruction caused additional costs. On the same day the disruption happened, Ukraine's parliament allocated 80 million Ukrainian Hryvnia (UAH) (about US$2.2 million at March 2023 exchange rates) to the parliament in emergency funding for "protection against hackers."[270] A sizable proportion of these emergency funds can be expected to have gone into the Ministry of Finance's mitigation efforts. In addition, the Ministry of Finance lost three terabytes of data, likely hampering future payment and transaction processing and leading to future losses and disruptions.[271] In short, despite moving fast and requiring minimal effort, the operation produced significant strategic value, weakening Ukraine's economic capacity and undermining public trust in its institutions.[272]

The apparent lack of correlation between intense effects and speed may suggest that Sandworm either found a way to overcome the subversive trilemma or sacrificed control for speed. However, neither is the case. The main reason this operation succeeded despite so little development is the apparent plenitude of vulnerabilities in Ukraine's government systems at the time. Hence, rather than having superhuman abilities, the hackers got lucky their target was so exceptionally vulnerable despite its importance. An information technology (IT) expert who works for an unnamed Ukrainian ministry and asked to remain anonymous describes the IT security situation among government agencies in 2018 as follows:

> One ministry, for example, has about 200–500 computers, but there are only one or two IT-guys for the whole organization, and they spend their time with changing printer cartridges, or repairing one computer with parts from another 10 very old, dead computers. . . . On older computers you just can't install modern software. Meanwhile, on modern computers newer software is mainly pirated, hence updates are impossible and not even attempted in many times. Some ministries have very old outdated solutions from the 2000s, where the vendor is already bankrupt, and you cannot migrate it. Many times, I faced a situation where I have a printer that is so old, maybe 20 years, and when you install Windows 10 there is no driver available. . . . [I]f you would like to deploy something really cool, IT guys are not ready. Most of the IT guys work for a 200 dollar salary, their average age is 50–60 years, or a student who just graduated.[273]

With such wide-open attack surfaces, the hackers could confidently rely on old tools and generic techniques. Accordingly, there are no signs Sandworm sacrificed control for speed and intensity. Unfortunately, evidence on the propagation mechanism of the malware involved remains scarce. However, there is no evidence of spread beyond the ministry, nor of a loss of control. Moreover, the hackers had used KillDisk before and knew how it worked.

To conclude, this operation pursued the same effect type as the 2015 power grid sabotage operation yet proceeded at more than ten times its speed while producing significantly greater strategic value. The operation pursued low-intensity effects against a single target; hence, as predicted, it required relatively little development time and afforded a high degree of control over effects. While the theory predicts that sensitive targets tend to be harder to compromise, in this case the hackers got lucky as security precautions were evidently minimal, and vulnerabilities abounded. Consequently, neither superior abilities by the hackers nor a solution to the trilemma explains this operation's effectiveness and strategic value; rather, target-specific enabling conditions do. An exceptionally "soft" target allowed for large-scale collateral effects of compromising this individual target despite exceptionally low development efforts. Accordingly, this operation indicates that cyber operations can produce significant strategic value despite the constraints of the trilemma—given the right set of conditions.

Sandworm IV: NotPetya and the Limits of Control

In their next act of disruption, Sandworm went for maximum-scale effects—and lost control. The 2017 NotPetya malware exploited vulnerabilities in the update server of a major accounting software vendor to spread malware to its entire user population at once. It destroyed data and disrupted business and public service at a massive scale, first in Ukraine but ultimately spreading to sixty-five countries. Like the Ministry of Finance disruption, NotPetya wiped data and disabled computers. Since it primarily affected the private sector, it had the same effect type of economic disruption without loss of life—overall of medium intensity. However, NotPetya was designed to spread as far and wide as possible, producing significant economic damage. Consequently, prevailing wisdom sees it as a resounding success. Yet NotPetya's massive scale was almost certainly an accident. Forensic evidence shows the hacker had no feasible way to predict its spread, nor means to curb it once released. As such, NotPetya underlines the limits of control the trilemma predicts. Sandworm maximized both speed and intensity and lost control over effects,

158 SUBVERSION

leading to collateral damage and unintended consequences that ultimately limited its strategic value. Moreover, as the analysis will show, Sandworm was only able to spread NotPetya because of an extraordinarily "soft" target—further underlining the importance of enabling conditions.

Again, this operation proceeded independently of military and diplomatic efforts. Former Ukrainian president Petro Poroshenko signed an executive order banning several popular Russian websites in Ukraine in May 2017, while military clashes in the Donbass continued their ebb and flow of violence.[274] No evidence indicates any coordination or linkage to NotPetya's deployment. Rather, the timing of its disruptive effect underlines its independent strategic role.

Insidiously, Sandworm had programmed NotPetya to activate its disk-wiping functionality on June 27—Ukraine's "Constitution Day" celebrating the day its democratic constitution entered into force, replacing the previous constitution approved under Soviet rule. By irreversibly encrypting all data on affected systems, NotPetya disabled systems and destroyed data.[275] Mimicking popular "ransomware" schemes in cybercrime, where users are asked to pay a ransom to decrypt their data, NotPetya prompted users to transfer bitcoin in order to "liberate" their data.[276] However, the bitcoin wallet where payments were to be sent was swiftly closed afterward, indicating that the ransom request masked the operation's destructive intent.[277] While NotPetya destroyed data, it did not damage computers but disabled their operation. Disabled computer systems, however, disrupted business and services at affected organizations. Initially, its proliferation was limited to Ukraine, but it rapidly spread across its borders. For example, shipping giant Maersk lost almost its entire IT infrastructure, resulting in a massive disruption to its shipping operations.[278]

For individual users, these disruptions were mostly a nuisance. Provided they had backups, re-enabling affected systems simply required installing all software from scratch. Accordingly, the CEO of national energy provider Ukrenergo stated, "The effect from it was insignificant. . . . [S]ome computers remained offline."[279] However, due to its massive scale, NotPetya produced more intense effects than any other cyber operation. Initial estimates suggested a mere twenty thousand computers were affected,[280] yet actual numbers are likely far higher. A cybersecurity expert employed by a large information security firm in Ukraine who was directly involved in mitigating NotPetya's disruption estimated that it crippled "more than half a million," noting that "our biggest clients who were affected lost about 45,000 computers each."[281]

Despite this massive scale of disruption, NotPetya required significantly less development time than the power grid sabotage operations. Forensic data indicates only seven months in total. Development started in December 2016 with the so-called Moonraker worm, a predecessor to NotPetya that evidently tested a mechanism to spread automatically through local networks and wipe data.[282] It affected only a small number of systems and passed by mostly unnoticed. Interestingly, Moonraker built mostly on GreenPetya, a popular ransomware used for cybercrime—underlining Sandworm's criminal heritage.[283] Next, between January and March 2017, Sandworm started experimenting with a "supply chain" propagation mechanism—infecting a third-party system, usually a software vendor, to automatically spread to all of the vendor's users. As ESET discovered, during that time Sandworm developed a new malware called Python/TeleBot.A that compromised an unknown software firm providing services to financial institutions.[284] Through an infected software update, it compromised the internal networks of two Ukrainian financial institutions and encrypted systems, extorting a ransom.[285] Target identities and the scale of disruption are unknown but likely minimal since the operation received little press coverage.

In May 2017, the next development stage commenced. Sandworm had now gained access to its final target: the server of the firm Intellect Services that propagated automated updates to users of the highly popular accounting software M.E.Doc.[286] The hackers had developed a new malware suite capable of encrypting data, called XData, and hid it in a software update that propagated across M.E.Doc customers.[287] XData spread rapidly—on May 18, the security researcher "MalwareHunter" alerted the public to the threat in a tweet,[288] and within twenty-four hours they had identified 134 infections within Ukraine.[289] At the time, this was considered a rapid spread, yet it was later dwarfed by the infection numbers of NotPetya, which would later compromise 12,500 systems within the same timeframe.[290] XData's purpose was likely to test propagation through the Intellect Services server. Since XData was highly targeted, going after specific entities, Victor Zhora speculated that the operation was both a "proof of concept" for the propagation mechanism in NotPetya and a means "mapping the network."[291]

Having tested the propagation mechanism, Sandworm now compiled NotPetya malware and integrated it into another M.E.Doc software update.

This update was "pushed" from the server to users on June 22.[292] Once inside their network, NotPetya then spread automatically to infect as many computers as possible, leveraging the infamous EternalBlue exploit (CVE-2017-0144) developed by the United States National Security Agency (NSA) that had been released by the ShadowBrokers group in April 2017.[293] Finally, its disk encryption module automatically activated on June 27.

The NotPetya worm itself was neither very complex nor advanced but used most of the codebase of the generic GreenPetya malware. In fact, NotPetya's disk encryption tool was only "slightly modified"—and, embarrassingly, ESET's analysis showed that the modifications included mistakes that precluded the decryption of data.[294] As Volodymyr Styran underlined, once Sandworm had access to the update server, inserting code in the update was relatively simple—yet the method of propagation via the official update server was "genius."[295]

The main challenge was thus establishing access to the server. However, as in the Ministry of Finance operation, Sandworm benefited from relatively lax security measures. As the Ukrainian hacker known under the alias "Sean Townsend" highlighted, most Western reporting on NotPetya neglected that "the attacked server of M.E.Doc company has not been updated since 2012. It was an easy target."[296] Other security researchers have echoed this assessment, as well as Ukrainian authorities, who seized M.E.Doc's servers in July 2017 and found "no updates had been installed since February 2013."[297]

In short, Sandworm maximized both speed and intensity, benefiting from a "soft" target. Because of the scale of disruption, NotPetya caused significant economic damage, widespread disruption, and significant psychological impact. Its main targets were businesses, but it also affected government organizations and other public entities, including transport and media.[298] ATMs stopped working, credit card payment systems went down, and overall business activity in Ukraine ground to a virtual standstill.[299] While the effect was temporary, Ukraine's finance minister Oleksandr Danyliuk nonetheless estimates that the disruption cost Ukraine 0.5% of its GDP, or 14 billion Ukrainian hryvnias,[300] about US$530 million at the exchange rate in May 2019. This estimate is possibly still conservative, considering that shipping giant Maersk and logistics firm FedEx each reported losses incurred due to NotPetya of around US$300 million,[301] and subsequent estimates have placed its global costs as high as US$53 billion.[302] Moreover, NotPetya also infected critical infrastructure, including the energy sector, although it did not affect the functionality of physical systems.[303] Accordingly, media reporting on NotPetya was much more extensive than on the energy sector operations, with the disruption covered in many general media outlets, causing wide public awareness, underlining its potential impact on public opinion.[304] NotPetya thus clearly achieved a strategically relevant effect, suggesting it produced significant strategic value to Russia—and thereby bypassed the constraints of the trilemma.

However, a closer look shows that is not the case. Rather, the hackers lost control and caused collateral damage that limited strategic value. As expected, moving fast while pursuing intense effects raised the risk of the latter. Accordingly, the development stage already shows evidence of Sandworm's limited familiarity with the target system and a remarkable loss of cover due to third-party intervention—a disgruntled cybercriminal whose code Sandworm had stolen. The XData "test" that spread through a software M.E.Doc update on May 15 revealed Sandworm's limited familiarity with the server they later used for NotPetya. Two days later, M.E.Doc had pushed out another, legitimate update free of the malware, however. Hence, when Sandworm activated the encryption module on May 18, only a small fraction of M.E.Doc users who had missed this update (for whatever reason) were affected. Sandworm had missed this update—ESET analysis concluded it was "an unexpected event for the attackers."[305]

Events took a curious turn three days after. On May 21, someone sent the XData decryption key to a hacker on a Russian online forum, who published them.[306] The author (whose name remains unknown) stated he published the keys because XData was based on code "stolen from him," and he feared he was "purposely being framed."[307] Apparently, Sandworm had used a cybercrime tool called AES-NI for disk encryption, purportedly to add an additional layer of plausible deniability. Yet they failed to anticipate its author's interests to avoid persecution.

In addition, this episode, and the disruption XData caused, increased the risk of premature discovery—which did occur. On May 23, 2017, ESET published a report on XData, also noting that it "appears to have been distributed through a Ukrainian document automation system widely used in accounting."[308] Although it did not name Intellect Services, it clearly indicated the victim and ESET notified them of the compromise. At this stage, the cover was effectively blown, giving the victim an opportunity to neutralize the compromise. Fortunately—for Sandworm—M.E.Doc apparently did little, or at least not enough, to neutralize Sandworm's control over their server. Again, Sandworm got lucky the victim evidently had such lax security practices in place, allowing them to proceed with NotPetya development.

Once they deployed NotPetya, however, Sandworm lost control over it and caused collateral damage, leading to unintended consequences. Because international businesses operating within Ukraine also used M.E.Doc, and because they had linked their Ukrainian-based systems to their corporate networks outside the country via virtual private networks (VPNs),[309] the malware spread far wider. Within twenty-four hours NotPetya spread to sixty-five different countries.[310] This rapid proliferation also included victims in Russia, even its state-controlled oil and gas giant Rosneft.[311] This collateral damage thus produced direct costs to Russia. While some may argue that Sandworm simply signaled their recklessness, it is hard to see why a Russian-sponsored campaign against Ukraine would intentionally cause damage to Russia—particularly against a firm owned by a powerful oligarch close to Russian intelligence service FSB.[312] In a curious twist, Russian state media used its uncontrolled spread as a propaganda opportunity, emphasizing disruption of Russian targets to deflect blame.[313] Considering that NotPetya started in Ukraine and 75% of all infected systems were located in Ukraine,[314] however, this claim is hardly plausible. Accordingly, there is now general consensus among cybersecurity researchers that the proliferation of NotPetya was an accident,[315] reflecting a loss of control. ESET's report notes forensic data showing that "the latest outbreak [referring to NotPetya] was directed against businesses in Ukraine, but they apparently underestimated the malware's spreading capabilities. That's why the malware went out of control."[316]

Because NotPetya proliferated automatically, gauging the extent of its spread and who the victims were would have required mapping compromised networks. Within the short timeframe involved, this was impossible, however. Mapping a complex network using the popular Nmap tool can take many hours, for example[317]—yet in this case the hackers only had seconds. NotPetya was designed to spread automatically within networks for the five days that passed between the initial infection and activation of its encryption module. For the 12,500 systems infected within the first 24 hours, even if they worked around the clock, the attackers would have thus had to map 104 targets per hour (5 days = 120 hours; 12,500 systems / 120 hours = 104.17 systems per hour), leaving only 34 seconds per target system. Considering the insider estimate of 500,000 total infected systems of NotPetya, it would leave merely 0.86 seconds per target—hardly enough time to determine the type of system, organization, geographic location, and its location within a network.

Not only the collateral damage to Russia produced costs, but also the response of Ukraine's allies. A US sanction package imposed on Russia in March 2018 explicitly references the operation.[318] The United Kingdom and the European Union followed suit in imposing sanctions.[319] Apart from larger economic costs, the sanctions specifically targeted individual leaders of the military intelligence service GRU, causing financial damage to its leadership, and by extension the GRU at large.[320] Considering the reportedly precarious budget situation of the GRU,[321] this impact will likely have further reduced its organizational and operational capacity—not least the affected leadership's tolerance for experimentation with cyber operations. The subsequent evolution of Sandworm's cyber operation supports this conclusion—more on this further below.

Before moving on to the discussion, it is worth considering alternate interpretations of NotPetya's purpose. Again, a dominant interpretation sees NotPetya as a signal. Some media reporting cast NotPetya as a highly effective economic and psychological warfare operation that demonstrated Russian strength, constituting the "grand finale" of Sandworm's campaigns and the "most devastating blow yet in the ongoing cyberwar" in Ukraine.[322] In this perception, NotPetya's disruption was a carefully calibrated act of coercion. As Greenberg's report underlines, "While many in the security community still see NotPetya's international victims as collateral damage, Cisco's Craig Williams argues that Russia knew full well the extent of the pain the worm would inflict internationally."[323] According to this narrative, its international spread was "meant to explicitly punish anyone who would dare even to maintain an office inside the borders of Russia's enemy."[324] Brandon Valeriano et al. echoed this argument in an op-ed, positing that NotPetya's purpose was "sending a signal. The primary goal instead appears to be limited destruction through malware wiping systems."[325] The problem with these interpretations is that, as discussed, Sandworm had no feasible way to predict NotPetya's spread or identify its targets. Its massive spread was an accident, and one that Sandworm later tried to rectify. It is unlikely a coincidence that Sandworm operations show clear efforts to control and limit the spread of disruptive disk wipers.[326]

Instead, a more plausible interpretation is that NotPetya's disruption was a cover-up for espionage gone awry. While, understandably, most reporting has focused on NotPetya's disruption, less attention has been paid to the activity in the weeks and months preceding this event. As Sergiy Markovets, director of the Ukrainian cybersecurity firm ISSP, underlines, "The level of penetration in the affected network has opened up much wider opportunities.... [I]t is likely that this [NotPetya's disk encryption] was a cover for leaving after a real attack that was aimed at espionage or data theft."[327] Moreover, Markovets stated that his company is aware Sandworm had exfiltrated data from at least one of the banks affected by NotPetya.[328] Similarly, a cybersecurity expert employed by a leading security vendor and personally involved in NotPetya mitigation efforts stated, "I know some case where they [Sandworm] used this access for critical means. They took some personal data, databases. There was some data exfiltration visible a couple of months before end of June."[329] Considering this broad access to sensitive data, the fact that Sandworm initiated the disruption at all, resulting in a loss of future access, is puzzling to some researchers. As Nikolay Koval put it, "You had a brilliant access to thousands of organizations, and fascinating for the adversary. But you decide to spy a little bit, exfiltrate a little bit, but then you decide to blow it up? Why? I don't know."[330] Unfortunately, only Sandworm currently knows why they decided to "blow it up." Nonetheless, in contrast to the dominant signaling interpretation, the cover-up interpretation is not only plausible but also supported by tangible evidence.

To conclude, as the analysis above has shown, NotPetya does confirm the scale advantage of cyber operations compared to traditional subversion. Yet it also demonstrates the increased risk of control loss when maximizing speed and intensity, limiting strategic value. Ultimately, NotPetya thus provides further evidence in support of the subversive trilemma. Interestingly, and in line with this conclusion, Sandworm's next operation shows clear efforts to balance the trilemma.

Sandworm V: BadRabbit—Balancing the Trilemma at the Cost of Strategic Relevance?

Sandworm's final disruptive cyber operation in this conflict phase shows clear efforts to improve control. "BadRabbit," as security researchers christened it, employed the same mechanism of encrypting data as NotPetya. Yet it propagated manually rather than automatically, and its encryption was reversible. With BadRabbit, Sandworm thus—intentionally or not— made an effort to balance the subversive trilemma. As expected, improving control over effects through the measures just mentioned lowered the operational speed and intensity of effects. Development took twice as long as for NotPetya, reflecting the extra measures taken to curb its spread. Consequently, the scale of disruption remained limited, affecting only several hundred victims. Circumstantial evidence suggests BadRabbit's limited spread obscured more surgical targeting of Ukrainian critical infrastructure. However, as I show below, even if this was the case, it failed to make any measurable impact. In short, BadRabbit remained strategically irrelevant. Evidently, Sandworm's efforts to balance the trilemma limited intensity to such a degree that it forfeited strategic value. The group's abandonment of active-effects cyber operations afterward indicates a possible recognition of this trade-off.

Like its predecessors, BadRabbit fulfilled an independent strategic role. There are no evident linkages to, or coordination with, diplomatic or military efforts. The key diplomatic event around this time, as already discussed, was the European Union–Ukraine Association Agreement entering into force. Meanwhile, there were no major developments on the military front.

In October 2017, a revamped version of NotPetya encrypted data and disrupted target systems in Ukraine and several other countries. Like NotPetya, it also displayed a ransom demand to victims, but unlike NotPetya, victims who paid the ransom reportedly had their files recovered.[331] Targets included the Kyiv metro, the Odessa airport and naval port, the Ukrainian ministries of infrastructure and finance, and additional targets in Ukraine as well as in Russia. The operation was quickly attributed to Sandworm due to its obvious linkages to NotPetya.[332] Like NotPetya, BadRabbit spread via a malicious software update, this time for the popular Adobe Flash Player, but in contrast this malware was not spread via an automated update service, but rather through multiple infected websites in Russia, Bulgaria, and Turkey.[333] Targets were located in multiple jurisdictions, including Russia, Ukraine, Bulgaria, Turkey, and Japan.[334]

BadRabbit relied on the same mechanism as NotPetya and thus shared its effect type, namely economic disruption without loss of life. In scope, its effects were comparable in intensity. In practice, however, it achieved far less intense effects because of its much smaller scale—affecting merely a few hundred computers—and the reversibility of the data encryption.[335] Hence, economic effects were also limited, and apparently concentrated on specific high-value targets in Ukraine. For example, the Kyiv metro temporarily lost its payment system, but the operation of trains remained undisrupted, while the Odessa airport had to cancel flights and experienced delays.[336] BadRabbit thus caused disruptions for individual victims but did not produce nationally and internationally significant effects of the kind NotPetya had achieved.

Nonetheless, BadRabbit required twice the development time of NotPetya. RiskIQ discovered forensic evidence indicating development had started at least a year earlier in September 2016.[337] Moreover, it found clear evidence that Sandworm strove to "improve upon previous mistakes" by making its encryption reversible, preventing the lasting data destruction of NotPetya.[338] As expected, increasing control increased development time. The second means of control was a manual proliferation mechanism. BadRabbit required each of its victims to navigate to one of the infected websites, accept a download of a fake Adobe Flash Player update, and confirm its installation by clicking on OK/Install.[339] Naturally, this took time, and hence the spread of the malware would have been much slower than NotPetya's near-instantaneous automatic proliferation. These added efforts paid off, as there is no data indicating that BadRabbit spread uncontrollably or of collateral damage and unintended consequences, nor are there indications that victims discovered it prematurely.[340] BadRabbit thus balanced intensity, operational speed, and control over effects.

Balancing the trilemma came at the cost of strategic relevance, however. Due to its limited scale, BadRabbit did not produce measurable economic impacts on Ukraine or any of the other countries affected. Its reversibility also facilitated restoration of service at affected systems, reducing the time of the disruption. Available evidence indicates that its disruptions were largely inconsequential.[341] In short, BadRabbit did not produce measurable strategic value.

Intriguingly, forensic evidence indicates that BadRabbit's already highly limited proliferation was meant to obscure an even more limited surgical disruption of Ukraine's critical infrastructure. Curiously, most targets (65%) were in Russia[342]—the reverse pattern of NotPetya, 75% of whose targets were in Ukraine.[343] One could think this was an accident. Yet BadRabbit spread manually via watering-hole websites, many of which were Russian. Hence, the inclusion of Russian targets was almost certainly intentional. Accordingly, ESET identified a suspicious pattern as Ukraine only makes up 12% of targets yet is the only affected country where targets included a concentration of high-value critical infrastructure entities—all of which were hit at the same time.[344] More intriguingly, ESET researchers found no evidence any of these targets had been compromised via the malicious Flash Player update. Consequently, ESET's report concludes that it is "possible that the group [Sandworm] already had a foot inside their [Ukrainian targets] network and launched the watering hole attack at the same time as a decoy."[345] The targeting of prominent media outlets in Russia, sure to maximize public attention, fits with this goal.[346]

Two further pieces of evidence support the decoy theory. First, BadRabbit was part of a long-running campaign exfiltrating information from infected targets. RiskIQ's researchers puzzled over the disruption it caused, noting that what "we do not understand at this point is why they decided to burn this information position to mass distribute the BadRabbit ransomware rather than save it for another type of malware."[347] This discovery confirms the pre-existing compromises among Ukrainian targets. Second, Russian news coverage of BadRabbit malware specifically emphasized Russian targeting. For example, on the day BadRabbit hit, Russia Today reported, "A new global cyber virus attack began on Tuesday and targeted corporate networks mainly in Russia, cybersecurity company Kaspersky Lab said. A number of companies in Germany, Turkey and Ukraine have been affected on a smaller scale."[348]

To be sure, these are circumstantial fragments of evidence, yet they do support the theory that BadRabbit's international spread (and reversible disk encryption) added a layer of plausible deniability to obscure targeted disruption of Ukrainian critical infrastructure.

Regardless of intent, however, the operation failed to produce strategic value. Sandworm had attempted to balance speed, intensity, and control—at the cost of strategic relevance. Consequently, and considering the underwhelming track record of its preceding operations, it is perhaps unsurprising that Sandworm abandoned active-effects cyber operations afterward. The group's last recorded activity was a detection of an updated version of the backdoor used in the 2016 energy sector sabotage in April 2018—yet it was evidently not targeting any industrial facilities.[349] Instead, the group exclusively focused on espionage, at least until the 2022 invasion.[350]

Tactical Sabotage? The Curious Case of the Artillery

Overall, cyber operations have been irrelevant to the military dimension of the conflict, and accordingly the operations discussed above constituted independent instruments. Yet one cyber operation stands out as a potential outlier since its evident purpose was to complement the use of force. In 2016, security vendor CrowdStrike published a report claiming Russia had compromised the phones of Ukrainian artillery units, allowing Russian forces to track the latter's location, and implying a resulting massive increase in casualties. Specifically, it claimed the Ukrainian military lost "over 80% of D-30 howitzers, the highest percentage of loss of any other artillery pieces in Ukraine's arsenal."[351] To achieve this feat, CrowdStrike reported, APT28 had compromised a smartphone app used by Ukrainian artillery officers to simplify targeting data, allowing the threat group to determine the location of Ukrainian units.[352] Based on a decline in the number of Ukrainian D-30 artillery pieces, the report suggests it is "possible that the deployment of this malware infected application may have contributed to the high-loss nature of this platform."[353] This report garnered much attention, seemingly providing the first evidence of force-multiplying effects of cyber operations.[354] In an essay for *Foreign Policy*, Elias Groll suggested that this hack illustrated no less than "the future of war."[355] Yet its findings were swiftly challenged.

Problematically, CrowdStrike had derived casualty estimates from data by the International Institute for Strategic Studies (IISS)—but the IISS refuted the interpretation of the data that CrowdStrike's conclusion relied upon: "The inference they make that reductions in Ukrainian D-30 artillery holdings between 2013 and 2016 were primarily the result of combat losses is not a conclusion that we have ever suggested ourselves, nor one we believe to be accurate."[356]

The Ukrainian Ministry of Defense subsequently disputed the cited casualty numbers in a statement, leading Jeffrey Carr to conclude that CrowdStrike had spread "false information."[357] Sean Townsend, a hacktivist at the Ukrainian Cyber Alliance, is more blunt, stating the CrowdStrike report "was complete bullshit" as the attempt to subvert the artillery units' smartphones failed to produce any consequence—yet at the same time he underlines that the incident "is alarming because the technique could have worked if it was done well."[358] In response to the criticism, CrowdStrike updated its report in March 2017, lowering the loss estimates of artillery units drastically, now stating that "Ukrainian Armed Forces lost between 15% and 20% of their pre-war D–30 inventory in combat operations."[359]

In short, this operation possibly had some impact on artillery casualties, but there is no conclusive evidence it actually did—on the contrary, available evidence indicates negligible impact on casualties. Pavlo Narozhnyy, an advisor to the Ukrainian military who claims he "personally knows hundreds of gunmen in the warzone," reported that "none of them told me of D-30 losses caused by hacking or any other reason."[360] Of course, this assessment is to be taken with a grain of salt considering it comes from Ukraine's military. However, the absence of evidence of the impact of this cyber operation, combined with the fierce rebuttal by the independent think tank IISS, whose data supposedly supported the conclusions of CrowdStrike's report, and the latter's subsequent revision of the report, strongly suggests this operation had at best a very limited impact, and possibly no impact at all. This limited impact stands in marked contrast to the significant lead time of the operation, reflecting considerable investments: CrowdStrike estimates that development of the malware agent took twenty months.[361]

Since this operation did not produce any active effects on targets but rather pursued only passive intelligence collection, it falls beyond the scope of the trilemma theory. However, it provides further illustration of the contrast between the theoretical possibilities of what cyber operations can achieve—which form the basis for the CrowdStrike report—and their practical limitations.

Discussion: New Technology, Old Limitations

Despite the use of new technologies, the strategic role and value of subversion in the Ukrainian case shows clear parallels to the Czechoslovakian case. Moreover, the analysis produced strong evidence of the constraining role of the trilemma across the cyber operations examined, underlining the continuity in the quality of subversion. Hence, there is no evidence indicating that information technology has fundamentally changed the quality of subversion. On the contrary, the findings showed that traditional rather than cyber-enabled subversion contributed to Russia's key strategic gains in this phase of the conflict, namely the takeover of Crimea and partial takeover of the Donbass. Contrary to prevailing conceptions of cyber-enabled hybrid war, active-effects cyber operations remained irrelevant both to the military dimension of the conflict and to the subversive campaigns that preceded and achieved these takeovers. Russia only deployed active-effects cyber operations after the military conflict had reached a bloody stalemate, reflecting a strategic shift toward a long-term subversive campaign attempting to exert influence and weaken Ukraine. Evidently, Russia had taken the use of force as far as it deemed beneficial at that stage, then switched to subversion as a strategic alternative—in line with its predicted role.

Throughout the seven cyber operations discussed, the analysis produced clear evidence of the persistently constraining role of the subversive trilemma and resulting limited strategic value. In a striking parallel to the initial experimentation with illegal agents in Czechoslovakia, the first set of operations pursued daringly intense effects. As expected, this resulted either in a failure to produce effects or the effects produced failing to provide strategic significance. With efforts to maximize effect intensity, both development time and risks of control loss increased. Accordingly, the two widely and sensationally reported power grid cyber sabotage operations in 2015 and 2016 required extensive development time yet only produced temporary outages that failed to produce any significant economic or psychological impact. In contrast, traditional sabotage operations during the same period produced far more intense effects with less development time and effort, providing significant strategic value.

A similar picture emerges when considering cumulative effects, challenging prevailing expectations of cyber operations providing superior value in this regard. Even if the cyber operations examined mostly failed to contribute toward Russia's specific strategic goals, they may have cumulatively stoked public fear and undermined public trust in the government. In fact, that was a common argument I heard in interviews in Ukraine and is in line with the interpretation of cyber operations as signaling tools. Survey data does not show any measurable change in public trust in the government that could be plausibly correlated to cyber campaigns, however. Rather, polls by the Kyiv International Institute for Sociology show a slight increase—despite overall remarkably low percentages—of trust throughout the period. As Figure 4.2 shows, Ukrainians' trust in their government increased from 8.7% in 2015 to 14% in 2020. In short, there is no evidence of any cumulative effect eroding public trust.

The situation is similar concerning economic effects. As discussed, in 2016 the subversive campaigns transitioned from infrastructure sabotage to economic warfare. Hence, it is plausible that there was a cumulative economic impact. Indeed, both the Ministry of Finance hack and NotPetya had a significant impact. Based on World Bank data from 2017, the estimated half percentage point of GDP NotPetya erased amounted to US$56 million at current exchange rates (March 2023). The Ministry of Finance hack cost a combined US$44 million (including recovery efforts, as discussed) at current

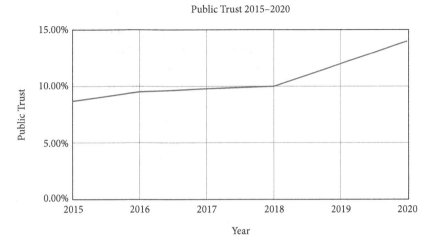

Figure 4.2 Public trust in the government of Ukraine 2015–2020.
From KIIS, "Press Releases and Reports—Trust in Social Institutions and Social Groups," 2015, https://kiis.com.ua/?lang=eng&cat=reports&id=579; KIIS, "Press Releases and Reports—Trust to Social Institutions," 2016, https://www.kiis.com.ua/?lang=eng&cat=reports&id=678; KIIS, "Press Releases and Reports—Trust to Social Institutes, December 2018," December 2018, https://www.kiis.com.ua/?lang=eng&cat=reports&id=817&page=2; KIIS, "Press Releases and Reports—Trust in Social Institutions and Parties," December 2020, https://kiis.com.ua/?lang=eng&cat=reports&id=1005.

exchange rates, bringing the total to US$100 million. Considering Ukraine's GDP in 2017 amounted to US$112 billion, that is just short of 1% of GDP—a measurable impact.[362] This cumulative impact, however, is dwarfed by the economic damage caused by a single traditional subversive operation, namely the takeover of Crimea. According to a study by the Center for Economic Strategy, a Ukrainian nongovernmental organization, the cumulative damage caused by Russia's takeover of Crimea amounted to 75% of Ukraine's GDP in 2013, or US$135 billion in total (at 2021 exchange rates).[363] Accordingly, Ukraine's GDP showed a drastic decrease between 2013 and 2015, more than halving from US$190 billion at March 2023 exchange rates to around US$90 billion.[364] Just as cyber operations picked up steam, so did Ukraine's GDP. From 2015 it grew consistently, increasing to around US$130 billion by 2018.[365] Hence, this paradigmatic case of cyber-enabled aggression short of war provides no indication that cyber operations enable superior cumulative effects compared to traditional subversion.

Comparing the scope of effects realized through cyber operations in Ukraine to those of traditional subversive operations in Czechoslovakia further underlines their relative limitations. In Czechoslovakia, the KGB pursued a range of effect types (albeit with decidedly mixed results) that the theory predicted to be beyond the range of cyber operations: assassination, kidnapping, government infiltration and manipulation, and regime change. Russian-sponsored cyber operations against Ukraine, on the other hand, pursued more limited and less intense effects, namely election interference and economic disruption without loss of life. Most importantly, cyber operations neither attempted nor achieved the same scope of influence over elites as traditional subversion both in Czechoslovakia and in Ukraine. In Czechoslovakia, illegal agents penetrated both the highest echelons of government and the leadership of its civil society. In Ukraine, Russian handlers cultivated and coordinated a set of subversive proxy actors who became key instruments in Russia's regime change operations in Crimea and the Donbass (unsuccessfully in the latter case). The irrelevance of cyber operations in the latter operations reflects their expected inability to achieve this kind of influence and corresponding effects.

Conversely, the Ukraine case provides evidence of the expected superior scale of cyber operations. The compromise of the Ministry of Finance and NotPetya both produced measurable economic disruptions at a scale beyond anything seen in Czechoslovakia. Moreover, comparing the efforts required for these operations to the cyber sabotage attempts that preceded them further cements the conclusion that cyber operations excel at large-scale effects. Sandworm's widely neglected compromise of the Ministry of Finance in 2016 produced significantly greater economic loss, societal disruption, and corresponding strategic value than the power grid sabotage operations of 2015 and 2016 with far less development time and effort. Instead of physical effects, the operation pursued less intense data destruction and reused generic tools yet produced by far the most favorable ratio between strategic value and efforts invested among the cyber operations examined. Perhaps unsurprisingly, Sandworm subsequently changed its approach, attempting further economic disruptions through data destruction while leveraging the scale advantage of cyber operations. With this approach, the NotPetya operation of 2017 achieved the greatest strategic impact of any cyber operation, producing massive economic disruption both domestically and internationally. Yet as the analysis showed, it maximized scale at the cost of control, producing unintended consequences and limiting its strategic value. The BadRabbit operation finally balanced the constraints of time, intensity, and control—yet at the cost of strategic relevance and corresponding utility.

Overall, the evidence thus strongly indicates that cyber operations continue to be subject to the constraints of the trilemma despite the use of new technology. Consequently, there is little evidence of a fundamental change in the nature of subversion. Rather, there are differences in degree concerning the scope and scale of effects. While the findings overall thus strongly support the theory, some of the evidence uncovered also indicate a potential limitation. Specifically, the success of the Crimean takeover compared to the partial failure of the Donbass operation based on the same playbook poses a puzzle for the theory. Both were implemented in relatively short timeframes, and both built on long-running preceding subversive campaign that nurtured and grew the networks of proxy actors these operations relied upon. Considering these parallels, the trilemma should constrain both operations in roughly similar ways. Yet one succeeded while the other failed, and the analysis showed an additional variable to be a key component of the prospects of subversive operations under the constraints of the trilemma: the extent of available vulnerabilities. The same applies to the compromise of the Ministry of Finance, which evidently succeeded because of the exceptional vulnerability of a target with such social and economic significance. Similarly, the NotPetya operation only became possible because of the victim's extraordinarily lax security practices.

How the presence of vulnerabilities interacts with the constraints of the trilemma, and specifically whether there is an identifiable threshold for success, is thus an important question for further research and refinement of the theory. So is the question of whether other external conditions may influence the relative significance of these constraints and the strategic value of cyber operations—foremost, shifting strategic contexts. The future evolution of the Russo-Ukrainian conflict does include a dramatic shift, as Russia invaded in 2022. The next chapter will examine what role subversion played in this escalation.

5

Subversion in War

Russia's full-scale Invasion of Ukraine since February 2022

Early in the morning on February 24, 2022, Russia invaded Ukraine (again). Rather than a few "little green men," however, this time tens of thousands of troops, columns of tanks, and armored personnel carriers marked with "Z" insignia started pouring across Ukraine's border. Russia's "hybrid war" strategy since 2014 had failed to achieve its goals, and therefore Moscow escalated. In its invasion, the Kremlin's core goals remained the same, namely to stop and reverse Ukraine's pro-Western foreign policy. Yet Moscow escalated both the means and objectives. Rather than the slow erosion of Ukraine's morale and capacity to resist Russia's subversive campaign had pursued, Russia now threw all its military might against its smaller neighbor to attempt a rapid decapitation strike. As Kremlin statements made clear, the aim was to topple Zelenskiy's government and install a puppet regime. This plan failed, however, and after initial rapid advances, the invasion ground to a halt. Nonetheless, Russia has made significant advances in its occupation, which it turned into territorial gains in annexing four Ukrainian regions it has (in some cases only partially) occupied in October 2022.

Subversion played an important role in these efforts, both as an independent instrument to continue to erode Ukraine's strength and as a direct complement to the use of force. This chapter will trace how Russia's hacking groups, intelligence services, and "shadow forces" that pervaded Ukraine's security services and local government attempted to help topple Zelenskiy, take over territory, erode Ukrainian's morale, sabotage its infrastructure, and guide Russian missiles to their target. Some of these operations played out like spy fiction, such as a Russian undercover agent escaping just before the invasion only to be caught in a luxury car loaded with cash and diamonds three months later in Serbia. Apart from laying out the remarkable audacity of some of these operations, and correspondingly catastrophic blunders, this analysis strives to piece together timelines, mechanisms, and constraints. Finally, it evaluates their strategic value. It will show that while cyber operations have received far greater attention, traditional subversion has achieved far greater strategic value.

With Russia's troop buildup along Ukraine's borders in the months before, cyberwar fears went into overdrive. Chris Stokel-Walker summed up these fears, writing on the day before the invasion that "Russia, Ukraine and the latter's Western allies have all built up the capability to launch huge state-sponsored cyberattacks. Are we lurching towards the world's biggest cyberwar?"[1] Some went as far as suggesting that Russia could achieve its goals through cyber operations alone, with Chatham House analyst Keir Giles speculating about "a destructive cyber onslaught" that "could target military command and control systems or civilian critical infrastructure and pressure Kyiv into concessions and its friends abroad into meeting Russia's demands."[2] In the background of these expectations has been the persistent notion that Russia had held back its most powerful capabilities—in line with alternative interpretations of the underwhelming impact of its preceding cyber operations as signals.[3] Accordingly, a Politico story warned that "the potential Russian invasion of Ukraine could give the world its first experience of a true cyber war."[4] Former director of the US Cyber Command General Keith Alexander went as far as asserting that "cyber warfare in Ukraine poses a threat to the global system."[5]

Yet these expectations do not match the evolution of this conflict. As the previous chapter showed, Russia had already tried, and failed, to get Ukraine to change course through its hybrid war strategy, of which cyber operations were an integral part. Strategically, that was the time to use its most powerful capabilities. In other words, why go through the costs and risks of full-scale invasion when there are still less costly and risky alternatives available? After all, those are supposedly the advantages of cyber operations driving cyberwar fears.

Unsurprisingly, catastrophic cyber war did not happen. Yet cyber operations became a key dimension of this invasion. As the analysis will show, Russia mounted a large number of cyber operations within a very short time—since the invasion far more cyber operations targeted Ukraine than during the preceding eight years of hybrid war combined. These operations contributed to a psychological and economic warfare campaign, a failed coup attempt, critical infrastructure sabotage, and attempts to gain advantages on the battlefield. With fast-moving operations happening in the fog of war, and with both sides running information wars, evidence on these operations and their impact is both scarce and scattered. Accordingly, this analysis remains preliminary. However, building on the evidence that is available, namely forensic reporting, local news reporting, and statements from government officials, it shows that cyber operations by and large fell short of providing measurable and significant strategic value. Except for a large-scale disruption of Ukraine's national Internet provider in March 2022, none of the operations discussed caused effects with a measurable strategic impact. Although data remains incomplete, piecing together operational timelines and mechanisms from the fragments of information that are available produces further evidence in support of the constraints and trade-offs posed by the trilemma limiting strategic value. In contrast, the analysis uncovers extensive evidence that traditional subversive operations contributed both to clear and measurable advantages on the battlefield, the achievement of invasion objectives, and to the territorial expansion overall. This contrast further cements the superior effectiveness of traditional subversion in producing more intense effects—and its resulting comparatively greater strategic value.

Kremlin Perception and Goals

Russia's subversive campaigns and hybrid war since 2014 had failed. As in Czechoslovakia, the Kremlin thus faced two options: accept failure or escalate to still get what it wanted. It opted for the latter and commenced a full-scale invasion. This outcome attests to the paradox role of subversion as an alternative to force whose shortcomings may yet ultimately increase the likelihood of escalation. Whether subversion facilitated or rather forestalled the use of force remains an open question that cannot be conclusively answered until evidence of decision-making within the Kremlin becomes available. However, the currently available evidence suggests that subversion did ultimately make the use of force more likely. In the counterfactual scenario where subversion and covert aggression were (for whatever reason) not an option in 2014, Russia might have mounted a full-scale invasion right away in response to Yanukovych's downfall. Consequently, one could reasonably conclude that subversion merely delayed, rather than contributed to, this eventual outcome. However, although the subversive operations examined during the hybrid war phase did not contribute to military operations, evidence discussed in this chapter indicates a more direct contribution to the outbreak of war. Russia's initial invasion aim of a "decapitation strike" built on slanted intelligence provided by its subversive assets within Ukraine.

Moreover, the broad subversion of Ukraine's security services and local government evidently played a role in Russia's war plans of a lightning offensive by facilitating the takeover of territory without protracted fighting. Both efforts likely, or at least plausibly, contributed to the decision in favor of using force by making the prospects of Russia's lightning decapitation strike strategy appear rosier.

Not only the apparent rationale behind the decision to intervene but also the course of the invasion show key parallels to Czechoslovakia. As in 1968, Moscow's invasion plan falsely anticipated broad public support, which did not materialize.[6] In contrast to Czechoslovakia, however, the Ukrainian armed forces and (volunteer) territorial defense forces resisted the invasion, which ground to a halt following initial rapid advances during the first few days and has seen Russia on the backfoot since.[7] There are currently no sources providing insights into Kremlin decision-making in the runup to the war; hence, only public statements offer evidence of leaders' perception. Available evidence about Russia's war plans and public statements by Kremlin leaders suggests they received slanted intelligence painting an unrealistically rosy picture of Ukrainian support for the invaders—another parallel to the Czechoslovakian case.[8]

With Russia's escalation in means came an escalation in objectives as well. Rather than attempting to shift Ukraine's foreign policy, manipulate public opinion, and erode its power, Russia attempted no less than to subjugate Ukraine. Russian president Vladimir Putin hinted at this goal already in his February 24 televised speech announcing the "special military operation" against Ukraine. Its goals, Putin stated, were "de-nazification and de-militarization"[9]—in line with preceding propaganda and disinformation efforts railing against the "Kyiv junta" and its alleged crimes.[10] Despite these aims, initially the Kremlin did not officially pursue regime change. In April 2022, Russian foreign minister Sergej Lavrov stated, "Ukrainians should decide themselves how to live their lives."[11] Three months later, he stated the opposite, however, namely that Russia's key goal in Ukraine was to "free its people from its unacceptable regime."[12] Meanwhile, Russia has shown a clear goal of territorial expansion as well, officially annexing provinces it had occupied—in some cases only partially—in October 2022.[13]

In short, Russia has pursued two complementary goals: territorial expansion and regime change in Kyiv. To achieve these ends, as before, Russia has relied on a range of different means. The primary instrument is force, aiming to defeat Ukraine's forces on the battlefields. However, Russia has also deployed broad subversive efforts to complement and facilitate the use of force. The next section will evaluate their impact.

Economic and Psychological (Cyber) Warfare: Defacements, Wipers, and Distributed Denial of Service

As Russian troops massed along Ukraine's borders, the first signs of an accompanying psychological and economic warfare campaign targeting Ukraine appeared. In January and February 2022, a series of website "defacements" with threatening messages were followed by disruptive wiper malware as well as distributed denial-of-service (DDoS) attacks. While there is (unsurprisingly) no tangible evidence from inside Russian intelligence services or Kremlin decision-making establishing these incidents as part of an orchestrated campaign, analysts have since uncovered growing evidence linking individual operations to Russian-sponsored actors. The means employed and the effects pursued correspond to a subversive "erosion" strategy, aiming to sow fear and confusion among Ukraine's population, causing economic dislocation and disrupting its government.

On January 14, visitors to the websites of many Ukrainian government agencies—seventy in total—were confronted with an unsettling message stating in Ukrainian, Russian, and Polish that "all their personal data has been uploaded" and warning them to "be afraid and expect worse."[14] Media reports called this a "massive cyber-attack."[15] However, as Ukraine's Computer Emergency Response Team (CERT-UA) soon clarified, no government data was affected, nor was there any leakage of personal data.[16] The hackers had gained access to website content management systems, but not to the servers involved—nor to the government's networks itself. While Ukraine's Foreign Ministry initially attributed this operation to Russia, subsequent investigations linked it to a Belarusian hacking group christened "UNC1151" by cybersecurity firm Mandiant, with possible links to Russian intelligence.[17]

Unfortunately, there is not enough data to fully assess operational challenges and constraints. Yet what is known points to a relatively simple, ad hoc operation. Subsequent analyses revealed that rather than coordinating the compromise of each of the seventy government websites affected—which would be difficult—the hackers had apparently exploited a vulnerability in a popular content management system called October CMS, as well as a

Ukrainian content management service, allowing them to gain instant access to all of the affected sites.[18] How they compromised this service and how long it took precisely are unknown. However, the evidence available on wiper software involved in this operation, discussed just below, indicates rather short preparation. Available evidence thus suggests this operation pursued a low-intensity effect and medium to high speed and maintained sufficient control over targets to achieve that effect, namely the defacement.

Yet it had no measurable impact on Ukrainian morale or the functioning of society. There were no reports of panicking Ukrainians flooding government agencies with emails and calls about their alleged loss of personal data. Rather, once the compromises became apparent, victims swiftly restored their websites while cybersecurity firms analyzed the methods used by the hackers and published them online, making clear both the falsehood of their claims and their association with a close Russian ally. Consequently, apart from a symbolic act of aggression against the government, this operation did not produce any measurable strategic value. While incomplete evidence prevents a full analysis of how the constraints of the trilemma contributed to this outcome, the very low intensity of effects and the high speed and control they allowed are at least in line with predictions.

Interestingly, later analyses showed these defacements involved destructive malware that attempted but failed to disrupt government servers. In a post on January 26, 2022, CERT-UA noted that contrary to initial claims that no data had been affected at the government agencies whose websites were defaced, "in some cases . . . attackers encrypted or deleted data."[19] To that end, it employed two individual malware programs, dubbed BootPatch and WhisperKill. Microsoft has since dubbed this operation WhisperGate.[20]

BootPatch overwrote the master boot record of hard drives, making recovery impossible, while WhisperKill overwrote any data with random values to further prevent recovery.[21] In an interesting parallel to NotPetya, this malware also displayed a fake ransom note, suggesting data could be recovered in return for payment—when in fact the malware involved was specifically designed to prevent recovery. Furthermore, Ukraine's State Service of Special Communications and Information Protection (SSSCIP) noted an apparent attempt to pin this operation on Ukraine. The ransom note displayed the national symbol of Ukraine, a trident, while the WhisperKill malware showed significant similarities to a publicly available ransomware program called WhiteBlackCrypt, previously used in a provocative and extortionist campaign against Russian targets.[22] In addition, there is evidence of an ongoing disinformation campaign to actively pin this operation on Ukrainian government agencies. The SSSCIP found a Telegram user under the alias "TomHunter" who, without evidence, claimed WhisperGate was run by Ukrainian intelligence and armed forces.[23]

Contrary to initial analyses of the website defacements, the WhisperGate operation that was linked to it thus pursued medium-intensity effects, namely data destruction. Accordingly, as one would expect, it thus took considerable time to prepare. The route to exploitation remains unclear, but evidence uncovered by Cisco Talos researchers indicates the hackers had access to target systems for months.[24] Meanwhile, they also mounted a disinformation operation aiming to falsely pin this operation on a Ukrainian military unit through posts on pro-Russian blogs and Telegram channels.[25] Significantly, the earliest of these posts appeared nine months before the WhisperGate operation delivered its destructive effect—hence at least the planning stage, and likely the development stage for the actual malware deployment, had already commenced. Considering the similarities between the techniques used in this operation and NotPetya, which required six months of preparation, such a timeline would be in line with expectations as well. WhisperGate shared not only the mechanism of irreversibly encrypting data and showing a false ransom note but also likely a similar means of exploitation, namely a supply chain compromise—that is, a compromise of a software or service used by the ultimate targets, in this case likely the OctoberCMS service.[26]

Yet in contrast to NotPetya, WhisperGate did not produce mass disruption or damage. There is no evidence indicating any significant impact on Ukraine's economy or the functioning of its government. Victor Zhora, SSSCIP deputy head, explained that their investigation showed this wiper was "intended to have an impact, but propagation was not as wide" as it only affected a "very limited number of PCs."[27]

Why WhisperGate's scale and impact remained limited remains unclear since neither the means of exploitation used nor how the hackers spread the malware is known. From what is known, there are two likely, and possibly complementary, explanations: a lack of skill, and efforts to control the spread. The (speculative) supply-chain-spreading mechanisms the hackers relied upon would have only provided access to a limited number of systems—in case of the OctoberCMS content management solution likely involved, these would only have been the systems used to manage content on the seventy-odd government websites targeted. Since there are no indications this malware caused government disruptions, it evidently did not spread within networks. Accordingly, contrary to NotPetya, which proliferated automatically, the hackers behind WhisperGate likely manually compromised individual OctoberCMS customers.[28] Perhaps they did so intentionally to keep the disruptions highly targeted and control the spread. This manual exploitation and infiltration mechanism would also explain the relatively long preparation time, taking (probably) 50% longer than NotPetya. In this scenario, similar to BadRabbit, efforts to control the malware's spread both extended the development time to produce a given effect type, namely data destruction, and reduced its relative scale.

Yet WhisperGate was (almost certainly) carried out by a different hacking group, and this group evidently lacked Sandworm's skills. While multiple forensic analyses underline similarities to NotPetya, there is consensus that WhisperGate is the work of a different group. And technical analyses underline that WhisperGate was significantly less advanced than NotPetya. CrowdStrike's analysis of the BootPatch component of WhisperGate highlighted that it is similar to NotPetya but "less sophisticated,"[29] while Secureworks underlines that "NotPetya was delivered indiscriminately via a more sophisticated supply chain attack."[30] Considering this situation, the hackers were perhaps simply unable to spread further in the time they had. Thus far, the operation has not been attributed to a specific actor. Possibly, it is the work of the same Belarusian actor behind the website defacements.

While WhisperGate's relative simplicity likely prevented a larger impact, the same is not the case for a very basic cyber operation targeting Ukraine subsequently. On February 15, a large DDoS attack—the biggest to hit Ukraine to date—targeted government institutions and banks. The US and UK governments have since attributed it to the Russian intelligence service GRU.[31] DDoS attacks are among the least complex types of cyber operations. Rather than exploiting systems, they simply overload target systems with fake requests that render them unresponsive to legitimate users (hence the "denial of service"). An analogy would be organizing a large flash mob at a government office, with people queueing with fake requests, preventing those with actual requests from getting served. To maximize scale, such attacks can be carried out from multiple systems at once, hence the "distributed" part. At first glance, this may not look like subversion but rather coercion since the target system is overpowered rather than exploited. However, there are two key subversive dimensions. First, this operation leveraged what is known as a "botnet," meaning a set of previously compromised computer systems. By compromising these systems with malware, in this case the Mirai strain,[32] hacking groups clandestinely repurpose them into "attack tools" without alerting users to that fact. To get there, the hackers of course first need to find a vulnerability that allows exploiting and manipulating these systems. The attack itself in turn exploits the openness of systems to respond to user requests from the general Internet to overload them.

Apart from the general mass requests sent, this operation specifically targeted the domain name servers (DNSs) of the gov.ua space, meaning all government websites whose domain ended with "gov.ua" were affected.[33] On top of that, the hackers sent SMS messages to Ukrainian citizens—at unknown scale—suggesting that ATMs were running out of money in an evident attempt to create a bank run.[34] The operation did succeed in disrupting targeted systems, and ATM operation at affected banks, for several hours.[35] Ukrainian media also reported on it prominently, with a sense of danger and urgency. The portal TSN, for example, put out a headline about "the largest cyberattack in Ukraine's history" and asserted it cost Ukraine "millions of dollars."[36] Reporting by Epravda quoted Ukraine's minister of digital transformation, Mykhailo Fedorov, stating the same.[37] While emphasizing the attack's scale (which, in international comparison, is rather moderate[38]), the same reporting also underlines a key point, however: the attack did not trigger panic and confusion among Ukrainians. Rather, people remained calm, and service was restored swiftly.[39] Consequently, the impact remained limited to monetary losses due to the outages. They were considerable for the individual organizations involved yet did not rise to a level of strategic significance comparable to NotPetya.

This operation pursued a low-intensity effect, namely temporary overload, but at large scale, while maintaining control over effects (the targeting of specific entities). Nonetheless, it proceeded very swiftly. Research by Cado Security indicates that the hackers compromised the systems with the botnet only days before the actual attack.[40] Moreover, the malware involved, a variation of the Mirai malware called Katana, is freely available online; hence, it required no development time whatsoever.[41] This operation proceeded fast, maintained control, and yet produced a measurable, albeit strategically insignificant, impact. This outcome suggests that DDoS attacks, due to their relative simplicity, may be relatively more efficient than more advanced cyber operations. However, and in line with the theory, their effects are of very low intensity and, with appropriate preventative measures, can be mitigated relatively easily.[42]

Contrary to "cyber onslaught" predictions, the cyber operations preceding the invasion thus only achieved minimal impact. Perhaps Russia had been holding back its most powerful capabilities until further escalation, as many commentators had suggested previously.[43] If so, the ideal time to sow panic among the population and cripple Ukraine's government was the moment of invasion itself—hampering Ukraine's ability to respond and resist the aggression.

And indeed, several cyber operations hit Ukraine around the invasion's start in the early hours of February 24. Yet they failed to make a mark, underlining the limitations of cyber operations.

The first operation involved another DDoS attack against government websites and banks, replicating the February 15 attack.[44] There are no reports indicating any significant impact. Rather, having learned from the previous operation, victims mitigated it faster and minimized the disruptions.[45] Around the same time, another destructive wiper activated across several hundred systems, according to ESET.[46] This malware, since christened "HermeticWiper" by SentinelOne researcher Juan Andres Guerrero-Saade,[47] used the same mechanism as WhisperGate, overwriting the master boot record of hard drives to effectively destroy data on them. There is no evidence it impacted the functioning of government, and there are no reports of any significant disruptions. It is still not clear who is behind this operation, but forensic evidence provides some clues about its development time. ESET shows the malware involved was compiled on December 28, that is, two months earlier.[48] Accordingly, it also took relatively little time to develop.

The first steps date back almost nine months. This operation used a false digital certificate to install itself as a driver in Windows—making it look like legitimate software—which was registered on April 21, 2021.[49] However, as Guerrero-Saade explained to me later, hacking groups often register such certificates for general-purpose use when they have the opportunity, then use them only when they are needed—and otherwise saw "no indication this would have taken very long to develop."[50] Development thus likely took little more than three to four months, which is still relatively fast.

HermeticWiper thus proceeded faster than WhisperGate, pursued somewhat more intense effects, and apparently maintained control over its spread. HermeticWiper also aimed at the same effect type, namely disruption of government and economic damage, but at greater scale—rather than dozens, it compromised hundreds of systems. This greater scale was likely the result of its ability to spread automatically within local networks[51]—albeit with significant limitations compared to NotPetya.[52] Yet it affected targets not only within Ukraine but also in Latvia and Lithuania in what initial analyses considered collateral damage.[53] Kim Zetter's follow-up reporting revealed, however, that victims in Latvia and Lithuania were in fact contractors of the Ukrainian government, underlining the "extremely targeted" nature of this operation.[54] Yet despite its greater scale, HermeticWiper does not seem to have caused any significant impact. This is puzzling, considering Juan Andres Guerrero-Saade's assessment that "this isn't a bullshit wiper like the last time [referring to WhisperGate]. This thing is meant to be devastating."[55]

Its lack of impact is less surprising, however, considering that HermeticWiper's scale of infections was roughly similar to BadRabbit, which also remained strategically irrelevant. Furthermore, according to subsequent research, the systems affected likely belonged to only five different organizations overall.[56] Hence, HermeticWiper underlines how efforts to control the scale of effects tend to reduce intensity and, consequently, strategic value. This outcome, parallel to BadRabbit, is thus in line with the theory.

On the same day that HermeticWiper was launched, another string of website defacements hit the same websites as on January 14 with the same message.[57] Unsurprisingly, considering the previous defacement wave's lack of impact, it barely registered in the media.[58] Overall, there are no signs indicating the operation discussed thus far caused confusion and fear even among immediate victims—bar the population at large.

Ukraine's minister of digital transformation Mykhail Fedorova put out a statement via Telegram on February 24 likely referring to HermeticWiper and the DDoS attacks, noting that, "We have been protecting cyberspace all night. Attacks on all basic information resources took place and continue without stops. So far everything is stable. All teams are in place. We are keeping calm."[59]

Of course, Ukraine's government may have an interest to downplay the impact, so this statement is to be taken with a grain of salt. Nonetheless, it is aligned with the absence of any evidence to the contrary.

The following day another wiper hit Ukrainian government systems—and again failed to leave a mark. This IsaacWiper also aimed to destroy data (but used a less advanced and less efficient mechanism of overwriting data with random numbers) and also affected several hundred systems.[60] As with HermeticWiper, there is no evidence indicating any significant impact on government operation, and no local media reporting in Ukraine mentioned the attack. ESET analysis, on the other hand, provides further evidence of the relative trade-offs in cyber operations. IsaacWiper required significantly less development time than HermeticWiper, only four months based on forensic evidence found by ESET.[61] Less time, however, resulted in less capable means of exploitation and manipulation. IsaacWiper, forensic analysts highlighted, was "way less sophisticated" than HermeticWiper.[62] Accordingly, while pursuing effects of similar intensity and scale as HermeticWiper, this operation apparently fell short in producing them. ESET's report notes a new version appearing on February 25 with debug logs, indicating that "the attackers were unable to wipe some of the targeted machines and added log messages to understand what was happening."[63] This circumstantial evidence suggests the hackers failed to produce the desired effects because they did not know the target systems well enough. As predicted, high speed and medium intensity came at the cost of control.

Despite the underwhelming record of preceding wipers, yet another appeared shortly after, on March 13.[64] Contrary to its predecessors, this CaddyWiper malware finally showed clear fingerprints of a known group: Sandworm.[65] It also had no code similarities with preceding wipers, suggesting Sandworm was not involved in the latter.[66] Concerning its mechanisms, effects, and impact, however, CaddyWiper was very similar to its earlier cousins. It destroyed data by corrupting hard drives, its spread was limited in scale, and it achieved no measurable strategic impact. ESET states that CaddyWiper affected "a few dozen systems in a limited number of organizations."[67] It is unclear how many of these were disrupted by the wiper before victims could neutralize it. Even in case all victims suffered data losses, however, its scale is still miniscule compared to an operation like NotPetya. Development time is also unclear since the malware was compiled on the same day it was deployed, yet its proliferation mechanism (manual, by exploiting a Windows network feature called Group Policy Objects) suggested the hackers had previous access to target systems.[68]

This manual mechanism suggests efforts to control spread. In line with that conclusion, ESET noted that the wiper would not activate on domain controllers in an apparent effort to make sure the hackers could continue their destructive operation within networks beyond these domain controllers.[69] Recall that in the 2015 Starlight Media operation, Sandworm had made the mistake of wiping domain controllers and consequently lost access to the target network—here the hackers showed clear signs of having learned from this mistake. While speed is unknown, Sandworm's efforts to control effects thus came with low intensity (and very low scale) of effects.

Like its predecessors, there is no evidence CaddyWiper measurably affected Ukraine's government. No Ukrainian media reporting mentions it. The same applies to subsequent deployments of CaddyWiper. According to research by Google's Threat Analysis Group, Sandworm deployed CaddyWiper nine additional times afterward against different targets.[70] This activity, combined with other strains of destructive malware observed, the researchers conclude, was "likely not as impactful as previous Russian cyberattacks in Ukraine."[71]

Similarly, other destructive malware disguised as ransomware that Sandworm used against organizations in Ukraine and its allies in October and November 2022 fell short of leaving a mark. The malware Prestige and RansomBoggs encrypted data and demanded a ransom payment—although curiously without stating an amount. Prestige focused on logistics and transportation firms in Ukraine as well as in Poland, suggesting an effort to hamper supply lines for Ukraine, while RansomBoggs aimed at unspecified organizations in Ukraine.[72] Ukrainian media reporting only cites cybersecurity firms and does not mention any impact on affected organizations.[73] As is the case with preceding data-destroying operations, these malware strains thus possibly caused some disruption at individual organizations, yet no evidence indicates any measurable impact on Ukraine's economy, government, or public life.

To sum up, rather than new and more powerful capabilities, the wake of the invasion saw Russian actors leverage the same techniques, and sometimes even the same tools, against the same targets in Ukraine as in preceding weeks. Considering the strategic context, this turn of events is not surprising as Russia had put considerable effort into eroding Ukrainian strength through cyber means and subversion for multiple years—and failed. Why hold back more powerful capabilities until the invasion, which only became necessary (from Moscow's perspective) because the hybrid war strategy since 2014 had fallen short? Regardless of strategic intent, and unsurprisingly, with victims having learned from previous actions, the impact of these operations was even less pronounced than their predecessors. Overall, they offered little strategic value. When I interviewed the SSSCIP's Victor Zhora in January 2023, he conceded that "compromises of individual databases and leaks of data happen, of course. You can see it on Telegram channels of Russian hackers where they share the data."[74] Yet these primarily concerned private sector targets, whereas government databases remained largely functional. Consequently, Zhora stressed, "after more than one year of cyber aggression, nothing very serious happened to government databases."[75]

Preliminary findings thus support the theory. Operations that formed part of the economic and psychological warfare campaign proceeded relatively fast while attempting to control targeting and avoiding runaway effects. In the words of security researcher Guerrero-Saade, these operations were "very fast, hodgepodge, and not sophisticated."[76] As the theory predicts, prioritizing speed and control tends to lower the intensity of effects—and that is evident here. Yet at least one wiper, WhisperGate, took more time than the devastating NotPetya worm of 2017. Plausibly, its manual proliferation mechanism and efforts to control its spread explain the increased development time. Yet considering WhisperGate's relative simplicity, the hacking group involved may have also simply lacked the skills required to move faster. Considering this possibility highlights the potential relevance of another variable outside the scope of the theory that is difficult to measure: there is no systematic framework to rank the skills of hacking groups, and the term "sophisticated cyber-attack" that private sector reports often use has little meaning except for sounding exciting.[77] Comparisons between unattributed and attributed operations concerning the trade-offs between speed, intensity, and control must thus remain preliminary—and suggest a potential alternative explanation for some of the findings, which I will discuss in the chapter conclusion in more detail.

The Clowns Fail to Take Over—A Botched Coup

As Russian troops crossed the border, a small detachment of commandos parachuted directly into Kyiv. Their apparent objective: assassinating president Zelenskiy. In a parallel to Czechoslovakia, Russian intelligence services had planned an operation to topple Zelenskiy's government at the moment of the invasion. However, rather than an internal coup from within, this plan foresaw a "decapitation" by force followed by the installation of a puppet regime. It failed.

Washington Post journalists Greg Miller and Catherine Belton provide a fascinating account of this plan based on records of the Russian intelligence service FSB.[78] It shows not only that the FSB provided the Kremlin with slanted intelligence overstating public support for Russia—just like in Czechoslovakia—but also that it had cultivated a network of agents within Ukraine's security services in the months preceding the invasion.[79] Yet the individuals involved were of questionable quality. According to one anonymous source, the Kremlin relied on "clowns" who "told the leadership what they wanted to hear."[80] Perhaps that is why the Kremlin ultimately deemed this network insufficient to take control of Ukraine and instead sent assassins after Zelenskiy.[81] Not only the assassins came from outside Ukraine, however, but also the members of the puppet regime Moscow aimed to install. In an unusual move, the United Kingdom's Foreign Office published intelligence findings on January 22, 2022, indicating that the "Russian Government is looking to install a pro-Russian leader in Kyiv as it considers whether to invade and occupy Ukraine" and specifying that "former Ukrainian MP Yevhen Murayev is being considered as a potential candidate."[82] The statement named four additional former Ukrainian politicians implicated in the scheme: Serhiy Arbuzov, Andriy Kluyev, Vladimir Sivkovich, and Mykola Azarov.[83] Importantly, they all lived in exile, having escaped Ukraine when Yanukovych's government collapsed in 2014. This decapitation plan collapsed with the failure of Russia's military to take control of Kyiv—forcing some FSB assets and agents to stop and turn around at the outskirts of Kyiv.[84]

This coup attempt was not subversive but rather involved brute force. Consequently, it is beyond the scope of the theory. However, the choice in favor of brute force and the key components of this plan provide circumstantial evidence in support of the limitations of subversion the theory predicts. With only a few months of preparation (at least according to the files obtained by the *Washington Post* journalists), the FSB was evidently not confident the network of agents it had developed in Ukraine could take over control from within. The choice of exiled politicians to lead the puppet government further attests to this limitation—and reflects the failures of the preceding subversive operations. The members of the proposed puppet regime were all assets who had to flee with its collapse in 2014. Recall that the Kremlin had prioritized the establishment of powerful subversive shadow forces in Ukraine, as stated in the "Complex of Measures" discussed in the preceding chapter. Evidently, these shadow forces were insufficient to attempt an internal takeover.

Subversion in the Service of Force

Moscow's shadow forces made important contributions to the use of force, however. Russian-sponsored subversive operations disrupted a key communication system used by Ukraine's army, made possible the takeover of the

Chernobyl nuclear plant early in the invasion, and facilitated the takeover of regions as well as identifying targets. Compared to the erosion campaign, this use of subversion as a "force multiplier" provided significant strategic value.

Early in the morning on February 24, one hour before Russian troops started streaming across Ukraine's borders, customers of Viasat's KA-SAT satellite internet service suddenly lost connectivity.[85] Significantly, one of these customers was Ukraine's military, for which this outage meant a "huge loss in communications" according to Victor Zhora from the SSSCIP.[86] Moreover, it soon became evident that a cyber operation was responsible.[87] Subsequent analysis has produced "non-trivial" forensic evidence linking this operation to Sandworm.[88] Since it disabled military communications and evidently succeeded, initial reactions suggested a significant strategic advantage. For example, Dmitry Alperovitch (founder of the cybersecurity firm CrowdStrike) suggested this was "perhaps the most strategically impactful cyber operation in wartime history."[89] However, Victor Zhora clarified later that the operation had no impact on military operations because of the existence of alternative, fallback communication channels.[90] Accordingly, when I interviewed him on January 26, 2023, Zhora underlined that the Viasat disruption had a "huge impact on infrastructure, but not on military coordination because satellite communication was a backup channel."[91]

Of course, Ukrainian officials might have an interest in downplaying communication problems. And, in fact, some reports suggest significant communication breakdown at the start of the invasion. A Ukrainian military officer stated that "military communications were completely paralyzed" in the first hours of the invasion.[92] More specifically, the report notes that satellite communications were affected as well but cites Russian "jamming," rather than cyber-attacks, as the cause.[93] Hence, circumstantial evidence suggests communications outages impacted some military operations.

To what extent the KA-SAT disruption contributed to these problems, however, is not clear—especially considering broad jamming efforts. It is certainly plausible the outage hampered coordination, especially in the initial rush to withstand the invasion. Accordingly, Jason Bateman from the Carnegie Endowment concluded that "the combination of Moscow's traditional electronic warfare and the Viasat hack seemed to give Russian forces an edge in many early engagements."[94] While tactical advantages are highly plausible, however, there is no evidence that communications problems, regardless of their specific cause, made an overall significant strategic difference. On the contrary, one month after the invasion, US Secretary of Defense

John Kirby stated in an interview that, despite jamming efforts, "Ukrainians still have good command and control over their forces in the field in ways that the Russians actually don't have."[95] In short, most available evidence indicates the KA-SAT operation did not provide significant strategic value.

The course of conflict aligns with this assessment as well. Russia already had such an overwhelming advantage in materiel that some predicted the war would be over "within days."[96] Considering that even broad jamming of Ukrainian military communications failed to prevent Ukrainian forces from mounting a resistance far more effective than most analysts had expected, even if this cyber operation contributed to communications losses, its impact would have been at the very best marginal and almost certainly insignificant.

The KA-SAT disruption thus most likely failed to impact its intended target yet produced significant collateral damage. It affected tens of thousands of the satellite service's customers across Europe. Among them was wind turbine operator Enercon, who lost connectivity to 5,800 of its turbines in Germany.[97] To be clear, the turbines continued to work normally; only the monitoring software was disrupted—meaning in practice the company had to "send a farmer out to look at the turbines and report back: 'Yep, they're still working.'"[98] Despite its relatively minor impact, this operation still produced considerable costs by corrupting firmware and rendering modems unusable. While Viasat's own press release suggested a factory reset could restore functionality,[99] a SentinelOne analysis questioned this assessment, noting replacement may be necessary.[100] Accordingly, subsequent reporting showed Enercon rushing to procure satellite modems in bulk.[101] Considering that a standard KA-SAT Surfbeam modem costs 269 euros,[102] total replacement costs may have been upward of 1 million euros. Viasat later confirmed it had to replace 30,000 modems.[103]

Its European customers were clearly not a relevant target at that stage (no sanctions had been imposed on Russia yet), and these pan-European disruptions were likely contrary to Russian interests. Not only did they trigger broad international attention by cybersecurity professionals who picked apart Russia's malware for all the world to see, but also they fostered a sense of unity among the Western alliance. The latter is illustrated by the North Atlantic Treaty Organization's (NATO) Secretary-General, Jens Stoltenberg, going as far as citing this case when discussing a potential scenario where cyber operations could trigger the body's collective defense clause (Article 5 of the NATO Charter).[104]

This operation's collateral damage attests to the growing risk of control loss that comes with increased intensity of effects—especially under tight timelines. The malware involved, now known as AcidRain, not only disabled physical hardware but also spread automatically across an entire class of devices used by an entire user population.[105] SentinelOne's analysis suggests the wiper involved leveraged a supply chain proliferation mechanism, likely using the management mechanism for the KA-SAT service to deploy a malicious update to affected devices.[106] Hence, both the scope and scale of effects were significantly greater than the preceding wipers. Consequently, AcidRain likely both required more development time and had a higher chance to run out of control.

Development time remains unclear since how the hackers got into Viasat's network remains uncertain. Ruben Santamarta, an independent security researcher, suggested the most likely vector for initial exploitation was an unpatched virtual private network (VPN) device run by Skylogic, an Italian firm administering the KA-SAT service.[107] Importantly, in 2021 a cyber operation targeted the VPN provider Fortinet also used by Skylogic—and the hackers behind it published access credentials for 87,000 VPN devices that made them vulnerable to exploitation.[108] Possibly, this operation thus commenced by exploiting an unpatched Fortinet VPN appliance, then using this initial access to spread within the Viasat network. The timeline remains incomplete, but if this most plausible scenario of initial infiltration to date holds true, it will have likely taken at least a year of preparation.[109]

Despite the added time, just as happened with the last self-spreading virus, NotPetya, the hackers lost control—or perhaps simply had no idea what the network they disrupted looked like. As Guerrero-Saade explained to me, the AcidRain malware is a "strange hybrid" consisting of around 60% of the robust code base of VPN Filter, a well-established malware, with an added 40% of new code stacked on top that is "not as good, not as quality-controlled."[110] Moreover, its design suggests the hackers did not know the specifics of the modems they ultimately targeted. Rather, AcidRain is a "brute force wiper" designed to corrupt any embedded Linux operating system, rather than its specific implementation in KA-SAT modems. This design, Guerrero-Saade highlighted, indicates the hackers had access to neither the modems nor the firmware involved, raising the bigger question—as in the NotPetya operation—of "whether they had any granular control within KA-SAT, if they actually knew what they were hitting."[111]

Circumstantial evidence thus aligns with the predictions of the theory. The KA-SAT operation pursued more intense effects and likely required more time than preceding wipers. It maximized intensity and spread uncontrollably, producing collateral damage. Moreover, while it produced at best very limited strategically relevant impact, and most likely none at all, against its intended target, the collateral damage against unintended targets triggered reactions contrary to Russia's interests. Hence, similar to NotPetya, it is questionable whether this operation produced a net strategic gain for Russia. In line with this conclusion, Jason Bateman's comprehensive analysis finds that cyber operations complementing military efforts fell short of providing significant military utility for Russia.[112]

In contrast, traditional subversion provided measurable and significant strategic value. The previous section alluded to Russia's shadow forces, subversive agents penetrating Ukraine's security services and government. While these shadow forces had insufficient influence to attempt an internal coup as in Czechoslovakia, they played an important role in facilitating the invasion. In some instances, they even enabled Russia to achieve objectives it would otherwise not have achieved without suffering greater costs. Overall, the Kremlin's subversive agents produced two main effect types: intelligence collection, especially on military targets, and facilitating the takeover of regions and facilities.

Similar to KGB illegals in Czechoslovakia, most Russian agents focused on intelligence collection. They targeted Ukraine's security services, government, and military. Captured agents provide a snapshot of some of these activities, and thus a hint of the overall campaign. In August 2022, Ukraine's intelligence service exposed an employee of Ukraine's parliament as a Russian asset tasked with gathering intelligence about visits by foreign delegations.[113] The individual involved resigned at the start of the invasion, attempting to gain employment at a "strategically important facility" but failing a background check as Ukrainian intelligence uncovered their collaboration with Russia—and then willingly surrendered.[114] It is not clear how long the operation took, but the SBU's terse statement suggests its duration fell within the "several months" of subversive efforts documented above.

Apart from this example, most intelligence collection focused on Ukraine's military. For example, in August 2022 the SBU discovered and arrested members of an FSB-sponsored agent network headed by an individual residing in Odessa nicknamed "the Professor."[115] Their primary task was providing targeting information on "decision-making centers and strategic objects of critical infrastructure" to their Russian handlers in exchange for payment.[116] The SBU caught the Professor doing precisely this, namely conducting reconnaissance around Odessa's military administration.[117] While such intelligence likely helped Russian forces, there is no evidence indicating what specific outcomes it enabled. Such information is available for another similar case, however, involving eight individuals the SBU captured in the Mykolaiv region in July 2022. These individuals transmitted locations of infrastructure and Ukrainian military units, which Russian subsequently attacked with missiles and artillery.[118] Meanwhile, no evidence has emerged of Russian cyber operations providing similar reconnaissance advantages—or even attempting to do so. Rather, Russian forces have primarily relied on drones, radar, electronic warfare, and acoustic reconnaissance to help artillery targeting.[119]

Some Russian agent networks also conducted active measures, however. One of the earliest examples involves a Ukrainian man caught by the SBU in May 2022 passing on intelligence and planning unspecified "subversive activities" in the Lviv region in western Ukraine.[120] Unfortunately, no further details are currently known. A month later, Ukrainian intelligence neutralized a far larger-scale operation, however. Andriy Derkach, a member of Ukraine's parliament since 1998—who, unsuspiciously, had studied at the KGB School in Moscow—had fostered a network of agents to help invading forces. Specifically, Derkach set up private security firms that were supposed to facilitate the takeover of Ukrainian cities, hand over equipment to Russian troops, and "sit on armor with Russian flags" to enable a "peaceful entry into the cities."[121] This subversive network's scale is unclear, but the GRU's investment indicates it was significant: the SBU reports "every few months" the GRU sent Derkach payments of around US$3 to 4 million.[122] How many cities were involved is also unclear. However, anecdotal evidence from Derkach's electoral district shows that at least in some cities local agents attempted to implement these plans. For example, in August 2022 Ukrainian intelligence arrested a local politician who had destroyed defensive structures in the city of Sumy and aimed to help "hand over" the city to invaders.[123] Multiple other locals were arrested in various cities for aiding the enemy, providing weapons, food, and housing.[124] Hence, this operation's scale and supporting anecdotal evidence make it both plausible and likely that it directly contributed to the capture of territory.

Moreover, its long duration and Derkach's influential position enabled a range of other effects. According to the SBU, Derkach worked for the GRU since 2016,[125] giving him five years to manipulate policy through votes. To give one example, in January 2014 Derkach voted in favor of draconian measures to restrict freedom of expression. Significantly, this law enabled an escalation of violence against Euromaidan protesters—culminating in the massacre of protestors in February 2014 that, according to Ukrainian law enforcement, bore the footprint of Russian intelligence.[126]

In short, this operation pursued increasingly intense effects—from manipulating government policy to facilitating the takeover of territory. While Johnson's escalation ladder does not include this specific scenario, it corresponds most closely to a coup d'etat, "involving the intelligence service in the overthrow of a foreign adversary" with "minimal intended bloodshed," near the top of the ladder on rung thirty-five of thirty-eight.[127] The fact that the GRU plan for the invasion also foresaw special forces deployment to Kyiv to "capture the Government Quarter and gather a crowd in the Verkhovna Rada that would vote for the creation of a new government" further underlines the parallels to this effect type.[128] As the theory would predict, this high effect intensity required significant time to prepare and involved high risks of control loss. The five years of preparation involved and the eventual capture of Derkach confirm these predictions. The types of effects this operation produced plausibly enabled significant contributions toward Russian strategic goals. Unfortunately, however, there is still too little evidence to conclusively assess its strategic value.

While the SBU ultimately intervened and started legal proceedings against Derkach, it is unclear whether the intensification of effects pursued by the subversive efforts he oversaw contributed to this discovery and neutralization—as the theory would predict. Interestingly, the SBU's press release suggests it had long been monitoring Derkach's efforts. Perhaps it assessed that the advantages of monitoring adversary activity outweighed the advantages of neutralizing it. There is a more sinister explanation though: the SBU's own leadership may have hampered efforts to neutralize Russian subversion. In fact, two months after Derkach's arrest, the SBU's very own director was implicated as part of a major Russian subversive operation.

On July 17, 2022, Ukrainian president Volodymyr Zelenskiy fired SBU head Ivan Bakanov and Ukraine's prosecutor general Irina Venediktova for collaboration with Russian intelligence and building a network of subversive agents.[129] Zelenskiy later specified that sixty agents close to Bakanov or Venediktova remained in occupied territories and "worked for the enemy."[130] Very likely, that meant facilitating the takeover of territory. Accordingly, one of Bakanov's close confidants, Brigadier General Serhiy Kryvoruchko, who headed the SBU department in Kherson, was stripped of his rank in April 2022 for treason.[131] However, as in Derkach's case, there is little systematic evidence of the operation's impact. Perhaps the most tangible outcome is the lack of action the SBU took against enemy agents within its ranks over the preceding years. The problem of subversion within its own ranks, as the previous chapter highlighted, was neither new nor recent. Yet the SBU made few arrests prior to Bakanov's removal. In contrast, under his successor, the SBU continued to discover large numbers of Russian agents not only within its ranks but also across Ukraine's government and military agencies—leading to 360 additional arrests within the following three months.[132]

The reason Zelenskiy fired Bakanov was almost certainly his involvement in an operation that provided the most significant strategic value to Russia among all subversive operations to date: the takeover of the Chernobyl nuclear ruin. In the early hours of the invasion, Russian forces took over the site, a strategically important location en route to Kyiv (and a place to keep forces protected from Ukrainian artillery fire unless they were willing to risk release nuclear radiation), without a fight.[133] This casualty-free takeover, it later became clear, was the result of long-running subversive efforts.

Andriy Naumov, the former head of the state-owned Center for Organizational, Technical, and Information Management of the Exclusion Zone, which managed the site, was a close confidant of Bakanov.[134] In fact, Bakanov had appointed him personally to the position of head of internal security at the SBU, namely the person in charge of hunting down Russian agents within its ranks.[135] Yet Naumov himself was a Russian agent, explaining why the SBU did so little to eradicate infiltration of its ranks during his tenure. Naumov also made a key contribution to the Chernobyl takeover, however. Hours before Russia's invasion started, Naumov escaped Ukraine—only to be caught four months later at the border between Serbia and North Macedonia in a BMW loaded with 607,990 euros and US$124,924 in cash as well as two precious gems.[136] An SBU investigation later found that Naumov had passed on secrets about security arrangements in Chernobyl to Russia.[137] This intelligence would have been highly useful for Russian forces aiming to take over the facility. Even more useful, however, was having infiltrated the security forces at Chernobyl itself. Valentin Viter, head of security at the facility, played a key role in its apparent handover. As a Reuters investigation revealed, when Russia's invasion commenced, Viter advised the commander of the Ukrainian National Guard unit tasked with protecting Chernobyl to lay down arms and "spare your people."[138] Russian intelligence services had deployed additional subversive agents to Chernobyl in the preceding months to bribe officials and prepare a bloodless handover.[139] Evidently, these combined efforts succeeded.

This operation produced significant strategic value by achieving a highly intense effect—territorial conquest—without being discovered or otherwise losing control. As the theory predicts, with very high effect intensity and control, it took significant time to prepare. Considering that Naumov was part of Bakanov's subversive network, overall preparation took at least five years. More importantly, Bakanov very likely prevented discovery by putting his acolyte Naumov in charge of internal investigations at the SBU. This role of high-level infiltration of security services in hampering counterintelligence, thereby ensuring subversive success, adds an important interaction effect among iterative operations that goes beyond the framework the theory provides. It also offers a possible way out of the trilemma by lowering the discovery risks that more intense effects would usually bring.

While subverting institutions by bribing high-level corrupt officials brings many opportunities, it also bears many risks. Russian intelligence services' reliance on Viktor Medvedchuk, oligarch and close friend of Vladimir Putin, provides an illustrative example. In the preceding months, Russian intelligence services provided Medvedchuk with up to US$1 billion to prepare the invasion by paying people who were supposed to become local officials after the takeover, as well as building a subversive movement within Ukraine.[140] Yet as an investigation by Ukraine's Ministry of Defense following Medvedchuk's arrest on April 12 revealed, he had embezzled—that is, pocketed—almost all of these funds himself.[141]

Despite this loss and the failure of the overall "decapitation" strategy, as this section has shown, Russian-sponsored subversive operations produced key strategic gains. Contrary to media hype around a "cyberwar," traditional subversion offered far more significant strategic value than cyber operations. In line with the theory, traditional subversion enabled effect types beyond the reach of cyber operations, namely manipulating government policy from within and taking over physical control over territory.

Critical Infrastructure Sabotage: Sandworm Strikes Back

While most cyber operations discussed so far went after "low-hanging fruits," some aimed higher and pursued complex compromises of critical infrastructure. Two major operations stand out: first, an attempt to disrupt Ukraine's national Internet provider Ukrtelecom, and second, an attempt to disrupt the power grid. The former succeeded, while the latter failed. This section will examine the causes of their relative success and failure and consider the implications for the future of "strategic cyber strikes."

The most impactful cyber operation in the conflict to date caused a fifteen-hour disruption to Internet connectivity for customers of Ukrtelecom. Outage monitor NetBlock first reported the disruption on March 28 at 5:28 p.m. local time via Twitter.[142] Initially the cause was unclear, but around an hour later, at 6:25 p.m., Ukrtelecom had confirmed a cyber attack on its "core infrastructure," constituting the "most severe disruption since the start of invasion."[143] Mitigation took considerable time, despite Ukraine's SSSCIP getting involved. Three hours later, at 9:35 p.m., the SSSCIP reported that the attack was "neutralized," while resumption of services was "underway."[144] Yet at noon the following day—around nineteen hours after the first report—mitigation efforts were evidently still underway as Ukrtelecom reported 85% of connectivity was restored.[145] This cyber operation thus disrupted Internet service for a vast number of Ukrainians for a significant amount of time—up to an entire day for some. Clearly, this disruption had an impact on ordinary Ukrainians as well as businesses depending on online services and transactions.

The way the hacking group behind this operation—whose identity remains unknown to date—managed to cause this outage illustrates an underappreciated consequence of territorial occupation: the distinct cyber threats it poses for organizations with infrastructure in such territory. Initially, it remained unclear whether another DDoS attack or some more cunning exploitation of Ukrtelecom's network itself caused this outage.[146] Ukrtelecom had been the victim of DDoS attacks before, some of which succeeded—the largest one on March 10, 2022, disrupted service for around forty minutes.[147] The long duration of the March 28 outage, combined with its apparently partial nature, however, suggested something else was at work here. DDoS attacks typically affect an entire network, but provided appropriate expertise and infrastructure, they can be mitigated relatively easily by blocking off traffic from the "offending" IP addresses.

The SSSCIP confirmed a week later this disruption was the result of a special type of insider attack enabled by territorial conquest.[148] It proceeded in two stages. First, the hackers "launched [the operation] from the Ukrainian territory recently temporarily occupied" using credentials of a local employee to conduct reconnaissance of Ukrtelecom's network, attempting to compromise additional employee accounts.[149] What exactly this means remains unclear, but most likely the hackers leveraged physical access to Ukrtelecom equipment in occupied territory—perhaps blackmailing or bribing a former employee to give up credentials. Intriguingly, a similar thing later happened to Ukraine's natural gas giant Naftogaz, which hired the security firm Mandiant to protect its network in the wake of the invasion. Mandiant swept the company's network for compromises and eliminated all threats—yet compromises kept occurring nonetheless.[150] As it turns out, by focusing only on technology, the cybersecurity experts missed other vectors of exploitation.[151] Ultimately, Ron Bushar, then chief technology officer at Mandiant, figured out the source of the threat, realizing that "they [the Russians] had physically captured that data center or that system so they could plug in their own systems and continue to attack other parts of the infrastructure. . . . It's almost like you're dealing with an insider threat."[152] The SSSCIP's description of what happened at Ukrtelecom suggests something similar at play.

In any case, after reconnaissance, the hackers moved on to disruption. While the SSSCIP statement puzzlingly claims the operation was neutralized at this stage, the hackers evidently still had access to Ukrtelecom's network since they commenced their efforts to disrupt it by attempting to "disable the company's equipment and servers and also to get control over Ukrtelecom's network and equipment."[153] The SSSCIP reports detection of this activity within fifteen minutes, when efforts to mitigate the impact started—which lasted until the next day, as we now know.

Unfortunately, there is not enough information available to fully reconstruct operational mechanisms and assess constraints. However, considering the attack vector chosen, development time could have been no more than a month since the invasion starting on February 24 provided access to the network and credentials the hackers then used. Despite this short development time, however, the operation achieved a highly intense effect. Internet outages are not included in Johnson's escalation ladder, which is unsurprising considering the World Wide Web that provided the foundation for the modern Internet only launched the year after the publication of his article.[154] Considering the importance of Internet communication not only for economic activity but also for a wide range of social and physical processes and interactions, universal nationwide Internet disruption constitutes a more intense effect than disruption of specific organizations and businesses through wipers or other means. Hence, both the scope and scale of effects are greater than any other cyber operation since the start of the war. And yet, despite proceeding fast and pursuing highly intense effects, the hackers did not lose control over the target network or fail in their manipulation. Yes, the SSSCIP mentions that the victim discovered the hackers within fifteen minutes of the start of their disruptive activity. However, that was clearly too late, as the hackers had remained undiscovered until the moment they commenced their manipulation of the target network and caused the disruption. At face value, this outcome challenges the theory, as a fast and intense operation maintained control.

As the previous theory "misses," this outcome cements the importance of enabling conditions. The physical access to network infrastructure, and likely employees as well, negated the need for complex and time-consuming remote exploitation of infrastructure. Moreover, this "insider attack" illustrates how the combination of traditional means of exploitation with cyber means can improve effectiveness beyond any of those possible by either of these individual instruments. Having a human asset at a target facility with physical access to computer systems significantly facilitates exploitation, and subverting the network itself then enables a scale of effects no human agent in place could achieve.

Despite its scale, the strategic impact of this operation is unclear. There are no estimates of economic losses due to the outage. Meanwhile, there are also no indications this breakdown of communications affected Ukraine's government and military communications. However, a subsequent statement by Ukrtelecom showed the large outage suffered by ordinary Ukrainians was the direct consequence of the company's efforts to maintain connectivity for the latter. In a statement on March 29, the company explained that "in order to preserve the network infrastructure and continue providing services to the Armed Forces, other military formations and users of critical infrastructure, we were forced to temporarily limit the provision of services for the majority of private users and business clients."[155] Consequently, military and government channels likely remained operational. Hence, the main impact was on economic activity and Ukrainians' personal lives.[156] Regardless of the specific measures of impact, however, it is safe to conclude that despite its short and relatively simple preparations (stealing account names and passwords), this operation provided measurable strategic value to Russia by causing economic losses and adding to the uncertainty people face in war by preventing communication and access to information, plausibly undermining morale.

In contrast to this marked success, another attempt to disrupt the power grid by the infamous Sandworm group ended in a complete failure. The plan, forensic evidence shows, was to shut down power in the Vinnytsia region in central Ukraine on the evening of April 8.[157] As a Ukrainian government official speculated, the timing had been chosen to "catch the employees responsible for the security of the IT infrastructure by surprise, and on the other hand, to achieve maximum psychological pressure on the population due to the lack of power supply on Friday evening."[158] To achieve this effect, Sandworm had—through unknown means—compromised the computer systems of the energy provider some time in February 2022.[159] The hackers had then spread within the network, installing a set of malicious software: an updated version of the Industroyer malware they used in the 2016 sabotage, an updated version of CaddyWiper, and two new wipers for the Linux and Solaris operating systems.[160] Evidently, Sandworm had planned to follow the same sequence as its previous power grid sabotage operations of first disrupting the power supply, then disabling the computer systems of the affected substations to delay restoration.

Yet things did not play out that way. Instead, CERT-UA detected the malware and helped victims neutralize it before it could produce any effects.[161] In short, the operation was a failure. This outcome is in line with the heightened risk of control loss for operations that maximize both speed and intensity. Sandworm had attempted to produce a similar intensity of effects as in 2016 but with a fraction of the preparation time: two months compared to nineteen. Reflecting this tight timeline, rather than developing new malware, the hackers had reused code and tools from previous operations, whose signatures were out in the open and thus had a high chance of being detected.[162] As Juan Andres Guerrero-Saade put it, this operation "looks like a rush job, you use tools you have lying around, and you use them to achieve whatever you can."[163] High speed and high intensity thus ended in control loss, as the theory would predict.

However, there is an important additional variable to consider: the effectiveness of Ukraine's detection and mitigation efforts, and its support by the private sector. The response to the detected intrusion constitutes a marked contrast to the (non)response by victims to the discovery of compromises in their systems in 2015. Within a short time, network defenders detected and mitigated the intrusion. ESET's reporting shows that the Industroyer2 malware used was compiled roughly two weeks before the intended time of the disruption.[164] Hence, within this relatively short time window (compared to both of the preceding power grid sabotage operations), defenders managed to detect the malware and neutralize it. Likely, private sector help was instrumental in facilitating this effective response as well—note that CERT-UA's statement thanks both Microsoft and ESET for their support.[165] The victim's improved counterintelligence processes and private sector help thus contributed to the failure of this operation, compounding the already heightened risk of control loss.

Discussion: Quantity over Quality

As its "hybrid war" fell short, Russia escalated to avoid strategic failure. With this strategic shift, the role of subversion also changed. Not only did subversive operations fulfill an independent role, as before, but also some directly supported military operations. Traditional subversion provided far greater strategic value in this context, underlining its continued relevance, and confirming its expected relative advantage in producing physical effects.

Cyberwar fears, meanwhile, did not materialize. Nonetheless, cyber operations have been an integral part of Russia's aggression. Accordingly, in the year that has passed since the start of the invasion, Ukraine has suffered more suspected or confirmed Russian-sponsored disruptive cyber operations than during the eight years before. Still, quantity does not make up for quality. As the analysis showed, most of these operations failed to measurably contribute to Russia's strategic goals. Most pursued less intense effects than their predecessors during the hybrid war phase, going after low-hanging fruit with relatively easy and fast-to-mount distributed denial-of-service (DDoS) attacks and disk wipers. Three exceptions, the Viasat compromise, the power grid sabotage, and the Ukrtelecom disruption did pursue more intense effects, but with mixed results. Only the Ukrtelecom disruption provided clear and measurable strategic value, while the power grid sabotage operation failed entirely, and the Viasat disruption most likely fell short of providing a strategic advantage while producing collateral damage.

The analysis produced further evidence of the trilemma's constraints and trade-offs limiting strategic value. The early website defacements and DDoS attacks used relatively simple methods that were easy and fast to implement—yet produced very low-intensity effects that remained strategically irrelevant. The waves of wipers Russia deployed next interestingly showed efforts to control their spread. Consequently, they took relatively long to prepare (compared to NotPetya) and yet achieved small-scale disruptions. Interestingly, security researcher Juan Andres Guerrero-Saade noted that these efforts to improve control suggested the hackers "learned something from NotPetya, namely that self-spreaders are just not good tools, because they tend produce collateral damage."[166]

In contrast, the Viasat compromise produced intense effects through self-spreading malware that disabled hardware, disrupting military communication. Accordingly, it required more time to prepare—probably around a year. With this high intensity and medium speed, the theory predicts, comes a heightened risk of control loss—and that is what happened. The operation almost certainly failed to achieve the desired effect on its intended target, while hitting unintended targets that likely ran counter to Russian interests. The power grid sabotage attempt in April 2022, meanwhile, underlined the doubly increased risk of control loss when maximizing both speed and intensity, as it was discovered and neutralized before producing any effect. It is the clearest example of a failed cyber operation to date.

While these findings broadly support the theory, the Ukrtelecom disruption challenged it. Moving fast and producing the most intense effects thus far, it nonetheless avoided premature discovery and maintained control over target systems long enough for a lasting outage. The reason, the analysis showed, was an enabling condition beyond the scope of the theory: physical access to Ukrenergo's employees and infrastructure within occupied territory. Territorial conquest thus facilitated cyber operations—an interaction between physical control over infrastructure and outcomes "in cyberspace" worth further research.

Overall, there is no evidence suggesting Russia's cyber operations enabled battlefield outcomes that otherwise would have been impossible, nor of significantly (or measurably) weakening Ukraine's capacity to resist, nor of undermining public morale. In line with this assessment, deputy head of Ukraine's State Service of Special Communications and Information Protection (SSSCIP), Victor Zhora, concluded that "in general, Russian cyber-attacks have not reached their goals in infecting and seriously affecting critical services and infrastructure."[167] Rather, these operations mostly produced individual inconveniences for Ukraine's citizens, some limited financial losses for businesses, and possibly temporary disruptions of government bureaucracy and military communications. One assessment by a North Atlantic Treaty Organization (NATO) analyst stressed that the "cumulative effects of these [cyber] attacks were striking," noting the large number of disruptive cyber operations against a broad set of targets during the start of the invasion. Yet as the analysis of these operations showed, just as the number of soldiers Russia sent over the border did not guarantee victory, the quantity of activity did not equal quality of strategic value. As these operations failed to produce measurable strategic value individually, it is challenging to provide a plausible causal mechanism producing a cumulative impact on economic activity, public trust, or military capabilities. Accordingly, no tangible evidence has come to light yet showing a measurable impact along either of those lines.

In contrast, traditional subversion provided significant strategic value both individually and cumulatively. Andriy Derkach's efforts to manipulate policy and facilitate the takeover of territory, Bakanov's capture of the SBU and his contributions toward the takeover of Chernobyl, and local subversive networks providing intelligence to Russian forces all made a plausible and measurable—in theory, yet in practice limited by the limited data—contribution toward achieving core Russian goals. These outcomes underline that traditional subversion retains an edge over cyber operations in producing a broader range of more intense effects.

These striking successes seem to challenge the theory. The *Washington Post*'s investigation indicated that the Chernobyl takeover only involved a few months preparation, for example. However, as the analysis showed, the infiltration of senior leadership of the institutions involved that made the operation possible took years of preparation—providing further evidence supporting the hypothesized correlation between intensity and speed. The apparent failure of the operation that had tasked Medvedchuk with building a "resistance" in turn illustrates the limits of control due to agents going rogue—in this case simply pocketing the money. Overall, the evidence thus broadly supports the theory.

Nonetheless, findings remain preliminary and subject to likely change as further evidence becomes available. Moreover, there are several alternate explanations that need to be considered. The first reflects the limited evidence and the source of the current evidence. Rather than proving the limited impact of cyber operations, one might argue that the absence of evidence of a more significant impact reflects Ukraine's successful "information warfare"—controlling the release of information on its own losses not only on the battlefield but also in general. It is certainly possible that the wipers, for example, had a more significant impact on Ukraine's government than is currently apparent. However, the fact that Ukraine allowed the publication of information on the impact of the far more damaging Ukrtelecom and Viasat disruptions challenges this interpretation. Accordingly, Deputy Head of the SSSCIP Victor Zhora underlined his agency's interest to "share as much data as we can to attract attention to Russian cyber aggression"—which is in line with observed disclosure behavior.[168] Hence, it is unlikely that evidence of more damaging operations is being withheld. Importantly, while a recent report by the Dutch intelligence service highlighted that many attempted Russian cyber operations have not become public knowledge, it nonetheless underlined that "large-scale disruption has so far failed to materialize, however, and the consequences of cyber sabotage are dwarfed by the impact of physical military operations."[169]

The second alternative explanation reflects the pervasiveness of cyberwar narratives that have persisted despite mounting evidence to the contrary, suggesting Russia is still holding back its capabilities—as multiple researchers have done.[170] If true, however, this situation begs a simple question: holding back for what? Cyber operations are supposedly cheap, low-risk, and effective means of offense. Yet if they are instead so precious or risky that actors hold back with their use until great power war or nuclear exchanges—the plausible scenarios for further escalation in this case—clearly assumptions about cyber operations that inform cyberwar fears do not hold. More importantly, there is no evidence indicating Russia has more powerful capabilities. The argument is entirely speculative. Conversely, extensive evidence exists supporting a more plausible explanation: following years of experimentation, Russian actors learned that cyber operations face significant constraints. Hence, what we see is Russian actors running cyber operations in what they perceive to be their most effective and efficient use within these constraints.

The third alternative explanation is that the capabilities of Ukraine's emergency response teams explain the shortcomings of these cyber operations. Since cyber operations involve an invisible struggle between those pursuing exploitation and detection, a failure of the former often reflects a success for the latter. Accordingly, Yurii Shchyhol, the head of Ukraine's SSSCIP, which also includes CERT-UA, stated in a recent interview that "other cybersecurity experts ... have been helpful in providing consultations ... especially in the energy sector and critical infrastructure sites. That's probably the reason none of the cyberattacks that were carried out in the past four months of this invasion has allowed the enemy to destroy any databases or cause any private data leakage."[171]

A key reason the wiper attacks discussed in this chapter did not have more of an impact, according to Shchyhol's deputy Victor Zhora, was a basic countermeasure government agencies took in response to the January 14 website defacements: taking important databases offline, at least their public-facing pages. One example is the national registry for state servants' assets, where the public can inquire about the assets of any public servant. This database, Zhora stated, has been "operating internally, but publicly it has been unavailable since the start of the invasion."[172]

On top of this internal expertise, help from international cybersecurity firms evidently also played a role in neutralizing some of these operations. Indeed, as noted above, two statements by CERT-UA emphasize the importance of private sector assistance. Moreover, when I interviewed Zhora, he underlined that private sector assistance has made a "huge difference," allowing his team to "avoid many more damaging outcomes by reaching out to notify us of a compromise before a cyber operation could produce an impact."[173] Accordingly, the skills of Ukraine's detection and mitigation teams and their allies are clearly an important variable explaining why Russian-sponsored cyber operations have fallen short of expectations.

Importantly, this interplay between hacking groups and network defenders is at the heart of the theory of the trilemma—exploitation and manipulation are challenging precisely because victims can detect, mitigate, and neutralize one's efforts. However, there is an interesting additional dimension as this interplay happens over time, with both hacking groups and defenders learning. In this light, considering the cumulative effects of cyber campaigns, it is important to note that the most tangible cumulative impact of Russia's combined cyber campaigns against Ukraine since 2014 may have been training its computer emergency response teams and cybersecurity experts—which further exacerbated the challenges and corresponding constraints involved in cyber operations, leading to diminishing returns.[174] Russia's continued cyber operations against Ukraine thus likely had the unintended consequence of reducing the availability of targets with suitable vulnerabilities. Zhora hints at this development, noting that "NotPetya in comparison [to the wipers discussed in this chapter] was unique; they [Sandworm] had the supply chain of a supplier of the largest number of customers in Ukraine. I don't know of any other suppliers with that number of customers."[175] Hence, Zhora continued, "I am not sure they can find anything of this scope for a similar attack."[176] Security researcher Juan Andres Guerrero-Saade challenged this assessment, however, stating "it is incredibly optimistic" and that despite the SSSCIP's "fantastic job on defense" it would "still be possible to do a NotPetya-style worm using the same mechanisms (namely Mimikatz andPSXX)" because the types of vulnerabilities exploited are inherent to the Windows operating system and thus remain.[177]

Fourth, considering that attribution remains incomplete, the divergences across some of the cyber operations during the invasion phase may be better explained by the varying skill levels and organizational capacities of the different hacking groups behind them rather than the constraints of the trilemma. Indeed, Guerrero-Saade underlined that technical indicators suggest Sandworm has likely undergone a significant evolution since 2018, being "either subdivided now, or serving multiple masters, or reorganized into multiple pieces."[178] This assessment is in line with ESET's assessment in 2018 of the group having split up.[179] This change, combined with the uncertain identity of the hacking groups involved in the operations examined here, some of which may simply be subcontractors according to Guerrero-Saade, underlines the preliminary nature of the findings presented here. Final conclusions will have to wait until more evidence becomes available.

Conclusion

New Possibilities and New Perils

Despite disruptive technological innovation, the quality of subversion has remained surprisingly stable. It is still a relatively slow, weak, and volatile instrument of power that fails far more often than it succeeds. I defined subversion by three core characteristics: first, its reliance on secret exploitation and manipulation of adversary systems, which I showed cyber operations share, and second, its promise as a low-risk, low-cost instrument capable of manipulating public opinion and policy, eroding institutions and infrastructure and capabilities, or overthrowing regimes. It can both fulfill an independent role as an alternative to force or complement the latter. Cyber operations fit within the same strategic mold, I showed, but fulfill a narrower role. Third, the same mechanism that enables subversion's strategic promise produces a trilemma involving a distinct set of trade-offs that limit its strategic value. I showed that cyber operations face the same trilemma. Rather than harbingers of a revolution in conflict, cyber operations are thus but the most recent step in the long evolution of subversion. They enable new possibilities to project power but also bring new perils as increasing complexity heightens the risk of control loss.

Moreover, compared to traditional subversion, cyber operations can achieve a more limited range of effects and struggles at higher-intensity, physical effects. Hence, contrary to prevailing expectations, I predicted cyber operations offer relatively less strategic value than traditional subversion.

Evidence from the case studies strongly supports these expectations—while also documenting several unexpected subversive successes that illustrate the importance of enabling conditions. This conclusion will start by briefly summarizing core findings before identifying six key implications of the argument for world politics. The final part addresses limitations of the study, considers alternate explanations for some of its findings, and lays out under what conditions the argument would change.

Findings: From Cold War to Hybrid War—and, Finally, War

Subversion against Czechoslovakia underlined both its potential and its limitations. When Czechoslovakia commenced liberalizing reforms in 1968, the Soviet Union mounted an ambitious subversive campaign to infiltrate and manipulate its government and undermine the reform movement. Yet the campaign failed to do so, and I showed the constraints and trade-offs of the trilemma to be key limiting factors.

An initial string of operations to disintegrate civil society, discredit its leading figures, and plant false evidence of armed revolution, known as the KHODOKI campaign, moved fast and pursued daringly intrusive effects. They mostly failed to produce effects, however, and had no measurable impact on the liberalization movement. As expected, the high speed and intensity of these operations came at the cost of control. Conversely, a parallel campaign to infiltrate government and civil society, codenamed PROGRESS, proceeded quickly and carefully, successfully infiltrating target organizations while avoiding discovery. Yet it failed to manipulate decisions and actions toward Soviet interests. As expected, maximizing speed and control came at the cost of effect intensity. Consequently, operations from both campaigns made little measurable contribution toward the Soviet Union's strategic goals, neither individually nor cumulatively.

Faced with failure, the Kremlin opted for escalation and invaded in full force. This invasion, the analysis showed, aimed to help the subversive campaign that had evolved into an attempt at regime change succeed—underlining subversion's limits as a standalone instrument. These limitations thus ultimately contributed to this escalation. The regime change attempt moved fast and pursued the most intense effect subversion can achieve. As expected with this combination, it also went off the rails and fell apart.

Subsequent operations to discredit the Dubcek administration and disintegrate civil society proceeded more slowly and, in line with predictions, produced more intense effects without losing control. Civil society lost key figures as infiltrating agents facilitated their arrest. Moreover, the subversive operation culminating in the Aeroflot incident likely helped trigger Dubcek's eventual resignation. Yet the "normalization" in Czechoslovakian politics these efforts helped achieved by 1973 proved incomplete and temporary, necessitating permanent military occupation. Subversion alone proved incapable of subduing Czechoslovakia.

In its "hybrid war" against Ukraine between 2013 and 2018, Russia deployed both traditional subversion and cyber operations to manipulate government policy and neutralize its pro-European social movement to keep Ukraine within its sphere of influence. Although there is still insufficient evidence to reconstruct Kremlin decision-making, its use of subversive operations showed clear parallels to Czechoslovakia. Subversion primarily fulfilled an independent role, initially aiming to manipulate policy and public opinion. Yet these efforts failed to bear fruit and faltered. Consequently, Moscow implemented contingency plans: using local proxy actors to conduct a subversive regime change operation aiming to take control over Crimea and the Donbass. As in Czechoslovakia, Russia also sent military forces to help this operation succeed—only covertly this time. These tactics succeeded in Crimea but met unexpected resistance in the Donbass—resulting in a protracted military conflict that lasted until the escalation in 2022. These diametrically opposed outcomes for operations with otherwise highly similar characteristics against similar targets challenged the theory. Clearly, factors beyond the trilemma shaped these diverging outcomes. Further analysis revealed the relevance of a key variable: the extent of available vulnerabilities.

Meanwhile, cyber operations played no role in both regime change operations, confirming their more limited scope. Contrary to expectations of cyber-enabled hybrid war in Ukraine, cyber operations also remained irrelevant to its military dimension. Instead, Russia deployed cyber operations only when this military conflict ground to a halt, and as independent instruments against those parts of Ukraine where it was unwilling to project force. Seven cyber operations targeting Ukraine between 2014 and 2017 produced some significant disruptions. Yet they produced little tangible strategic value, both individually and cumulatively. Overall, the constraining role of the *antedaa* ran like a golden thread through these operations, explaining their limited impact—albeit with some exceptions.

The initial cyber operations were daring experiments pursuing increasingly intense effects—culminating in the attempted destruction of critical infrastructure. Yet they fell short of achieving them. The first operation, attempting cyber-enabled election interference in 2014, failed to produce any effect because hackers missed a basic security —measure—backups. High speed and intensity came at the cost of control. Two subsequent attempts at sabotaging the power grid instead maximized intensity. As expected, they required extensive development time yet had only fleeting effects. Victims neutralized these blackouts swiftly, minimizing economic or psychological impact. Moreover, the 2016 operation failed to produce the physical damage it was capable of in theory because of a basic error, further underlining the volatility of cyber operations. As expected, cyber operations struggle when pursuing physical effects, and their relative ineffectiveness became clear in comparison to two traditional sabotage operations. These involved far less development time and efforts yet produced vastly more intense effects and corresponding strategic value.

As if in recognition of these limitations, Sandworm changed its approach and pivoted toward economic warfare, maximizing scale rather than scope of effects. The 2016 disruption of the Ministry of Finance underlined the large-scale impact cyber operations can produce at a relatively swift pace. Sandworm achieved high speed and intensity without losing control, causing significant economic disruption and damage. This outcome challenged the theory. Sandworm had not solved the trilemma, however, but as the analysis showed, it benefited from an exceptional level of vulnerability in the target compared to its economic significance.[1] This outcome underlined the importance of available vulnerabilities as an enabling condition for subversive success. Its successor, the 2017 NotPetya operation, further maximized scale and produced the largest strategic impact of all cyber operations. At first glimpse, this outcome also challenges the theory. However, a closer look revealed NotPetya involved a significant control loss, in line with expectations—and ultimately undermining its strategic value. Finally, BadRabbit used the same mechanisms yet showed efforts to improve control, implying an attempt to balance the trilemma. It succeeded on the latter front but forfeited any strategic relevance. Tellingly, Russian-sponsored actors ceased any disruptive cyber operations afterward.

As in Czechoslovakia, subversion had thus failed. Ukraine's government continued its popular pro-European foreign policy. Contrary to prevailing expectations of cyber operations providing unprecedented strategic value in conflict short of war, they made little contribution toward achieving Moscow's goals. Neither did the evidence support the expectation that cyber operations produce superior cumulative gains. On the contrary, it showed that cumulative gains of all cyber operations combined were dwarfed by those of a single traditional operation: the takeover of Crimea.

Faced with failure, Moscow again chose to escalate: commencing a full-scale invasion. As before, the shortcomings of subversion likely contributed to this outcome. Of course, one could argue subversion merely postponed the inevitable. Perhaps Putin was always planning to invade. If so, however, why invest all the time and effort into these expansive subversive efforts?

Furthermore, all available evidence indicates this invasion lacked adequate long-term planning. In short, all evidence indicates Moscow attempted to get what it wanted without using force and failed.

Events have unfolded rapidly, and evidence remains incomplete, hidden behind the fog of war. Hence, findings and conclusions about the use of subversion in this invasion remain preliminary. Yet what evidence is available provides further support for the theory. First, there was no "cyber onslaught" and strategic cyber strikes of the kind many journalists and analysts had predicted in the wake of the invasion. Evidence showed a lot of disruptive cyber activity, far more than in the preceding years, and some of it clearly had an impact on targeted organizations. Yet quantity is not quality. Strategically, the cyber operations suspected or confirmed to be carried out by Russian actors failed to measurably contribute toward the attainments of Moscow's goals. Overall, the operations examined reflect priorities to maximize speed and intensity, and correspondingly high rates of control loss and failure. Two operations stood out through their impact, the Viasat hack and the Ukrtelecom disruption. The former underlined the risk of control loss and collateral damage, however. The latter, meanwhile, revealed the importance of an enabling condition unique to the context of an invasion: physical access to employees and infrastructure of targeted organizations. Overall, there is (currently) no evidence suggesting a contribution to battlefield outcomes or strategic gains—that is, outcomes that would not have been possible without cyber operations—Both individually and cumulatively. This finding stands in marked contrast to traditional subversion, which made clear and tangible contributions to key strategic gains—foremost the takeover of the Chernobyl nuclear plant without a fight.

In short, subversion remains promising in theory but challenging in practice. Despite technological advances, the subversive trilemma persists. Findings also confirmed that cyber operations face further constraints due to their dependence on target systems. Consequently, they struggle to produce more intense, physical effects and offer even more limited value than traditional subversion.

Implications for World Politics

This theory and its findings have six important implications for world politics:

First, subversion will likely remain an attractive option for leaders but will rarely affect the balance of power. This situation poses an apparent puzzle, namely if subversion falters so often, why do leaders continue to bet on it? As discussed, the tendency to overestimate the effectiveness of subversion persisted throughout the Cold War despite a string of failures. A comprehensive explanation of this puzzle would require archival research into the decision-making processes behind the use of subversion and could easily fill a book of its own. Hence, doing so is beyond the scope of this project. However, there are two complementary explanations that are supported by existing knowledge. On the one hand, policymakers may receive incomplete and biased information on the prospects of subversion that distorts their perception. The activity itself is secret; hence, there is generally little publicly available information. Instead, assessments of its own and hostile subversive operations are the purview of intelligence services—which, as the literature on the pathologies of intelligence shows, have clear incentives to overstate their own successes as well as adversary capabilities.[2] In the absence of alternative sources of information, policymakers may thus receive slanted reports, explaining their overestimates of the effectiveness of subversion. Conversely, even if policymakers do perceive the chance of subversive success as relatively low, its low risks and costs still likely pale in comparison to the perceived significant gains in case of success. In other words, since it is relatively cheap and easy, especially if the alternative is going to war, subversion may simply appear worth a try in most circumstances.

Hence, we can expect subversion to be used frequently and broadly. This applies to both traditional subversion and cyber operations. The relatively lower resource requirements for cyber operations, which usually do not require local infrastructure in the target country, are likely to make them even more attractive. Consequently, we can expect to see a lot of activity, but only a small percentage—if any—will provide measurable strategic value. Meanwhile, the secrecy surrounding subversive operations is likely to perpetuate widespread overestimates of their efficacy among policymakers and the public.

The complexity, fast development pace, and growing spread of information technology within societies adds further potential for perceptions of shadowy threats lurking within this technological infrastructure. The pervasiveness of "cyber doom" scenarios and their influence on policymakers attest to this influence.[3] Business incentives behind "cyber threat reporting" by the private sector, which generates most publicly available information on cyber operations, prioritize the most dramatic operations and further drive threat inflation.[4] Media reporting further stokes the flames by selecting the most dramatic stories from this already biased sample, publishing them with attention-grabbing headlines about the latest developments in global "cyberwar."[5] Correctives offered by academics are unlikely to stem this tide of thrilling reporting. Even if more level-headed reporting pointing out the shortcomings of cyber-enabled subversion takes hold[6]—unlikely in the face of the countervailing incentives—the secrecy of subversion will continue to help obscure its failings. Without full certainty about who was behind an operation, with what motives, and pursuing which objectives, there is always potential to interpret mission failures as cunning schemes and experiments heralding threats to come. The 2016 power sabotage operation in Ukraine, widely held as a successful signal and demonstration of capabilities despite its clearly documented failings, offered a case in point. An alternative interpretation of the findings would be that leaders may opt for subversion to achieve substrategic goals—such as demonstrating they are capable of cyber sabotage. It is certainly possible that leaders choose subversion to achieve more modest goals. This would be entirely in line with the theory, however. In fact, one would expect leaders to limit the scope of the goals as they become more aware of subversion's limitations.

Second, while subversion can destabilize targeted societies it likely plays a stabilizing role in world politics overall. Since subversion offers a strategic alternative to force, in theory its use can avoid military escalation. The more actors opt for subversion, the less world politics involves the chaos and destruction of war. In practice, however, subversion's shortcomings limit its stabilizing potential. As discussed, subversion often falls short of fulfilling strategic goals—leaving actors with the option to either accept failure or escalate to the use of force. Hence, rather than avoid escalation altogether, in most cases subversion is more likely to delay it. However, even such delays offer added opportunities for diplomatic solutions to disputes. Time pressure is a key cause of escalation as it increases the risk of misperception and miscalculation.[7] With its relatively slow pace, the use of subversion thus likely reduces the risk of escalation by lowering the chance of miscalculations under pressure and widening the window for diplomatic solutions.

The same applies even in cases where actors covertly deploy force to support subversive regime change operations, as was the case in both conflicts examined. Even though using force to support an instrument whose purpose is to avoid the former may seem paradoxical, doing so helps alleviate subversion's shortcomings to increase the likelihood of success in regime change, for example, correspondingly decreasing the likelihood of further escalation. Important caveats apply in this context as well. For example, success depends on the strength of potential armed resistance and the effectiveness of the strategies and tactics involved—and, particularly, the maintenance of secrecy. Deploying force against a capable adversary who is aware of the regime change attempt and prepared to mount armed resistance thus raises the likelihood of escalation. The relatively weaker the forces deployed are in such contexts, the likelier escalation becomes. On the other hand, the larger the force deployment, the harder it will be to keep this deployment, or the sponsorship of this deployment, secret—thus again raising escalation risks as the adversary discovers the covert intervention. Finally, even if the covert force deployment remains a success, the subversive regime change itself may fail, leaving the sponsor in the awkward position of having armed forces within the adversary's territory without explanation. Victims are likely to respond militarily in such contexts, even if not commencing a retaliatory strike against the sponsor, engaging the forces covertly deployed within the victim's territory.

In short, covert deployment of force in support of subversion can increase the likelihood of success yet also increases the risk of military escalation in the different cases of failure just discussed. Still, such military escalation is likely to remain more limited than all-out war for two reasons. First, due to the constraints of secrecy, the number of forces deployed will remain relatively small—one of the key limitations of regime change operations.[8] Second, with their choice in favor of covertly using force, the sponsor signals intent to limit escalation, just as is the case in full-on secret wars.[9]

Considering the latter point, choosing subversion likely constitutes a stronger de-escalatory signal than using covert force as it indicates an intent to avoid military engagement altogether. This aspect of subversion is particularly relevant considering the pervasive expectations of the escalatory nature of cyber conflict or its destabilizing role as a new form of conflict and competition.[10] Rather than destabilizing world politics by enabling a new dimension of conflict, cyber operations offer a way to pursue goals without escalating to the use of force. As such, the availability of cyber operations is more likely to decrease rather than increase the prevalence of armed conflict. Moreover, considering this strategic purpose, in effect actors who use cyber operations tacitly signal intent to avoid military escalation, or indeed any use of force. Considering their narrower scope of effects compared to traditional subversion, cyber operations likely carry a lower risk of triggering retaliatory responses. However, their superior scale and corresponding potential for mass disruption may at least partially offset this stabilizing role. Moreover, intent determines neither outcomes nor victim perceptions—things can go wrong, leading to unintended consequences. This point leads to the third implication.

Third, the proliferation of cyber operations brings a heightened risk of destabilizing mass effects and systemic disruption despite the stabilizing logic of subversion. Control loss has always been a problem in subversion. However, the superior scale of cyber operations increases the risks of mass effects, possibly reaching the level of systemic disruption. Self-proliferating viruses can spread out of control, and have done so often, infecting systems they are not intended to infect and proliferating far beyond the intended target(s). If the virus is designed to disrupt systems, furthermore, this disruption can similarly spread out of control. Although cyber operations are capable of a narrower scope of effects than subversion, within this range of effects their superior scalability produces new risks of mass disruptions or other unintended consequences that threaten stability.

Importantly, the very shortcomings that limit the strategic value of cyber operations in international conflict also raise this risk of inadvertent destabilization. Causing massively scaled yet carefully calibrated effects against a specific target country is hard because it is easy to lose control over the capabilities that make such effects possible. The greater the scale of global networked computer systems and the deeper their embeddedness within modern societies, the greater the risk thus becomes that such control loss produces systemic disruptions or other unintended consequences. Of course, the risk that collateral damage affects oneself might dissuade actors from deploying tools and techniques capable of such proliferating disruption, as Joe Nye argues.[11] Yet the deeper problem, this book has shown, is that rather than a calculable risk, the volatility of cyber operations means their sponsors face fundamental uncertainty about effects.

Imagine a virus designed and deployed to manipulate computer systems of a specific financial institution by infecting a popular trading application. To limit its targeting, the designers added a set of conditions that target systems must fulfill for the virus to install itself. Yet due to a configuration error, the virus skips these conditions and spreads through the Internet, infecting a large number of financial institutions around the globe. When activated, rather than the surgical disruption of a single organization, this virus causes massive disruptions of the financial system, producing significant economic damage. Because hackers face the same human fallibility that enables hacking in the first place, the code they write to manipulate systems will inevitably contain logical flaws. Sometimes these flaws may be discovered before deployment, but often they will not. Consequently, the actual effects cyber operations produce can be markedly different from their sponsors' intentions. Even less malicious intentions than in the above example can cause massive havoc, as illustrated by the Morris worm discussed earlier. In short, these pathologies can produce destabilizing effects despite the overall stabilizing logic of cyber operations.

As actors experiment with the new opportunities for power projection that cyber operations offer, one might expect they increasingly become aware of their limitations in scope. Consequently, they may aim to maximize their relative advantage in scale. In this case, and given the continuing computerization of ever more aspects of social life, the chance of cyber operations spiraling out of control and producing massive, possibly systemic disruption increases. Conversely, as they become increasingly aware of the risks of control loss, actors may increase their efforts to avoid it. Interestingly, Russia's use of cyber operations corresponds to this—suggesting the hackers or their handlers may have concluded that the risk of control loss inherent in scale-maximizing disruption is not worth the added damage. Optimistically, the self-interested pursuit of strategic gains may thus at least partially alleviate the risk of mass effects and their risk of unintended consequences and mass losses.

Fourth, in some circumstances the limitations of subversion increase the risk of unintended or inadvertent escalation—especially when deployed to contribute to military goals. When subversion falls short of achieving strategic goals, leaders face a choice of accepting failure or escalating efforts. On the one hand, as discussed above, subversion may delay escalation and diffuse crises by buying extra time. Yet on the other hand, the need to respond to failed subversive campaigns is likely to present leaders with a situation involving increased time pressures, threat perception, and a perceived pressure to prevent impending losses—all factors that research on decision-making has shown to increase risk-taking and impulsiveness.[12] Such situations are especially likely if subversion fails unexpectedly—a probable scenario considering prevailing expectations. Hence, the failure of subversion may indirectly contribute to escalation by producing a crisis and choices for leaders whose characteristics increase the likelihood of escalatory actions.

Conversely, the shortcomings of subversion may directly contribute to escalation when actors use it to complement military goals. As in its independent use, when it succeeds, subversion can contribute to victory and reduce escalation risks. For example, in Czechoslovakia the Soviets used their infiltration of the government to minimize resistance against the invasion. Getting the supreme commander of a military to order his troops not to resist foreign invasion, as the Soviets managed to do, provides great complementary support for military objectives while minimizing escalation risks. Even less impactful manipulations of command structures can complement military campaigns and provide tactical, operational, and strategic advantages. Having a few officers within adversary forces who give nonsensical orders or lose their cool in crucial moments may turn the tide of battle, for instance. Similarly, using subversive agents to sabotage military equipment can provide key tactical advantages. Accordingly, sabotage has long been a routine dimension of military campaigns—such as "Lawrence of Arabia's" operations against Ottoman supply lines.[13]

Importantly, because the trilemma is inherent in the subversive mechanism of exploitation, however, its constraints apply independently of strategic context. Accordingly, subversion can certainly provide advantages but is unlikely to be a game changer in most circumstances. This point is especially germane considering prevailing expectations about cyber operations as "force-multiplying" complements to military operations that may improve the latter's effectiveness and strategic value. The Viasat hack provides a key example, yet its evident lack of strategic impact also attests to the limitations of subversion. In short, subversion deployed in the service of force will still tend to be relatively slow, weak, and volatile—and actors would be ill-advised to stake victory on its success.

More critically, the more sensitive the targets chosen, the more likely the pathologies of subversion are to not only lead to failure but also produce unintended consequences. In particular, when going after military targets, the result can be inadvertent escalation. Secrecy and the limits of control create uncertainty not only for the adversary but also for oneself. Because subversive actors strive to maintain secrecy and hide their involvement, victims who discover intrusions in their system face significant uncertainty about the intruder's intention. This uncertainty increases the risk of misperception and miscalculation in the victim's response, especially considering the distinct tradeoffs and interactions involved in intelligence contests.[14] In the worst case, it may produce a security dilemma where actors retaliate pre-emptively in response to intrusion, as Ben Buchanan has shown.[15] The more sensitive the targets are, the likelier such escalation becomes due to the perceived risks of nonaction for the victim. Consider a victim discovering widespread compromises in key military hardware, say its fleet of F-35 fighter jets.[16] Now consider the victim attributes these compromises to its key adversary with whom the victim is currently engaged in a tense territorial dispute marked by mutual threats. The victim is likely to interpret these intrusions as signs of impending military action, perhaps responding to the compromises detected and launching a pre-emptive military offensive to avoid being caught off-guard with disabled hardware. The sponsor of the intrusion may have had nonescalatory aims, such as simply monitoring the deployment of these fighter jets or their weapons status in order to reduce uncertainty—and thus similarly be caught off-guard. In military contexts, the cybersecurity dilemma resulting from this uncertainty about intentions identified by Buchanan is thus a likely cause of escalation.[17]

The volatility of cyber operations further exacerbates uncertainty. Not only is the victim uncertain of the intention of the adversary whose presence it detects in its own systems, but also the adversary cannot be certain about the effects and reliability of their manipulation. In an alternative version of the scenario above, the sponsor of the intrusion into F-35 jets may be aiming to disable these planes by subverting their software. Reflecting the tendency to overestimate the strategic promise of subversion, the sponsor may be confident enough in its hackers' ability to succeed and launch a military offensive in the conviction that the adversary (the victim of the cyber operation) is unable to use its fighter jets. In this scenario, military escalation becomes more likely, and the use of subversion thus has a destabilizing rather than stabilizing effect. Yet the hackers may have missed something when developing the virus aimed to disable the aircraft, leading to failure, and forfeiting the expected advantage. As a result, the victim of the operation would have a sudden tactical advantage, being able to use planes the sponsor of the cyber operations expected to be disabled. There is a significant chance the victim would be able to turn these tactical advantages into a strategic advantage, and possibly victory in the ensuing military clash.

The risks involved in relying on cyber operations to shift the balance of power in war are thus great, while payoffs are uncertain. The potential consequences of miscalculation resulting from the use of cyber sabotage is particularly catastrophic when nuclear weapons are involved.[18] As is the case with the risk of unintended mass effects, the same characteristics that limit the strategic value of cyber operations exacerbate the potential for devastating strategic impacts when actors push their limits. Therefore, deploying cyber operations to complement military force may backfire spectacularly, and possibly catastrophically.

Fifth, strategists must recognize the continued relevance of traditional subversion, especially when integrated with cyber means. Findings confirmed the expectation that traditional subversion not only enables a greater scope of effects but also is more effective at producing more intense, physical effects. Consequently, in comparison, traditional subversion provided more strategic value than cyber operations and campaigns. Importantly, this situation is evident beyond the cases discussed in this book. The devastating explosion at Iran's Natanz nuclear enrichment facility in April 2021 offers a telling example.[19] A decade earlier, the same site had been the target of the Stuxnet cyber operation then widely seen as a harbinger of future cyber war.[20] Considering this background, it is unsurprising that many analysts and commentators initially speculated that the 2021 explosion was another cyber attack.[21] Yet it soon became clear this had been a traditional sabotage operation using undercover agents who had planted explosives at the site—confirmed by a story published in the *Jewish Chronicle* in December 2021 describing minute operational details—suggesting an intentional disclosure by Israel's intelligence service to claim responsibility and signal its capabilities.[22] This operation against the same targets is illustrative of the relative strength of traditional subversion. While the highly complex—and expensive—cyber operation damaged around a thousand centrifuges, the traditional sabotage in 2021 destroyed four times as many, while also causing massive structural damage to the complex housing them.[23] Such effects are beyond the reach of cyber operations, and will likely remain so—at least as long as there are no computer systems with built-in explosives.

Accordingly, it is important to consider the continuing threat posed by traditional subversion in strategy—especially when integrated with cyber operations. The theory and strategy of persistent engagement correctly identifies the primary suitability of cyber operations for long-term erosion campaigns that pursue cumulative effects on the balance of power. Yet it errs in assuming that this strategic role is the result of cyber operations' relative strengths compared to traditional subversion. I argue the opposite is the case, namely that cyber operations are primarily suitable for erosion campaigns because of their limited scope and intensity. Fischerkeller, Goldman, and Harknett start from the premise that subversion is not strategically relevant in the way cyber operations are. The latter, they argue, use a "fundamentally different strategic logic" that is "of a strategic rather than tactical, subversive or only intelligence-gathering nature."[24] Yet as this book has shown, traditional subversion not only is more effective at more intense effects but also can produce effects cyber operations and campaigns cannot. Consequently, traditional subversion has demonstrated far superior strategic value. Dismissing its significance puts the strategy at peril of prioritizing the lesser threat. Rather than focus on cyber campaigns in isolation, a more effective counterstrategy would treat cyber operations as part of larger subversive campaigns and consider the corresponding threats of campaigns integrating both traditional and cyber means.

Considering these relative strengths and weaknesses, actors can be expected to increasingly combine cyber operations with traditional subversion. Such "blended operations," as security researcher "The Grugq" calls them, allow maximizing the strengths of both while helping to alleviate their relative weaknesses.[25] The rise of so-called insider threats in cybersecurity—referring simply to infiltrating agents or personnel recruited by adversarial actors—is a key indicator for this development.[26] As discussed, having a human agent in place provides greater scope of access and influence than cyber means alone. Conversely, cyber means, such as self-proliferating malware, provide superior scale of access and manipulation. Combining cyber-enabled and traditional subversion thus offers the best of both worlds. Rational actors aiming to maximize gains should thus increasingly use such combined operations where feasible—and effective counterstrategies must consider such integrated threats or risk missing them, as the Naftogaz case illustrated.

Thinking a step further, integrated subversive campaigns that combine both traditional and cyber operations to pursue the effect types both are most effective at (large-scale disruption plus in-depth infiltration and manipulation or sabotage) promise potentially significant strategic value. Successfully carrying out such integrated campaigns requires significant organizational capacity, systematic coordination between different branches of the intelligence services, and discipline. Findings suggest Russia has struggled along all of these dimensions, just as it has with implementing combined arms maneuvers on the battlefield in Ukraine. Yet other actors may not; hence, it is important to consider the threat posed by both traditional subversion and its integration with cyber campaigns and to adjust strategy accordingly to counter subversion at large, not just in the cyber "domain."

CONCLUSION   221

Sixth, while cyber operations do not fundamentally transform international security, there are clear indications they significantly impact state-society relations and the relationship between states and nonstate actors. Even if its strategic value may be limited, subversion can have a significant impact on the organizations, political groups, and individuals targeted. The global interconnectedness of the Internet and the scalability of cyber operations, meanwhile, both facilitate its use and expand its impact on targets. The NotPetya operation illustrated the devastating impact large-scale disruptions can have on individual organizations, such as Maersk. Because cyber operations facilitate scale, smaller firms are especially at risk of becoming unwitting and unwilling pawns in global intelligence contests whose rules they are unlikely to be familiar with. While private sector firms face financial damage, for political actors, and especially civil society in repressive regimes, the impact can be far more severe—reaching threats to life. The Czechoslovakian case illustrated the use of subversive agents to identify and arrest individuals, resulting in incarceration, possible torture, or even death.

Cyber operations, meanwhile, allow repressive regimes to subvert civil society far more efficiently than they could do with spies, from afar and relying on tools and malware that can be easily repurposed from international espionage and active measures campaigns.[27] Moreover, the Internet allows reaching across borders to subvert diasporas. Meanwhile, private vendors sell increasingly capable tools and malware. In particular, the spyware market provides subversion capabilities on par with leading states to anyone willing to pay—including authoritarian regimes using these tools for repression both within and across borders.[28] On top of this, private firms offer a broadening set of tools for "subversion as a service," including disinformation campaigns.[29] In short, information technology expands the targets of subversion, the range of subversive actors, and, correspondingly, the range of threats to nonstate actors. In the long run, this development may have the more consequential impact on world politics.

Alternate Explanations and Limitations

Before concluding, it is important to consider potential limitations of the theory and case studies as well as alternative explanations. Overall, the analysis provided strong support for the theory of subversion and its trilemma. However, the course and outcome of a few subversive operations confounded the theory, underlining the importance of enabling conditions that lay beyond the scope of the theory—in particular, the extent of available vulnerabilities. As these outliers illustrate, given a distinct set of circumstances, subversive actors can produce intense effects quickly while maintaining control. Consequently, going forward it will be useful to integrate such enabling conditions into threat assessments, as well as indexes of relative subversive power, or cyber power.

Even if the theory thus explains key findings, there are alternate explanations worth considering. In the analysis I already touched upon possible alternate explanations for some of the findings based on creative interpretations of adversary intent, namely treating cyber operations that fell short of leaving a mark as just "proofs of concept" or means of signaling. In a similar vein, some analysts have argued that Russia has been exercising restraint in its use of cyber operations—motivated by deterrence. These arguments have resurged recently as cyberwar scenarios many analysts had predicted in the wake of the invasion failed to materialize.[30] As long as there is no publicly available evidence on decision-making processes in the Kremlin concerning cyber operations against Ukraine, it is impossible to conclusively establish its intentions and operational objectives. Hence, these interpretations remain plausible in theory.

There are two problems with this argument though. First, if cyber capabilities are too valuable to use even in a major war that is significantly depleting the aggressor's material capabilities, then what is their strategic role? Consider that current expectations hold them to be highly efficient and effective instruments below the threshold of war. Yet this strain of restraint interpretations suggests that "real" cyber capabilities only become relevant in scenarios of great power (nuclear) conflict. If so, however, the same hacker groups who have struggled to make a mark in relatively low-urgency situations of conflict short of war are then expected to deliver far superior effects in far more dire straits. Unless there are still unknown "super" hacker groups that have capabilities that far outstrip anything we have seen, which will have consumed far more time and resources than the cyber operations we have thus far seen, this is highly improbable. In fact, restraint interpretations are overall improbable because the rich evidence on the cyber operations uncovered does not contain any tangible indicators of restraint—such as capabilities remaining unused. Conversely, it is full of tangible instances documenting the constraints and trade-offs of the trilemma.

Alternatively, one could argue, the lack of observed strategic value reflects incomplete indicators used to measure it, emphasizing especially the importance of more diffuse second-order cumulative effects of erosion campaigns. Erosion campaigns aim to undermine trust, and while I have included public trust in governments as an indicator, subversion also plausibly undermines trust among the members of institutions targeted, and within entire societies. On top of these effects, cyber operations can erode trust in information technology itself.[31] While plausible, there are several issues with this explanation. First, it is extremely hard to prove. Measuring these diffuse types of effects is challenging, especially within sensitive organizations. Doing so *and* isolating the causal impact of subversion, especially over multiple years where many relevant circumstances may change as well, is extremely difficult to impossible. Second, assuming, for the sake of argument, that measuring it is possible, however, even if one can prove this causal impact, it is unlikely to change the main conclusion concerning the limited strategic value subversion offers. On the contrary, if all that subversion is good for is throwing sand into the gears of institutions and societies at large, it is unlikely to significantly affect the balance of power—that is, unless the resulting inefficiencies measurably affect economic growth, in which case the indicators used here would measure it.

Third, however, and most importantly, past evidence indicates such trust erosion tends to affect the subverter itself as well—underlining the persistent challenge of controlling effects. Michael Herman has pointed out how adversary infiltration and the threat of it is akin to "putting a virus into the bloodstream of its intelligence target."[32] The result, he continued, is "the special counterintelligence mentality: slightly paranoid, considering the possibility of manipulation and deception everywhere."[33] Accordingly, one could argue, an adversary's discovery of one's subversive operations is not necessarily a failure but may still provide tactical, or even strategic, advantages.[34] The problem is, however, that just as with biological weapons, this virus may easily spread into one's own bloodstream. The Czechoslovakian case has already illustrated how the KGB and the Soviet leadership came to believe in its own deceptions. Mitrokhin's note revealed how this spirit of paranoia spread through the KGB as a whole. Over the course of the Cold War, it became increasingly occupied with the hunt for perceived traitors—not only distracting it but also drawing actual resources away from its covert operations against the "main adversary" (the United States).[35] Consequently, subversive campaigns may erode trust not only among the adversary's society and institutions but also within one's own ranks. In other words, erosion campaigns may cause collateral cognitive damage to oneself—possibly negating any strategic gains. This risk, combined with the general tendency of authoritarian regimes and closed societies to breed paranoia,[36] is an important potential vulnerability to consider compared to the transparency of democratic and open societies that likely renders them more resilient.

Before concluding, potential limitations of the argument must be considered. Since this book focuses on one "subverter," Russia, one may question the generalizability of findings. That is certainly a limitation, especially considering the distinct history of its intelligence services, their tradecraft, and pathologies.[37] Yet, on the other hand, Russia is one of the most, if not the most, prolific actors pursuing subversion and, more recently, cyber operations. Covering Russia thus means covering a large proportion of the universe of cases. More importantly, as discussed, in general Russia is held to be one of the most capable actors, and in Ukraine it faced close to ideal conditions for subversive success. If even under these conditions the shortcomings of the trilemma are so readily apparent and limit strategic value, one must wonder why we would expect other actors not to be subject to them in other contexts, especially less ideal ones. Moreover, especially in cyber conflict there are only a small handful of politically motivated cyber operations pursued by actors other than Russia, most of which are already included as illustrative examples in chapter two. There is currently no other conflict including even a small proportion of the number of cyber operations we have seen against Ukraine. Consequently, and considering that the involvement of one individual actor (Sandworm) in most of these operations allowed direct comparison concerning the constraints and trade-offs of the trilemma, as well as efforts to escape them through learning, under given circumstances this case provides the best available evidence to test the theory.

Moreover, if the theory is right, the constraints and trade-offs it identifies are inherent to the mechanism of exploitation, and thus independent of actor-specific variables such as preferences, intent, and culture. Consequently, these constraints should apply irrespective of which specific actor(s) are involved. Accordingly, I have mentioned several such examples throughout the book. Of course, different preferences, risk acceptances, and goals mean different actors will use cyber operations in different ways. Hence, which of the three variables of speed, intensity, and control they will strive to maximize, and the trade-offs they are willing to accept in the process, will vary significantly as well. However, and this is the key point, regardless of these differences, actors will not be able to escape the trilemma—within the threshold of their skill level, resource endowment and organizational capacity. Accordingly, I would expect to see evidence of the constraining role of the trilemma across a large variety of cases. Adding further case studies, and ideally a quantitative study of the universe of available cases, is thus a key priority for further research.

Finally, subversion can conceivably provide strategic value beyond the archetypical means this book has focused on, namely operations that produce active effects through undercover spies vis-à-vis hacking. There are two relevant use cases of subversion beyond the scope of the analysis. First is the covert spread of propaganda and disinformation via the exploitation of media organizations and platforms. Currently, there is grave concern among both policymakers and academics about the threat of fake accounts, automated "bots," or paid ads spreading disinformation with the potential to sway public opinion.[38] Undoubtedly, social media provide significant new opportunities to spread disinformation and manipulate audiences by exploiting the design of platforms, underlying business models, and user pathologies. Hence, examining its effectiveness, and comparing it to traditional means, requires urgent attention. While I could not do so in this book for simple reasons of space, I have done so elsewhere and showed a similar mismatch between expectations and evidence.[39] This finding is in line with further emerging research underlining the challenges involved in social media disinformation and the continued relevance and superior effectiveness of traditional mass media, foremost television.[40] More systematic research of this kind is urgently needed.

Second, subversive actors can leverage access to adversary systems for intelligence collection. Secret exploitation establishes access to parts of organizations otherwise out of bounds, and in doing so provides access to sensitive information as well. US doctrine draws a clear line between collection and interference (covert action), and some scholars similarly exclude intelligence collection from the objectives of subversion.[41] However, this separation is artificial since a key advantage of infiltrating an adversary with subversive agents is their dual-use capacity for both collection and interference, a central tenet of Soviet doctrine. As Johnson and Wirtz highlight, "In the Soviet view these 'active measures' were complementary to espionage and doctrinally inseparable from it in the communist struggle."[42] Gavin Wilde shows the same to be the case in contemporary Russia with its expansive conception of "information warfare."[43] This dual purpose of subversion adds to its strategic promise. The same applies to cyber operations, and considering their limitations in producing the active effects the findings showed, intelligence collection may actually be their most effective use. An upcoming study of the cyber dimension of Russia's invasion of Ukraine by security researcher The Grugq comes to the same conclusion.[44] Consequently, assessing the strategic value of cyber espionage, both in general and compared to traditional means, is a key topic worthy of further research. This question is especially pertinent since the theory and strategy of persistent engagement build on the assumption that cyber espionage, both individual operations and cumulatively, produces greater strategic value than traditional espionage.[45]

The final open question this book has not answered is under what circumstances the predictions of the theory would change and what developments could render the theory irrelevant. The vulnerabilities that traditional subversion exploits are created and shaped by human nature and fallibility, which are (unfortunately) not apparently subject to change within timescales relevant to political inquiry. Cyber operations, on the other hand, target information technologies subject to rapid development and sometimes disruptive change. Hence, one might expect the predictions of this theory to be as fleeting as technological trends. However, a deeper look has shown that cyber operations ultimately exploit human fallibility, either directly via social engineering or indirectly by leveraging flaws in the design and logical rules that determine machine behavior. Even if the technologies change, as long as humans design them, this source of vulnerability and its manifestations will remain the same. Therefore, the trilemma can be expected to apply to cyber operations as long as humans remain in the loop.

Similarly, decisions concerning the design and proliferation of interconnected information technologies can shift the constraints of the trilemma. For example, a state might decide to build a network of small and nimble "smart" nuclear reactors connected via the Internet to respond to changes in consumption in real time, maximizing efficiency. If these reactors follow a standardized design (as one would expect), in doing so that state has lowered the bar for adversaries to produce intense physical effects (i.e., nuclear meltdowns) at scale through cyber operations. However, while the baseline maximum level of intensity of effects is now greater compared to a state where such reactors do not exist, attempting to produce these effects will still require significant efforts and corresponding time, while involving a nonzero risk of control loss.

Consequently, the main conceivable technological change that could render the theory invalid or irrelevant is removing humans from the loop.

Accordingly, predictions that the rise of artificial intelligence will upend and transform cybersecurity through automated and inhumanly fast offense and defense abound. These visions reproduce the same tendencies to ascribe all-transforming powers to new technologies—focusing on theoretical possibilities while neglecting practical feasibility—that underpin prevailing expectations about cyber operations. For example, Kott and Stump posit that exploitation of critical systems can be prevented through "artificial cyber hunters—intelligent, autonomous, mobile agents specialized in active cyber defense.... [S]uch agents will stealthily patrol the networks, detect the enemy malware while remaining concealed, and then destroy or degrade the enemy malware."[46] While it sounds exciting, such visions are far removed from current applications of artificial intelligence and, considering the need for creativity and cunning required to succeed, likely impossible until the advent of human-level generalized artificial intelligence. Considering the transformative nature of such a development on human societies, and indeed the survival of the human species, questions of cybersecurity will at best be a footnote. Existing automated techniques to detect compromises meanwhile face significant limitations.[47] Similarly, existing machine learning techniques powering artificial intelligence applications suffer from critical vulnerabilities that are inherent to the technology—thus extending the potential for subversion.[48] As such, artificial intelligence algorithms provide yet another new and complex target for subversion, where the same types of constraints identified here can be expected to apply. Targets change, but the trilemma persists.

Notes

Introduction

1. According to a popular definition, hybrid war involves "multidimensional activities by a state actor just below the threshold of aggressive use of military forces." Frank G. Hoffman, "The Contemporary Spectrum of Conflict: Protracted, Gray Zone, Ambiguous, and Hybrid Modes of War," 2016, 26, https://www.heritage.org/sites/default/files/2019-08/2016_Index_of_US_Military_Strength_ESSAYS_ALL.pdf.
2. Defined as the exploitation of vulnerabilities in computer systems or services to produce detrimental effects against an adversary. Effects are varied, ranging from information exfiltration (espionage) to active effects such as manipulation, disruption, and damage. They commence with the infiltration of a target, proceed by developing means to establish access and temporary control, and conclude with the production of the desired effect and/or loss of access.
3. Michael J. Mazarr, "Mastering the Gray Zone: Understanding a Changing Era of Conflict," 2015, 3, https://apps.dtic.mil/sti/citations/AD1000186.
4. Christopher S. Chivvis, "Hybrid War: Russian Contemporary Political Warfare," *Bulletin of the Atomic Scientists: How Dangerous Is Hybrid War?* 73, no. 5 (2017): 316, doi:10.1080/00963402.2017.1362903.
5. Rod Thornton, "The Changing Nature of Modern Warfare," *RUSI Journal* 160, no. 4 (July 2015): 44, doi:10.1080/03071847.2015.1079047.
6. Oliver Fitton, "Cyber Operations and Gray Zones: Challenges for NATO," *Connections* 15, no. 2 (2016): 109–119.
7. Andy Greenberg, "How an Entire Nation Became Russia's Test Lab for Cyberwar," *Wired*, June 2017, https://www.wired.com/story/russian-hackers-attack-ukraine/.
8. Jack S. Levy, "The Causes of War and the Conditions of Peace," *Annual Review of Political Science* 1, no. 1 (1998): 139–165, doi:10.1146/annurev.polisci.1.1.139.
9. Michael Kofman and Matthew Rojansky, "A Closer Look at Russia's 'Hybrid War,'" *Kennan Cable* 7 (2015); Alexander Lanoszka, "Russian Hybrid Warfare and Extended Deterrence in Eastern Europe," *International Affairs* 92, no. 1 (January 2016): 175–195, doi:10.1111/1468-2346.12509; Chiara Libiseller, "'Hybrid Warfare' as an Academic Fashion," *Journal of Strategic Studies* 0, no. 0 (February 2023): 1–23, doi:10.1080/01402390.2023.2177987.
10. NATO, "Closing Press Conference by NATO Secretary General Jens Stoltenberg Following the Meetings of NATO Foreign Ministers in Antalya, Turkey," May 2015, http://www.nato.int/cps/en/natohq/opinions_119432.htm; Susan Landau, "Russia's Hybrid Warriors Got the White House. Now They're Coming for America's Town Halls," *Foreign Policy* (blog), 2017, https://foreignpolicy.com/2017/09/26/russ

ias-hybrid-warriors-are-coming-for-american-civil-society-hacking-trump-clinton/; BBC, "Nato to Counter 'Hybrid Warfare' from Russia," *BBC News*, May 2015, sec. Europe, https://www.bbc.com/news/world-europe-32741688; John Vandiver, "SACEUR: Allies Must Prepare for Russia 'Hybrid War,'" *Stars and Stripes*, accessed December 14, 2020, https://www.stripes.com/news/saceur-allies-must-prepare-for-russia-hybrid-war-1.301464.

11. Mark Galeotti, "The 'Gerasimov Doctrine' and Russian Non-Linear War," *In Moscow's Shadows* (blog), July 2014, https://inmoscowsshadows.wordpress.com/2014/07/06/the-gerasimov-doctrine-and-russian-non-linear-war/.
12. Lawrence W. Beilenson, *Power through Subversion* (Washington, DC: Public Affairs Press, 1972), 139.
13. Beilenson, *Power through Subversion*, 251.
14. Michael P. Fischerkeller, Emily O. Goldman, and Richard J. Harknett, *Cyber Persistence Theory: Redefining National Security in Cyberspace*, Bridging the Gap (New York: Oxford University Press, 2022), 25.
15. Ben Buchanan, *The Hacker and the State: Cyber Attacks and the New Normal of Geopolitics* (Cambridge, MA: Harvard University Press, 2020), 7, 3.
16. Christopher M. Andrew and Vasili Mitrokhin, *The Sword and the Shield: The Mitrokhin Archive and the Secret History of the KGB* (New York: Basic Books, 1999).
17. Paul W. Blackstock, *The Strategy of Subversion: Manipulating the Politics of Other Nations* (Chicago: Quadrangle Books, 1964), 304.
18. Buchanan, *The Hacker and the State*, 202.
19. Thomas Rid, *Cyber War Will Not Take Place* (Oxford: Oxford University Press, 2013); Erik Gartzke and Jon R. Lindsay, "Weaving Tangled Webs: Offense, Defense, and Deception in Cyberspace," *Security Studies* 24, no. 2 (April 2015): 316–348, doi:10.1080/09636412.2015.1038188; Aaron Franklin Brantly, *The Decision to Attack: Military and Intelligence Cyber Decision-Making* (University of Georgia Press, 2016), http://muse.jhu.edu/book/45365; Brandon Valeriano, Benjamin Jensen, and Ryan C. Maness, *Cyber Strategy: The Evolving Character of Power and Coercion* (New York: Oxford University Press, 2018); Joshua Rovner, "Cyber War as an Intelligence Contest," *War on the Rocks* (University of Georgia Press, September 2019), https://warontherocks.com/2019/09/cyber-war-as-an-intelligence-contest/; Michael Warner, "A Matter of Trust: Covert Action Reconsidered," *Studies in Intelligence* 63, no. 4 (2019), https://web.archive.org/web/20201016162622/https://www.cia.gov/library/center-for-the-study-of-intelligence/csi-publications/csi-studies/studies/vol-63-no-4/pdfs/Covert-Action-Reconsidered.pdf; Buchanan, *The Hacker and the State*; Richard J. Harknett and Max Smeets, "Cyber Campaigns and Strategic Outcomes," *Journal of Strategic Studies* 45, no. 4 (March 2020): 1–34, doi:10.1080/01402390.2020.1732354.
20. Austin Carson, "Facing Off and Saving Face: Covert Intervention and Escalation Management in the Korean War," *International Organization* 70, no. 1 (2016): 103–131, doi:10.1017/S0020818315000284.
21. Michael Poznansky, *In the Shadow of International Law: Secrecy and Regime Change in the Postwar World* (Oxford: Oxford University Press, 2020).

22. Langdon Winner, *The Whale and the Reactor* (Chicago: University of Chicago Press, 1986), 20–21.
23. Stephen Biddle, *Military Power: Explaining Victory and Defeat in Modern Battle* (Princeton, NJ: Princeton University Press, 2010).
24. Erika Solomon, Steven Erlanger, and Christopher F. Schuetze, "Scrounging for Tanks for Ukraine, Europe's Armies Come Up Short," *New York Times*, February 28, 2023, sec. World, https://www.nytimes.com/2023/02/28/world/europe/ukraine-tanks.html; "The West Is Struggling to Forge a New Arsenal of Democracy," *The Economist*, February 19, 2023, https://www.economist.com/briefing/2023/02/19/the-west-is-struggling-to-forge-a-new-arsenal-of-democracy.
25. United States Cyber Command, "Achieve and Maintain Cyberspace Superiority—Command Vision for US Cyber Command," April 2018, https://www.cybercom.mil/Portals/56/Documents/USCYBERCOM%20Vision%20April%202018.pdf?ver=2018-06-14-152556-010; Paul M. Nakasone, "A Cyber Force for Persistent Operations," *Joint Force Quarterly* 92 (2019): 10–15.
26. Fischerkeller, Goldman, and Harknett, *Cyber Persistence Theory*.
27. Robert Gorwa and Max Smeets, "Cyber Conflict in Political Science: A Review of Methods and Literature," preprint (SocArXiv, July 2019), doi:10.31235/osf.io/fc6sg.
28. Lennart Maschmeyer, Ronald J. Deibert, and Jon R. Lindsay, "A Tale of Two Cybers—How Threat Reporting by Cybersecurity Firms Systematically Underrepresents Threats to Civil Society," *Journal of Information Technology & Politics* 18, no. 1 (January 2021): 1–20, doi:10.1080/19331681.2020.1776658.
29. Building on Pape's definition. Robert A. Pape, *Bombing to Win: Air Power and Coercion in War* (Ithaca and London: Cornell University Press, 1996), 56.
30. Susan Strange, *States and Markets*, 2nd rev. ed. (London: Bloomsbury Academic, 1998); Michael Barnett and Raymond Duvall, "Power in International Politics," *International Organization* 59, no. 1 (2005): 39–75; Stefano Guzzini, "The Concept of Power: A Constructivist Analysis," *Millennium—Journal of International Studies* 33, no. 3 (June 2005): 495–521.
31. I argue that this form of power is best conceptualized as a reversal of structural power. Lennart Maschmeyer, "Subversion, Cyber Operations, and Reverse Structural Power in World Politics," *European Journal of International Relations* 29, no. 1 (March 2023): 79–103, doi:10.1177/13540661221117051.
32. Lindsey A. O'Rourke, *Covert Regime Change: America's Secret Cold War*, Cornell Studies in Security Affairs (Ithaca, NY: Cornell University Press, 2018); Poznansky, *In the Shadow of International Law*.
33. Dov H. Levin, *Meddling in the Ballot Box: The Causes and Effects of Partisan Electoral Interventions* (New York: Oxford University Press, 2020).
34. Melissa M. Lee, *Crippling Leviathan: How Foreign Subversion Weakens the State* (Ithaca, NY: Cornell University Press, 2020).
35. William C. Wohlforth, "Realism and Great Power Subversion," *International Relations* 34, no. 4 (December 2020): 459–481, doi:10.1177/0047117820968858.
36. Frank Kitson, *Low Intensity Operations: Subversion, Insurgency, Peacekeeping* (London: Faber, 1971), 3; Beilenson, *Power through Subversion*.

37. Blackstock, *The Strategy of Subversion*, 121–122.
38. Michael Warner, "Wanted: A Definition of 'Intelligence,'" *Studies in Intelligence* 46, no. 3 (2002): 21, https://web.archive.org/web/20170501023714/https://www.cia.gov/library/center-for-the-study-of-intelligence/csi-publications/csi-studies/studies/vol46no3/article02.html.
39. Austin Carson, *Secret Wars: Covert Conflict in International Politics*, Princeton Studies in International History and Politics (Princeton, NJ: Princeton University Press, 2018), 18.
40. Michael E. DeVine and Heidi M. Peters, *Covert Action and Clandestine Activities of the Intelligence Community: Selected Definitions in Brief* (Washington, DC: US Congressional Research Service, July 2019).
41. Jeffrey Richelson, *A Century of Spies: Intelligence in the Twentieth Century* (New York: Oxford University Press, 1995); Stephen Grey, *The New Spymasters: Inside the Modern World of Espionage from the Cold War to Global Terror* (New York: St. Martin's Press, 2015).
42. Loch K. Johnson, "On Drawing a Bright Line for Covert Operations," *American Journal of International Law* 86, no. 2 (1992): 284–309, doi:10.2307/2203235.
43. Johnson, "On Drawing a Bright Line for Covert Operations," 286.
44. Johnson, "On Drawing a Bright Line for Covert Operations."
45. Blackstock, *The Strategy of Subversion*, 303.
46. Beilenson, *Power through Subversion*, 139.
47. Kitson, *Low Intensity Operations*; Ian Greig, *Subversion: Propaganda, Agitation and the Spread of People's War* (London: Tom Stacey, 1973).
48. R. Anderson, "Why Information Security Is Hard—An Economic Perspective," in *Proceedings of the 17th Annual Computer Security Applications Conference (ACSAC '01)* (Washington, DC: IEEE Computer Society, 2001), 358, http://dl.acm.org/citation.cfm?id=872016.872155; Nicholas Tsagourias, "Cyber Attacks, Self-Defence and the Problem of Attribution," *Journal of Conflict and Security Law* 17, no. 2 (2012): 229–244.
49. Warner, "A Matter of Trust," 38.
50. Harknett and Smeets, "Cyber Campaigns and Strategic Outcomes," 24.
51. Sarah-Jane Corke, *US Covert Operations and Cold War Strategy: Truman, Secret Warfare, and the CIA, 1945–1953*, Studies in Intelligence Series (New York: Routledge, 2008), 98–99.
52. James Callanan, *Covert Action in the Cold War: US Policy, Intelligence and CIA Operations* (London: I. B. Tauris, 2009), 70–85.
53. Harknett and Smeets, "Cyber Campaigns and Strategic Outcomes," 13–23; Fischerkeller, Goldman, and Harknett, *Cyber Persistence Theory*, 68–74.
54. Jon R. Lindsay, "The Impact of China on Cybersecurity: Fiction and Friction," *International Security* 39, no. 3 (2014): 7–47; Andrea Gilli and Mauro Gilli, "Why China Has Not Caught Up Yet: Military-Technological Superiority and the Limits of Imitation, Reverse Engineering, and Cyber Espionage," *International Security* 43, no. 3 (February 2019): 141–189, doi:10.1162/isec_a_00337.
55. Buchanan, *The Hacker and the State*, 3.

56. Adam P. Liff, "Cyberwar: A New 'Absolute Weapon'? The Proliferation of Cyberwarfare Capabilities and Interstate War," *Journal of Strategic Studies* 35, no. 3 (June 2012): 401–428, doi:10.1080/01402390.2012.663252; Kim Zetter, "An Unprecedented Look at Stuxnet, the World's First Digital Weapon," *Wired*, March 2014, http://www.wired.com/2014/11/countdown-to-zero-day-stuxnet/.
57. "Stuxnet Malware Is 'Weapon' Out to Destroy . . . Iran's Bushehr Nuclear Plant?," *Christian Science Monitor*, September 2010, https://www.csmonitor.com/USA/2010/0921/Stuxnet-malware-is-weapon-out-to-destroy-Iran-s-Bushehr-nuclear-plant.
58. Ralph Langner, "To Kill a Centrifuge," November 2013, https://www.langner.com/wp-content/uploads/2017/03/to-kill-a-centrifuge.pdf.
59. David Sanger, *Confront and Conceal: Obama's Secret Wars and Surprising Use of American Power* (New York: Broadway Paperbacks, 2012), 190.
60. Committee on Foreign Relations, "Chain Reaction: Avoiding a Nuclear Arms Race in the Middle East," Report to the US Senate Committee on Foreign Relations, February 2008, https://www.govinfo.gov/content/pkg/CPRT-110SPRT39674/html/CPRT-110SPRT39674.htm.
61. Jon R. Lindsay, "Stuxnet and the Limits of Cyber Warfare," *Security Studies* 22, no. 3 (2013): 390, doi:10.1080/09636412.2013.816122.
62. Rebecca Slayton, "What Is the Cyber Offense-Defense Balance? Conceptions, Causes, and Assessment," *International Security* 41, no. 3 (January 2017): 72–109, doi:10.1162/ISEC_a_00267.
63. Myriam Dunn Cavelty, "From Cyber-Bombs to Political Fallout: Threat Representations with an Impact in the Cyber-Security Discourse," *International Studies Review* 15, no. 1 (2013): 105–122, doi:10.1111/misr.12023; Sean Lawson and Michael K. Middleton, "Cyber Pearl Harbor: Analogy, Fear, and the Framing of Cyber Security Threats in the United States, 1991–2016," *First Monday*, March 2019, doi:10.5210/fm.v24i3.9623.
64. Thomas Dullien, "Weird Machines, Exploitability, and Provable Unexploitability," *IEEE Transactions on Emerging Topics in Computing* 8, no. 2 (April 2020): 391–403, doi:10.1109/TETC.2017.2785299.
65. Jon Erickson, *Hacking: The Art of Exploitation* (San Francisco: No Starch Press, 2003), 115.
66. Maschmeyer, "Subversion, Cyber Operations, and Reverse Structural Power in World Politics."
67. Norbert Wiener, *Cybernetics or Control and Communication in the Animal and the Machine*, 2nd ed. (Cambridge, MA: MIT Press, 2000).
68. Translated by a native speaker.
69. Known in German as the "Bundesbeauftragte für die Unterlagen des Staatssicherheitsdienstes der ehemaligen Deutschen Demokratischen Republik."
70. Alexander L. George and Andrew Bennett, *Case Studies and Theory Development in the Social Sciences* (Cambridge, MA: MIT Press, 2005), 73.
71. "Russia Accuses U.S. of Increasing Subversion," *Irish Times*, May 1968.
72. Greenberg, "How an Entire Nation Became Russia's Test Lab for Cyberwar."

73. Andy Greenberg, *Sandworm: A New Era of Cyberwar and the Hunt for the Kremlin's Most Dangerous Hackers* (New York: Doubleday, 2019).

Chapter 1

1. David A. Baldwin, *Power and International Relations: A Conceptual Approach* (Princeton, NJ: Princeton University Press, 2016), 2.
2. Steven Lukes, *Power: A Radical View*, 2nd ed. (Houndmills, Basingstoke, Hampshire: Palgrave Macmillan, 2004), 30.
3. Baldwin, *Power and International Relations*, 18–20.
4. Robert A. Dahl, "The Concept of Power," *Behavioral Science* 2, no. 3 (1957): 203–204.
5. Max Weber, *Max Weber: The Theory of Social and Economic Organization*, ed. A. M. Henderson and Talcott Parsons (New York; London: Free Press; Collier Macmillan, 1964), 152.
6. In the words of Biddle, "Both realists and liberals view capability as a product of material wherewithal; some (mainly offense-defense theorists) see the materiel's nature as key, but for most it is the relative mass of troops, population, military expenditure, or economic potential that creates capability." Biddle, *Military Power*, 192. Kenneth Waltz proposes capability as a universal measure of relative power, since "economic, military, and other capabilities of nations cannot be sectored and separately weighed. States are not placed in the top rank [of relative power] because they excel in one way or another. Their rank depends on how they score on all of the following items: size of population and territory, resource endowment, economic capability, military strength, political stability and competence." Kenneth N. Waltz, *Theory of International Politics*, reissue ed. (Long Grove, IL: Waveland Press, 2010), 131.
7. Hans J. Morgenthau, *Politics among Nations: The Struggle for Power and Peace* (New York: Alfred A. Knopf, 1948), 341.
8. John J. Mearsheimer, "The False Promise of International Institutions," *International Security* 19, no. 3 (1994): 9, doi:10.2307/2539078.
9. Levy, "The Causes of War and the Conditions of Peace."
10. Dahl, "The Concept of Power."
11. Carl von Clausewitz, *On War*, Oxford World's Classics, ed. Beatrice Heuser, trans. Michael Howard and Peter Paret (New York: Oxford University Press, 2006), 13.
12. Morgenthau, *Politics among Nations*, 52.
13. Carson, *Secret Wars*.
14. Bull Hedley, *The Anarchical Society: A Study of Order in World Politics* (New York: Columbia University Press, 1977), 163.
15. Jürgen Habermas, *The Theory of Communicative Action* (Boston: Beacon Press, 1984); Thomas Risse, "'Let's Argue!': Communicative Action in World Politics," *International Organization* 54, no. 1 (2000): 1–39.
16. Barbara Koremenos, Charles Lipson, and Duncan Snidal, "The Rational Design of International Institutions," *International Organization* 55, no. 4 (Autumn 2001): 761–799; Christopher Jönsson, "Diplomacy, Bargaining and Negotiation," in *Handbook*

of International Relations, 2nd ed., ed. Walter Carlsnaes, Thomas Risse-Kappen, and Beth A. Simmons (Los Angeles: SAGE, 2013).
17. Thomas C. Schelling, *Arms and Influence* (New Haven, CT: Yale University Press, 2008), chap. 1.
18. Biddle, *Military Power*.
19. David A. Baldwin, "Power Analysis and World Politics: New Trends versus Old Tendencies," *World Politics* 31, no. 2 (1979): 161–194.
20. John Prados, *Safe for Democracy: The Secret Wars of the CIA* (Chicago: Ivan R. Dee, 2006); Corke, *US Covert Operations and Cold War Strategy*; Alexander B. Downes and Mary Lauren Lilley, "Overt Peace, Covert War?: Covert Intervention and the Democratic Peace," *Security Studies* 19, no. 2 (May 2010): 266–306, doi:10.1080/09636411003795756; J. Patrice McSherry, *Predatory States: Operation Condor and Covert War in Latin America* (Lanham, MD: Rowman & Littlefield Publishers, 2012); Rory Cormac, "Coordinating Covert Action: The Case of the Yemen Civil War and the South Arabian Insurgency," *Journal of Strategic Studies* 36, no. 5 (October 2013): 692–717, doi:10.1080/01402390.2011.651534; Carson, *Secret Wars*.
21. Bull, *The Anarchical Society*, 163.
22. A. Maurice Low, "The Vice of Secret Diplomacy," *North American Review* 207, no. 747 (1918): 209–220; Corneliu Bjola and Stuart Murray, *Secret Diplomacy: Concepts, Contexts and Cases* (London: Routledge, 2016).
23. Habermas, *The Theory of Communicative Action*; Risse, "Let's Argue!"
24. Henry Kissinger, *Diplomacy*, A Touchstone Book (New York: Simon & Schuster, 1995); Koremenos, Lipson, and Snidal, "The Rational Design of International Institutions."
25. Schelling, *Arms and Influence*.
26. Schelling, *Arms and Influence*.
27. Bull, *The Anarchical Society*, 70.
28. Joseph S. Nye, "Soft Power," *Foreign Policy*, no. 80 (1990): 166, doi:10.2307/1148580.
29. To be sure, more recent literature distinguishes a wider range of instruments, as discussed in the next section.
30. The use of political proxy groups described by Melissa Lee in *Crippling Leviathan* is a key instance of such exploitation. Lee, *Crippling Leviathan*.
31. Blackstock, *The Strategy of Subversion*, 56.
32. Melissa Lee's theory does this as well by emphasizing the crucial importance of delegation to proxy actors.
33. Blackstock, *The Strategy of Subversion*, 121–122.
34. Blackstock, *The Strategy of Subversion*, 49–50.
35. James G. March and Johan P. Olsen, "The Institutional Dynamics of International Political Orders," *International Organization* 52, no. 4 (1998): 946.
36. Mahoney, James, and Kathleen Thelen, eds. 'A Theory of Gradual Institutional Change'. In *Explaining Institutional Change: Ambiguity, Agency, and Power*, 1–37 (Cambridge: Cambridge University Press, 2009). https://doi.org/10.1017/CBO9780511806414.003; Falleti, Tulia G. 'Infiltrating the State: The Evolution of Health Care Reforms in Brazil, 1964–1988'. In *Explaining Institutional Change: Ambiguity,*

Agency, and Power, edited by James Mahoney and Kathleen Thelen, 38–62. (Cambridge: Cambridge University Press, 2009). https://doi.org/10.1017/CBO9780511806414.004

37. James Mahoney and Kathleen Ann Thelen, eds., *Explaining Institutional Change: Ambiguity, Agency, and Power* (Cambridge: Cambridge University Press, 2010), 25–26.
38. Defined as "more or less stable patterns of interaction among a set of internally related elements based on shared understandings, knowledge, rules, and practices that evolve in a mutually constitutive iterative process where interaction shapes the identities of agents, while agents in turn shape structure." Maschmeyer, "Subversion, Cyber Operations, and Reverse Structural Power in World Politics," 86.
39. As previously mentioned, population is a key measure of state capability in both realist and liberal theory.
40. Strange, *States and Markets*; Barnett and Duvall, "Power in International Politics."
41. Maschmeyer, "Subversion, Cyber Operations, and Reverse Structural Power in World Politics."
42. Maschmeyer, "Subversion, Cyber Operations, and Reverse Structural Power in World Politics."
43. Rory Cormac and Richard J. Aldrich, "Grey Is the New Black: Covert Action and Implausible Deniability," *International Affairs* 94, no. 3 (May 2018): 477–494, doi:10.1093/ia/iiy067.
44. Beilenson, *Power through Subversion*, 63. This risk will be discussed in further detail in the operational section further below.
45. Beilenson, *Power through Subversion*, vi.
46. Christopher M. Andrew, *The Mitrokhin Archive: The KGB in Europe and the West* (London: Allen Lane, 2000).
47. Andrew and Mitrokhin, *The Sword and the Shield*, 360.
48. Richelson, *A Century of Spies*, 140; Andrew and Mitrokhin, *The Sword and the Shield*, 400.
49. O'Rourke, *Covert Regime Change*, 65–66; Lee, *Crippling Leviathan*, 9–10.
50. Johnson, "On Drawing a Bright Line for Covert Operations," 286.
51. Wohlforth, "Realism and Great Power Subversion," 461.
52. Shultz, Richard H., and Roy Godson. *Dezinformatsia: Active Measures in Soviet Strategy* (Washington: Pergamon-Brassey's, 1984)..
53. US Department of State, "Soviet 'Active Measures' Report No. 88 Forgery, Disinformation, Political Operations," 1981, https://www.cia.gov/library/readingroom/docs/CIA-RDP84B00049R001303150031-0.pdf.
54. Eckard Michels, *Guillaume, Der Spion: Eine Deutsch-Deutsche Karriere* (Berlin: Ch. Links Verlag, 2013).
55. Howard Douthit III, "The Use and Effectiveness of Sabotage as a Means of Unconventional Warfare" (Master's Thesis: Air University, 1987); Ian Dear, *Sabotage & Subversion: Stories from the Files of the SOE and OSS* (London: Arms and Armour, 1996).
56. Johnson, "On Drawing a Bright Line for Covert Operations," 288.

57. OSS, "Simple Sabotage Field Manual," 1944.
58. Callanan, *Covert Action in the Cold War*; O'Rourke, *Covert Regime Change*.
59. Blackstock, *The Strategy of Subversion*, 159.
60. Blackstock, *The Strategy of Subversion*, 161–165.
61. The operation was never executed, for unknown reasons.
62. Andrew and Mitrokhin, *The Sword and the Shield*, 374–376.
63. Prados, *Safe for Democracy*; O'Rourke, *Covert Regime Change*; Poznansky, *In the Shadow of International Law*.
64. Lennart Maschmeyer, "A New and Better Quiet Option? Strategies of Subversion and Cyber Conflict," *Journal of Strategic Studies* 46, no. 3 (July 2022): 1–25, doi:10.1080/01402390.2022.2104253.
65. Maschmeyer, "A New and Better Quiet Option?," 7–8.
66. Maschmeyer, "A New and Better Quiet Option?," 8–9.
67. J. C. Wylie and John B. Hattendorf, *Military Strategy: A General Theory of Power Control*, Classics of Sea Power (Annapolis, MD: Navel Institute Press, 2014), 51.
68. Maschmeyer, "A New and Better Quiet Option?," 10–12.
69. Beilenson, *Power through Subversion*, 251.
70. M. J. Heale, "Controlling Communist Subversion, 1948–1956," in *McCarthy's Americans: Red Scare Politics in State and Nation, 1935–1965*, American History in Depth, ed. M. J. Heale (London: Macmillan Education UK, 1998), 234–253, doi:10.1007/978-1-349-14546-1_11.
71. O'Rourke, *Covert Regime Change*, 5.
72. Blackstock, *The Strategy of Subversion*, 303.
73. Beilenson, *Power through Subversion*, 94.
74. Beilenson, *Power through Subversion*, 94.
75. Beilenson, *Power through Subversion*, 251.
76. Blackstock, *The Strategy of Subversion*, 303.
77. James D. Fearon, "Rationalist Explanations for War," *International Organization* 49, no. 3 (1995): 382.
78. Michael Poznansky, "Feigning Compliance: Covert Action and International Law," *International Studies Quarterly* 63, no. 1 (March 2019): 72–84, doi:10.1093/isq/sqy054.
79. To be sure, subversion can also support warfare and diplomacy, yet as discussed in the previous section the increasing destructiveness of war has raised its attractiveness as an alternative to force—in line with its perceived strategic promise. That is why I expect subversion to be primarily used as an independent instrument.
80. Blackstock, *The Strategy of Subversion*, 301; Beilenson, *Power through Subversion*, 160.
81. Blackstock, *The Strategy of Subversion*, 70.
82. Blackstock, *The Strategy of Subversion*, 75.
83. Blackstock, *The Strategy of Subversion*, 76.
84. Beilenson, *Power through Subversion*, 74, 83, 251.
85. Blackstock, *The Strategy of Subversion*, 70.

86. Michael Herman, *Intelligence Power in Peace and War* (Cambridge: Cambridge University Press, 1996), 64; Helen Womack, ed., *Undercover Lives: Soviet Spies in the Cities of the World* (London: Weidenfeld & Nicolson, 1998).
87. Scope refers to the sensitivity of processes, while scale refers to the proportion of relevant processes of a given system and the corresponding scale of effects.
88. Beilenson, *Power through Subversion*, 63.
89. Raymond J. Batvinis, "The Future of FBI Counterintelligence through the Lens of the Past Hundred Years," in *The Oxford Handbook of National Security Intelligence*, Oxford Handbooks, ed. Loch K. Johnson (Oxford: Oxford University Press, 2010), 511ff; Arthur S. Hulnick, "What's Wrong with the Intelligence Cycle?," in *Strategic Intelligence*, vol. 2: *The Intelligence Cycle*, ed. Loch K. Johnson (Westport, CT: Praeger Security International, 2007), 15.
90. O'Rourke, *Covert Regime Change*, 8.
91. Andrew, *The Mitrokhin Archive*, 200–201.
92. David A. Graham, "Rumsfeld's Knowns and Unknowns: The Intellectual History of a Quip," *The Atlantic*, March 2014, http://www.theatlantic.com/politics/archive/2014/03/rumsfelds-knowns-and-unknowns-the-intellectual-history-of-a-quip/359719/.
93. Lee, *Crippling Leviathan*, 56.
94. Callanan, *Covert Action in the Cold War*, 193; Lee, *Crippling Leviathan*, 55–56.
95. Gregory F. Treverton, *Covert Action: The Limits of Intervention in the Postwar World* (New York, Basic Books: I. B. Tauris, 1987), 9, doi:10.5040/9780755612529.
96. Herman, *Intelligence Power in Peace and War*, 65; Grey, *The New Spymasters*, 279.
97. For more details, see Stephen A. Ross, "The Economic Theory of Agency: The Principal's Problem," *American Economic Review* 63, no. 2 (1973): 134–139.

Chapter 2

1. Daniel T. Kuehl, "From Cyberspace to Cyberpower: Defining the Problem," in Franklin D. Kramer, Stuart H. Starr, and Larry K. Wentz, eds. *Cyberpower and National Security* (Washington, DC: Potomac Books, 2009), 38; Joseph S. Nye, *The Future of Power* (New York: PublicAffairs, 2011), 123; Liff, "Cyberwar"; Dale Peterson, "Offensive Cyber Weapons: Construction, Development, and Employment," *Journal of Strategic Studies* 36, no. 1 (2013): 120–124, doi:10.1080/01402390.2012.742014.
2. Max Smeets, *NO SHORTCUTS: Why States Struggle to Develop a Military Cyber-Force* (S.l.: Hurst & Company, 2022).
3. Wiebe E. Bijker and John Law, eds., *Shaping Technology/Building Society: Studies in Sociotechnical Change*, Inside Technology, repr. (Cambridge, MA: MIT Press, 2010).
4. David I. Bainbridge, "Hacking: The Unauthorised Access of Computer Systems; The Legal Implications," *Modern Law Review* 52, no. 2 (1989): 236–245.
5. Ronald Deibert, *Parchment, Printing, and Hypermedia: Communication in World Order Transformation* (New York: Columbia University Press, 1997); Laura DeNardis, *Protocol Politics: The Globalization of Internet Governance* (Cambridge, MA: MIT Press, 2009), http://myaccess.library.utoronto.ca/login?url=http://site.ebrary.com/

lib/utoronto/Doc?id=10326187; Thierry Balzacq and Myriam Dunn Cavelty, "A Theory of Actor-Network for Cyber-Security," *European Journal of International Security* 1, no. 2 (July 2016): 176–198, doi:10.1017/eis.2016.8; Rebecca Slayton and Brian Clarke, "Trusting Infrastructure: The Emergence of Computer Security Incident Response, 1989–2005," *Technology and Culture* 61, no. 1 (2020): 173–206, doi:10.1353/tech.2020.0036.

6. Mary Thornton, "'Hackers' Ignore Consequences of Their High-Tech Joy Rides," *Washington Post*, May 21, 1984, https://www.washingtonpost.com/archive/politics/1984/05/21/hackers-ignore-consequences-of-their-high-tech-joy-rides/6ab0d2fa-68dd-44af-89fe-7dd30927133b/.

7. Katie Hafner and John Markoff, *Cyberpunk: Outlaws and Hackers on the Computer Frontier* (New York: Simon & Schuster, 1991), 60–61.

8. Prashanth Rajivan and Cleotilde Gonzalez, "Creative Persuasion: A Study on Adversarial Behaviors and Strategies in Phishing Attacks," *Frontiers in Psychology* 9 (February 2018): 135, doi:10.3389/fpsyg.2018.00135.

9. The initial email suggests one's email account is compromised, indicating a failed login attempt from Ukraine, triggering an emotional response (fear), while the failed login attempt exploits the human aversion of loss and indicates a sense of urgency (stopping the third party from access). This email contains a link to a password recovery page, which is coded to look like Google's recovery page, including its URL, yet is hosted on an entirely different server and sends the changed login information—purportedly restoring account integrity—to the Russian intelligence operatives behind it. The recovery page exploits the trust of users in Google, which is impersonated by replicating the visual design of its website despite the different underlying code. Lorenzo Franceschi-Bicchierai, "How Hackers Broke Into John Podesta and Colin Powell's Gmail Accounts," *Motherboard*, October 2016, https://motherboard.vice.com/en_us/article/how-hackers-broke-into-john-podesta-and-colin-powells-gmail-accounts; Lisa Vaas, "How Hackers Broke Into John Podesta, DNC Gmail Accounts," *Naked Security* (blog), October 2016, https://nakedsecurity.sophos.com/2016/10/25/how-hackers-broke-into-john-podesta-dnc-gmail-accounts/.

10. Lawrence Lessig, "Code Is Law," *Harvard Magazine*, January 2000, http://harvardmagazine.com/2000/01/code-is-law-html.

11. Technopedia, "Source Code Definition," n.d., accessed July 20, 2017, https://www.techopedia.com/definition/547/source-code#:~:text=Source%20code%20is%20the%20set,referred%20to%20as%20object%20code.

12. Jack Ganssle, *The Firmware Handbook* (Boston: Elsevier, 2004).

13. Erickson, *Hacking*, 115.

14. Erickson, *Hacking*, 320.

15. James P. Anderson, "Computer Security Technology Planning Study (Volume II)," October 1972, 3, https://csrc.nist.rip/publications/history/ande72.pdf.

16. Philip A. Myers, "Subversion: The Neglected Aspect of Computer Security" (master's thesis, Naval Postgraduate School, 1980), 10.

17. Susan Young and Dave Aitel, *The Hacker's Handbook: The Strategy behind Breaking Into and Defending Networks* (Boca Raton, FL: CRC Press, 2004), chap. 2.

18. Byungho Min and Vijay Varadharajan, "A Novel Malware for Subversion of Self-Protection in Anti-Virus," *Software: Practice and Experience* 46, no. 3 (2016): 361–379, doi:10.1002/spe.2317.
19. RSA, "Kingslayer—A Supply Chain Attack," 2017, 6, http://www.rsa.com/en-us/blog/2017-02/kingslayer-a-supply-chain-attack.
20. Rid, *Cyber War Will Not Take Place*.
21. Rid, *Cyber War Will Not Take Place*, 114.
22. Jon R. Lindsay, "Restrained by Design: The Political Economy of Cybersecurity," *Digital Policy, Regulation and Governance* 19, no. 6 (July 2017): 505, doi:10.1108/DPRG-05-2017-0023.
23. In some cases, remote conduct is not possible, requiring physical access. Particularly sensitive systems tend to be air-gapped, meaning they lack any physical connection to a network. Hence, physical access to the system is required to install malicious code, for example via a portable drive such as a USB key. In fact, the infamous Stuxnet operation very probably relied on this means to infect the air-gapped systems at the Natanz nuclear enrichment plan. Nicolas Falliere, Liam O. Murchu, and Eric Chien, "W32.Stuxnet Dossier," Symantec, 2011, 25. http://www.symantec.com/security_response/writeup.jsp?docid=2010-071400-3123-99.
24. Martin C. Libicki, *Cyberdeterrence and Cyberwar* (Santa Monica, CA: Rand, 2009), xiv.
25. Jason Healey and Karl Grindal, eds., *A Fierce Domain: Conflict in Cyberspace, 1986 to 2012* (Vienna, VA: Cyber Conflict Studies Association, 2013), 221; Langner, "To Kill a Centrifuge," 11.
26. Lindsay, "Stuxnet and the Limits of Cyber Warfare."
27. Bernd J. Krämer, "Evolution of Cyber-Physical Systems: A Brief Review," in *Applied Cyber-Physical Systems*, ed. Sang C. Suh et al. (New York: Springer New York, 2014), 1–3, doi:10.1007/978-1-4614-7336-7; Lukas Esterle and Radu Grosu, "Cyber-Physical Systems: Challenge of the 21st Century," *E & i Elektrotechnik Und Informationstechnik* 133, no. 7 (2016): 299–303, doi:10.1007/s00502-016-0426-6.
28. Kello, *Virtual Weapon and International Order*; see also Harknett and Smeets, "Cyber Campaigns and Strategic Outcomes," 9–10.
29. Warner, "A Matter of Trust: Covert Action Reconsidered," 39–40.
30. Buchanan, *The Hacker and the State*, 290.
31. Michael P. Fischerkeller and Richard J. Harknett, "Deterrence Is Not a Credible Strategy for Cyberspace," *Orbis* 61, no. 3 (January 2017): 386, doi:10.1016/j.orbis.2017.05.003.
32. Harknett and Smeets, "Cyber Campaigns and Strategic Outcomes," 24.
33. Jürgen Kraus, "Selbstreproduktion Bei Programmen" (diploma thesis, Universität Dortmund, 1980), http://83.133.184.251/virensimulation.org/lib/mjk00.html; Fred Cohen, "Computer Viruses: Theory and Experiments," *Computers & Security* 6, no. 1 (1987): 22–35.
34. Jon R. Lindsay and Erik Gartzke, "Coercion through Cyberspace: The Stability-Instability Paradox Revisited," in *The Power to Hurt: Coercion in Theory and in Practice*, ed. Peter Krause (New York: Oxford University Press, 2018), 185–187; Max

Smeets, "The Strategic Promise of Offensive Cyber Operations," *Strategic Studies Quarterly* 12, no. 3 (2018): 90–113.
35. Maschmeyer, "A New and Better Quiet Option?"
36. Harknett and Smeets, "Cyber Campaigns and Strategic Outcomes"; Fischerkeller, Goldman, and Harknett, *Cyber Persistence Theory*.
37. Robert S. Mueller III, "Report on the Investigation into Russian Interference in the 2016 Presidential Election," March 2019, https://www.justice.gov/storage/report.pdf.
38. Of course, influence on public opinion can also influence government policy, especially in democratic regimes. Yet this is an indirect influence through the public rather than subverting the government itself, as is possible with human agents in traditional subversion.
39. Philip N. Howard, *Pax Technica: How the Internet of Things May Set Us Free or Lock Us Up* (New Haven, CT: Yale University Press, 2015).
40. Ray Y. Zhong et al., "Intelligent Manufacturing in the Context of Industry 4.0: A Review," *Engineering* 3, no. 5 (October 2017): 616–630, doi:10.1016/J.ENG.2017.05.015; Hugh Boyes et al., "The Industrial Internet of Things (IIoT): An Analysis Framework," *Computers in Industry* 101 (October 2018): 1–12, doi:10.1016/j.compind.2018.04.015.
41. Laura Tyson and Susan Lund, "The Promise of Digital Finance," *European Financial Review*, 2017, http://www.europeanfinancialreview.com/?p=16598.
42. O'Rourke, *Covert Regime Change*.
43. Hopefully for quite some time.
44. Lillian Ablon and Andy Bogart, *Zero Days, Thousands of Nights* (Santa Monica, CA: Rand, 2017), https://www.rand.org/pubs/research_reports/RR1751.html.
45. McDonald, Geoff, Liam O. Murchu, Stephen Doherty, and Eric Chien. "Stuxnet 0.5: The Missing Link." *Symantec*, February 2013. https://web.archive.org/web/20150112172930/http://www.symantec.com/content/en/us/enterprise/media/security_response/whitepapers/stuxnet_0_5_the_missing_link.pdf.
46. Slayton, "What Is the Cyber Offense-Defense Balance?," 91–93.
47. Andy Greenberg, "The US Sanctions Russians for Potentially 'Fatal' Triton Malware," October 2020, https://www.wired.com/story/russia-sanctions-triton-malware/.
48. FireEye, "Attackers Deploy New ICS Attack Framework 'TRITON' and Cause Operational Disruption to Critical Infrastructure," *FireEye* (blog), December 2017, https://www.fireeye.com/blog/threat-research/2017/12/attackers-deploy-new-ics-attack-framework-triton.html.
49. FireEye, "Attackers Deploy New ICS Attack Framework 'TRITON' and Cause Operational Disruption to Critical Infrastructure."
50. Anderson, "Why Information Security Is Hard—An Economic Perspective"; William J. Lynn III, "Defending a New Domain," *Foreign Affairs*, 2010, https://www.foreignaffairs.com/articles/united-states/2010-09-01/defending-new-domain.
51. Anti-Virus.by, "News: VirusBlokAda," 2010, http://www.anti-virus.by/en/tempo.shtml.
52. Florian J. Egloff, "Contested Public Attributions of Cyber Incidents and the Role of Academia," *Contemporary Security Policy* 41, no. 1 (January 2020): 55–81,

242   NOTES

doi:10.1080/13523260.2019.1677324; Sasha Romanosky and Benjamin Boudreaux, "Private-Sector Attribution of Cyber Incidents: Benefits and Risks to the U.S. Government," *International Journal of Intelligence and CounterIntelligence* 34, no. 3 (August 2020): 1–31, doi:10.1080/08850607.2020.1783877.

53. FireEye, "M-Trends," 2020, https://content.fireeye.com/m-trends/rpt-m-trends-2020; Florian Roth et al., "APT Groups and Operations," accessed July 3, 2022, https://docs.google.com/spreadsheets/d/1H9_xaxQHpWaa4O_Son4Gx0YOIzlcBWMsdvePFX68EKU/edit?usp=embed_facebook.
54. Ronald Deibert, Rafal Rohozinski, and Masashi Crete-Nishihata, "Cyclones in Cyberspace: Information Shaping and Denial in the 2008 Russia–Georgia War," *Security Dialogue* 43, no. 1 (2012): 3–24, doi:10.1177/0967010611431079; Florian J. Egloff, *Semi-State Actors in Cybersecurity* (New York: Oxford University Press, 2022).
55. Herman, *Intelligence Power in Peace and War*, 65; Grey, *The New Spymasters*, 279.
56. Andy Sudduth, "The Morris Internet Worm," 1988, https://snowplow.org/tom/worm/worm.html.
57. Hafner and Markoff, *Cyberpunk*, 290–310.
58. Hafner and Markoff, *Cyberpunk*, 303.
59. Slayton, "What Is the Cyber Offense-Defense Balance?," 92.

Chapter 3

1. Philip Windsor and Adam Roberts, *Czechoslovakia, 1968: Reform, Repression, and Resistance* (London: Columbia University Press, for the Institute for Strategic Studies, 1969), 9–10.
2. CIA Office of National Estimates, "Czechoslovakia: A New Direction," Special Memorandum, CIA, January 1968, 1.
3. Kieran Williams, *Prague Spring and Its Aftermath: Czechoslovak Politics, 1968–1970*. (Cambridge: Cambridge University Press, 2011), 29, http://public.eblib.com/choice/publicfullrecord.aspx?p=4641036.
4. Jiri Valenta, *Soviet Intervention in Czechoslovakia, 1968: Anatomy of a Decision*, 2nd rev. and expanded ed. (Baltimore, MD: Johns Hopkins University Press, 1991), 186.
5. Günter Bischof, Stefan Karner, and Peter Ruggenthaler, eds., *The Prague Spring and the Warsaw Pact Invasion of Czechoslovakia in 1968*, Harvard Cold War Studies Book Series (Lanham, MD: Lexington Books, 2010), 4.
6. Valenta, *Soviet Intervention in Czechoslovakia, 1968*, 12.
7. Ladislav Bittman, *The Deception Game* (New York: Ballantine Books, 1981), 185.
8. Karen Dawisha, *The Kremlin and the Prague Spring*, International Crisis Behavior Series, vol. 4 (Berkeley: University of California Press, 1984), 21–31; Valenta, *Soviet Intervention in Czechoslovakia, 1968*, 15–16; M. Mark Stolarik, ed., *The Prague Spring and the Warsaw Pact Invasion of Czechoslovakia, 1968: Forty Years Later* (Mundelein, IL: Bolchazy-Carducci Publishers, 2010), 28–29.
9. Bittman, *The Deception Game*, 185.
10. Williams, *Prague Spring and Its Aftermath*, 54–56.
11. Williams, *Prague Spring and Its Aftermath*, 63.

12. Mikhail Prozumenshchikov, "Politburo Decision-Making on the Czechoslovak Crisis in 1968," in *The Prague Spring and the Warsaw Pact Invasion of Czechoslovakia in 1968*, Harvard Cold War Studies Book Series, ed. Günter Bischof, Stefan Karner, and Peter Ruggenthaler (Lanham, MD: Lexington Books, 2010), 105; Nikita Petrov, "The KGB and the Czechoslovak Crisis of 1968," in *The Prague Spring and the Warsaw Pact Invasion of Czechoslovakia in 1968*, Harvard Cold War Studies Book Series, ed. Günter Bischof, Stefan Karner, and Peter Ruggenthaler (Lanham, MD: Lexington Books, 2010), 159.
13. Williams, *Prague Spring and Its Aftermath*, 64.
14. Andrew and Mitrokhin, *The Sword and the Shield*, 250; Dawisha, *The Kremlin and the Prague Spring*, 32; Prozumenshchikov, "Politburo Decision-Making on the Czechoslovak Crisis in 1968," 104.
15. Prozumenshchikov, "Politburo Decision-Making on the Czechoslovak Crisis in 1968," 108.
16. Alexander Dubcek, *Hope Dies Last: The Autobiography of Alexander Dubcek*, ed. Jiri Hochman (New York: Kodansha USA, 1993), 134.
17. Dubcek, *Hope Dies Last*, 135.
18. Williams, *Prague Spring and Its Aftermath*, 66.
19. Dubcek, *Hope Dies Last*, 138.
20. Dubcek, *Hope Dies Last*, 138.
21. Bittman, *The Deception Game*, 184.
22. Petrov, "The KGB and the Czechoslovak Crisis of 1968," 149.
23. Brad D. Williams, "How Russia Adapted KGB 'Active Measures' to Cyber Operations, Part I," Fifth Domain: Cyber, March 2017, 66–67, http://fifthdomain.com/2017/03/19/how-russia-adapted-kgb-active-measures-to-cyber-operations-part-i/.
24. Dubcek, *Hope Dies Last*, 130.
25. Williams, *Prague Spring and Its Aftermath*, 113.
26. Williams, *Prague Spring and Its Aftermath*, 34.
27. Petrov, "The KGB and the Czechoslovak Crisis of 1968," 105.
28. Stolarik, *The Prague Spring and the Warsaw Pact Invasion of Czechoslovakia, 1968*, 20.
29. Petrov, "The KGB and the Czechoslovak Crisis of 1968," 105.
30. Dawisha, *The Kremlin and the Prague Spring*, 37.
31. Dubcek, *Hope Dies Last*, 142.
32. Williams, *Prague Spring and Its Aftermath*, 71.
33. Williams, *Prague Spring and Its Aftermath*, 113.
34. Williams, *Prague Spring and Its Aftermath*, 113.
35. Miklós Kun, *Prague Spring, Prague Fall: Blank Spots of 1968* (Budapest: Akadémiai Kiadó, 1999), 138.
36. Petrov, "The KGB and the Czechoslovak Crisis of 1968," 151; Andrew and Mitrokhin, *The Sword and the Shield*, 251.
37. Matthew J. Ouimet, "Reconsidering the Soviet Role," in *The Prague Spring and the Warsaw Pact Invasion of Czechoslovakia, 1968: Forty Years Later*, ed. M. Mark Stolarik (Mundelein, IL: Bolchazy-Carducci Publishers, 2010), 22.
38. "Russia Accuses U.S. of Increasing Subversion."
39. Andrew and Mitrokhin, *The Sword and the Shield*, 252.

40. Andrew and Mitrokhin, *The Sword and the Shield*, 251.
41. Andrew and Mitrokhin, *The Sword and the Shield*, 252.
42. Andrew and Mitrokhin, *The Sword and the Shield*, 248.
43. Z. A. B. Zeman, *Prague Spring* (New York: Hill and Wang, 1969); Dimitri K. Simes, "The Soviet Invasion of Czechoslovakia and the Limits of Kremlinology," *Studies in Comparative Communism* 8, no. 1–2 (1975): 174–180, doi:10.1016/0039-3592(75)90026-5; Dawisha, *The Kremlin and the Prague Spring*.
44. Valenta, *Soviet Intervention in Czechoslovakia, 1968*, 64.
45. Petrov, "The KGB and the Czechoslovak Crisis of 1968," 149–150.
46. Kun, *Prague Spring, Prague Fall*, 139.
47. Prozumenshchikov, "Politburo Decision-Making on the Czechoslovak Crisis in 1968," 111.
48. Bittman, *The Deception Game*, 185.
49. CIA, "Intelligence Memorandum: Czechoslovakia in Transition," April 1968, 4.
50. Prozumenshchikov, "Politburo Decision-Making on the Czechoslovak Crisis in 1968," 111.
51. Fred H. Eidlin, *The Logic of "Normalization": The Soviet Intervention in Czechoslovakia of 21 August 1968 and the Czechoslovak Response* (Boulder, Colorado: Eastern European Monographs, 1980), 28.
52. Jaromír Navrátil, *The Prague Spring 1968: A National Security Archive Documents Reader* (Budapest: Central European University Press, 1998), 502.
53. Kieran Williams, "New Sources on Soviet Decision Making during the 1968 Czechoslovak Crisis," *Europe-Asia Studies* 48, no. 3 (May 1996): 457.
54. Bischof, Karner, and Ruggenthaler, *The Prague Spring and the Warsaw Pact Invasion of Czechoslovakia in 1968*, 20.
55. Andrew and Mitrokhin, *The Sword and the Shield*, 255; Petrov, "The KGB and the Czechoslovak Crisis of 1968," 153; Jiri Valenta, "The Bureaucratic Politics Paradigm and the Soviet Invasion of Czechoslovakia," *Political Science Quarterly* 94, no. 1 (1979): 33, doi:10.2307/2150156.
56. Andrew and Mitrokhin, *The Sword and the Shield*, 253; Petrov, "The KGB and the Czechoslovak Crisis of 1968," 152. There is some ambiguity in the literature as to the precise division of labor between PROGRESS and KHODOKI: Andrew and Mitrokhin seem to suggest that KHODOKI operations were an overall part of PROGRESS. While this may be the case, it does not pose a problem for the distinction between active measures and infiltration operations made here for the sake of clarity.
57. Andrew and Mitrokhin, *The Sword and the Shield*, 252; Pavel Žáček, "The KGB and the Czechoslovak State Security Apparatus in August 1968," *Journal of Slavic Military Studies* 29, no. 4 (2016): 628, doi:10.1080/13518046.2016.1232561.
58. Andrew, *The Mitrokhin Archive*, 329.
59. Valenta, "The Bureaucratic Politics Paradigm and the Soviet Invasion of Czechoslovakia," 23; Ouimet, "Reconsidering the Soviet Role," 22.
60. Herman, *Intelligence Power in Peace and War*, 64; Womack, *Undercover Lives*.
61. Andrew and Mitrokhin, *The Sword and the Shield*, 252.
62. Petrov, "The KGB and the Czechoslovak Crisis of 1968," 152.

63. Andrew and Mitrokhin, *The Sword and the Shield*, 252.
64. Petrov, "The KGB and the Czechoslovak Crisis of 1968," 152.
65. Andrew and Mitrokhin, *The Sword and the Shield*, 252.
66. Christopher M. Andrew and Oleg Gordievsky, *KGB: The Inside Story of Its Foreign Operations from Lenin to Gorbachev* (New York: Harper Collins Publishers, 1990), 483.
67. Ithiel De Sola Pool, "Public Opinion in Czechoslovakia," *Public Opinion Quarterly* 34, no. 1 (1970): 15.
68. Johnson, "On Drawing a Bright Line for Covert Operations."
69. Johnson, "On Drawing a Bright Line for Covert Operations," 290.
70. Navrátil, *The Prague Spring 1968*, 96.
71. Navrátil, *The Prague Spring 1968*, 97.
72. Navrátil, *The Prague Spring 1968*, 97.
73. Moreover, the timing of the operation coincides with Andropov's order to dispatch illegal agents to Czechoslovakia in March 1968. However, if these agents had penetrated Cerny and Prochizka's group at that time, it would indicate a very short lead time of only a few days. Hence, this report indicates that KGB infiltration of opposition groups may have proceeded earlier than suggested by Andrew and Mitrokhin. An alternative explanation is that the information in the report came from a pre-existing agent who had infiltrated the group prior to the start of PROGRESS operations.
74. Andrew and Mitrokhin, *The Sword and the Shield*, 254.
75. Andrew and Mitrokhin, *The Sword and the Shield*, 254–255.
76. CIA, "The Situation in Czechoslovakia 10/5/1968, 10am," May 1968.
77. Andrew and Mitrokhin, *The Sword and the Shield*, 254.
78. Andrew and Mitrokhin, *The Sword and the Shield*, 254–255.
79. Johnson, "On Drawing a Bright Line for Covert Operations," 286.
80. Petrov, "The KGB and the Czechoslovak Crisis of 1968," 153, 162.
81. Andrew and Mitrokhin, *The Sword and the Shield*, 256.
82. Andrew and Mitrokhin, *The Sword and the Shield*, 256.
83. Andrew and Mitrokhin, *The Sword and the Shield*, 254.
84. Dawisha, *The Kremlin and the Prague Spring*, 196.
85. Andrew and Mitrokhin, *The Sword and the Shield*, 255.
86. Andrew and Mitrokhin, *The Sword and the Shield*, 255.
87. Johnson, "On Drawing a Bright Line for Covert Operations," 286.
88. Andrew and Mitrokhin, *The Sword and the Shield*, 256.
89. Valenta, "The Bureaucratic Politics Paradigm and the Soviet Invasion of Czechoslovakia," 64; Andrew and Mitrokhin, *The Sword and the Shield*, 255.
90. Dawisha, *The Kremlin and the Prague Spring*, 233.
91. Dawisha, *The Kremlin and the Prague Spring*, 196.
92. Alexsei Filitov, "The USSR, the Federal Republic of Germany, and the Czechoslovak Crisis of 1968," in *The Prague Spring and the Warsaw Pact Invasion of Czechoslovakia in 1968*, Harvard Cold War Studies Book Series, ed. Günter Bischof, Stefan Karner, and Peter Ruggenthaler (Lanham, MD: Lexington Books, 2010), 322.
93. Filitov, "The USSR, the Federal Republic of Germany, and the Czechoslovak Crisis of 1968," 322.

246   NOTES

94. Valenta, "The Bureaucratic Politics Paradigm and the Soviet Invasion of Czechoslovakia," 65.
95. Andrew and Mitrokhin, *The Sword and the Shield*, 256; Dawisha, *The Kremlin and the Prague Spring*, 196; Ladislav Bittman, *The KGB and Soviet Disinformation: An Insider's View* (Washington, DC: Pergamon-Brassey's, 1985), 14.
96. J. Řezábek, "Let Us Pay Attention," *Mladá Fronta*, July 23, 1968; "Unsubstantiated Reports," *Zemědělské Noviny*, July 1968.
97. Bittman, *The Deception Game*, 195.
98. As will be discussed in more detail below, these reports contain meticulously collected and highly comprehensive summaries of individual opinions and perceptions by a wide range of the population in both countries. If the deception had an impact, it should be visible in these reports: they provide the clearest window into public perception that is available.
99. Based on all available material in the CIA archive collection on the "Czech Invasion," available online at https://www.cia.gov/readingroom/collection/strategic-warning-and-role-intelligence-lessons-learned-1968-soviet-invasion.
100. Foreign Broadcast Information Service, "FBIS Special Report on Communist Propaganda—The I. Aleksandrov Article," July 1968.
101. Williams, *Prague Spring and Its Aftermath*.
102. Andrew and Mitrokhin, *The Sword and the Shield*, 256.
103. Petrov, "The KGB and the Czechoslovak Crisis of 1968," 153.
104. Andrew and Mitrokhin, *The Sword and the Shield*, 5.
105. Lead time refers to the period between the start of first preparations for an operation and the production of the effect under examination. If an operation pursues multiple effects over a period of time, lead time is measured for each of these effects.
106. Dawisha, *The Kremlin and the Prague Spring*, 233.
107. Prozumenshchikov, "Politburo Decision-Making on the Czechoslovak Crisis in 1968," 116–118.
108. Prozumenshchikov, "Politburo Decision-Making on the Czechoslovak Crisis in 1968," 118.
109. Prozumenshchikov, "Politburo Decision-Making on the Czechoslovak Crisis in 1968," 118.
110. Andrew and Mitrokhin, *The Sword and the Shield*, 256.
111. Valenta, "The Bureaucratic Politics Paradigm and the Soviet Invasion of Czechoslovakia," 64.
112. Andrew and Mitrokhin, *The Sword and the Shield*, 256.
113. Richard H. Shultz and Roy Godson, *Dezinformatsia: Active Measures in Soviet Strategy* (Washington, DC: Pergamon-Brassey's, 1984); US Department of State, "Soviet 'Active Measures' Report No. 88 Forgery, Disinformation, Political Operations," 2.
114. Andrew and Mitrokhin, *The Sword and the Shield*, 257.
115. Andrew and Mitrokhin, *The Sword and the Shield*, 253.
116. Andrew and Mitrokhin, *The Sword and the Shield*, 253.

117. Valenta, *Soviet Intervention in Czechoslovakia, 1968*, 40–41; Bischof, Karner, and Ruggenthaler, *The Prague Spring and the Warsaw Pact Invasion of Czechoslovakia in 1968*, 374–375.
118. Andrew and Mitrokhin, *The Sword and the Shield*, 256.
119. KGB Ukrainian SSR, "F.16-Op.01-Spr.0979-0056," October 1968, Archive Department of the Security Service of Ukraine—Former KGB Archive.
120. In September 1968, the KGB noticed a pattern in letters by Czechoslovak schoolchildren to their pen pals in Ukraine that condemned the Soviet invasion. KGB Ukrainian SSR, "F.16-Op.01-Spr.0979-0079," September 1968, Archive Department of the Security Service of Ukraine—Former KGB Archive. These children were not happy about the invasion, telling their pen pals what the KGB called "fabrications," such as how Soviet tanks had destroyed the National Museum in Prague (which was in fact subjected to heavy machine gun fire, being mistaken for the Communist Party headquarters). Helen Womack and Kate Connolly, "Previously Unseen Photos Depict Drama of 1968 Soviet Invasion of Prague," *The Observer*, August 17, 2008, sec. World News, https://www.theguardian.com/world/2008/aug/17/1968theyearofrevolt.russia. KGB investigators smelled a rat, noting, "the monotony of the structure of the majority of the letters is suspicious." KGB Ukrainian SSR, "F.16-Op.01-Spr.0979-0079." Hence, they concluded, these letters were coordinated by anti-Soviet forces to misinform the Soviet public. To defend against this threat, the Ukrainian KGB proposed exactly what it accused the Czechoslovakian anti-Soviets of doing: organizing a mass writing of response letters, coordinated by the Ukrainian Communist Party and educational organizations, laying out the correct ideology. Whether it was ever carried out is not clear—the operation is never mentioned again in later reports.
121. Žáček, "The KGB and the Czechoslovak State Security Apparatus in August 1968," 627.
122. Petrov, "The KGB and the Czechoslovak Crisis of 1968," 151.
123. Žáček, "The KGB and the Czechoslovak State Security Apparatus in August 1968," 627.
124. Petrov, "The KGB and the Czechoslovak Crisis of 1968," 152.
125. Dawisha, *The Kremlin and the Prague Spring*, 72–77.
126. Williams, *Prague Spring and Its Aftermath*, 115.
127. Petrov, "The KGB and the Czechoslovak Crisis of 1968," 151.
128. Williams, *Prague Spring and Its Aftermath*, 116.
129. CIA, "The Situation in Czechoslovakia 10/5/1968, 10am."
130. Petrov, "The KGB and the Czechoslovak Crisis of 1968," 151–152.
131. KGB Ukrainian SSR, "F.16.Op.01-Spr.0974-0338," July 1968, Archive Department of the Security Service of Ukraine—Former KGB Archive.
132. Valenta, *Soviet Intervention in Czechoslovakia, 1968*, 38.
133. Williams, *Prague Spring and Its Aftermath*, 120.
134. Cynthia R Grabo, "Soviet Deception in the Czechoslovak Crisis," *Studies in Intelligence*, Fall 2000, 81.
135. CIA, "The Crisis in Czechoslovakia," July 1968, 2.

136. Foreign Broadcast Information Service, "FBIS Special Report on Communist Propaganda—The I. Aleksandrov Article," 5.
137. Prozumenshchikov, "Politburo Decision-Making on the Czechoslovak Crisis in 1968," 111.
138. Pool, "Public Opinion in Czechoslovakia," 15.
139. Andrew and Mitrokhin, *The Sword and the Shield*, 256.
140. Bischof, Karner, and Ruggenthaler, *The Prague Spring and the Warsaw Pact Invasion of Czechoslovakia in 1968*, 153.
141. Williams, *Prague Spring and Its Aftermath*, 99.
142. Andrew and Mitrokhin, *The Sword and the Shield*, 256.
143. Williams, *Prague Spring and Its Aftermath*, 102.
    Williams, *Prague Spring and Its Aftermath*, 103.
    Grabo, "Soviet Deception in the Czechoslovak Crisis," 81.
144. Williams, *Prague Spring and Its Aftermath*, 102.
145. Williams, *Prague Spring and Its Aftermath*, 103.
146. Prozumenshchikov, "Politburo Decision-Making on the Czechoslovak Crisis in 1968," 121.
147. CIA, "Intelligence Memorandum: The Soviet Decision to Intervene in Czechoslovakia," August 1968, 2.
148. Williams, *Prague Spring and Its Aftermath*, 121.
149. Williams, *Prague Spring and Its Aftermath*, 122.
150. Valenta, "The Bureaucratic Politics Paradigm and the Soviet Invasion of Czechoslovakia," 126.
151. Valenta, *Soviet Intervention in Czechoslovakia, 1968*, 180.
152. Williams, *Prague Spring and Its Aftermath*, 122.
153. Williams, *Prague Spring and Its Aftermath*, 125.
154. Prozumenshchikov, "Politburo Decision-Making on the Czechoslovak Crisis in 1968," 127.
155. Kun, *Prague Spring, Prague Fall*, 146.
156. Andrew and Mitrokhin, *The Sword and the Shield*, 256.
157. Andrew and Mitrokhin, *The Sword and the Shield*, 257.
158. Oleg Kalugin, *Spymaster: My Thirty-Two Years in Intelligence and Espionage against the West* (New York: Basic Books, 2009), 120.
159. Williams, *Prague Spring and Its Aftermath*, 33.
160. Williams, *Prague Spring and Its Aftermath*, 33.
161. Valenta, *Soviet Intervention in Czechoslovakia, 1968*, 184.
162. Valenta, "The Bureaucratic Politics Paradigm and the Soviet Invasion of Czechoslovakia," 183.
163. Valenta, *Soviet Intervention in Czechoslovakia, 1968*, 178.
164. Williams, *Prague Spring and Its Aftermath*, 110.
165. Williams, *Prague Spring and Its Aftermath*, 106–107.
166. Williams, *Prague Spring and Its Aftermath*, 32.
167. Windsor and Roberts, *Czechoslovakia, 1968*, 105–110; Simes, "The Soviet Invasion of Czechoslovakia and the Limits of Kremlinology"; Dawisha, *The Kremlin and the Prague Spring*, 319–332.

168. Dubcek, *Hope Dies Last*, 128.
169. Eidlin and Eidlin, *The Logic of "Normalization,"* 208.
170. Kun, *Prague Spring, Prague Fall*, 151.
171. Williams, *Prague Spring and Its Aftermath*, 130–131.
172. Dawisha, *The Kremlin and the Prague Spring*, 321.
173. Dawisha, *The Kremlin and the Prague Spring*, 322.
174. Williams, *Prague Spring and Its Aftermath*, 127.
175. Dawisha, *The Kremlin and the Prague Spring*, 322.
176. Callanan, *Covert Action in the Cold War*, chap. 6.
177. Johnson, "On Drawing a Bright Line for Covert Operations," 286.
178. Herman, *Intelligence Power in Peace and War*, 197.
179. Žáček, "The KGB and the Czechoslovak State Security Apparatus in August 1968," 633–634.
180. Dawisha, *The Kremlin and the Prague Spring*, 322.
181. Williams, *Prague Spring and Its Aftermath*, 128.
182. Prozumenshchikov, "Politburo Decision-Making on the Czechoslovak Crisis in 1968," 128.
183. Petrov, "The KGB and the Czechoslovak Crisis of 1968," 156.
184. Prozumenshchikov, "Politburo Decision-Making on the Czechoslovak Crisis in 1968," 128.
185. Bittman, *The Deception Game*, 205.
186. Prozumenshchikov, "Politburo Decision-Making on the Czechoslovak Crisis in 1968," 129.
187. BND, "Dokumente Des Bundesnachrichtendienstes Zum Prager Frühling 1968," Mitteilungen Der Forschungs-Und Arbeitsgruppe "Geschichte Des BND," 2016, 285, https://web.archive.org/web/20201108155812/http://uzsi.cz/files/spolkova-zpravodajska-sluzba-prazske-jaro-1968.pdf.
188. Žáček, "The KGB and the Czechoslovak State Security Apparatus in August 1968."
189. Robert Littell, ed., *The Czech Black Book* (Westport, CT: Praeger, 1968), 65.
190. Žáček, "The KGB and the Czechoslovak State Security Apparatus in August 1968," 650–654.
191. Žáček, "The KGB and the Czechoslovak State Security Apparatus in August 1968," 634; Bittman, *The Deception Game*, 202.
192. Williams, *Prague Spring and Its Aftermath*, 129.
193. Bittman, *The Deception Game*, 203; Dawisha, *The Kremlin and the Prague Spring*, 329.
194. Williams, *Prague Spring and Its Aftermath*, 140–143.
195. Petrov, "The KGB and the Czechoslovak Crisis of 1968," 158.
196. Williams, *Prague Spring and Its Aftermath*, 126.
197. KGB Ukrainian SSR, "F.16-Op.01-Spr.0976-0244," July 1968, Archive Department of the Security Service of Ukraine—Former KGB Archive.
198. Littell, *The Czech Black Book*, 175.
199. Littell, *The Czech Black Book*, 176.
200. Dawisha, *The Kremlin and the Prague Spring*, 327.

250 NOTES

201. Williams, *Prague Spring and Its Aftermath*, 140.
202. Quoted in Petrov, "The KGB and the Czechoslovak Crisis of 1968," 152.
203. Monika Tantzscher, "Maßnahme »Donau« und Einsatz »Genesung«. Die Niederschlagung Des Prager Frühlings 1968/69 Im Spiegel Der MfS-Akten," Analysen Und Berichte, Reihe B (BStU, 1998), 39, https://d-nb.info/1036332 25X/34.
204. Petrov, "The KGB and the Czechoslovak Crisis of 1968," 158.
205. Žáček, "The KGB and the Czechoslovak State Security Apparatus in August 1968," 655.
206. Andrew and Mitrokhin, *The Sword and the Shield*, 260.
207. Andrew and Mitrokhin, *The Sword and the Shield*, 260.
208. Andrew and Mitrokhin, *The Sword and the Shield*, 252.
209. Žáček, "The KGB and the Czechoslovak State Security Apparatus in August 1968," 634; Bittman, *The Deception Game*, 202.
210. Robert K. Evanson, "Political Repression in Czechoslovakia, 1948–1984," *Canadian Slavonic Papers / Revue Canadienne Des Slavistes* 28, no. 1 (1986): 13.
211. Vladimir V. Kusin, *From Dubček to Charter 77: A Study of "Normalization" in Czechoslovakia, 1968–1978* (New York: St. Martin's Press, 1978), 112.
212. Tantzscher, "Maßnahme »Donau« und Einsatz »Genesung«. Die Niederschlagung Des Prager Frühlings 1968/69 Im Spiegel Der MfS-Akten," 43.
213. KGB Ukrainian SSR, "F.16-Op.01-Spr.0981-0350," December 1968, Archive Department of the Security Service of Ukraine—Former KGB Archive.
214. KGB Ukrainian SSR, "F.16-Op.01-Spr.0981-0350."
215. KGB Ukrainian SSR, "F.16-Op.01-Spr.0982-0410," January 1969, Archive Department of the Security Service of Ukraine—Former KGB Archive.
216. Windsor and Roberts, *Czechoslovakia, 1968*, 129.
217. Eidlin and Eidlin, *The Logic of "Normalization,"* 56.
218. Bittman, *The KGB and Soviet Disinformation*, 156.
219. Pool, "Public Opinion in Czechoslovakia," 15.
220. KGB Ukrainian SSR, "F.16-Op.01-Spr.0979-0267," October 1968, Archive Department of the Security Service of Ukraine—Former KGB Archive.
221. KGB Ukrainian SSR, "F.16-Op.01-Spr.0979-0267."
222. KGB Ukrainian SSR, "F.16-Op.01-Spr.0979-0267."
223. Ukrainian KGB Records at the SBU Archive in Kyiv, document range: F.16-Op.01-Spr.0979-0267 until F.16-Op.01-Spr.0979-0289.
224. Pavel Tigrid, *Why Dubcek Fell* (London: Macdonald and Co., 1971), 156.
225. Oldrich Tuma et al., "The (Inter-Communist) Cold War on Ice: Soviet-Czechoslovak Ice Hockey Politics, 1967–1969," CWIHP Working Paper #69 12, February 2014, 26.
226. Dubcek, *Hope Dies Last*, 237.
227. Dubcek, *Hope Dies Last*, 237.
228. Dubcek, *Hope Dies Last*, 237.
229. Dubcek, *Hope Dies Last*, 237.
230. Dubcek, *Hope Dies Last*, 237.
231. Dubcek, *Hope Dies Last*, 239.

232. Andrew and Mitrokhin, *The Sword and the Shield*, 262.
233. Williams, *Prague Spring and Its Aftermath*, 225.
234. Tuma et al., "The (Inter-Communist) Cold War on Ice," 26.
235. Tuma et al., "The (Inter-Communist) Cold War on Ice," 27.
236. Tuma et al., "The (Inter-Communist) Cold War on Ice," 27.
237. Tuma et al., "The (Inter-Communist) Cold War on Ice," 28.
238. Linda Holmes, "The Sports Riot: First We Lose (or Win), Then We Set This Sucker on Fire," *NPR*, 2011, https://www.npr.org/2011/06/16/137219581/the-sports-riot-first-we-lose-or-win-then-we-set-this-sucker-on-fire; Melvin M. Mark, Fred B. Bryant, and Darrin R. Lehman, "Perceived Injustice and Sports Violence," in *Sports Violence*, Springer Series in Social Psychology, ed. Jeffrey H. Goldstein (New York: Springer New York, 1983), 83–109, doi:10.1007/978-1-4612-5530-7_6; CBC, "Riots Erupt in Vancouver after Canucks Loss," *CBC News*, June 2011, https://www.cbc.ca/news/canada/british-columbia/riots-erupt-in-vancouver-after-canucks-loss-1.993707.
239. Williams, *Prague Spring and Its Aftermath*, 224.
240. Josef Frolík, John Bok, and Přemysl Vachalovský, *Špion vypovídá II: jasná zpráva o konci jednoho světa* (Praha: J. W. Hill, 2000), 283 (English translation by a professional translator).
241. Dawisha, *The Kremlin and the Prague Spring*, 368–369.
242. Dubcek, *Hope Dies Last*, 237.
243. Kusin, *From Dubček to Charter 77*, 90–106; Williams, *Prague Spring and Its Aftermath*, 227–240.
244. Andrew and Mitrokhin, *The Sword and the Shield*, 263; Dylan Loeb McClain, "Ludek Pachman, 78, Chess Star Imprisoned after 'Prague Spring,'" *New York Times*, March 13, 2003, sec. World, https://www.nytimes.com/2003/03/13/world/ludek-pachman-78-chess-star-imprisoned-after-prague-spring.html.
245. ZA, Sekretariat des Ministers (SdM) 1469, "Information Nr. 942/69 Der ZAIG Über Die Ereignisse in Der CSSR Anläßlich Des Ersten Jahrestages Der Militärischen Hilfsaktion Der Sozialistischen Länder," n.d., BStU.
246. Andrew and Mitrokhin, *The Sword and the Shield*, 265.
247. Andrew and Mitrokhin, *The Sword and the Shield*, 265.
248. Petrov, "The KGB and the Czechoslovak Crisis of 1968," 158.
249. Petrov, "The KGB and the Czechoslovak Crisis of 1968," 158.
250. Andrew and Mitrokhin, *The Sword and the Shield*, 265.
251. Andrew and Mitrokhin, *The Sword and the Shield*, 265.
252. Andrew and Mitrokhin, *The Sword and the Shield*, 265.
253. "Political Repression in Czechoslovakia, 1948–1984," 13.
254. CIA, "National Intelligence Survey 18; Czechoslovakia; The Society," 1974, 1, https://www.cia.gov/library/readingroom/docs/CIA-RDP01-00707R000200110015-7.pdf.
255. CIA, "National Intelligence Survey 18; Czechoslovakia; The Society."
256. Williams, *Prague Spring and Its Aftermath*, 46.
257. Williams, *Prague Spring and Its Aftermath*, 46.
258. Kusin, *From Dubček to Charter 77*, 273–304.

259. Rick Fawn and Jiří Hochman, *Historical Dictionary of the Czech State* (Lanham, MD: Scarecrow Press, 2010), 174.
260. Pool, "Public Opinion in Czechoslovakia," 15.
261. Prozumenshchikov, "Politburo Decision-Making on the Czechoslovak Crisis in 1968," 127.
262. Lewis A. Coser, *Functions of Social Conflict* (New York: Simon and Schuster, 1964).
263. Prozumenshchikov, "Politburo Decision-Making on the Czechoslovak Crisis in 1968," 127.
264. CIA, "Eastern Europe and the USSR in the Aftermath of the Invasion of Czechoslovakia," November 1968, 1.

Chapter 4

1. Rajan Menon and Eugene B. Rumer, *Conflict in Ukraine: The Unwinding of the Post-Cold War Order*, Boston Review Originals (Cambridge, MA: MIT Press, 2015); András Rácz, "Russia's Hybrid War in Ukraine," Finnish Institute of International Affairs, June 2015, https://www.fiia.fi/en/publication/russias-hybrid-war-in-ukraine; Yuriy Radkovets, "Lessons of Russia's 'Hybrid War' against Ukraine," (Santa Monica, California), accessed March 23, 2020, http://bintel.com.ua/en/article/10-13-lessons/; Michael Kofman et al., *Lessons from Russia's Operations in Crimea and Eastern Ukraine* (Rand, 2017).
2. Andy Greenberg, *Sandworm: A New Era of Cyberwar and the Hunt for the Kremlin's Most Dangerous Hackers* (New York: Doubleday, 2019); David E. Sanger, *The Perfect Weapon: War, Sabotage, and Fear in the Cyber Age* (New York: Broadway Books, 2019); Julia Voo et al., "National Cyber Power Index," Belfer Center of International Affairs, 2020, https://www.belfercenter.org/publication/national-cyber-power-index-2020.
3. Mark Clayton, "Ukraine Election Narrowly Avoided 'Wanton Destruction' from Hackers (+Video)," *Christian Science Monitor*, June 17, 2014, http://www.csmonitor.com/World/Passcode/2014/0617/Ukraine-election-narrowly-avoided-wanton-destruction-from-hackers-video; Jose Pagliery, "Scary Questions in Ukraine Energy Grid Hack," *CNNMoney*, January 18, 2016, https://money.cnn.com/2016/01/18/technology/ukraine-hack-russia/index.html; Andy Greenberg, "The Untold Story of NotPetya, the Most Devastating Cyberattack in History," *Wired*, August 2018, https://www.wired.com/story/notpetya-cyberattack-ukraine-russia-code-crashed-the-world/.
4. Laurens Cerulus, "How Ukraine Became a Test Bed for Cyberweaponry," Politico, February 2019, https://www.politico.eu/article/ukraine-cyber-war-frontline-russia-malware-attacks/.
5. Mark Galeotti, "Controlling Chaos: How Russia Manages Its Political War in Europe," August 2017, 6, http://www.ecfr.eu/publications/summary/controlling_chaos_how_russia_manages_its_political_war_in_europe.

6. Elias Götz, "Russia, the West, and the Ukraine Crisis: Three Contending Perspectives," *Contemporary Politics* 22, no. 3 (2016): 249–266, doi:10.1080/13569775.2016.1201313.
7. "О Комплексе Мер По Вовлечению Украины в Евразийский Интеграционный Процесс," *ZN.Ua*, August 2013, https://zn.ua/internal/o-komplekse-mer-po-vovlecheniyu-ukrainy-v-evraziyskiy-integracionnyy-process-_.html.
8. "О Комплексе Мер По Вовлечению Украины в Евразийский Интеграционный Процесс."
9. "О Комплексе Мер По Вовлечению Украины в Евразийский Интеграционный Процесс."
10. Oleg Tsarev, "О Комплексе Мер По Вовлечению Украины в Евразийский Интеграционный Процесс," *LB.Ua* (blog), accessed August 16, 2021, https://lb.ua/blog/oleg_tsarev/220762_komplekse_mer_vovlecheniyu_ukraini.html.
11. Levhen Solonya, "Russia's Plan for Ukraine: Purported Leaked Strategy Document Raises Alarm," Radio Free Europe/Radio Liberty, August 2013, https://www.rferl.org/a/russia-ukraine-leaked-strategy-document/25081053.html.
12. "FrolovLeaks: Church-Going Kremlin Influence Expert in Ukraine. Episode 1," *Inform Napalm* (English) (blog), January 2017, https://informnapalm.org/en/frolovleaks-church-going-kremlin-influence-expert-in-ukraine-episode-1/.
13. svv@materik.ru, "Re: Nedeli Opublikovalo Tekst, Pokhozhe Na Utechku," August 2013.
14. V. V. Shtol, "Geopoliticheskiye Zadachi Rossii Na Postsovetskom Prostranstve," *Vestnik Moskovskogo Gosudarstvennogo Oblastnogo Universiteta*, no. 3S (2014): 176.
15. See also Шабловский Владислав Станиславович, "Отношения России и Нато в Контексте Кризиса На Украине," *Постсоветские Исследования* 2, no. 2 (2019).
16. E. Shturba and M. Makhalkina, "Territorial'nyye Anklavy Byvshego SSSR v Kontekste Natsional'noy Bezopasnosti Sovremennoy Rossii," *Istoricheskaya i Sotsial'no-Obrazovatel'naya Mysl* 2, no. 1C (2016): 26.
17. Shaun Walker, "Ukraine's EU Trade Deal Will Be Catastrophic, Says Russia," *The Guardian*, September 22, 2013, sec. World News, https://www.theguardian.com/world/2013/sep/22/ukraine-european-union-trade-russia.
18. Steven Erlanger, "Putin, at NATO Meeting, Curbs Combative Rhetoric," *New York Times*, April 5, 2008, sec. Europe, https://www.nytimes.com/2008/04/05/world/europe/05nato.html.
19. "Putin Says Russia, Ukraine Torn Apart to Prevent Major Rival from Emerging," TASS, accessed March 1, 2021, https://tass.com/politics/1122727.
20. Kremlin, "Address by President of the Russian Federation," President of Russia, March 2014, http://en.kremlin.ru/events/president/news/20603.
21. Graeme P. Herd, "Russia and the 'Orange Revolution': Response, Rhetoric, Reality?," *Connections* 4, no. 2 (2005): 15–28.
22. Mark Galeotti, "Putin's Hydra: Inside Russia's Intelligence Services," European Council on Foreign Relations, May 2016, 8, http://www.ecfr.eu/page/-/ECFR_169_-_PUTINS_HYDRA_INSIDE_THE_RUSSIAN_INTELLIGENCE_SERVICES_1513.pdf.

23. Dmitri Trenin, "The Putin Doctrine," Carnegie Moscow Center, February 2013, https://carnegie.ru/2013/02/01/putin-doctrine-pub-51085.
24. Menon and Rumer, *Conflict in Ukraine*, 77.
25. Spiegel Staff, "Putin's Gambit: How the EU Lost Ukraine," *Spiegel Online*, November 2013, sec. International, https://www.spiegel.de/international/europe/how-the-eu-lost-to-russia-in-negotiations-over-ukraine-trade-deal-a-935476.html.
26. Oksana Grytsenko and Ian Traynor, "Ukraine U-Turn on Europe Pact Was Agreed with Vladimir Putin," *The Guardian*, November 26, 2013, sec. World News, https://www.theguardian.com/world/2013/nov/26/ukraine-u-turn-eu-pact-putin.
27. Menon and Rumer, *Conflict in Ukraine*, 77.
28. "EuroMaidan Rallies in Ukraine—Nov. 21–23 Coverage," *Kyiv Post*, November 2013, https://www.kyivpost.com/post/7612.
29. Katya Gorchinskaya and Darina Marchak, "Russia Gives Ukraine Cheap Gas, $15 Billion in Loans," *Kyiv Post*, December 2013, https://www.kyivpost.com/article/content/ukraine-politics/russia-gives-ukraine-cheap-gas-15-billion-in-loans-333852.html.
30. Yana, "Opinion: 'We Were Trapped': Eyewitness to the Massacre in Kiev," *CNN*, accessed August 18, 2021, https://edition.cnn.com/2014/02/24/opinion/yana-ukraine-eyewitness/index.html.
31. Ian Traynor, "Ukraine Protests: End Nears for Viktor Yanukovych despite Concessions," *The Guardian*, February 21, 2014, sec. World News, https://www.theguardian.com/world/2014/feb/21/ukraine-protests-viktor-yanukovych-election.
32. The entire archive of emails is available at https://ordilo.org/wp-content/uploads/2016/12/frolov_moskva@mail.ru.rar (last accessed May 17, 2019).
33. "FrolovLeaks."
34. "FrolovLeaks."
35. "FrolovLeaks."
36. Email from frolov_moskva@mail.ru to v.granovski@granovski.com from August 22, 2013, 5:01 p.m., quoted in email from v.granosvki@granovski.com to frolov_moskva@mail.ru from August 28, 2013, 5:34 a.m.
37. Email from frolov_moskva@mail.ru to v.granovski@granovski.com from August 22, 2013, 5:01 p.m., quoted in email from v.granosvki@granovski.com to frolov_moskva@mail.ru from August 28, 2013, 5:34 a.m.
38. Email from glaziev@bk.ru to frolov_moskva@mail.ru, September 13, 2013, 9:45 a.m.
39. BBC, "Putin Strategist Returns to Kremlin," *BBC News*, September 2013, sec. Europe, https://www.bbc.com/news/world-europe-24178947.
40. For more details, see Sean Townsend's summary of these interactions. Sean Townsend, "FrolovLeaks VI: Tomorrow Was the War," *Inform Napalm* (English) (blog), November 2018, https://informnapalm.org/en/frolovleaks-vi-tomorrow-was-the-war/.
41. Sanshiro Hosaka, "The Kremlin's 'Active Measures' Failed in 2013: That's When Russia Remembered Its Last Resort—Crimea," *Demokratizatsiya; Washington* 26, no. 3 (Summer 2018): 354.
42. "Press Releases and Reports—'The European Union' and 'the Customs Union,'" KIIS, March 2013, http://kiis.com.ua/?lang=eng&cat=reports&id=186&page=32&t=3.

43. "Press Releases and Reports—Consequences of Ukraine's Accession to Integration Associations," KIIS, November 2013, http://kiis.com.ua/?lang=eng&cat=reports&id=206&page=31&t=3.
44. Hosaka, "The Kremlin's 'Active Measures' Failed in 2013," 337.
45. Interfax-Ukraine, "Kolesnichenko Denies Combining His Parliamentary Work with Advocacy," *Kyiv Post*, March 5, 2013, https://www.kyivpost.com/article/content/verkhovna-rada/kolesnichenko-denies-combining-his-parliamentary-work-with-advocacy-321307.html; "Ukraine's Party of Regions Expels Presidential Hopefuls Tigipko, Tsariov and Boiko," Interfax-Ukraine, accessed November 18, 2022, https://en.interfax.com.ua/news/general/199490.html.
46. Andrei Lipsky, "«Представляется Правильным Инициировать Присоединение Восточных Областей Украины к России»," *Новая Газета—Novayagazeta.Ru*, February 2015, https://www.novayagazeta.ru/articles/2015/02/24/63168-171-predstavlyaetsya-pravilnym-initsiirovat-prisoedinenie-vostochnyh-oblastey-ukrainy-k-rossii-187.
47. UNIAN, "Novaya Gazeta's 'Kremlin Papers' Article: Full Text in English," February 2015, https://www.unian.info/politics/1048525-novaya-gazetas-kremlin-papers-article-full-text-in-english.html.
48. UNIAN, "Novaya Gazeta's 'Kremlin Papers' Article."
49. UNIAN, "Novaya Gazeta's 'Kremlin Papers' Article."
50. UNIAN, "Novaya Gazeta's 'Kremlin Papers' Article."
51. UNIAN, "Novaya Gazeta's 'Kremlin Papers' Article."
52. Kofman et al., *Lessons from Russia's Operations in Crimea and Eastern Ukraine*, 7.
53. Howard Amos, "Ukraine: Sevastopol Installs Pro-Russian Mayor as Separatism Fears Grow," *The Guardian*, February 25, 2014, sec. World News, https://www.theguardian.com/world/2014/feb/25/ukraine-sevastopol-installs-pro-russian-mayor.
54. Kofman et al., *Lessons from Russia's Operations in Crimea and Eastern Ukraine*, 7.
55. Haroon Siddique, Tom McCarthy, and Alan Yuhas, "Crimean Parliament Seizure Inflames Russian-Ukrainian Tensions—Live," *The Guardian*, February 25, 2014, sec. World News, https://www.theguardian.com/world/2014/feb/27/ukraine-pro-russian-gunmen-seize-crimea-parliament-live-updates.
56. Siddique, McCarthy, and York, "Crimean Parliament Seizure Inflames Russian-Ukrainian Tensions—Live."
57. Kofman et al., *Lessons from Russia's Operations in Crimea and Eastern Ukraine*, 8.
58. "Why Surkov Needs Private Army: Union of Donbas Volunteers (UDV) as Reserve of National Guard of Russia," *Inform Napalm* (English) (blog), April 2017, https://informnapalm.org/en/surkov-needs-private-army-union-donbas-volunteers-reserve-russian-guard/.
59. Roman Sohn, "[Opinion] Ukraine: The Empire Strikes Back," *EUobserver* (blog), September 2014, https://euobserver.com/opinion/123339.
60. "Glazyev Tapes, Continued: New Details of Russian Occupation of Crimea and Attempts to Dismember Ukraine," *Euromaidan Press* (blog), May 2019, http://euromaidanpress.com/2019/05/16/glazyev-tapes-continued-ukraine-presents-new-details-of-russian-takeover-of-crimea-and-financing-of-separatism/.

61. Kofman et al., *Lessons from Russia's Operations in Crimea and Eastern Ukraine*, 9.
62. Kofman et al., *Lessons from Russia's Operations in Crimea and Eastern Ukraine*, 9.
63. Kathy Lally, Will Englund, and William Booth, "Russian Parliament Approves Use of Troops in Ukraine," *Washington Post*, March 1, 2014, sec. Europe, https://www.washingtonpost.com/world/europe/russian-parliament-approves-use-of-troops-in-crimea/2014/03/01/d1775f70-a151-11e3-a050-dc3322a94fa7_story.html.
64. Kofman et al., *Lessons from Russia's Operations in Crimea and Eastern Ukraine*, 9.
65. Email from priestnov@icloud.com to frolov_moskva@mail.ru, March 4, 2014, 7:49 a.m. EST.
66. Vitaly Shevchenko, "'Little Green Men' or 'Russian Invaders'?," *BBC News*, March 2014, sec. Europe, https://www.bbc.com/news/world-europe-26532154.
67. Shaun Walker and Ian Traynor, "Ukraine Crisis: Crimea Now Part of Russia, Local Parliament Declares," *The Guardian*, March 6, 2014, sec. World News, https://www.theguardian.com/world/2014/mar/06/ukraine-crisis-crimea-part-of-russia-local-parliament-declares.
68. "Ukraine Publishes Video Proving Kremlin Directed Separatism in Eastern Ukraine and Crimea," *Euromaidan Press* (blog), August 2016, http://euromaidanpress.com/2016/08/23/ukraine-publishes-video-proving-kremlin-directed-separatism-in-ukraine/.
69. Russia Today, "95.7% of Crimeans in Referendum Voted to Join Russia—Preliminary Results," *RT International*, March 2014, 7, https://www.rt.com/news/crimea-vote-join-russia-210/.
70. Kremlin, "Подписан Указ о Признании Республики Крым," Президент России, March 2014, http://kremlin.ru/events/president/news/20596.
71. NPR, "Ukrainian Servicemen Reported Shot by Masked Soldiers in Crimea," *NPR*, March 2014, https://www.npr.org/sections/thetwo-way/2014/03/18/291148781/ukrainian-servicemen-reported-shot-by-masked-soldiers-in-crimea; "Pro-Russia Forces Enter Ukraine Naval Base," *Al Jazeera*, March 2014, https://www.aljazeera.com/news/europe/2014/03/pro-russia-forces-enter-ukraine-naval-base-20143198741233396.html.
72. David M. Herszenhorn and Andrew E. Kramer, "Ukraine Plans to Withdraw Troops from Russia-Occupied Crimea," *New York Times*, March 20, 2014, sec. World, https://www.nytimes.com/2014/03/20/world/europe/crimea.html.
73. Johnson, "On Drawing a Bright Line for Covert Operations," 286.
74. "FrolovLeaks."
75. Denis Trifonov, "Russian Intelligence Presence in the CIS," *CACI Analyst*, December 2003, http://www.cacianalyst.org/publications/analytical-articles/item/8615-analytical-articles-caci-analyst-2003-12-17-art-8615.html.
76. Ivan Kapsamun, "СБУ Проти ФСБ," April 2015, https://day.kyiv.ua/uk/article/podrobyci/sbu-proty-fsb.
77. "30% of Ukrainian SBU Officers Were Russian FSB and GRU Agents," Euromaidan Press, April 2014, http://euromaidanpress.com/2014/04/24/30-of-ukrainian-sbu-officers-were-russian-fsb-and-gru-agents/.
78. Interviewed by the author in Kyiv on April 11, 2018.

79. GfK Ukraine, "Public Opinion Survey in Crimea," March 2014, https://avaazpress.s3.amazonaws.com/558_Crimea.Referendum.Poll.GfK.pdf.
80. GfK Ukraine, "Public Opinion Survey in Crimea."
81. Georgiy Brusov, E-Mail to Vladislav Surkov on July 16, 2014. This E-Mail comes from the "Surkov Leaks" archive published by Informnapalm.org via Google Drive at https://drive.google.com/drive/folders/0BxCzAWE6sxSfRXVjdm1pV2c3WXc?resourcekey=0-VuOAohjNfpasdEMoYH2t3g.
82. Leonid Peisakhin and Arturas Rozenas, "Electoral Effects of Biased Media: Russian Television in Ukraine," *American Journal of Political Science* 62, no. 3 (2018): 535–550, doi:10.1111/ajps.12355.
83. "Russophone Identity in Ukraine," Ukraine Center for Independent Political Research, 2017, http://www.ucipr.org.ua/publicdocs/RussophoneIdentity_EN.pdf.
84. Importantly, vulnerability in this context refers to the receptiveness for propaganda and acceptance of the takeover it apparently prepared. It emphatically does not refer to the presence of a population with diverse ethnic or other identities. I am grateful to Jesse Driscoll for pointing out this potential misinterpretation of the argument.
85. Kofman et al., *Lessons from Russia's Operations in Crimea and Eastern Ukraine*, 38.
86. "Ukraine Protesters Urge Yanukovych's Return at Rally in Donetsk," Bloomberg, March 2014, https://www.bloomberg.com/news/articles/2014-03-22/ukraine-protesters-urge-yanukovych-s-return-at-rally-in-donetsk.
87. Adam Withnall, "Ukraine Crisis: Donetsk 'Declares Independence from Kiev' and Sets Date for Referendum on Joining Russia," *The Independent*, April 2014, https://www.independent.co.uk/news/world/europe/ukraine-crisis-officials-in-eastern-city-of-donetsk-proclaim-independence-from-kiev-and-set-date-for-9243750.html.
88. Olga Rudenko, "Separatist Crisis Flares Again Today in Ukraine's Eastern Regions," *Kyiv Post*, April 7, 2014, https://www.kyivpost.com/article/content/war-against-ukraine/separatist-crisis-flares-again-today-in-ukraines-eastern-regions-342351.html.
89. Yuri Butusov, "День кризи: 6 квітня 2014 року російські спецслужби атакували органи влади на південному сході України," Цензор.НЕТ, April 2017, https://censor.net.ua/ua/resonance/435372/den_kryzy_6_kvitnya_2014_roku_rosiyiski_spetsslujby_atakuvaly_organy_vlady_na_pivdennomu_shodi_ukrayiny.
90. Kofman et al., *Lessons from Russia's Operations in Crimea and Eastern Ukraine*, 39.
91. There are no references to any of these operations in Surkov and Frolov's emails either.
92. Sergei L. Loiko, "Ukraine Cracks Down on Demonstrators; Russia Issues Warning," *Latimes.com*, April 8, 2014, https://www.latimes.com/world/worldnow/la-fg-wn-ukraine-raid-russia-supporters-20140408-story.html.
93. Email from priestnov@icloud.com to frolov.moskva@mail.ru, April 9, 2014, 10:33 a.m. EST.
94. On April 20, the Ukrainian government published official evidence of Russian special forces in Donbass. "Ukraine Provides Evidence of Russian Military in Civil Unrest," *New York Times*, April 20, 2014, sec. World, https://www.nytimes.com/interactive/2014/04/20/world/europe/ukraine-provides-evidence-of-russian-military-in-civil-unrest.html.

95. Alexander J. Motyl, "The Weakness of Eastern Ukraine's Pro-Russian Separatists," *Al Jazeera*, April 2014, http://america.aljazeera.com/opinions/2014/4/eastern-ukraine-prorussianseparatistsdonetskdonbas.html.
96. "Ukrainian Clashes with Pro-Russian Separatists Turn Deadly," *Denver Post*, April 13, 2014, https://www.denverpost.com/2014/04/13/ukrainian-clashes-with-pro-russian-separatists-turn-deadly/.
97. Tom McCarthy and Alan Yuhas, "Ukraine Crisis: Kiev Launches 'Anti-Terror Operation' in East—Live Updates," *The Guardian*, April 15, 2014, https://www.theguardian.com/world/2014/apr/15/ukraine-military-forces-russia-live-blog.
98. Alison Smale and Andrew Roth, "Ukraine Says That Militants Won the East," *New York Times*, May 1, 2014, sec. World, https://www.nytimes.com/2014/05/01/world/europe/ukraine.html.
99. "Rebels Declare Victory in East Ukraine Vote on Self-Rule," Reuters, May 2014, https://www.reuters.com/article/us-ukraine-crisis-idUSBREA400LI20140511.
100. "У Донецьку Ідеї Сепаратизму Несподівано Виявилися Непопулярними," *Українська Правда*, April 2014, https://www.pravda.com.ua/news/2014/04/9/7021883/.
101. Harriet Salem, "Kiev Hits Back at Pro-Russia Rebels as Ukraine Moves towards Civil War," *The Observer*, May 3, 2014, sec. World News, https://www.theguardian.com/world/2014/may/03/ukraine-civil-war-kiev-russia-slavyansk; Alexander Vasovic, "Ukraine Rebels Speak of Heavy Losses in Battle against Government Troops," Reuters, June 2014, https://www.reuters.com/article/us-ukraine-crisis-fighting/ukraine-rebels-speak-of-heavy-losses-in-battle-against-government-troops-idUSKBN0EU0K320140619; Isabel Gorst, "Russians Invading, Says Ukraine Leader; Tanks Reported Crossing Border," *Latimes.com*, August 28, 2014, https://www.latimes.com/world/europe/la-fg-ukraine-president-russian-forces-20140828-story.html; "Two Servicemen Killed in Past 24 Hours in East Ukraine: Kiev Military," Reuters, April 2015, https://www.reuters.com/article/us-ukraine-crisis-casualties/two-servicemen-killed-in-past-24-hours-in-east-ukraine-kiev-military-idUSKBN0MZ0UN20150408; "Minsk Contact Group Reaches Agreement on Complete Ceasefire in Donbas, Starting from Easter," Interfax-Ukraine, April 2016, https://en.interfax.com.ua/news/general/340994.html; Anna Matveeva, *Through Times of Trouble: Conflict in Southeastern Ukraine Explained from Within*, Russian, Eurasian, and Eastern European Politics (Lanham, MD: Lexington Books, 2018).
102. A. F. Brantly, N. Cal, and D. Winkelstein, "Defending the Borderland," Army Cyber Institute, December 2017, https://vtechworks.lib.vt.edu/handle/10919/81979; N. Kostyuk and Y. M. Zhukov, "Invisible Digital Front: Can Cyber Attacks Shape Battlefield Events?," *Journal of Conflict Resolution* 63, no. 2 (2017): 317–347, doi:10.1177/0022002717737138.
103. Johnson, "On Drawing a Bright Line for Covert Operations," 286–288.
104. Katya Gorchinskaya, Olga Rudenko, and William Schreiber, "Authorities: Hackers Foiled in Bid to Rig Ukraine Presidential Election Results," *Kyiv Post*, May 25, 2014, https://www.kyivpost.com/article/content/may-25-presidential-election/authorities-hackers-foiled-in-bid-to-rig-ukraine-presidential-election-results-349288.html.

105. Nikolay Koval, "Revolution Hacking," in *Cyber War in Perspective: Russian Aggression against Ukraine*, ed. Kenneth Geers (Tallinn, Estonia: NATO Cooperative Cyber Defence Centre of Excellence, 2015), 57, https://ccdcoe.org/sites/default/files/multimedia/pdf/CyberWarinPerspective_full_book.pdf.
106. Personal correspondence, May 9, 2019.
107. Berkut is a reference to the name of riot police units, some of which were engaged in the violence on the Maidan.
108. "Cyber Berkut: Кибер Беркут," May 2014, http://www.cyber-berkut.ru/en/index_02.php.
109. Adam Hulcoop et al., "Tainted Leaks: Disinformation and Phishing with a Russian Nexus," May 2017, https://citizenlab.ca/2017/05/tainted-leaks-disinformation-phish/; National Cyber Security Centre, "Reckless Campaign of Cyber Attacks by Russian Military Intelligence Service Exposed," October 2018, https://www.ncsc.gov.uk/news/reckless-campaign-cyber-attacks-russian-military-intelligence-service-exposed.
110. Koval, "Revolution Hacking."
111. Victor Zhora, interviewed by the author in Kyiv in April 2018.
112. Victor Zhora, interviewed by the author in Kyiv in April 2018.
113. Koval, "Revolution Hacking," 56.
114. Personal correspondence, May 9, 2019.
115. Victor Zhora, personal correspondence, May 9, 2019.
116. "International Election Observation Mission," OSCE, May 2014, 1, https://www.osce.org/odihr/elections/ukraine/119078?download=true.
117. "International Election Observation Mission," 15.
118. Victor Zhora, interviewed by the author in Kyiv in April 2018.
119. Victor Zhora, interviewed by the author in Kyiv in April 2018; Koval, "Revolution Hacking," 57.
120. Reuters Staff, "Ukraine, Separatists to Strive for Full Ceasefire from September 1," Reuters, August 2015, https://www.reuters.com/article/us-ukraine-crisis-ceasefire/ukraine-separatists-to-strive-for-full-ceasefire-from-september-1-idUSKCN0QV29A20150826; "Deadly Ambush Ends Lull in Ukraine," *BBC News*, September 2015, sec. Europe, https://www.bbc.com/news/world-europe-34128085.
121. Yulia Silina, "Ukraine, Pro-Russia Rebels Begin Donetsk Arms Withdrawal," October 2015, http://news.yahoo.com/ukraine-pro-russia-rebels-begin-donetsk-arms-withdrawal-152455026.html.
122. Greenberg, *Sandworm*.
123. ESET, "BlackEnergy by the SSHBearDoor: Attacks against Ukrainian News Media and Electric Industry," *We Live Security* (blog), January 2016, https://www.welivesecurity.com/2016/01/03/blackenergy-sshbeardoor-details-2015-attacks-ukrainian-news-media-electric-industry/; CERT-UA, "Ukrainian Media Are Attacked with Black Energy," January 2016, https://web.archive.org/web/20160116110418/http://cert.gov.ua/?p=2370; CysCentrum, "Киберугроза BlackEnergy2/3," 2016, https://cys-centrum.com/ru/news/black_energy_2_3.
124. Cerulus, "How Ukraine Became a Test Bed for Cyberweaponry."

125. Personal correspondence via online messenger app, May 9, 2019.
126. CysCentrum, "Киберугроза BlackEnergy2/3."
127. There are three known versions of this malware suite, 1, 2, and 3. The Sandworm group switched to the newest version of this suite some time in 2015, but it is not clear when this switch occurred.
128. CysCentrum, "Киберугроза BlackEnergy2/3"; Aleksey Yasinskiy, "Dismantling Blackenergy, Part 2—The Mark,'" *SOC Prime* (blog), March 2016, https://socprime.com/en/blog/dismantling-blackenergy-part2-the-mark/.
129. Aleksey Yasinskiy, "Dismantling Blackenergy, Part 3—All Aboard!," *SOC Prime* (blog), March 2016, https://socprime.com/blog/dismantling-blackenergy-part-3-all-aboard/.
130. Yasinskiy, "Dismantling Blackenergy, Part 3."
131. Yasinskiy, "Dismantling Blackenergy, Part 3."
132. Volodymyr Styran, interviewed by the author in Kyiv in April 2018.
133. Aleksey Yasinskiy, "Dismantling KillDisk: Reverse of the BlackEnergy Destructive Component," *SOC Prime* (blog), February 2016, https://socprime.com/en/blog/dismantling-killdisk-reverse-of-the-blackenergy-destructive-component/.
134. Aleksey Yasinskiy, "BlackEnergy Phase 2: From Media and Electric Companies to Darknet and TTPs," *SOC Prime* (blog), January 2016, https://socprime.com/en/blog/blackenergy-phase-2-from-media-and-electric-companies-to-darknet-and-ttps/.
135. Yasinskiy, "Dismantling Blackenergy, Part 3."
136. See, for example, Elias Groll, "Did Russia Knock Out Ukraine's Power Grid?," *Foreign Policy* (blog), January 2016, https://foreignpolicy.com/2016/01/08/did-russia-knock-out-ukraines-power-grid/; Pagliery, "Scary Questions in Ukraine Energy Grid Hack"; Kim Zetter, "Inside the Cunning, Unprecedented Hack of Ukraine's Power Grid," *Wired*, March 2016, https://www.wired.com/2016/03/inside-cunning-unprecedented-hack-ukraines-power-grid/.
137. Johnson, "On Drawing a Bright Line for Covert Operations," 286.
138. Johnson, "On Drawing a Bright Line for Covert Operations," 286, 288.
139. "The Ukraine Crisis Timeline," CSIS, accessed April 12, 2019, http://ukraine.csis.org/#478.
140. "Deadly Clashes in Ukraine Despite Truce," Radio Free Europe/Radio Liberty, December 2015, https://www.rferl.org/a/deadly-clashes-in-ukraine-despite-holiday-truce/27452015.html.
141. Ivan Nechepurenko and Neil MacFarquhar, "As Sabotage Blacks Out Crimea, Tatars Prevent Repairs," *New York Times*, November 24, 2015, sec. Europe, https://www.nytimes.com/2015/11/24/world/europe/crimea-tatar-power-lines-ukraine.html.
142. Kim Zetter, "Everything We Know about Ukraine's Power Plant Hack," *Wired*, January 2016, https://www.wired.com/2016/01/everything-we-know-about-ukraines-power-plant-hack/.
143. Oleg Sych, "Zillya! Антивирус провела анализ кибератак на инфраструктурные объекти Украины," February 2016, https://zillya.ua/ru/zillya-antivirus-provela-analiz-kiberatak-na-infrastrukturnye-obekti-ukrainy; Zetter, "Inside the Cunning, Unprecedented Hack of Ukraine's Power Grid."

144. Sych, "Zillya! Антивирус провела анализ кибератак на инфраструктурные объекти Украины."
145. CysCentrum, "Киберугроза BlackEnergy2/3"; Sych, "Zillya! Антивирус провела анализ кибератак на инфраструктурные объекти Украины"; Zetter, "Inside the Cunning, Unprecedented Hack of Ukraine's Power Grid."
146. Zetter, "Inside the Cunning, Unprecedented Hack of Ukraine's Power Grid."
147. CysCentrum, "Киберугроза BlackEnergy2/3."
148. CysCentrum, "Киберугроза BlackEnergy2/3."
149. CysCentrum, "Киберугроза BlackEnergy2/3."
150. Zetter, "Inside the Cunning, Unprecedented Hack of Ukraine's Power Grid."
151. Meaning a vulnerability that is still unknown both to the vendor of the software in question and to its users.
152. "ISIGHT Discovers Zero-Day Vulnerability CVE-2014-4114 Used in Russian Cyber-Espionage Campaign," iSight, October 2014, https://web.archive.org/web/20141015001101/https://www.isightpartners.com/2014/10/cve-2014-4114/.
153. Iain Thomson, "So You've Got a Zero-Day—Do You Sell to Black, Grey or White Markets?," April 2018, https://www.theregister.co.uk/2018/04/15/mature_bug_bounty_market_bsidessf/.
154. TrendMicro, "Sandworm to Blacken: The SCADA Connection," *TrendLabs Security Intelligence* (blog), October 2014, https://blog.trendmicro.com/trendlabs-security-intelligence/sandworm-to-blacken-the-scada-connection/.
155. Dragos, "CRASHOVERRIDE Analysis of the Threat to Electric Grid Operations," 2017, 10, https://dragos.com/blog/crashoverride/CrashOverride-01.pdf.
156. Dragos, "CRASHOVERRIDE Analysis of the Threat to Electric Grid Operations," 10.
157. CysCentrum, "Киберугроза BlackEnergy2/3."
158. IDC Security Roadshow in Kyiv, February 17, 2016.
159. Volodymyr Styran, interviewed by the author in Kyiv in April 2018.
160. Holly Williams, "Russian Hacks into Ukraine Power Grids a Sign of Things to Come for U.S.?," *CBS News*, December 2016, https://www.cbsnews.com/news/russian-hacks-into-ukraine-power-grids-may-be-a-sign-of-things-to-come/; Groll, "Did Russia Knock Out Ukraine's Power Grid?"
161. Lee, Robert M., Michael J. Assante, and Tim Conway. "Analysis of the Cyber Attack on the Ukrainian Power Grid" (SANS. E-ISAC), March 2016. https://nsarchive.gwu.edu/sites/default/files/documents/3891751/SANS-and-Electricity-Information-Sharing-and.pdf.
162. Greenberg, "How an Entire Nation Became Russia's Test Lab for Cyberwar."
163. Dragos, "CRASHOVERRIDE Analysis of the Threat to Electric Grid Operations," 10.
164. Sych, "Zillya! Антивирус провела анализ кибератак на инфраструктурные объекти Украины."
165. Sean Lawson, "Beyond Cyber-Doom: Assessing the Limits of Hypothetical Scenarios in the Framing of Cyber-Threats," *Journal of Information Technology & Politics* 10, no. 1 (2013): 86–103, doi:10.1080/19331681.2012.759059; Elisabeth Bumiller and Thom Shanker, "Panetta Warns of Dire Threat of Cyberattack on U.S.," *New York Times*, October 12, 2012, sec. World, https://www.nytimes.com/2012/10/12/world/panetta-warns-of-dire-threat-of-cyberattack.html.

166. Zetter, "Inside the Cunning, Unprecedented Hack of Ukraine's Power Grid"; Groll, "Did Russia Knock Out Ukraine's Power Grid?"; Alex Hern, "Ukrainian Blackout Caused by Hackers That Attacked Media Company, Researchers Say," *The Guardian*, January 7, 2016, sec. Technology, https://www.theguardian.com/technology/2016/jan/07/ukrainian-blackout-hackers-attacked-media-company.
167. Pagliery, "Scary Questions in Ukraine Energy Grid Hack."
168. "СБУ Предупредила Хакерскую Атаку Российских Спецслужб На Энергообъекты Украины—112 Украина," *112.Ua*, December 2015, https://112.ua/kriminal/sbu-predupredila-hakerskuyu-ataku-rossiyskih-specsluzhb-na-energoobekty-ukrainy-281811.html; Obozrevatel, "Після кібератаки на 'Прикарпаттяобленерго' в США переглянуть захист енергомереж," *Політика*, January 2016, https://www.obozrevatel.com/ukr/news/58420-pislya-kiberataki-na-prikarpattyaoblenergo-v-ssha-pereglyanut-zahist-energomerezh.htm; Sergey Martynets, "США підозрюють Росію у причетності до кібератак на українські електромережі," Інформаційне агентство Українські Національні Новини (УНН), Всі онлайн новини дня в Україні за сьогодні—найсвіжіші, останні, головні., January 2016, https://www.unn.com.ua/uk/news/1536191-ssha-pidozryuyut-rosiyu-u-prichetnosti-do-kiberatak-na-ukrayinski-elektromerezhi.
169. The report by 112 briefly quotes a press release by the Ukrainian intelligence service, the *Політика* story covers US plans to improve its own power grid in response to the operation, and the Martynets article quotes several US media reports attributing the power outage to a Russian cyber operation.
170. "СБУ Попередила Спробу Російських Спецслужб Вивести з Ладу Об'єкти Енергетики України," SBU, December 2015, https://web.archive.org/web/20160103175824/http://www.sbu.gov.ua/sbu/control/uk/publish/article?art_id=170951&cat_id=39574.
171. "Deadly Clashes in Ukraine despite Truce."
172. anonymous government advisor interviewed by the author in Kyiv in April 2018.
173. Sych, "Zillya! Антивирус провела анализ кибератак на инфраструктурные объекти Украины."
174. Joseph S. Nye, "Deterrence and Dissuasion in Cyberspace," *International Security* 41, no. 3 (January 2017): 49, doi:10.1162/ISEC_a_00266.
175. Nicole Perlroth and David E. Sanger, "Cyberattacks Put Russian Fingers on the Switch at Power Plants, U.S. Says," *New York Times*, March 15, 2018, sec. U.S., https://www.nytimes.com/2018/03/15/us/politics/russia-cyberattacks.html; Alyza Sebenius, "Will Ukraine Be Hit by Yet Another Holiday Power-Grid Hack?," *The Atlantic*, December 2017, https://www.theatlantic.com/technology/archive/2017/12/ukraine-power-grid-hack/548285/.
176. Schelling, *Arms and Influence*.
177. Greenberg, "How an Entire Nation Became Russia's Test Lab for Cyberwar."
178. ESET, "GREYENERGY," October 2018, https://www.welivesecurity.com/wp-content/uploads/2018/10/ESET_GreyEnergy.pdf.
179. ESET, "GREYENERGY."

180. Alisa Sopova and Neil MacFarquhar, "Russia and Ukraine in a Standoff over Crimea Power Outage," *New York Times*, 26 November 2015, sec. World, https://www.nytimes.com/2015/11/26/world/europe/russia-and-ukraine-in-a-standoff-over-crimea-power-outage.html.
181. "Ukraine Sees First Direct Combat in Two Months before EU Meeting," November 2015, https://www.bloomberg.com/news/articles/2015-11-09/ukraine-sees-first-direct-combat-in-two-months-before-eu-meeting; Yulia Silina, "Fears of New Flareup in Ukraine as Violence Grows on Frontline," November 2015, http://news.yahoo.com/fears-flareup-ukraine-violence-grows-frontline-080945741.html; "Soldier Killed in E. Ukraine Clashes," *VOA*, November 2015, https://www.voanews.com/a/soldier-killed-in-clashes-in-eastern-ukraine/3058960.html.
182. "Russia Decides to Impose Food Embargo against Ukraine—Minister," TASS, November 2015, http://tass.com/economy/837503.
183. Volodymyr Verbyany, Elena Mazneva, and Eduard Gismatullin, "Twin Ukraine Power Cable Blasts Leave Crimeans in the Dark," November 2015, https://www.bloomberg.com/news/articles/2015-11-22/crimea-declares-emergency-as-1-9-million-people-lose-electricity.
184. BBC, "Crimea Blackout 'Sabotage by Ukraine,'" *BBC News*, November 2015, sec. Europe, https://www.bbc.com/news/world-europe-34967093.
185. Maxim Tucker, "Coal Cutoff Escalates Russia-Ukraine Tensions," Politico, November 2015, https://www.politico.eu/article/coal-russia-ukraine-crimea-sanctions-putin-turkey/.
186. "In the Kherson Region, the Military Stole and Tried to Sell Anti-Tank Mines with TNT," *Ukrop News 24* (blog), February 2017, https://ukropnews24.com/in-the-kherson-region-the-military-stole-and-tried-to-sell-anti-tank-mines-with-tnt/.
187. Sopova and MacFarquhar, "Russia and Ukraine in a Standoff over Crimea Power Outage."
188. "Crimea Power Cut 'Caused by Blast,'" *BBC News*, December 2015, sec. Europe, http://www.bbc.com/news/world-europe-35204304.
189. Ivan Nechepurenko, "Crimea to Face Power Shortages for Months, Officials Say," *New York Times*, 8 January 2016, sec. World, https://www.nytimes.com/2016/01/09/world/europe/crimea-power-ukraine-russia.html.
190. Johnson, "On Drawing a Bright Line for Covert Operations," 289.
191. "Ukraine Resumes Power Supply to Crimea," Euractiv, December 2015, https://www.euractiv.com/section/energy/news/ukraine-resumes-power-supply-to-crimea/.
192. Interfax, "Kakhovka-Titan Power Transmission Line Feeding Crimea Fixed," Russia Beyond, January 2016, https://www.rbth.com/news/2016/01/02/kakhovka-titan-power-transmission-line-feeding-crimea-fixed_557037.
193. I am grateful to Kimberly Martens for pointing out this explanation.
194. Margarita Kraminska, "Росія не погоджується укласти договір на постачання електроенергії до Криму через формулювання—М.Джемілєв," *UNN*, accessed November 24, 2022, https://www.unn.com.ua/uk/news/1537754-rosiya-ne-pogodzhuyetsya-uklasti-dogovir-na-postachannya-elektroenergiyi-do-krimu-cherez-formulyuvannya-m-dzhemilyev.

195. Nechepurenko, "Crimea to Face Power Shortages for Months, Officials Say."
196. "Putin Says Crimea Now Free of Reliance on Kiev for Its Power," Reuters, May 2016, https://www.reuters.com/article/us-russia-crimea-power-idUSKCN0Y21K5.
197. "Massive Power Outage Hits Crimea," Radio Free Europe/Radio Liberty, 2018, https://www.rferl.org/a/massive-power-outages-hit-crimea-cause-unclear/29288821.html.
198. Nechepurenko, "Crimea to Face Power Shortages for Months, Officials Say."
199. Johnson, "On Drawing a Bright Line for Covert Operations," 290.
200. Jack Losh, "Ukrainian Rebel Leaders Divided by Bitter Purge," *Washington Post*, accessed 3 October 2016, https://www.washingtonpost.com/world/europe/ukrainian-rebel-leaders-divided-by-bitter-purge/2016/10/03/2e0076ac-8429-11e6-b57d-dd49277af02f_story.html; Andrew E. Kramer, "Bomb Kills Pro-Russian Rebel Commander in Eastern Ukraine," *New York Times*, December 2017, sec. World, https://www.nytimes.com/2016/10/18/world/europe/ukraine-rebel-arsen-pavlov-motorola-killed.html.
201. anonymous government advisor, interviewed by the author in Kyiv in 2018.
202. "Причиной обесточивания части Киева может быть атака хакеров," Fakty.ua, December 2016, https://fakty.ua/227538-prichinoj-obestochivaniya-chasti-kieva-mozhet-byt-ataka-hakerov.
203. In the United States, one megawatt typically provides enough power for about 750 households. California Energy Commission, "California ISO Glossary," n.d., https://www.energy.ca.gov/glossary/ISO_GLOSSARY.PDF. Hence, total outage of 202.9 megawatt would equal power loss for 152,175 standard US households. Since in 2016 average energy consumption per capita in Ukraine was only about a quarter of that in the United States (3.2 MWh versus 12.8 MWh; International Energy Agency, "Statistics: World—Total Primary Energy Supply [TPES] by Source [Chart]," accessed May 11, 2019, https://www.iea.org/statistics/?country=WORLD&year=2016&category=Energy%20supply&indicator=TPESbySource&mode=chart&dataTable=BALANCES), the number of households affected could be up to 600,000. The actual number is most likely somewhere in the middle, according to a statement by Ukrenergy, which stated that the loss of power amounted to about a fifth of power consumption in Kyiv at this time. BBC, "Ukraine Power Cut 'Was Cyber-Attack,'" *BBC News*, January 2017, sec. Technology, https://www.bbc.com/news/technology-38573074. At a population of 2.88 million, a fifth would equal 576,000 individuals. However, the precise number will depend on the specific configuration of the power grid, which is not known.
204. Vsevolod Kovalchuk, "Цієї Ночі На Підстанції 'Північна' Відбувся Збій . . .—Vsevolod Kovalchuk," December 2016, https://www.facebook.com/permalink.php?story_fbid=1798082313797621&id=100007876094707.
205. ESET, "Win32/Industroyer," 2017, 15, https://www.welivesecurity.com/wp-content/uploads/2017/06/Win32_Industroyer.pdf.
206. Neither the initial attack vector nor the precise timeframe of this compromise is known; hence, the only known timeframe is the gap between the 2015 operation and

the 2016 operation, building directly on the knowledge acquired during this operation. Because the 2016 operation applied knowledge gathered through the 2015 operation and was significantly more advanced, it is reasonable to assume a continuous development process.
207. Dragos, "CRASHOVERRIDE Analysis of the Threat to Electric Grid Operations," 11.
208. ESET, "Win32/Industroyer," 2.
209. Anonymous cybersecurity researchers interviewed by the author in Kyiv in April 2018 s April 2018.
210. Dragos, "CRASHOVERRIDE Analysis of the Threat to Electric Grid Operations," 23.
211. Dragos, "CRASHOVERRIDE Analysis of the Threat to Electric Grid Operations," 23.
212. Dragos, "CRASHOVERRIDE Analysis of the Threat to Electric Grid Operations," 24.
213. Johnson, "On Drawing a Bright Line for Covert Operations," 286.
214. Kovalchuk, "Цієї Ночі На Підстанції 'Північна' Відбувся Збій . . .—Vsevolod Kovalchuk."
215. The only news story mentioning this event is the following on the UNN network: "В 'Укренерго' не виключають кібератаку на підстанцію 'Північна', через яку частину Києву було знеструмлено," Інформаційне агентство Українські Національні Новини (УНН), Всі онлайн новини дня в Україні за сьогодні—найсвіжіші, останні, головні, *UNN*, December 2016, https://www.unn.com.ua/uk/news/1628435-v-ukrenergo-ne-viklyuchayut-kiberataku-na-pidstantsiyu-pivnichna-cherez-yaku-chastinu-kiyevu-bulo-znestrumleno.
216. "Відключення Електроенергії в Україні Було Хакерською Атакою—Експерти," Hromadske.ua, January 2017, https://hromadske.ua/posts/vidkliuchennia-elektro enerhii-v-ukraini-bulo-khakerskoiu-atakoiu.
217. Dragos, "CRASHOVERRIDE Analysis of the Threat to Electric Grid Operations," 11.
218. Benjamin Jensen and J. D. Work, "Cyber Civil-Military Relations: Balancing Interests on the Digital Frontier," *War on the Rocks*, September 2018, https://waront herocks.com/2018/09/cyber-civil-military-relations-balancing-interests-on-the-digital-frontier/.
219. Greenberg, "How an Entire Nation Became Russia's Test Lab for Cyberwar."
220. Greenberg, "How an Entire Nation Became Russia's Test Lab for Cyberwar."
221. Rebecca Smith, "Cyberattacks Raise Alarm for U.S. Power Grid," *Wall Street Journal*, December 30, 2016, sec. US, https://www.wsj.com/articles/cyberattacks-raise-ala rms-for-u-s-power-grid-1483120708.
222. Daniel W. Drezner, "Why Vladimir Putin's Strategic Genius Scares the Heck Out of Me," *Washington Post*, July 30, 2014, sec. PostEverything, https://www.washingtonp ost.com/posteverything/wp/2014/07/30/why-vladimir-putins-strategic-genius-sca res-the-heck-out-of-me/; Mark Hertling and Molly K. Mckew, "Putin's Attack on the U.S. Is Our Pearl Harbor," *Politico Magazine*, 2018, https://politi.co/2L1gYOS; Kathleen Hall Jamieson, *Cyberwar: How Russian Hackers and Trolls Helped Elect a President What We Don't, Can't, and Do Know* (New York: Oxford University Press, 2018).
223. Personal correspondence on February 25, 2021.

224. Symantec, "Dragonfly: Western Energy Companies under Sabotage Threat," *Symantec Security Response* (blog), accessed August 23, 2017, http://www.symantec.com/connect/blogs/dragonfly-western-energy-companies-under-sabotage-threat.
225. Schelling, *Arms and Influence*.
226. Dragos, "CRASHOVERRIDE Analysis of the Threat to Electric Grid Operations," 25.
227. Sean Townsend (pseudonym), interviewed by the author in Kyiv in April 2018.
228. Victor Zhora, interviewed by the author in Kyiv in April 2018.
229. Volodymyr Styran, interviewed by the author in Kyiv in April 2018.
230. Nikolay Koval, April 2018.
231. Dragos, "CRASHOVERRIDE: Reassessing the 2016 Ukraine Electric Power Event as a Protection-Focused Attack," 2019, 9, https://dragos.com/wp-content/uploads/CRASHOVERRIDE.pdf.
232. Dragos, "CRASHOVERRIDE: Reassessing the 2016 Ukraine Electric Power Event as a Protection-Focused Attack," 9.
233. Dragos, "CRASHOVERRIDE: Reassessing the 2016 Ukraine Electric Power Event as a Protection-Focused Attack," 11.
234. Dragos, "CRASHOVERRIDE: Reassessing the 2016 Ukraine Electric Power Event as a Protection-Focused Attack," 12.
235. Kurt Baumgartner, "BE2 Extraordinary Plugins, Siemens Targeting, Dev Fails," February 2015, https://securelist.com/be2-extraordinary-plugins-siemens-targeting-dev-fails/68838/.
236. Dragos, "CRASHOVERRIDE: Reassessing the 2016 Ukraine Electric Power Event as a Protection-Focused Attack," 5.
237. "Стратегічні Об'єкти Мають Бути Захищені, а Винні у Вибухах На Військових Складах Притягнуті До Відповідальності—Президент Щодо Ситуації Під Калинівкою," Офіційне інтернет-представництво Президента України, PResident.gov.ua, September 2017, https://www.president.gov.ua/news/strategichni-obyekti-mayut-buti-zahisheni-vinni-u-vibuhah-na-43610; "Ukrainian Leaders Blame 'Sabotage' for Huge Blast at Munitions Depot," Radio Free Europe/Radio Liberty, September 2017, https://www.rferl.org/a/artillery-warehouses-explode-evacuations-ordered-around-vinnitsa-ukraine-kalinovka-evacuated/28759382.html.
238. "Начальника пожежної охорони арсеналу в Калинівці не було покарано за недбалість через закінчення термінів притягнення до адмінвідповідальності," *Цензор.НЕТ*, Censor.net, October 2018, https://censor.net.ua/ua/news/3091002/nachalnyka_pojejnoyi_ohorony_arsenalu_v_kalynivtsi_ne_bulo_pokarano_za_nedbalist_cherez_zakinchennya.
239. "The EU-Ukraine Association Agreement Enters into Force on 1 September 2017," EEAS—European External Action Service, European Commission, accessed April 16, 2019, https://eeas.europa.eu/delegations/ukraine/30478/eu-ukraine-association-agreement-enters-force-1-september-2017_en.
240. Johnson, "On Drawing a Bright Line for Covert Operations," 289.
241. Johnson, "On Drawing a Bright Line for Covert Operations," 290.

242. "Вибухи в Калинівці: Майора, Який Пропустив Сторонніх На Військові Склади, Оштрафували На 2,5 Тисячі," Espreso.tv, November 2017, https://espreso.tv/news/2017/11/22/vybukhy_v_kalynivci_mayora_yakyy_propustyv_storonnikh_osib_na_viyskovi_sklady_oshtrafuvaly_na_2_5_tysyachi.
243. "Начальника пожежної охорони арсеналу в Калинівці не було покарано за недбалість через закінчення термінів притягнення до адмінвідповідальності."
244. "Вибухи в Калинівці."
245. "2 Ukrainian Border Guards Killed in Mine Explosion; Military Prosecutor Finds 'No Saboteurs' at Ammo Depot," *The Interpreter*, September 2017, http://www.interpretermag.com/day-1319/.
246. "2 Ukrainian Border Guards Killed in Mine Explosion."
247. "У Російських Диверсантів Могли Бути Спільники На Складах у Калинівці,— Генерал Розвідки," Espreso.tv, September 2017, https://espreso.tv/news/2017/09/27/u_rosiyskykh_dyversantiv_mogly_buty_spilnyky_na_skladakh_u_kalynivci_general_rozvidky.
248. "Начальника пожежної охорони арсеналу в Калинівці не було покарано за недбалість через закінчення термінів притягнення до адмінвідповідальності."
249. "Вибухи в Калинівці."
250. "Вибухи в Калинівці."
251. Olena Holubeva, "How Much Do Ukrainian Soldiers Earn?," March 2019, https://112.international/opinion/how-much-do-ukrainian-soldiers-earn-38268.html.
252. Roland Oliphant and Charlotte Krol, "Huge Explosion at Ukraine Ammunition Depot Prompts Mass Evacuation," *The Telegraph*, September 27, 2017, https://www.telegraph.co.uk/news/2017/09/27/fire-ukraine-ammunition-depot-prompts-mass-evacuation/; Iuliia Mendel, "In Ukraine, a Huge Ammunition Depot Catches Fire," *New York Times*, 27 September 2019, sec. World, https://www.nytimes.com/2017/09/27/world/europe/ukraine-ammunition-depot-explosion.html.
253. "Слідчі розглядають 4 версії вибухів на складі боєприпасів під Вінницею," Hromadske.ua, September 2017, https://hromadske.ua/posts/slidchi-rozhliadaiut-4-versii-vybukhiv-na-skladi-boieprypasiv-pid-vinnytseiu; "Тероризм чи недбалість: як в Україні розслідуються вибухи на військових складах," Hromadske.ua, October 2018, https://hromadske.ua/posts/iak-v-ukraini-rozslid uiutsia-vybukhy-na-viiskovykh-skladakh.
254. "Ukrainian Leaders Blame 'Sabotage' for Huge Blast at Munitions Depot."
255. Tony Wesolowsky, "Ukraine's Exploding Munition Depots Give Ammunition to Security Concerns," Radio Free Europe/Radio Liberty, https://www.rferl.org/a/ukraine-exploding-munitions-security-concerns-russia/28777991.html.
256. The causes of the explosion in March have not been as conclusively established yet, however, leaving open the possibility of a simple accident. "Terrorism or Negligence? Inside the Investigation into Ukraine's Exploding Military Warehouses," Hromadske.ua, October 2017, https://en.hromadske.ua/posts/terrorism-or-negligence-inside-the-investigation-into-ukraines-exploding-military-warehouses.

268 NOTES

257. "Ukraine Says Ammo Depot Explosions Huge Blow to Combat Capability," Reuters, September 2017, https://www.reuters.com/article/us-ukraine-explosions-idUSKC N1C316Z.
258. "Blasts at Ukrainian Munitions Depot Let $800 Mln of Weapons Go Up in Smoke," TASS, September 2017, http://tass.com/world/967814.
259. "Кабінет Міністрів України—Щодо роботи інформаційно-телекомунікаційної системи Казначейства," KMU, December 2016, https://www.kmu.gov.ua/ua/news/249559690 (translated from Ukrainian).
260. Specifically, its successor group TeleBots.
261. ESET, "The Rise of TeleBots: Analyzing Disruptive KillDisk Attacks," *We Live Security* (blog), December 2016, https://www.welivesecurity.com/2016/12/13/rise-telebots-analyzing-disruptive-killdisk-attacks/.
262. ESET, "The Rise of TeleBots."
263. ESET, "The Rise of TeleBots."
264. ESET, "The Rise of TeleBots."
265. ESET, "The Rise of TeleBots."
266. ESET, "The Rise of TeleBots."
267. ESET, "The Rise of TeleBots."
268. Dmitry Dubov, interviewed by the author in Kyiv in April 2018.
269. "Кабінет Міністрів України—Щодо роботи інформаційно-телекомунікаційної системи Казначейства."
270. Vsevolod Nekrasov, "Украина Проигрывает Кибервойну. Хакеры Наносят Удар По Минфину," Экономическая правда, December 2016, http://www.epravda.com.ua/rus/publications/2016/12/9/613957/.
271. "Из-За Кибератаки Минфин и Госказначейство Потеряли 3 Терабайта Информации," accessed October 13, 2021, https://biz.nv.ua/economics/iz-za-kiberataki-minfin-i-goskaznachejstvo-poterjali-3-terabajta-informatsii-330784.html.
272. There is insufficient survey data to establish a clear causal linkage to the attack, yet the assessments provided by analysts and the scale of the disruption strongly indicate an impact on morale among those affected.
273. Anonymous government employee, interviewed by the author in Kyiv in April 2018.
274. Cassandra Allen, "Mapping Media Freedom: Ukrainian Journalists Subjected to Malicious Cyber-Attacks," *Index on Censorship* (blog), July 2017, https://www.indexoncensorship.org/2017/07/journalists-ukraine-cyber-attacks/; Patrice Hill, "Monitor Says Ukraine Cease-Fire, Weapons Withdrawal Not Being Honored," Radio Free Europe/Radio Liberty, accessed August 31, 2020, https://www.rferl.org/a/monitor-osce-says-ukraine-cease-fire-heavy-weapons-withdrawal-not-honored/28324012.html.
275. ESET, "TeleBots Are Back: Supply-Chain Attacks against Ukraine," *We Live Security* (blog), June 2017, https://www.welivesecurity.com/2017/06/30/telebots-back-supply-chain-attacks-against-ukraine/.
276. ESET, "TeleBots Are Back."

277. Alex Hern, "Hackers Who Targeted Ukraine Clean Out Bitcoin Ransom Wallet," *The Guardian*, July 5, 2017, sec. Technology, https://www.theguardian.com/technology/2017/jul/05/notpetya-ransomware-hackers-ukraine-bitcoin-ransom-wallet-motives; Dan Goodin, "Tuesday's Massive Ransomware Outbreak Was, in Fact, Something Much Worse," *Ars Technica*, June 2017, https://arstechnica.com/information-technology/2017/06/petya-outbreak-was-a-chaos-sowing-wiper-not-profit-seeking-ransomware/.
278. Greenberg, "The Untold Story of NotPetya, the Most Devastating Cyberattack in History."
279. "Ukraine Power Company Says It Was Hit by a Second Cyber Attack," *Fortune*, June 30, 2017, http://fortune.com/2017/06/30/ukraine-power-station-cyber-attack/.
280. Ionut Arghire, "NotPetya Connected to BlackEnergy/KillDisk: Researchers," Security Week, July 2017, https://www.securityweek.com/notpetya-connected-blackenergykilldisk-researchers.
281. Anonymous cybersecurity expert interviewed by the author in Kyiv in April 2018.
282. ESET, "GREYENERGY," 21.
283. ESET, "GREYENERGY," 21; "Keeping Up with the Petyas: Demystifying the Malware Family," Malwarebytes Labs, July 2017, https://blog.malwarebytes.com/cybercrime/2017/07/keeping-up-with-the-petyas-demystifying-the-malware-family/.
284. ESET, "TeleBots Are Back: Supply-Chain Attacks against Ukraine."
285. ESET, "TeleBots Are Back."
286. ESET, "TeleBots Are Back."
287. ESET, "TeleBots Are Back."
288. Dell Cameron, "In WannaCry's Wake, a New Rapidly Spreading Ransomware Attack Appeared Today," *Gizmodo*, May 2017, https://gizmodo.com/in-wannacrys-wake-a-new-rapidly-spreading-ransomware-a-1795385418.
289. MalwareHunterTeam (@malwrhunterteam), "XData Is Still Going, Even Closer to Cerber's 24 Hours Numbers . . .," Twitter, May 2017, https://twitter.com/malwrhunterteam/status/865618366412849157.
290. Bill Chappell, "'Petya' Ransomware Hits at Least 65 Countries; Microsoft Traces It to Tax Software," *NPR*, June 2017, https://www.npr.org/sections/thetwo-way/2017/06/28/534679950/petya-ransomware-hits-at-least-65-countries-microsoft-traces-it-to-tax-software.
291. Victor Zhora, interviewed by the author in Kyiv in April 2018.
292. Meaning the update will have installed automatically on client systems unless they opted out of this service.
293. FireEye, "SMB Exploited: WannaCry Use of 'EternalBlue'" May 2017, https://www.fireeye.com/blog/threat-research/2017/05/smb-exploited-wannacry-use-of-eternalblue.html.
294. ESET, "TeleBots Are Back: Supply-Chain Attacks against Ukraine."
295. Volodymyr Styran, interviewed by the author in Kyiv in April 2018.

296. Sean Townsend (pseudonym), interviewed by the author in Kyiv in April 2018.
297. Catalin Cimpanu, "M.E.Doc Software Was Backdoored 3 Times, Servers Left without Updates since 2013," Bleeping Computer, 2017, https://www.bleepingcomputer.com/news/security/m-e-doc-software-was-backdoored-3-times-servers-left-without-updates-since-2013/.
298. Anonymous government employee, interviewed by the author in Kyiv in April 2018.
299. Greenberg, "The Untold Story of NotPetya, the Most Devastating Cyberattack in History."
300. Igor Burdiga, "«Чорний вівторок» українського ІТ: яких збитків завдала кібератака, та хто її вчинив," July 2017, https://hromadske.ua/posts/naslidki-kiberataki.
301. MKA Cyber, "Maersk Replaces IT Infrastructure after NotPetya Ransomware Infection," *MKACyber, Inc.* (blog), January 2018, https://mkacyber.io/news/maersk-shipping-reinstalled-entire-infrastructure-after-notpetya-ransomware/; John Leyden, "FedEx: TNT NotPetya Infection Blew a $300m Hole in Our Numbers," September 2017, https://www.theregister.co.uk/2017/09/20/fedex_notpetya_damages/.
302. "Global Cyber Attack Could Spur $53 Billion in Losses: Lloyd's Of . . .," Reuters, July 2017, https://www.reuters.com/article/us-cyber-lloyds-report/global-cyber-attack-could-spur-53-billion-in-losses-lloyds-of-london-idUSKBN1A20AB.
303. Anonymous government employee, interviewed by the author in Kyiv in April 2018.
304. "Масова Хакерська Атака: Під Удар Потрапив Навіть Кабмін—5 Канал," 5.ua, June 2017, https://www.5.ua/suspilstvo/masova-khakerska-ataka-pid-udar-potrapyv-kabmin-metropoliten-nyzka-bankiv-ta-pidpryiemstv-148971.html; "Очільник СБУ Розповів Про Мотив Хакерів, Які Атакували Україну Вірусом Petya," TCN.ua, July 2017, https://tsn.ua/ukrayina/ochilnik-sbu-rozpoviv-pro-motiv-hakeriv-yaki-atakuvali-ukrayinu-virusom-petya-955817.html; "Підсумки 2017 Року: Найгучніші Вбивства в Україні," 24 Канал, accessed May 13, 2019, https://24tv.ua/news/showNews.do?pidsumki_2017_roku_v_ukrayini_vbivstva_2017&objectId=895499.
305. ESET, "Analysis of TeleBots' Cunning Backdoor," *We Live Security* (blog), July 2017, https://www.welivesecurity.com/2017/07/04/analysis-of-telebots-cunning-backdoor/.
306. Lawrence Adams, "AES-NI Ransomware Dev Releases Decryption Keys amid Fears of Being Framed for XData Outbreak," Bleeping Computer, May 2017, https://www.bleepingcomputer.com/news/security/aes-ni-ransomware-dev-releases-decryption-keys-amid-fears-of-being-framed-for-xdata-outbreak/.
307. Adams, "AES-NI Ransomware Dev Releases Decryption Keys amid Fears of Being Framed for XData Outbreak."
308. ESET, "XData Ransomware Making Rounds amid Global WannaCryptor Scare," *We Live Security* (blog), May 2017, https://www.welivesecurity.com/2017/05/23/xdata-ransomware-making-rounds-amid-global-wannacryptor-scare/.
309. VPNs enable private and encrypted connections via the public Internet, effectively linking remote computers as in a local network.

310. Chappell, "'Petya' Ransomware Hits at Least 65 Countries; Microsoft Traces It to Tax Software."
311. Greenberg, "The Untold Story of NotPetya, the Most Devastating Cyberattack in History."
312. "Russia: The FSB Branches Out," *Stratfor* (blog), 2008, https://worldview.stratfor.com/article/russia-fsb-branches-out.
313. Russia Today, "US Blames Moscow for NotPetya Malware, Which Hit Russia Too," *RT International*, February 2018, https://www.rt.com/news/418955-us-blames-russia-notpetya-cyber-attack/.
314. Burdiga, "«Чорний вівторок» українського IT."
315. Greenberg, "The Untold Story of NotPetya, the Most Devastating Cyberattack in History."
316. ESET, "TeleBots Are Back: Supply-Chain Attacks against Ukraine."
317. "Timing and Performance," Nmap Network Scanning, accessed March 29, 2023, https://nmap.org/book/man-performance.html.
318. US Treasury, "Treasury Sanctions Russian Cyber Actors for Interference with the 2016 U.S. Elections and Malicious Cyber-Attacks," US Department of the Treasury, March 2018, https://home.treasury.gov/news/press-releases/sm0312.
319. European Council, "EU Imposes the First Ever Sanctions against Cyber-Attacks," July 2020, https://www.consilium.europa.eu/en/press/press-releases/2020/07/30/eu-imposes-the-first-ever-sanctions-against-cyber-attacks/.
320. US Treasury, "Treasury Sanctions Russian Cyber Actors for Interference with the 2016 U.S. Elections and Malicious Cyber-Attacks."
321. Michael Schwirtz, "Top Secret Russian Unit Seeks to Destabilize Europe, Security Officials Say," *New York Times*, October 8, 2019, sec. World, https://www.nytimes.com/2019/10/08/world/europe/unit-29155-russia-gru.html.
322. Greenberg, "The Untold Story of NotPetya, the Most Devastating Cyberattack in History."
323. Greenberg, "The Untold Story of NotPetya, the Most Devastating Cyberattack in History."
324. Greenberg, "The Untold Story of NotPetya, the Most Devastating Cyberattack in History."
325. Brandon Valeriano, Ryan C. Maness, and Benjamin Jensen, "Analysis: Cyberwarfare Has Taken a New Turn. Yes, It's Time to Worry," *Washington Post*, July 13, 2017, https://www.washingtonpost.com/news/monkey-cage/wp/2017/07/13/cyber-warfare-has-taken-a-new-turn-yes-its-time-to-worry/.
326. See the next chapter for an extended discussion of this point.
327. Burdiga, "«Чорний вівторок» українського IT."
328. Burdiga, "«Чорний вівторок» українського IT."
329. Anonymous cybersecurity expert, interviewed in Kyiv in April 2018.
330. Nikolay Koval, interviewed by the author in Kyiv in April 2018.
331. "What Is Bad Rabbit Ransomware?," *Proofpoint* (blog), February 2021, https://www.proofpoint.com/us/threat-reference/bad-rabbit.

332. ESET, "Bad Rabbit: Not-Petya Is Back with Improved Ransomware," *We Live Security* (blog), October 2017, https://www.welivesecurity.com/2017/10/24/bad-rabbit-not-petya-back/; "Ukraine Cyber Police Chief Says Ukraine Hit by 'Badrabbit' Malware," Reuters, October 2017, https://www.reuters.com/article/us-ukraine-cyber-police-idUSKBN1CT27G; Cisco Talos, "Threat Spotlight: Follow the Bad Rabbit," 2017, http://blog.talosintelligence.com/2017/10/bad-rabbit.html; Kaspersky, "Bad Rabbit Ransomware," October 2017, https://securelist.com/bad-rabbit-ransomware/82851/.
333. Cisco Talos, "Threat Spotlight."
334. ESET, "Bad Rabbit."
335. ESET, "Kiev Metro Hit with a New Variant of the Infamous Diskcoder Ransomware," *We Live Security* (blog), October 2017, https://www.welivesecurity.com/2017/10/24/kiev-metro-hit-new-variant-infamous-diskcoder-ransomware/.
336. "Ukraine Cyber Police Chief Says Ukraine Hit by 'Badrabbit' Malware."
337. "Tracking the BadRabbit Ransomware to an Ongoing Campaign of Target Selection," RiskIQ, October 2017, https://www.riskiq.com/blog/labs/badrabbit/.
338. Hasherezade, "BadRabbit: A Closer Look at the New Version of Petya/NotPetya," Malwarebytes Labs, October 2017, https://blog.malwarebytes.com/threat-analysis/2017/10/badrabbit-closer-look-new-version-petyanotpetya/.
339. Cisco Talos, "The MeDoc Connection," 2017, http://blog.talosintelligence.com/2017/07/the-medoc-connection.html.
340. Eduard Kovacs, "Files Encrypted by Bad Rabbit Recoverable Without Paying Ransom," Security Week, October 2017, https://www.securityweek.com/files-encrypted-bad-rabbit-recoverable-without-paying-ransom.
341. John Leyden, "Hop on, Average Rabbit: Latest Extortionware Menace Flopped," October 2017, https://www.theregister.co.uk/2017/10/26/bad_rabbit_post_mortem/.
342. ESET, "Bad Rabbit."
343. Burdiga, "«Чорний вівторок» українського ІТ."
344. ESET, "Bad Rabbit."
345. ESET, "Bad Rabbit."
346. Kaspersky, "Bad Rabbit Ransomware."
347. RiskIQ, "Tracking the BadRabbit Ransomware to an Ongoing Campaign of Target Selection."
348. Russia Today, "Bad Rabbit Cryptoware Attack: New Virus Hits Companies in Russia, Turkey, Germany & Ukraine," *RT International*, October 2017, https://www.rt.com/news/407655-bad-rabbit-cryptoware-attack/.
349. ESET, "New TeleBots Backdoor: First Evidence Linking Industroyer to NotPetya," *We Live Security* (blog), October 2018, https://www.welivesecurity.com/2018/10/11/new-telebots-backdoor-linking-industroyer-notpetya/.
350. ESET, "GREYENERGY"; ESET, "New TeleBots Backdoor."

351. CrowdStrike, "Fancy Bear Tracking of Ukrainian Field Artillery Units," December 2016, http://web.archive.org/web/20161223065425/https://www.crowdstrike.com/wp-content/brochures/FancyBearTracksUkrainianArtillery.pdf.
352. CrowdStrike, "Fancy Bear Tracking of Ukrainian Field Artillery Units."
353. CrowdStrike, "Fancy Bear Tracking of Ukrainian Field Artillery Units."
354. Dustin Volz, "Russian Hackers Tracked Ukrainian Artillery Units Using Android Implant: Report," Reuters, December 2016, https://www.reuters.com/article/us-cyber-ukraine-idUKKBN14B0CU; David Martin, "Russian Hacking Proves Lethal after Ukrainian Military App Hijacked," *CBS News*, December 2016, https://www.cbsnews.com/news/russian-hacking-proves-lethal-after-ukrainian-military-app-compromised/; Patrick Tucker, "DNC Hackers Linked to Russian Activity against Ukraine Two Years Ago," *Defense One* (blog), December 2016, https://www.defenseone.com/technology/2016/12/dnc-hackers-linked-russian-hacks-ukraine-two-years-ago/134098/.
355. Elias Groll, "In a Hacked Ukrainian App, a Picture of the Future of War," *Foreign Policy* (blog), December 2016, https://foreignpolicy.com/2016/12/22/in-a-hacked-ukrainian-app-a-picture-of-the-future-of-war/.
356. Oleksiy Kuzmenko, "Think Tank: Cyber Firm at Center of Russian Hacking Charges Misread Data," *VOA*, 2017, https://www.voanews.com/a/crowdstrike-comey-russia-hack-dnc-clinton-trump/3776067.html.
357. Jeffrey Carr, "The GRU-Ukraine Artillery Hack That May Never Have Happened," *Medium* (blog), January 2017, https://medium.com/@jeffreyscarr/the-gru-ukraine-artillery-hack-that-may-never-have-happened-820960bbb02d. The author has since deleted the story—for unknown reasons—but an archived version can be found here: https://web.archive.org/web/20180816101157/https://medium.com/@jeffreyscarr/the-gru-ukraine-artillery-hack-that-may-never-have-happened-820960bbb02d.
358. Sean Townsend (pseudonym), interviewed by the author in Kyiv in April 2018.
359. CrowdStrike, "Fancy Bear Tracking of Ukrainian Field Artillery Units," March 2017, https://www.crowdstrike.com/wp-content/brochures/FancyBearTracksUkrainianArtillery.pdf.
360. Kuzmenko, "Think Tank."
361. CrowdStrike, "Danger Close," March 2017. https://www.crowdstrike.com/blog/danger-close-fancy-bear-tracking-ukrainian-field-artillery-units/
362. World Bank, "GDP (Current US$)—Ukraine: Data," 2023, https://data.worldbank.org/indicator/NY.GDP.MKTP.CD?locations=UA.
363. "Assessment of Ukraine's Economic Losses from the Temporary Occupation of the Crimean Peninsula," Center for Economic Strategy, July 2021, https://ces.org.ua/assessment-of-ukraines-economic-losses-from-crimea/.
364. World Bank, "GDP (Current US$)—Ukraine: Data."
365. World Bank, "GDP (Current US$)—Ukraine: Data."

Chapter 5

1. Chris Stokel-Walker, "Will Russia's Invasion of Ukraine Trigger a Massive Cyberwar?," *New Scientist*, February 2022, https://www.newscientist.com/article/2309369-will-russias-invasion-of-ukraine-trigger-a-massive-cyberwar/.
2. Keir Giles, "Putin Does Not Need to Invade Ukraine to Get His Way," *Chatham House—International Affairs Think Tank* (blog), December 2021, https://www.chathamhouse.org/2021/12/putin-does-not-need-invade-ukraine-get-his-way.
3. See preceding chapter.
4. Maggie Miller, "Russian Invasion of Ukraine Could Redefine Cyber Warfare," Politico, January 2022, https://www.politico.com/news/2022/01/28/russia-cyber-army-ukraine-00003051.
5. Keith Alexander, "Cyber Warfare in Ukraine Poses a Threat to the Global System," *Financial Times*, February 2022, https://www.ft.com/content/8e1e8176-2279-4596-9c0f-98629b4db5a6.
6. Luke Harding and Luke Harding Lviv, "Demoralised Russian Soldiers Tell of Anger at Being 'Duped' into War," *The Guardian*, March 4, 2022, sec. World News, https://www.theguardian.com/world/2022/mar/04/russian-soldiers-ukraine-anger-duped-into-war; Ksenya Oksamytna, "Ukraine: Russian Attitudes to Ukrainians Can Help to Explain the Atrocities," King's College London, June 2022, https://www.kcl.ac.uk/ukraine-russian-attitudes-to-ukrainians-can-help-to-explain-the-atrocities.
7. Maksym Butchenko, "Ukraine's Territorial Defence on a War Footing," *ICDS* (blog), April 2022, https://icds.ee/en/ukraines-territorial-defence-on-a-war-footing/; Paul Sonne et al., "Battle for Kyiv: Ukrainian Valor, Russian Blunders Combined to Save the Capital," *Washington Post*, accessed January 13, 2023, https://www.washingtonpost.com/national-security/interactive/2022/kyiv-battle-ukraine-survival/.
8. Greg Miller and Catherine Belton, "Russia's Spies Misread Ukraine and Misled Kremlin as War Loomed," *Washington Post*, 19 August 2022, https://www.washingtonpost.com/world/interactive/2022/russia-fsb-intelligence-ukraine-war/.
9. Andrew Osborn, Polina Nikolskaya, and Polina Nikolskaya, "Russia's Putin Authorises 'Special Military Operation' against Ukraine," Reuters, February 2022, sec. Europe, https://www.reuters.com/world/europe/russias-putin-authorises-military-operations-donbass-domestic-media-2022-02-24/.
10. Lennart Maschmeyer et al., "Donetsk Don't Tell—'Hybrid War' in Ukraine and the Limits of Social Media Influence Operations," *Journal of Information Technology and Politics*, online first, May 2023, https://doi.org/10.1080/19331681.2023.2211969.
11. "Russia Not Seeking Regime Change in Ukraine, People Should Have Freedom of Choice—Lavrov," TASS, April 2022, https://tass.com/politics/1439823.
12. "Russia Says It Wants to End Ukraine's 'Unacceptable Regime,'" AP News, July 2022, https://apnews.com/article/russia-ukraine-zelenskyy-kyiv-black-sea-arab-league-b5c583e8d057897cfdef6b407e113339.

13. "Ukraine War: Putin Signs Ukraine Annexation Laws amid Military Setbacks," *BBC News*, October 2022, sec. Europe, https://www.bbc.com/news/world-europe-63149156.
14. Kim Zetter, "What We Know and Don't Know about the Cyberattacks against Ukraine (Updated)," Substack newsletter, *Zero Day* (blog), January 2022, https://zetter.substack.com/p/what-we-know-and-dont-know-about.
15. Luke Harding, "Ukraine Hit by 'Massive' Cyber-Attack on Government Websites," *The Guardian*, January 14, 2022, sec. World News, https://www.theguardian.com/world/2022/jan/14/ukraine-massive-cyber-attack-government-websites-suspected-russian-hackers; Pavel Polityuk, "Massive Cyberattack Hits Ukrainian Government Websites as West Warns on Russia Conflict," Reuters, January 2022, sec. Technology, https://www.reuters.com/technology/massive-cyberattack-hits-ukrainian-government-websites-amid-russia-tensions-2022-01-14/.
16. CERT-UA, "Cyber Attack on Websites of State Bodies," January 2022, https://cert.gov.ua/.
17. Pavel Polityuk, "EXCLUSIVE: Ukraine Suspects Group Linked to Belarus Intelligence over Cyberattack," Reuters, January 2022, sec. Europe, https://www.reuters.com/world/europe/exclusive-ukraine-suspects-group-linked-belarus-intelligence-over-cyberattack-2022-01-15/; Mandiant, "UNC1151 Assessed with High Confidence to Have Links to Belarus, Ghostwriter Campaign Aligned with Belarusian Government Interests," November 2021, https://www.mandiant.com/resources/unc1151-linked-to-belarus-government.
18. CERT-UA, "Cyber Attack on Websites of State Bodies"; Zetter, "What We Know and Don't Know about the Cyberattacks against Ukraine (Updated)."
19. CERT-UA, "A Fragment of the Research on Cyber Attacks 01.14.2022," January 2022, https://cert.gov.ua/article/18101.
20. Microsoft, "Destructive Malware Targeting Ukrainian Organizations," *Microsoft Security* (blog), January 2022, https://www.microsoft.com/security/blog/2022/01/15/destructive-malware-targeting-ukrainian-organizations/; CrowdStrike, "Technical Analysis of the WhisperGate Malicious Bootloader," January 2022, https://www.crowdstrike.com/blog/technical-analysis-of-whispergate-malware/; "WhisperGate Malware Corrupts Computers in Ukraine," *Recorded Future* (blog), January 2022, https://www.recfut.com/whispergate-malware-corrupts-computers-ukraine/.
21. CERT-UA, "A Fragment of the Research on Cyber Attacks 01.14.2022."
22. "Information on the Possible Provocation," accessed February 3, 2022, https://cip.gov.ua/en/news/informaciya-shodo-imovirnoyi-provokaciyi.
23. SSCIP, "Державна Служба Спеціального Зв'язку Та Захисту Інформації України," January 2022, https://cip.gov.ua/ua/news/informaciya-shodo-imovirnoyi-provokaciyi.
24. Cisco Talos, "Ukraine Campaign Delivers Defacement and Wipers, in Continued Escalation," *Cisco Talos* (blog), January 2022, https://blog.talosintelligence.com/ukraine-campaign-delivers-defacement/.

25. Cisco Talos, "Ukraine Campaign Delivers Defacement and Wipers, in Continued Escalation."
26. CERT-UA, "A Fragment of the Research on Cyber Attacks 01.14.2022."
27. Victor Zhora, interviewed by the author via Zoom on January 26, 2023.
28. Secureworks, "WhisperGate: Not NotPetya," January 2022, https://www.secureworks.com/blog/whispergate-not-notpetya.
29. CrowdStrike, "Technical Analysis of the WhisperGate Malicious Bootloader."
30. Secureworks, "WhisperGate."
31. Adrienne Watson, Twitter, "The U.S. has technical information linking Russian GRU to this week's distributed denial of service attacks in Ukraine. Known GRU infrastructure has been noted transmitting high volumes of communications to Ukraine-based IP addresses and associated banking-related domains." February 2022, https://twitter.com/NSC_Spox/status/1494796573959725057.
32. Chris Doman, "Technical Analysis of the DDoS Attacks against Ukrainian Websites," Cado Security: Cloud Investigation, February 2022, https://www.cadosecurity.com/technical-analysis-of-the-ddos-attacks-against-ukrainian-websites/.
33. CERT-UA, "Information on Cyber Attacks on February 15, 2022," accessed January 12, 2023, https://cert.gov.ua/.
34. CERT-UA, "Information on Cyber Attacks on February 15, 2022."
35. Katerina Kuznetsova, "'ПриватБанк' Та 'Ощадбанк' Повністю Відновили Роботу Після Другої Потужної Кібератаки," TCH.Ua, February 2022, https://tsn.ua/ukrayina/privatbank-ta-oschadbank-povnistyu-vidnovili-robotu-pislya-drugoyi-potuzhnoyi-kiberataki-1979029.html.
36. Kateryna Kuznetsova, "Найпотужніша Кібератака За Всю Історію України: Ціль Хакерів, Кого Підозрюють і Які Наслідки Для Держави," TCH.Ua, February 17, 2022, https://tsn.ua/ukrayina/naypotuzhnisha-kiberataka-za-vsyu-istoriyu-ukrayini-cil-hakeriv-kogo-pidozryuyut-i-yaki-naslidki-dlya-derzhavi-1979239.html.
37. Dana Gordiichuk, "Кібератака за мільйони доларів: за нападом може стояти РФ," Економічна правда, February 2022, https://www.epravda.com.ua/news/2022/02/16/682428/.
38. Raphael Satter and James Pearson, "Recent Ukraine Outage Caused by Modest Cyberattack, Data Shows," Reuters, February 2022, sec. Technology, https://www.reuters.com/technology/recent-ukraine-outage-caused-by-modest-cyberattack-data-shows-2022-02-17/.
39. As an illustrative example of the prevailing mood, see this Facebook post by the CEO of Monobank (one of the affected institutions) lamenting the outage, with users (some of them evidently bank customers) making jokes in the comments: https://www.facebook.com/oleg.gorohovsky/posts/pfbid09MB75nCSJYhLM48kuVfvPykMdCdJ3bzdmJ54kT8cpdg1V22wY7rLFr2DnHpkaKfml.
40. Doman, "Technical Analysis of the DDoS Attacks against Ukrainian Websites."
41. Doman, "Technical Analysis of the DDoS Attacks against Ukrainian Websites."

42. ASERT Team, "The Anatomy of the DDoS Attack Campaign Targeting Organizations in Ukraine," *NETSCOUT* (blog), February 2022, https://www.netscout.com/blog/asert/ddos-attack-campaign-targeting-multiple-organizations-ukraine.
43. Nye, "Deterrence and Dissuasion in Cyberspace"; Valeriano, Maness, and Jensen, "Analysis: Cyberwarfare Has Taken a New Turn. Yes, It's Time to Worry"; Miller, "Russian Invasion of Ukraine Could Redefine Cyber Warfare."
44. Lauren Feiner, "Cyberattack Hits Ukrainian Banks and Government Websites," *CNBC*, February 2022, https://www.cnbc.com/2022/02/23/cyberattack-hits-ukrainian-banks-and-government-websites.html.
45. NIKCENTER, "Веб-сайти Кабміна не відкриваються - Мінцифри повідомляють о масовій DDoS-атаці," February 2022, https://nikcenter.org/newsItem/65950.
46. ESET Research (@ESETresearch), Twitter, "Breaking. #ESETResearch discovered a new data wiper malware used in Ukraine today. ESET telemetry shows that it was installed on hundreds of machines in the country. This follows the DDoS attacks against several Ukrainian websites earlier today 1/n." February 2022, https://twitter.com/ESETresearch/status/1496581903205511181.
47. J. A. Guerrero-Saade (@juanandres_gs), "Ok, Folks, We're Clearly Missing the *MOST* Important Part of All of This. Seeing as Neither @threatintel nor @ESETresearch Have Named This Monster, Let's Call This #HermeticWiper," Twitter, February 2022, https://twitter.com/juanandres_gs/status/1496607141888724997.
48. ESET Research (@ESETresearch), Twitter, "We observed the first sample today around 14h52 UTC / 16h52 local time. The PE compilation timestamp of one of the sample is 2021-12-28, suggesting that the attack might have been in preparation for almost two months. 2/n." February 2022, https://twitter.com/ESETresearch/status/1496581904916754435.
49. Juan Andrés Guerrero-Saade, "HermeticWiper: New Destructive Malware Used In Cyber Attacks on Ukraine," *SentinelOne* (blog), accessed February 28, 2022, https://www.sentinelone.com/labs/hermetic-wiper-ukraine-under-attack/.
50. Juan Andres Guerrero-Saade, interviewed by the author on February 20, 2023.
51. ESET Research, "IsaacWiper and HermeticWizard: New Wiper and Worm Targeting Ukraine," *We Live Security* (blog), March 2022, https://www.welivesecurity.com/2022/03/01/isaacwiper-hermeticwizard-wiper-worm-targeting-ukraine/.
52. As Juan Andres Guerrero-Saade explained when I interviewed him via Zoom on February 20, 2023, HermeticWiper was spread through a separate worm called HermeticWizard that did not include any exploits (in contrast to NotPetya), had no credential harvester (which collects access credentials, and which NotPetya did), and only focused on local subnets rather than entire corporate networks linked through different routers.
53. Reliaquest, "Threat Advisory: HermeticWiper," *Legacy* (blog), February 2022, https://www.reliaquest.com/i/blog/threat-advisory-hermeticwiper/.
54. Kim Zetter, "Second Wiper Attack Strikes Systems in Ukraine and Two Neighboring Countries," Substack newsletter, *Zero Day* (blog), February 2022, https://zetter.substack.com/p/second-wiper-attack-strikes-systems.

55. J. A. Guerrero-Saade (@juanandres_gs), "Ok. This Isn't a Bullshit Wiper like the Last Time. This Thing Is Meant to Be Devastating. Https://T.Co/EvP0g3jjvU," Twitter, February 2022, https://twitter.com/juanandres_gs/status/1496599932966510600.
56. ESET Research, "IsaacWiper and HermeticWizard."
57. Secureworks, "Disruptive HermeticWiper Attacks Targeting Ukrainian Organizations," February 2022, https://www.secureworks.com/blog/disruptive-hermeticwiper-attacks-targeting-ukrainian-organizations.
58. Ukrinform, "Українські Урядові Сайти Знову Зазнали Кібератаки," February 2022, https://www.ukrinform.ua/rubric-technology/3410832-ukrainski-uradovi-sajti-znovu-zaznali-kiberataki.html.
59. Hromadske.ua, "У Ніч На 24 Лютого На Україну Була Здійснена Кібератака— Федоров," *Громадське Радіо*, February 2022, https://hromadske.radio/news/2022/02/24/u-nich-na-24-liutoho-na-ukrainu-bula-zdiysnena-kiberataka-fedorov.
60. ESET Research, "IsaacWiper and HermeticWizard."
61. ESET Research, "IsaacWiper and HermeticWizard."
62. ESET Research, "IsaacWiper and HermeticWizard."
63. ESET Research, "IsaacWiper and HermeticWizard."
64. ESET, "CaddyWiper: New Wiper Malware Discovered in Ukraine," *We Live Security* (blog), March 2022, https://www.welivesecurity.com/2022/03/15/caddywiper-new-wiper-malware-discovered-ukraine/.
65. ESET, "Sandworm Uses a New Version of ArguePatch to Attack Targets in Ukraine," *We Live Security* (blog), May 2022, https://www.welivesecurity.com/2022/05/20/sandworm-ukraine-new-version-arguepatch-malware-loader/.
66. ESET Research (@ESETresearch), "CaddyWiper Does Not Share Any Significant Code Similarity with #HermeticWiper, #IsaacWiper or Any Other Malware Known to Us. The Sample We Analyzed Was Not Digitally Signed. 3/7 Https://T.Co/EGp9NnctD9," Twitter, March 2022, https://twitter.com/ESETresearch/status/1503436425676705807.
67. ESET Research (@ESETresearch), Twitter, "This new malware erases user data and partition information from attached drives. #ESET telemetry shows that it was seen on a few dozen systems in a limited number of organizations. 2/7." March 2022, https://twitter.com/ESETresearch/status/1503436423818534915.
68. ESET Research (@ESETresearch), Twitter, "Similarly to HermeticWiper deployments, we observed CaddyWiper being deployed via GPO, indicating the attackers had prior control of the target's network beforehand. 4/7." March 2022, https://twitter.com/ESETresearch/status/1503436428096716800.
69. ESET Research (@ESETresearch), "Interestingly, CaddyWiper Avoids Destroying Data on Domain Controllers. This Is Probably a Way for the Attackers to Keep Their Access inside the Organization While Still Disturbing Operations. 5/7 Https://T.Co/XiXgOMe5wr," Twitter, March 2022, https://twitter.com/ESETresearch/status/1503436433134129158.
70. Google TAG, "Fog of War: How the Ukraine Conflict Transformed the Cyber Threat Landscape," Google, February 2023, 14, https://services.google.com/fh/files/blogs/google_fog_of_war_research_report.pdf.

71. Google TAG, "Fog of War," 14.
72. Paul Oliveria, "New 'Prestige' Ransomware Impacts Organizations in Ukraine and Poland," *Microsoft Security Blog* (blog), October 2022, https://www.microsoft.com/en-us/security/blog/2022/10/14/new-prestige-ransomware-impacts-organizations-in-ukraine-and-poland/; ESET, "RansomBoggs: New Ransomware Targeting Ukraine," *We Live Security* (blog), November 2022, https://www.welivesecurity.com/2022/11/28/ransomboggs-new-ransomware-ukraine/; Jeff Burt, "Sandworm Gang Launches Monster Ransomware Attacks on Ukraine," November 2022, https://www.theregister.com/2022/11/29/russia_ransomboggs_ransomware_ukraine/.
73. Ulyana Senko, "Російські Хакери Здійснюють Кібератаки На Логістичні Компанії України Та Польщі," LVIV.MEDIA, December 2022, https://lviv.media/viyna/62344-rosijski-hakeri-zdijsnyuyut-kiberataki-na-logistichni-kompaniyi-ukrayini-ta-polshi/; "Хакери Атакували Транспортні Та Логістичні Компанії в Україні й Польщі," Microsoft—Delo.Ua, October 2022, https://delo.ua/telecom/xakeri-atakuvali-transportni-ta-logisticni-kompaniyi-v-ukrayini-i-polshhi-microsoft-405412/; Natalia Zarudnia, "Російська Програма-Вимагач RansomBoggs Націлилася На Кілька Українських Організацій," November 2022, https://cybercalm.org/novyny/rosijska-programa-vymagach-ransomboggs-natsilylasya-na-kilka-ukrayinskyh-organizatsij/.
74. Victor Zhora, interviewed by the author via Zoom on January 26, 2023.
75. Victor Zhora, interviewed by the author via Zoom on January 26, 2023.
76. Juan Andres Guerrero-Saade, interviewed by the author via Zoom on February 20, 2023.
77. Ben Buchanan, "The Legend of Sophistication in Cyber Operations," *Belfer Center for Science and International Affairs* (blog), 2017, https://www.belfercenter.org/publication/legend-sophistication-cyber-operations.
78. Miller and Belton, "Russia's Spies Misread Ukraine and Misled Kremlin as War Loomed."
79. Miller and Belton, "Russia's Spies Misread Ukraine and Misled Kremlin as War Loomed."
80. Mari Saito and Maria Tsvetkova, "How Russia Spread a Secret Web of Agents across Ukraine," Reuters, accessed July 29, 2022, https://www.reuters.com/investigates/special-report/ukraine-crisis-russia-saboteurs/.
81. "Russians Twice Tried to Storm Zelensky's Compound in Early Hours of War, Aide Says," *Times of Israel*, April 2022, https://www.timesofisrael.com/russians-twice-tried-to-storm-zelensky-compound-in-early-hours-of-war-report/.
82. UK Foreign Office, "Kremlin Plan to Install Pro-Russian Leadership in Ukraine Exposed," January 2022, https://www.gov.uk/government/news/kremlin-plan-to-install-pro-russian-leadership-in-ukraine-exposed.
83. UK Foreign Office, "Kremlin Plan to Install Pro-Russian Leadership in Ukraine Exposed."
84. Miller and Belton, "Russia's Spies Misread Ukraine and Misled Kremlin as War Loomed."

85. NetBlocks (@netblocks), Twitter, "Commercial satellite operator Viasat is investigating a suspected cyberattack that caused a partial outage of its KA-SAT network in Europe." February 2022, https://twitter.com/netblocks/status/1498365220107997191.
86. Raphael Satter, "Satellite Outage Caused 'Huge Loss in Communications' at War's Outset—Ukrainian Official," Reuters, March 2022, sec. World, https://www.reuters.com/world/satellite-outage-caused-huge-loss-communications-wars-outset-ukrainian-official-2022-03-15/.
87. UK NCSC, "Russia behind Cyber Attack with Europe-Wide Impact an Hour before Ukraine Invasion," May 2022, https://www.ncsc.gov.uk/news/russia-behind-cyber-attack-with-europe-wide-impact-hour-before-ukraine-invasion.
88. Juan Andrés Guerrero-Saade, "AcidRain: A Modem Wiper Rains Down on Europe," *SentinelOne* (blog), March 2022, https://www.sentinelone.com/labs/acidrain-a-modem-wiper-rains-down-on-europe/.
89. Dmitri Alperovitch, "Perhaps the Most Strategically Impactful Cyber Operation in Wartime History . . .," Twitter, @Dalperovitch. August 2022, https://twitter.com/DAlperovitch/status/1562560980105584640.
90. Victor Zhora (@VZhora), "@lukasmaeder @LenMaschmeyer @lukOlejnik Huge Loss in Communications! = Huge Loss in Coordination. The Impact Was Direct, but the Goal Wasn't Reached," Twitter, June 2022, https://twitter.com/VZhora/status/1534279624347230208; Kim Zetter, "Viasat Hack 'Did Not' Have Huge Impact on Ukrainian Military Communications, Official Says," Substack newsletter, *Zero Day* (blog), September 2022, https://zetter.substack.com/p/viasat-hack-did-not-have-huge-impact.
91. Victor Zhora, interviewed by the author via Zoom on January 26, 2023.
92. Sonne et al., "Battle for Kyiv."
93. Sonne et al., "Battle for Kyiv."
94. Jon Bateman, "Russia's Wartime Cyber Operations in Ukraine: Military Impacts, Influences, and Implications," December 2022, 10, https://carnegieendowment.org/files/Bateman_Cyber-FINAL21.pdf.
95. Andrew Eversden and Jaspreet Gill, "Why Hasn't Russia Used Its 'Full Scope' of Electronic Warfare?," *Breaking Defense* (blog), March 2022, https://breakingdefense.sites.breakingmedia.com/2022/03/why-hasnt-russia-used-its-full-scope-of-electronic-warfare/.
96. "Ukraine Tensions: US Sources Say Russia 70% Ready to Invade," *BBC News*, February 2022, sec. Europe, https://www.bbc.com/news/world-europe-60276342.
97. "Satellite Outage Knocks Out Thousands of Enercon's Wind Turbines," Reuters, February 2022, sec. Energy, https://www.reuters.com/business/energy/satellite-outage-knocks-out-control-enercon-wind-turbines-2022-02-28/.
98. Kim Zetter, "So What This Means Is That Now They Have to Send a Farmer Out to Look at the Turbines and Report Back: 'Yep, They're Still Working,'" Twitter, @KimZetter. March 2022, https://twitter.com/KimZetter/status/1507389719411236871.

99. Viasat, "KA-SAT Network Cyber Attack Overview," March 2022, https://news.viasat.com/blog/corporate/ka-sat-network-cyber-attack-overview.
100. Guerrero-Saade, "AcidRain: A Modem Wiper Rains Down on Europe."
101. "Enercon: Thousands of Wind Turbines Need New Hardware," Energate Messenger, March 2022, https://www.energate-messenger.com/news/220914/enercon-thousands-of-wind-turbines-need-new-hardware.
102. "Viasat Surfbeam 2+ KA-SAT Modem inkl. WLAN Router", Sat_Speed+, accessed January 13, 2023, https://web.archive.org/web/20200921120922/https://www.satspeed.com/internet-via-satellit/satellitemodem-tria-antenna/viasat-surfbeam-2plus-tooway-kasat-modem.html.
103. Viasat, "KA-SAT Network Cyber Attack Overview."
104. NATO, "Keynote Address by NATO Secretary General at the NATO Cyber Defence Pledge Conference," November 2022, https://www.nato.int/cps/en/natohq/opinions_208925.htm.
105. Guerrero-Saade, "AcidRain: A Modem Wiper Rains Down on Europe."
106. Guerrero-Saade, "AcidRain: A Modem Wiper Rains Down on Europe."
107. ReverseMode, "VIASAT Incident: From Speculation to Technical Details," March 2022, https://www.reversemode.com/2022/03/viasat-incident-from-speculation-to.html.
108. crypto-cypher, "Fortinet Victim List—'Hackers Leak Passwords for 500,000 Fortinet VPN Accounts' #TrackThePlanet," Gist, 2021, https://gist.github.com/crypto-cypher/f216d6fa4816ffa93c5270b001dc4bdc.
109. Brigadier General Yurii Shchygol, head of Ukraine's State Special Communications Service, stated as much in a recent interview: *Юрій Щиголь.Як Вдалося Зберегти Зв`язок, Кібератаки На Україну,Відключені Військові Супутники*, 2022, https://www.youtube.com/watch?v=-K9OyhGWDRI.
110. Juan Andres Guerrero-Saade, interviewed by the author on February 20, 2023.
111. Juan Andres Guerrero-Saade, interviewed by the author on February 20, 2023.
112. Bateman, "Russia's Wartime Cyber Operations in Ukraine."
113. SSU, "СБУ Викрила Спробу Фсб Встановити «жучки» в Кулуарах Верховної Ради (Відео)," SSU, August 2022, https://ssu.gov.ua/novyny/sbu-vykryla-sprobu-fsb-vstanovyty-zhuchky-v-kuluarakh-verkhovnoi-rady-video.
114. SSU, "СБУ Викрила Спробу Фсб Встановити «жучки» в Кулуарах Верховної Ради (Відео)."
115. SBU, "СБУ Припинила Діяльність Агентурної Мережі Фсб Рф, Яка Діяла в Декількох Областях України (Відео)," SSU, August 2022, https://ssu.gov.ua/novyny/sbu-prypynyla-diialnist-ahenturnoi-merezhi-fsb-rf-yaka-diiala-v-dekilkokh-oblastiakh-ukrainy-video.
116. SBU, "СБУ Припинила Діяльність Агентурної Мережі Фсб Рф, Яка Діяла в Декількох Областях України (Відео)."
117. SBU, "СБУ Припинила Діяльність Агентурної Мережі Фсб Рф, Яка Діяла в Декількох Областях України (Відео)."

118. "СБУ Задержала Российских Агентов, Которые Корректировали Обстрелы Николаевской Области. Ими Оказались Местные Жители / ВОЙНА В УКРАИНЕ / Новости," Gordon.ua, July 2022, https://gordonua.com/amp/news/war/sbu-zaderzhala-rossiyskih-agentov-kotorye-korrektirovali-obstrely-nikolaevskoy-oblasti-imi-okazalis-mestnye-zhiteli-1617219.html.

119. Jack Watling and Nick Reynolds, "Ukraine at War: Paving the Road from Survival to Victory," RUSI, July 2022, file:///C:/Users/lenna/OneDrive%20-%20ETH%20Zurich/Sources/Articles/Ukraine/special-report-202207-ukraine-final-web.pdf.

120. Markiyan Klimkovetsky, "СБУ Разоблачила Еще Одного Агента Спецслужб Рф: Планировал Подрывную Деятельность Во Львовской Области," May 2022, https://hromadske.ua/ru/posts/sbu-razoblachila-eshe-odnogo-agenta-specsluzhb-rf-planiroval-podryvnuyu-deyatelnost-vo-lvovskoj-oblasti.

121. SBU, "СБУ Викрила Агентурну Мережу ГРУ Рф, До Якої Входив Народний Депутат України (Відео)," SSU, June 2022, https://ssu.gov.ua/novyny/sbu-vykryla-ahenturnu-merezhu-hru-rf-do-yakoi-vkhodyv-narodnyi-deputat-ukrainy-video.

122. SBU, "СБУ Викрила Агентурну Мережу ГРУ Рф, До Якої Входив Народний Депутат України (Відео)."

123. СУМСЬКА ОБЛАСТЬ, "Хотів 'Здати' Місто Росіянам: Голова Громади в Сумській Області Піде Під Суд," РБК-Украина, accessed January 20, 2023, https://www.rbc.ua/ukr/news/hotel-sdat-selo-rossiyanam-glava-obshchiny-1661518671.html.

124. ОЛЕНА БУРКАЛО, "На Сумщине Мэра Бурыни и Его Пособников Задержали За Коллаборационизм—Korrespondent.Net," March 2022, https://korrespondent.net/amp/4473984-na-sumschyne-mera-buryny-y-eho-posobnykov-zaderzhaly-za-kollaboratsyonyzm; "СБУ підозрює старосту села Сумського району в колабораціонізмі," June 2022, https://debaty.sumy.ua/news/sbu-pidozryuye-starostu-sela-sumskogo-rajonu-v-kolaboratsionizmi.

125. SBU, "СБУ Викрила Агентурну Мережу ГРУ Рф, До Якої Входив Народний Депутат України (Відео)."

126. Segodnya, "В 'Зачистке' Майдана Участвовали Сотрудники ФСБ России—СБУ," April 2014, https://www.segodnya.ua/criminal/v-zachistke-maydana-uchastvovali-sotrudniki-fsb-rossii-sbu-509753.html; "Russia Provided 5 Tons of Explosives and Weapons to Yanukovych in January to Disperse the Maidan," Ukrainian Week, April 2014, https://ukrainianweek.com/News/106701.

127. Johnson, "On Drawing a Bright Line for Covert Operations," 290.

128. SBU, "СБУ Викрила Агентурну Мережу ГРУ Рф, До Якої Входив Народний Депутат України (Відео)."

129. Tanya Matyash, "Зеленський Відсторонив Венедіктову Та Усунув Баканова," LB.ua, July 2022, https://lb.ua/news/2022/07/17/523439_zelenskiy_vidstoroniv_venediktovu.html.

130. New Voice of Ukraine, "Why Zelenskyy Removed the Heads of the SBU and PGO," July 2022, https://english.nv.ua/nation/why-zelenskyy-sacked-the-prosecutor-general-and-sbu-chief-ukraine-news-50257409.html.

131. "Zelensky Says Two Generals Stripped of Their Rank Due to Treason," *Kyiv Independent*, March 2022, https://kyivindependent.com/uncategorized/zelensky-says-two-generals-stripped-of-their-rank-due-to-treason.
132. "Бывший Офицер КГБ Попов: Агентов в Украине Россия Выращивала. Это 'Парничок'. Завербовать Человека, Когда Он Уже На Самом Верху, Намного Сложнее / ПОЛИТИКА / Новости," October 2022, https://gordonua.com/amp/news/politics/byvshij-ofitser-kgb-popov-agentov-v-ukraine-rossija-vyrashchivala-eto-parnichok-zaverbovat-cheloveka-kogda-on-uzhe-na-samom-verhu-namnogo-slozhnee-1637706.html.
133. "Russia Takes Control of Chernobyl Nuclear Power Plant," *USA Today*, 2022, https://www.youtube.com/watch?v=lpYoxBTyRec.
134. Радіо Свобода, "Ексначальник з СБУ Наумов Міг Передавати Спецслужбам РФ Секретні Дані Щодо Чорнобильської АЕС—«Схеми»," *Радіо Свобода*, June 2022, sec. Новини: Політика, https://www.radiosvoboda.org/a/news-skhemy-sbu-naumov-chaes/31902729.html.
135. Валерія Єгошина, "Таємний Кадр СБУ: Alter Ego Головного «контролера Порядності» Спецслужби Андрія Наумова (Розслідування)," *Радіо Свобода*, October 2020, sec. Політика, https://www.radiosvoboda.org/a/schemes/30919292.html.
136. "The Head of the Ukrainian Intelligence Service DENIED CULPABILITY! Tried to Transfer Huge Money and Emeralds across the Border, Arrested at the Preševo Crossing!," Republika.rs, Srpski telegraf, June 2022, https://www.republika.rs/top-news/serbia-news/366730/andriy-naumov-arrest-serbia; Радіо Свобода, "У Сербії Офіційно Підтвердили Затримання Ексначальника в СБУ, Який Фігурував у Розслідуванні «Схем»," *Радіо Свобода*, sec. Новини: Суспільство, https://www.radiosvoboda.org/a/nws-serbia-zatrymannia-naumova/31893820.html.
137. Свобода, "Ексначальник з СБУ Наумов Міг Передавати Спецслужбам РФ Секретні Дані Щодо Чорнобильської АЕС—«Схеми»."
138. Saito and Tsvetkova, "How Russia Spread a Secret Web of Agents across Ukraine."
139. Saito and Tsvetkova, "How Russia Spread a Secret Web of Agents across Ukraine."
140. Olena Cherkasets, "Медведчук Отримав Від ФСБ Мільярд На Підготовку Війни," July 2022, https://umoloda.kyiv.ua/number/0/2006/168191.
141. Pavlo Dak, "Як Віктор Медведчук Причетний До Війни в Україні: Відповідь Буданова," *Інформаційне Агентство Вголос/Vgolos*, October 1, 2022, accessed January 16, 2023, https://vgolos.ua/news/yak-viktor-medvedchuk-prichetniy-do-viyni-v-ukrayini-vidpovid-budanova_1428157.html.
142. NetBlocks (@netblocks), Twitter, "Confirmed: A major internet disruption has been registered across #Ukraine on national provider #Ukrtelecom; real-time network data show connectivity collapsing to 13% of pre-war levels; the provider reports issues assigning new sessions." March 2022, https://twitter.com/netblocks/status/1508453511176065033.
143. NetBlocks (@netblocks), *Twitter*, "Update: Ukraine's national internet provider Ukrtelecom has confirmed a cyberattack on its core infrastructure." March 2022, https://twitter.com/netblocks/status/1508465391244304389.

144. SSSCIP Ukraine (@dsszzi), *Twitter*, "Today, the enemy launched a powerful cyber-attack against #Ukrtelecom 's IT-infrastructure. According to Yurii Shchyhol, the Chairman of the @dsszzi, at the moment massive cyberattack against #Ukrtelecom is neutralized. Resuming services is under way. #Ukraine #CyberAttack #war." March 2022, https://twitter.com/dsszzi/status/1508528209075257347.

145. Melanie Mingas, "Ukrtelecom Restores 85% of Services after 'Powerful Cyberattack,'" *Capacity Media* (blog), March 2022, https://www.capacitymedia.com/article/29wch971qqy0z3dyifx8g/ukrtelecom-restores-85-of-services-after-powerful-cyberattack.

146. Thomas Brewster, "'Most Severe' Cyberattack since Russian Invasion Crashes Ukraine Internet Provider," *Forbes*, March 28, 2022, sec. Cybersecurity, https://www.forbes.com/sites/thomasbrewster/2022/03/28/huge-cyberattack-on-ukrtelecom-biggest-since-russian-invasion-crashes-ukraine-telecom/.

147. Doug Madory (@DougMadory), *Twitter*, "Large outages today in #Ukraine." March 2022, https://twitter.com/DougMadory/status/1501910709734678529.

148. SSCIP, "Cyberattack against Ukrtelecom on March 28: The Details," April 2022, https://cip.gov.ua/en/news/kiberataka-na-ukrtelekom-28-bereznya-detali.

149. SSCIP, "Cyberattack against Ukrtelecom on March 28."

150. "EXCLUSIVE: Rounding up a Cyber Posse for Ukraine," *The Record by Recorded Future* (blog), November 2022, https://therecord.media/exclusive-rounding-up-a-cyber-posse-for-ukraine/.

151. "EXCLUSIVE: Rounding up a Cyber Posse for Ukraine."

152. "EXCLUSIVE: Rounding up a Cyber Posse for Ukraine."

153. SSCIP, "Cyberattack against Ukrtelecom on March 28."

154. "The Birth of the Web," CERN, accessed January 18, 2023, https://home.web.cern.ch/science/computing/birth-web.

155. Darya Kiepova, "Потужна Кібератака На Укртелеком Вивела з Ладу Інтернет," Зеркало недели, Дзеркало тижня, *Mirror Weekly*, March 2022, https://zn.ua/ukr/TECHNOLOGIES/potuzhna-kiberataka-na-ukrtelekom-vivela-z-ladu-internet.html.

156. Comments under a Facebook post by Ukrtelecom informing customers of the outage illustrate some of these impacts, while also reflecting the relative calm of people. There are no signs of panic, but rather annoyance at the disruption. https://www.facebook.com/Ukrtelecom/posts/pfbid02ueDshhyHXdma5enzkShAJqQsiohBh8Z6fs3kCVcunqro6cAzn1wagN2X2ryJ8sofl (last accessed on January 18, 2022).

157. Павло Красномовець, "Російські Хакери Із ГРУ Спробували Залишити Без Світла Вінницьку Область, Як у 2017 Київ. Чому Їм Не Вдалося," Forbes.ua, April 2022, https://forbes.ua/innovations/rosiyski-khakeri-namagalis-zalishiti-bez-svitla-vinnitsku-oblast-atatsi-vdalos-zapobigti-12042022-5409.

158. Timur Yagofarov, "Кібератака на енергосектор розвивалася півтора місяці," *Computernoe Obozrenie*, April 2022, https://ko.com.ua/kiberataka_na_energosektor_rozvivalasya_pivtora_misyaci_140789.

159. CERT-UA, "Кібератака Групи Sandworm (UAC-0082) На Об'єкти Енергетики України з Використанням Шкідливих Програм INDUSTROYER2 Та CADDYWIPER (CERT-UA#4435)," April 2022, https://cert.gov.ua/.

160. "Industroyer2: Industroyer Reloaded," *We Live Security* (blog), April 2022, https://www.welivesecurity.com/2022/04/12/industroyer2-industroyer-reloaded/.
161. CERT-UA, "Heavy Cyberattack on Ukraine's Energy Sector Prevented," April 2022, https://cip.gov.ua/en/news/poperedzhena-masshtabna-kiberataka-na-energetichnii-sektor-ukrayini.
162. Kim Zetter, Twitter, "They used the same code they used in 2016 grid attack and the same wiper they used against a bank in February - so they kind of foiled themselves." April 2022, https://twitter.com/KimZetter/status/1514508733908348930.
163. Juan Andres Guerrero-Saade, interviewed by the author via Zoom on February 20, 2023.
164. "Industroyer2."
165. CERT-UA, "Heavy Cyberattack on Ukraine's Energy Sector Prevented."
166. Juan Andres Guerrero-Saade, interviewed by the author via Zoom on February 20, 2023.
167. Interviewed by the author via Zoom on January 26, 2023.
168. Interviewed by the author via Zoom on January 26, 2023.
169. AIVD and MIVD, "De Russische Aanval Op Oekraïne: Een Keerpunt in de Geschiedenis," February 2023, 21, https://www.defensie.nl/binaries/defensie/documenten/publicaties/2023/02/20/publicatie-aivd-en-mivd-24-2/Brochure_24-2+De+Russiche+aanval+op+Oekraine_TG_web.pdf.
170. Elizabeth Gibney, "Where Is Russia's Cyberwar? Researchers Decipher Its Strategy," *Nature* 603, no. 7903 (March 2022): 775–776, doi:10.1038/d41586-022-00753-9.
171. Kenneth R. Rosen, "The Man at the Center of the New Cyber World War," Politico, July 2022, https://www.politico.com/news/magazine/2022/07/14/russia-cyberattacks-ukraine-cybersecurity-00045486.
172. Victor Zhora, interviewed by the author via Zoom on January 26, 2023.
173. Interviewed by the author via Zoom on January 26, 2023.
174. See also The Grugq, "Foghorn: Signals through the Fog of War," Substack newsletter, *Info Op* (blog), June 2022, https://grugq.substack.com/p/foghorn-signals-through-the-fog-of?utm_campaign=post_embed.
175. Victor Zhora, interviewed by the author via Zoom on January 26, 2023.
176. Victor Zhora, interviewed by the author via Zoom on January 26, 2023.
177. Juan Andres Guerrero-Saade, interviewed by the author via Zoom on February 23, 2022.
178. Juan Andres Guerrero-Saade, interviewed by the author via Zoom on February 23, 2022.
179. ESET, "GREYENERGY."

Conclusion: New Possibilities and New Perils

1. The theory assumes that the more capable a target is of producing significant effects, the more protected and thus the less vulnerable the target will tend to be. In this case, as the analysis showed, that assumption turned out to be unfounded.

2. Richard K. Betts, *Enemies of Intelligence: Knowledge and Power in American National Security* (New York: Columbia University Press, 2007); Hulnick, "What's Wrong with the Intelligence Cycle?"; Joshua Rovner, *Fixing the Facts: National Security and the Politics of Intelligence* (Ithaca, New York: Cornell University Press, 2011).
3. Dunn Cavelty, "From Cyber-Bombs to Political Fallout: Threat Representations with an Impact in the Cyber-Security Discourse"; Lawson, "Beyond Cyber-Doom"; Miguel Alberto Gomez and Eula Bianca Villar, "Fear, Uncertainty, and Dread: Cognitive Heuristics and Cyber Threats," *Politics and Governance* 6, no. 2 (June 2018): 61–72, doi:10.17645/pag.v6i2.1279.
4. Maschmeyer, Deibert, and Lindsay, "A Tale of Two Cybers—How Threat Reporting by Cybersecurity Firms Systematically Underrepresents Threats to Civil Society."; Work, J. D. "Evaluating Commercial Cyber Intelligence Activity," *International Journal of Intelligence and CounterIntelligence* 33, no. 2 (2 April 2020): 278–308. https://doi.org/10.1080/08850607.2019.1690877.
5. Bill Blunden and Violet Cheung, *Behold a Pale Farce: Cyberwar, Threat Inflation, & the Malware Industrial Complex* (Waterville, Oregon: Trine Day, 2014); Lawson and Middleton, "Cyber Pearl Harbor."
6. See, for example, "Lessons from Russia's Cyber-War in Ukraine," *The Economist*, November 30, 2022, https://www.economist.com/science-and-technology/2022/11/30/lessons-from-russias-cyber-war-in-ukraine.
7. Robert Jervis, *Perception and Misperception in International Politics: New Edition* (Princeton, NJ: Princeton University Press, 2017), 194–196, doi:10.2307/j.ctvc77bx3.
8. O'Rourke, *Covert Regime Change*.
9. Carson, *Secret Wars*.
10. Lucas Kello, "The Meaning of the Cyber Revolution: Perils to Theory and Statecraft," *International Security* 38, no. 2 (2013): 7–40; Kello, *The Virtual Weapon and International Order*; Jason Healey and Robert Jervis, "The Escalation Inversion and Other Oddities of Situational Cyber Stability," *Texas National Security Review* 3, no. 4 (Fall 2020), doi:10.26153/tsw/10962.
11. Nye, "Deterrence and Dissuasion in Cyberspace."
12. Amos Tversky and Daniel Kahneman, "The Framing of Decisions and the Psychology of Choice," *Science* 211 (1981): 453; Carol Gordon and Asher Arian, "Threat and Decision Making," *Journal of Conflict Resolution* 45, no. 2 (April 2001): 196–215, doi:10.1177/0022002701045002003.
13. Jason Healey, "Preparing for Inevitable Cyber Surprise," *War on the Rocks* (blog), January 2022, https://warontherocks.com/2022/01/preparing-for-inevitable-cyber-surprise/.
14. Work, J. D. 'Burned and Blinded: Escalation Risks of Intelligence Loss from Countercyber Operations in Crisis,' *International Journal of Intelligence and CounterIntelligence* 35, no. 4 (2 October 2022): 806–833. https://doi.org/10.1080/08850607.2022.2081904
15. Ben Buchanan, *The Cybersecurity Dilemma: Hacking, Trust and Fear between Nations.* (Oxford: Oxford University Press, 2017).
16. A realistic scenario, considering the known vulnerabilities of these jets. See, for example, "Uncorrected Design Flaws, Cyber-Vulnerabilities, and Unreliability Plague

the F-35 Program," Project on Government Oversight, accessed October 10, 2021, https://www.pogo.org/analysis/2020/03/uncorrected-design-flaws-cyber-vulnerabilities-and-unreliability-plague-the-f-35-program/.
17. Buchanan, *The Cybersecurity Dilemma*.
18. Erik Gartzke and Jon R. Lindsay, "Thermonuclear Cyberwar," *Journal of Cybersecurity* 3, no. 1 (2017): 37–48, doi:10.1093/cybsec/tyw017.
19. Ronen Bergman, Rick Gladstone, and Farnaz Fassihi, "Blackout Hits Iran Nuclear Site in What Appears to Be Israeli Sabotage," *New York Times*, April 11, 2021, sec. World, https://www.nytimes.com/2021/04/11/world/middleeast/iran-nuclear-natanz.html.
20. J. P. Farwell and R. Rohozinski, "Stuxnet and the Future of Cyber War," *Survival* 53, no. 1 (2011): 23–40, doi:10.1080/00396338.2011.555586.
21. Martin Chulov and Martin Chulov, "Israel Appears to Confirm It Carried Out Cyberattack on Iran Nuclear Facility," *The Guardian*, April 2021, sec. World News, https://www.theguardian.com/world/2021/apr/11/israel-appears-confirm-cyberattack-iran-nuclear-facility.
22. Jake Wallis Simons, "EXCLUSIVE: Mossad Recruited Top Iranian Scientists to Blow up Key Nuclear Facility," *Jewish Chronicle*, December 2021, https://www.thejc.com/news/world/exclusive-mossad-recruited-top-iranian-scientists-to-blow-up-key-nuclear-facility-1.523163.
23. "Natanz Enrichment Complex," *Nuclear Threat Initiative* (blog), accessed January 7, 2022, https://www.nti.org/education-center/facilities/natanz-enrichment-complex/; Simons, "EXCLUSIVE: Mossad Recruited Top Iranian Scientists to Blow up Key Nuclear Facility."
24. Fischerkeller, Goldman, and Harknett, *Cyber Persistence Theory*, 22.
25. The Grugq, "Day 2 Keynote: A Short Course in Cyber Warfare," YouTube, April 2018, https://www.youtube.com/watch?v=gvS4efEakpY.
26. Dawn Cappelli, Andrew Moore, and Randall Trzeciak, *The CERT Guide to Insider Threats: How to Prevent, Detect, and Respond to Information Technology Crimes (Theft, Sabotage, Fraud)*, Sei Series in Software Engineering (Upper Saddle River, NJ: Addison-Wesley, 2012); McKinsey, "Insider Threat: The Human Element of Cyberrisk," 2019, https://www.mckinsey.com/business-functions/risk/our-insights/insider-threat-the-human-element-of-cyberrisk.
27. Jakub Dalek Crete-Nishihata et al., "Communities @Risk: Targeted Digital Threats against Civil Society," Citizen Lab, November 2014, https://targetedthreats.net/; Ronald Deibert, *Reset: Reclaiming the Internet for Civil Society* (Toronto, Canada: House of Anansi Press, 2020).
28. Bill Marczak and John Scott-Railton, "The Million Dollar Dissident: NSO Group's iPhone Zero-Days Used against a UAE Human Rights Defender," *Citizen Lab* (blog), August 2016, https://citizenlab.org/2016/08/million-dollar-dissident-iphone-zero-day-nso-group-uae/; Sarah McKune et al., "Commercial Spyware: The Multibillion Dollar Industry Built on an Ethical and Legal Quagmire," Citizen Lab, December 2017, https://citizenlab.ca/2017/12/legal-overview-ethiopian-dissidents-targeted-spyware/.

29. Ronald Deibert, "Subversion Inc: The Age of Private Espionage," *Journal of Democracy* 33, no. 2 (April 2022): 28–44.
30. Jaspreet Gill, "Russia May Be Holding Cyber Capabilities in Reserve, so US Must Keep Its Shields Up: Experts," *Breaking Defense* (blog), March 2022, https://breakingdefense.sites.breakingmedia.com/2022/03/russia-may-be-holding-cyber-capabilities-in-reserve-so-us-must-keep-its-shields-up-experts/; Beth Maundrill, "Why Russia Has Refrained from a Major Cyber-Attack against the West," Cyber Security Hub, June 2022, https://www.cshub.com/attacks/articles/why-russia-has-refrained-from-a-cyber-attack-against-the-west.
31. Jacquelyn Schneider, "A World without Trust," *Foreign Affairs*, December 2021, https://www.foreignaffairs.com/articles/world/2021-12-14/world-without-trust.
32. Herman, *Intelligence Power in Peace and War*, 197.
33. Herman, *Intelligence Power in Peace and War*, 198.
34. I am grateful to one of the anonymous reviewers for highlighting this point.
35. Andrew and Mitrokhin, *The Sword and the Shield*, 366–370.
36. Robert H. Dix, "The Breakdown of Authoritarian Regimes," *Western Political Quarterly* 35, no. 4 (December 1982): 554–573, doi:10.1177/106591298203500407.
37. Bittman, *The KGB and Soviet Disinformation*; Andrew and Mitrokhin, *The Sword and the Shield*; John Earl. Haynes, *Spies: The Rise and Fall of the KGB in America* (New Haven, CT: Yale University Press, 2009); Galeotti, "Putin's Hydra."
38. Yochai Benkler, Robert Faris, and Hal Roberts, *Network Propaganda: Manipulation, Disinformation, and Radicalization in American Politics* (New York: Oxford University Press, 2018), https://www.oxfordscholarship.com/view/10.1093/oso/9780190923624.001.0001/oso-9780190923624; W. Lance Bennett and Steven Livingston, "The Disinformation Order: Disruptive Communication and the Decline of Democratic Institutions," *European Journal of Communication* 33, no. 2 (April 2018): 122–139. doi:10.1177/0267323118760317; Philip N. Howard, *Lie Machines: How to Save Democracy from Troll Armies, Deceitful Robots, Junk News Operations, and Political Operatives* (New Haven, CT: Yale University Press, 2020).
39. Maschmeyer et al., "Donetsk Don't Tell—'Hybrid War' in Ukraine and the Limits of Social Media Influence Operations."
40. Roy L. Behr and Shanto Iyengar, "Television News, Real-World Cues, and Changes in the Public Agenda," *Public Opinion Quarterly* 49, no. 1 (January 1985): 38–57, doi:10.1086/268900; Peisakhin and Rozenas, "Electoral Effects of Biased Media"; Thomas Rid, *Active Measures: The Secret History of Disinformation and Political Warfare* (New York: Farrar, Straus and Giroux, 2020).
41. Beilenson, *Power through Subversion*, vi.
42. Loch K. Johnson and James J. Wirtz, eds., *Intelligence: The Secret World of Spies: An Anthology*, 4th ed. (Oxford: Oxford University Press, 2015), 8.
43. Wilde, Gavin. "Cyber Operations in Ukraine: Russia's Unmet Expectations," *Carnegie Endowment for International Peace*. 12 December 2022. https://carnegieendowment.org/files/202212-Wilde_RussiaHypotheses-v2.pdf
44. The Grugq, "Towards an Analysis of Russian Cyber Warfare in Ukraine Feb 2022–Dec 2022" (Kings College London, forthcoming).

45. Fischerkeller, Goldman, and Harknett, *Cyber Persistence Theory*, 58.
46. Alexander Kott and Ethan Stump, "Intelligent Autonomous Things on the Battlefield," in *Artificial Intelligence for the Internet of Everything*, ed. William Lawless et al. (London, UK: Academic Press, 2019), 51, doi:10.1016/B978-0-12-817636-8.00003-X.
47. Fernando Maymí and Scott Lathrop, "AI in Cyberspace: Beyond the Hype," *Cyber Defense Review* 3, no. 3 (2018): 71–82.
48. Lennart Maschmeyer, "Subverting Skynet: The Strategic Promise of Lethal Autonomous Weapons and the Perils of Exploitation," in *2022 14th International Conference on Cyber Conflict: Keep Moving! (CyCon)*, vol. 700, 2022, 155–171, doi:10.23919/CyCon55549.2022.9811008.

Bibliography

"2 Ukrainian Border Guards Killed in Mine Explosion; Military Prosecutor Finds 'No Saboteurs' at Ammo Depot." *The Interpreter*, September 2017. http://www.interpretermag.com/day-1319/.

5.ua. "Масова Хакерська Атака: Під Удар Потрапив Навіть Кабмін—5 Канал." June 2017. https://www.5.ua/suspilstvo/masova-khakerska-ataka-pid-udar-potrapyv-kabmin-metropoliten-nyzka-bankiv-ta-pidpryiemstv-148971.html.

24tv.ua. "Підсумки 2017 Року: Найгучніші Вбивства в Україні." 24 Канал. Accessed May 13, 2019. https://24tv.ua/news/showNews.do?pidsumki_2017_roku_v_ukrayini_vbivstva_2017&objectId=895499.

112.ua. "СБУ Предупредила Хакерскую Атаку Российских Спецслужб На Энергообъекты Украины—112 Украина." *112.Ua*, December 2015. https://112.ua/kriminal/sbu-predupredila-hakerskuyu-ataku-rossiyskih-specsluzhb-na-energoobekty-ukrainy-281811.html.

Ablon, Lillian, and Andy Bogart. "Zero Days, Thousands of Nights." Rand, 2017. https://www.rand.org/pubs/research_reports/RR1751.html.

Adams, Lawrence. "AES-NI Ransomware Dev Releases Decryption Keys amid Fears of Being Framed for XData Outbreak." Bleeping Computer, May 2017. https://www.bleepingcomputer.com/news/security/aes-ni-ransomware-dev-releases-decryption-keys-amid-fears-of-being-framed-for-xdata-outbreak/.

AIVD and MIVD. "De Russische Aanval Op Oekraïne: Een Keerpunt in de Geschiedenis." February 2023. https://www.defensie.nl/binaries/defensie/documenten/publicaties/2023/02/20/publicatie-aivd-en-mivd-24-2/Brochure_24-2+De+Russiche+aanval+op+Oekraine_TG_web.pdf.

Alexander, Keith. "Cyber Warfare in Ukraine Poses a Threat to the Global System." *Financial Times*, February 2022. https://www.ft.com/content/8e1e8176-2279-4596-9c0f-98629b4db5a6.

Allen, Cassandra. "Mapping Media Freedom: Ukrainian Journalists Subjected to Malicious Cyber-Attacks." *Index on Censorship* (blog), July 2017. https://www.indexoncensorship.org/2017/07/journalists-ukraine-cyber-attacks/.

Alperovitch, Dmitri. "Perhaps the Most Strategically Impactful Cyber Operation in Wartime History . . ." Twitter, @DAlperovitch. August 2022. https://twitter.com/DAlperovitch/status/1562560980105584640.

Amos, Howard. "Ukraine: Sevastopol Installs Pro-Russian Mayor as Separatism Fears Grow." *The Guardian*, February 25, 2014, sec. World News. https://www.theguardian.com/world/2014/feb/25/ukraine-sevastopol-installs-pro-russian-mayor.

Anderson, James P. "Computer Security Technology Planning Study (Volume II)." October 1972. https://csrc.nist.rip/publications/history/ande72.pdf.

Anderson, R. "Why Information Security Is Hard-An Economic Perspective." In *Proceedings of the 17th Annual Computer Security Applications Conference (ACSAC '01)*, 358. Washington, DC: IEEE Computer Society, 2001. http://dl.acm.org/citation.cfm?id=872016.872155.

Andrew, Christopher M. *The Mitrokhin Archive: The KGB in Europe and the West.* London: Allen Lane, 2000.

Andrew, Christopher M., and Oleg Gordievsky. *KGB: The inside Story of Its Foreign Operations from Lenin to Gorbachev.* New York: Harper Collins Publishers, 1990.

Andrew, Christopher M., and Vasili Mitrokhin. *The Sword and the Shield: The Mitrokhin Archive and the Secret History of the KGB.* New York: Basic Books, 1999.

Anti-Virus.by. "News: VirusBlokAda." 2010. http://www.anti-virus.by/en/tempo.shtml.

Arghire, Ionut. "NotPetya Connected to BlackEnergy/KillDisk: Researchers." Security Week, July 2017. https://www.securityweek.com/notpetya-connected-blackenergyk illdisk-researchers.

ASERT Team. "The Anatomy of the DDoS Attack Campaign Targeting Organizations in Ukraine." *NETSCOUT* (blog), February 2022. https://www.netscout.com/blog/asert/ddos-attack-campaign-targeting-multiple-organizations-ukraine.

"Assessment of Ukraine's Economic Losses from the Temporary Occupation of the Crimean Peninsula." Center for Economic Strategy, July 2021. https://ces.org.ua/ass essment-of-ukraines-economic-losses-from-crimea/.

Bainbridge, David I. "Hacking. The Unauthorised Access of Computer Systems: The Legal Implications." *Modern Law Review* 52, no. 2 (1989): 236–245.

Baldwin, David A. "Power Analysis and World Politics: New Trends versus Old Tendencies." *World Politics* 31, no. 2 (1979): 161–194.

Baldwin, David A. *Power and International Relations: A Conceptual Approach.* Princeton, NJ: Princeton University Press, 2016.

Balzacq, Thierry, and Myriam Dunn Cavelty. "A Theory of Actor-Network for Cyber-Security." *European Journal of International Security* 1, no. 2 (July 2016): 176–198. https://doi.org/10.1017/eis.2016.8.

Barnett, Michael, and Raymond Duvall. "Power in International Politics." *International Organization* 59, no. 1 (2005): 39–75.

Bateman, Jon. "Russia's Wartime Cyber Operations in Ukraine: Military Impacts, Influences, and Implications." December 2022. https://carnegieendowment.org/files/Bateman_Cyber-FINAL21.pdf.

Batvinis, Raymond J. "The Future of FBI Counterintelligence through the Lens of the Past Hundred Years." In *The Oxford Handbook of National Security Intelligence*, Oxford Handbooks, edited by Loch K. Johnson, 505–517. Oxford: Oxford University Press, 2010.

Baumgartner, Kurt. "BE2 Extraordinary Plugins, Siemens Targeting, Dev Fails." February 2015. https://securelist.com/be2-extraordinary-plugins-siemens-targeting-dev-fails/68838/.

BBC. "Crimea Blackout 'Sabotage by Ukraine.'" *BBC News*, November 2015, sec. Europe. https://www.bbc.com/news/world-europe-34967093.

BBC. "Nato to Counter 'Hybrid Warfare' from Russia." *BBC News*, May 2015, sec. Europe. https://www.bbc.com/news/world-europe-32741688.

BBC. "Putin Strategist Returns to Kremlin." *BBC News*, September 2013, sec. Europe. https://www.bbc.com/news/world-europe-24178947.

BBC. "Ukraine Power Cut 'Was Cyber-Attack.'" *BBC News*, January 2017, sec. Technology. https://www.bbc.com/news/technology-38573074.

Behr, Roy L., and Shanto Iyengar. "Television News, Real-World Cues, and Changes in the Public Agenda." *Public Opinion Quarterly* 49, no. 1 (January 1985): 38–57. https://doi.org/10.1086/268900.

Beilenson, Lawrence W. *Power through Subversion*. Washington, DC: Public Affairs Press, 1972.
Benkler, Yochai, Robert Faris, and Hal Roberts. *Network Propaganda: Manipulation, Disinformation, and Radicalization in American Politics*. New York, NY: Oxford University Press, 2018. https://www.oxfordscholarship.com/view/10.1093/oso/9780190923624.001.0001/oso-9780190923624.
Bennett, W. Lance, and Steven Livingston. "The Disinformation Order: Disruptive Communication and the Decline of Democratic Institutions." *European Journal of Communication*, 33, no. 2 (April 2018). https://doi.org/10.1177/0267323118760317.
Bergman, Ronen, Rick Gladstone, and Farnaz Fassihi. "Blackout Hits Iran Nuclear Site in What Appears to Be Israeli Sabotage." *New York Times*, April 2021, sec. World. https://www.nytimes.com/2021/04/11/world/middleeast/iran-nuclear-natanz.html.
Betts, Richard K. *Enemies of Intelligence: Knowledge and Power in American National Security*. New York: Columbia University Press, 2007.
Biddle, Stephen. *Military Power: Explaining Victory and Defeat in Modern Battle*. Princeton, NJ: Princeton University Press, 2010.
Bijker, Wiebe E., and John Law, eds. *Shaping Technology/Building Society: Studies in Sociotechnical Change*, Inside Technology, repr. Cambridge, MA: MIT Press, 2010.
"The Birth of the Web." CERN. Accessed January 18, 2023. https://home.web.cern.ch/science/computing/birth-web.
Bischof, Günter, Stefan Karner, and Peter Ruggenthaler, eds. *The Prague Spring and the Warsaw Pact Invasion of Czechoslovakia in 1968*, Harvard Cold War Studies Book Series. Lanham, MD: Lexington Books, 2010.
Bittman, Ladislav. *The Deception Game*. New York: Ballantine Books, 1981.
Bittman, Ladislav. *The KGB and Soviet Disinformation: An Insider's View*. Washington, DC: Pergamon-Brassey's, 1985.
Bjola, Corneliu, and Stuart Murray. *Secret Diplomacy: Concepts, Contexts and Cases*. London, UK: Routledge, 2016.
Blackstock, Paul W. *The Strategy of Subversion: Manipulating the Politics of Other Nations*. Chicago: Quadrangle Books, 1964.
"Blasts at Ukrainian Munitions Depot Let $800 Mln of Weapons Go Up in Smoke." TASS, September 2017. http://tass.com/world/967814.
Bloomberg. "Ukraine Protesters Urge Yanukovych's Return at Rally in Donetsk." March 2014. https://www.bloomberg.com/news/articles/2014-03-22/ukraine-protesters-urge-yanukovych-s-return-at-rally-in-donetsk.
Blunden, Bill, and Violet Cheung. *Behold a Pale Farce: Cyberwar, Threat Inflation, & the Malware Industrial Complex*. Waterville, OR: Trine Day, 2014.
BND. "Dokumente Des Bundesnachrichtendienstes Zum Prager Frühling 1968." Mitteilungen Der Forschungs-Und Arbeitsgruppe „Geschichte Des BND,»2016. http://uzsi.cz/files/spolkova-zpravodajska-sluzba-prazske-jaro-1968.pdf.
Boyes, Hugh, Bil Hallaq, Joe Cunningham, and Tim Watson. "The Industrial Internet of Things (IIoT): An Analysis Framework." *Computers in Industry* 101 (October 2018): 1–12. https://doi.org/10.1016/j.compind.2018.04.015.
Brantly, Aaron F., Nerea M. Cal, and Devlin P. Winkelstein. "Defending the Borderland." Army Cyber Institute, December 2017. https://vtechworks.lib.vt.edu/handle/10919/81979.
Brantly, Aaron Franklin. *The Decision to Attack: Military and Intelligence Cyber Decision-Making*. Athens, Georgia: University of Georgia Press, 2016. http://muse.jhu.edu/book/45365.

Brewster, Thomas. "'Most Severe' Cyberattack Since Russian Invasion Crashes Ukraine Internet Provider." *Forbes*, March 2022, sec. Cybersecurity. https://www.forbes.com/sites/thomasbrewster/2022/03/28/huge-cyberattack-on-ukrtelecom-biggest-since-russian-invasion-crashes-ukraine-telecom/.

Buchanan, Ben. *The Cybersecurity Dilemma Hacking, Trust and Fear between Nations*. Oxford: Oxford University Press, 2017.

Buchanan, Ben. *The Hacker and the State: Cyber Attacks and the New Normal of Geopolitics*. Cambridge, MA: Harvard University Press, 2020.

Buchanan, Ben. "The Legend of Sophistication in Cyber Operations." *Belfer Center for Science and International Affairs* (blog), 2017. https://www.belfercenter.org/publication/legend-sophistication-cyber-operations.

Bull, Hedley. *The Anarchical Society: A Study of Order in World Politics*. New York: Columbia University Press, 1977.

Bumiller, Elisabeth, and Thom Shanker. "Panetta Warns of Dire Threat of Cyberattack on U.S." *New York Times*, October 12, 2012, sec. World. https://www.nytimes.com/2012/10/12/world/panetta-warns-of-dire-threat-of-cyberattack.html.

Burdiga, Igor. "«Чорний вівторок» українського ІТ: яких збитків завдала кібератака, та хто її вчинив." July 2017. https://hromadske.ua/posts/naslidki-kiberataki.

Burt, Jeff. "Sandworm Gang Launches Monster Ransomware Attacks on Ukraine." November 2022. https://www.theregister.com/2022/11/29/russia_ransomboggs_ransomware_ukraine/.

Butchenko, Maksym. "Ukraine's Territorial Defence on a War Footing." *ICDS* (blog), April 2022. https://icds.ee/en/ukraines-territorial-defence-on-a-war-footing/.

Butusov, Yuri. "День кризи: 6 квітня 2014 року російські спецслужби атакували органи влади на південному сході України." Цензор.НЕТ, April 2017. https://censor.net.ua/ua/resonance/435372/den_kryzy_6_kvitnya_2014_roku_rosiyiski_spetsslujby_atakuvaly_organy_vlady_na_pivdennomu_shodi_ukrayiny.

California Energy Commission. "California ISO Glossary." n.d. https://www.energy.ca.gov/glossary/ISO_GLOSSARY.PDF.

Callanan, James. *Covert Action in the Cold War: US Policy, Intelligence and CIA Operations*. London: I. B. Tauris, 2009.

Cameron, Dell. "In WannaCry's Wake, a New Rapidly Spreading Ransomware Attack Appeared Today." *Gizmodo*, May 2017. https://gizmodo.com/in-wannacrys-wake-a-new-rapidly-spreading-ransomware-a-1795385418.

Cappelli, Dawn, Andrew Moore, and Randall Trzeciak. *The CERT Guide to Insider Threats: How to Prevent, Detect, and Respond to Information Technology Crimes (Theft, Sabotage, Fraud)*, Sei Series in Software Engineering. Upper Saddle River, NJ: Addison-Wesley, 2012.

Carr, Jeffrey. "The GRU-Ukraine Artillery Hack That May Never Have Happened." *Medium* (blog), January 2017. https://medium.com/@jeffreyscarr/the-gru-ukraine-artillery-hack-that-may-never-have-happened-820960bbb02d.

Carson, Austin. "Facing Off and Saving Face: Covert Intervention and Escalation Management in the Korean War." *International Organization* 70, no. 1 (2016): 103–131. https://doi.org/10.1017/S0020818315000284.

Carson, Austin. *Secret Wars: Covert Conflict in International Politics*, Princeton Studies in International History and Politics. Princeton, NJ: Princeton University Press, 2018.

CBC. "Riots Erupt in Vancouver after Canucks Loss." *CBC News*, June 2011. https://www.cbc.ca/news/canada/british-columbia/riots-erupt-in-vancouver-after-canucks-loss-1.993707.

Censor.net. "Начальника пожежної охорони арсеналу в Калинівці не було покарано за недбалість через закінчення термінів притягнення до адмінвідповідальності." *Цензор.НЕТ*, October 2018. https://censor.net.ua/ua/news/3091002/nachalnyka_pojejnoyi_ohorony_arsenalu_v_kalynivtsi_ne_bulo_pokarano_za_nedbalist_cherez_zakinchennya.

CERT-UA. "Cyber Attack on Websites of State Bodies." January 2022. https://cert.gov.ua/.

CERT-UA. "A Fragment of the Research on Cyber Attacks 01.14.2022." January 2022. https://cert.gov.ua/article/18101.

CERT-UA. "Heavy Cyberattack on Ukraine's Energy Sector Prevented." April 2022. https://cip.gov.ua/en/news/poperedzhena-masshtabna-kiberataka-na-energetichnii-sektor-ukrayini.

CERT-UA. "Information on Cyber Attacks on February 15, 2022." Accessed January 12, 2023. https://cert.gov.ua/.

CERT-UA. "Ukrainian Media Are Attacked with Black Energy." January 2016. https://web.archive.org/web/20160116110418/http://cert.gov.ua/?p=2370.

CERT-UA. "Кібератака Групи Sandworm (UAC-0082) На Об'єкти Енергетики України з Використанням Шкідливих Програм INDUSTROYER2 Та CADDYWIPER (CERT-UA#4435)." April 2022. https://cert.gov.ua/.

Cerulus, Laurens. "How Ukraine Became a Test Bed for Cyberweaponry." Politico, February 2019. https://www.politico.eu/article/ukraine-cyber-war-frontline-russia-malware-attacks/.

Chappell, Bill. "'Petya' Ransomware Hits at Least 65 Countries; Microsoft Traces It to Tax Software." *NPR*, June 2017. https://www.npr.org/sections/thetwo-way/2017/06/28/534679950/petya-ransomware-hits-at-least-65-countries-microsoft-traces-it-to-tax-software.

Cherkasets, Olena. "Медведчук Отримав Від ФСБ Мільярд На Підготовку Війни." July 2022. https://umoloda.kyiv.ua/number/0/2006/168191.

Chivvis, Christopher S. "Hybrid War: Russian Contemporary Political Warfare." *Bulletin of the Atomic Scientists: How Dangerous Is Hybrid War?* 73, no. 5 (2017): 316–321. https://doi.org/10.1080/00963402.2017.1362903. Chulov, Martin. "Israel Appears to Confirm It Carried Out Cyberattack on Iran Nuclear Facility." *The Guardian*, April 11, 2021, sec. World News. https://www.theguardian.com/world/2021/apr/11/israel-appears-confirm-cyberattack-iran-nuclear-facility.

CIA. "The Crisis in Czechoslovakia." July 1968.

CIA. "Eastern Europe and the USSR in the Aftermath of the Invasion of Czechoslovakia." November 1968.

CIA. "Intelligence Memorandum: Czechoslovakia in Transition." April 1968.

CIA. "Intelligence Memorandum: The Soviet Decision to Intervene in Czechoslovakia." August 1968.

CIA. "National Intelligence Survey 18; Czechoslovakia; The Society." 1974. https://www.cia.gov/library/readingroom/docs/CIA-RDP01-00707R000200110015-7.pdf.

CIA. "The Situation in Czechoslovakia 10/5/1968, 10am." May 1968.

CIA Office of National Estimates. "Czechoslovakia: A New Direction." Special Memorandum, CIA, January 1968.

Cimpanu, Catalin. "M.E.Doc Software Was Backdoored 3 Times, Servers Left without Updates Since 2013." Bleeping Computer, 2017. https://www.bleepingcomputer.com/news/security/m-e-doc-software-was-backdoored-3-times-servers-left-without-updates-since-2013/.

Cisco Talos. "The MeDoc Connection." 2017. http://blog.talosintelligence.com/2017/07/the-medoc-connection.html.

Cisco Talos. "Threat Spotlight: Follow the Bad Rabbit." 2017. http://blog.talosintelligence.com/2017/10/bad-rabbit.html.

Cisco Talos. "Ukraine Campaign Delivers Defacement and Wipers, in Continued Escalation." *Cisco Talos* (blog), January 2022. https://blog.talosintelligence.com/ukraine-campaign-delivers-defacement/.

Clausewitz, Carl von. *On War*, Oxford World's Classics. Edited by Beatrice Heuser. Translated by Michael Howard and Peter Paret. New York: Oxford University Press, 2006.

Clayton, Mark. "Ukraine Election Narrowly Avoided 'Wanton Destruction' from Hackers (+Video)." *Christian Science Monitor*, June 2014. http://www.csmonitor.com/World/Passcode/2014/0617/Ukraine-election-narrowly-avoided-wanton-destruction-from-hackers-video.

Cohen, Fred. "Computer Viruses: Theory and Experiments." *Computers & Security* 6, no. 1 (1987): 22–35.

Committee on Foreign Relations. "Chain Reaction: Avoiding a Nuclear Arms Race in the Middle East." Report to the US Senate Committee on Foreign Relations, February 2008. https://www.govinfo.gov/content/pkg/CPRT-110SPRT39674/html/CPRT-110SPRT39674.htm.

Connolly, Helen, and Kate Womack. "Previously Unseen Photos Depict Drama of 1968 Soviet Invasion of Prague." *The Observer*, August 17, 2008, sec. World News. https://www.theguardian.com/world/2008/aug/17/1968theyearofrevolt.russia.

Corke, Sarah-Jane. *US Covert Operations and Cold War Strategy: Truman, Secret Warfare, and the CIA, 1945–1953*, Studies in Intelligence Series. New York: Routledge, 2008.

Cormac, Rory. "Coordinating Covert Action: The Case of the Yemen Civil War and the South Arabian Insurgency." *Journal of Strategic Studies* 36, no. 5 (October 2013): 692–717. https://doi.org/10.1080/01402390.2011.651534.

Cormac, Rory, and Richard J. Aldrich. "Grey Is the New Black: Covert Action and Implausible Deniability." *International Affairs* 94, no. 3 (May 2018): 477–494. https://doi.org/10.1093/ia/iiy067.

Coser, Lewis A. *Functions of Social Conflict*. New York, NY: Simon and Schuster, 1964.

Crete-Nishihata, Masashi, Jakub Dalek, Ronald Deibert, Seth Hardy, Katherine Kleemola, Sarah McKune, Irene Poetranto, et al. "Communities @Risk: Targeted Digital Threats against Civil Society." Citizen Lab, November 2014. https://targetedthreats.net/.

"Crimea Power Cut 'Caused by Blast.'" *BBC News*, December 2015, sec. Europe. http://www.bbc.com/news/world-europe-35204304.

CrowdStrike. "Fancy Bear Tracking of Ukrainian Field Artillery Units." December 2016. http://web.archive.org/web/20161223065425/https://www.crowdstrike.com/wp-content/brochures/FancyBearTracksUkrainianArtillery.pdf.

CrowdStrike. "Fancy Bear Tracking of Ukrainian Field Artillery Units." March 2017. https://www.crowdstrike.com/wp-content/brochures/FancyBearTracksUkrainianArtillery.pdf.

CrowdStrike. "Technical Analysis of the WhisperGate Malicious Bootloader | CrowdStrike." January 2022. https://www.crowdstrike.com/blog/technical-analysis-of-whispergate-malware/.

Crypto-cypher. "Fortinet Victim List—'Hackers Leak Passwords for 500,000 Fortinet VPN Accounts' #TrackThePlanet." Gist, 2021. https://gist.github.com/crypto-cypher/f216d6fa4816ffa93c5270b001dc4bdc.

CSIS. "The Ukraine Crisis Timeline." Accessed April 12, 2019. http://ukraine.csis.org/#478.

Cyber Berkut. "Cyber Berkut: Кибер Беркут." May 2014. http://www.cyber-berkut.ru/en/index_02.php.

CysCentrum. "Киберугроза BlackEnergy2/3." 2016. https://cys-centrum.com/ru/news/black_energy_2_3.

Dahl, Robert A. "The Concept of Power." *Behavioral Science* 2, no. 3 (1957): 201–215.

Dak, Pavlo. "Як Віктор Медведчук Причетний До Війни в Україні: Відповідь Буданова." *Інформаційне Агентство Вголос/Vgolos*, October 1, 2022 edition. Accessed January 16, 2023. https://vgolos.ua/news/yak-viktor-medvedchuk-prichetniy-do-viyni-v-ukrayini-vidpovid-budanova_1428157.html.

Dawisha, Karen. *The Kremlin and the Prague Spring*, International Crisis Behavior Series. Vol. 4. Berkeley: University of California Press, 1984.

"Deadly Ambush Ends Lull in Ukraine." *BBC News*, September 2015, sec. Europe. https://www.bbc.com/news/world-europe-34128085.

"Deadly Clashes in Ukraine Despite Truce." Radio Free Europe/Radio Liberty, December 2015. https://www.rferl.org/a/deadly-clashes-in-ukraine-despite-holiday-truce/27452015.html.

Dear, Ian. *Sabotage & Subversion: Stories from the Files of the SOE and OSS*. London: Arms and Armour, 1996.

Deibert, Ronald. *Parchment, Printing, and Hypermedia: Communication in World Order Transformation*. New York: Columbia University Press, 1997.

Deibert, Ronald. *Reset: Reclaiming the Internet for Civil Society*. Toronto, Canada: House of Anansi Press, 2020.

Deibert, Ronald. "Subversion Inc: The Age of Private Espionage." *Journal of Democracy* 33, no. 2 (April 2022): 28–44.

Deibert, Ronald, Rafal Rohozinski, and Masashi Crete-Nishihata. "Cyclones in Cyberspace: Information Shaping and Denial in the 2008 Russia–Georgia War." *Security Dialogue* 43, no. 1 (2012): 3–24. https://doi.org/10.1177/0967010611431079.

DeNardis, Laura. *Protocol Politics: The Globalization of Internet Governance*. Cambridge, MA: MIT Press, 2009. http://myaccess.library.utoronto.ca/login?url=http://site.ebrary.com/lib/utoronto/Doc?id=10326187.

DeVine, Michael E., and Heidi M. Peters. *Covert Action and Clandestine Activities of the Intelligence Community: Selected Definitions in Brief*. Washington, DC: US Congressional Research Service, July 2019.

Dix, Robert H. "The Breakdown of Authoritarian Regimes." *Western Political Quarterly* 35, no. 4 (December 1982): 554–573. https://doi.org/10.1177/106591298203500407.

Doman, Chris. "Technical Analysis of the DdoS Attacks against Ukrainian Websites." Cado Security: Cloud Investigation, February 2022. https://www.cadosecurity.com/technical-analysis-of-the-ddos-attacks-against-ukrainian-websites/.

Madory, Doug (@DougMadory). Twitter, "Large outages today in #Ukraine." March 2022. https://twitter.com/DougMadory/status/1501910709734678529.

Douthit, Howard, III. "The Use and Effectiveness of Sabotage as a Means of Unconventional Warfare." Master's Thesis: Air University, 1987.

Downes, Alexander B., and Mary Lauren Lilley. "Overt Peace, Covert War?: Covert Intervention and the Democratic Peace." *Security Studies* 19, no. 2 (May 2010): 266–306. https://doi.org/10.1080/09636411003795756.

Dragos. "CRASHOVERRIDE Analysis of the Threat to Electric Grid Operations." 2017. https://dragos.com/blog/crashoverride/CrashOverride-01.pdf.

Dragos. "CRASHOVERRIDE: Reassessing the 2016 Ukraine Electric Power Event as a Protection-Focused Attack." 2019. https://dragos.com/wp-content/uploads/CRASHOVERRIDE.pdf.

Drezner, Daniel W. "Why Vladimir Putin's Strategic Genius Scares the Heck Out of Me." *Washington Post*, July 30, 2014, sec. PostEverything. https://www.washingtonpost.com/posteverything/wp/2014/07/30/why-vladimir-putins-strategic-genius-scares-the-heck-out-of-me/.

Dubcek, Alexander. *Hope Dies Last: The Autobiography of Alexander Dubcek*. Edited by Jiri Hochman. New York: Kodansha USA, 1993.

Dullien, Thomas. "Weird Machines, Exploitability, and Provable Unexploitability." *IEEE Transactions on Emerging Topics in Computing* 8, no. 2 (April 2020): 391–403. https://doi.org/10.1109/TETC.2017.2785299.

Dunn Cavelty, Myriam. "From Cyber-Bombs to Political Fallout: Threat Representations with an Impact in the Cyber-Security Discourse." *International Studies Review* 15, no. 1 (2013): 105–122. https://doi.org/10.1111/misr.12023.

Egloff, Florian J. "Contested Public Attributions of Cyber Incidents and the Role of Academia." *Contemporary Security Policy* 41, no. 1 (January 2020): 55–81. https://doi.org/10.1080/13523260.2019.1677324.

Egloff, Florian J. *Semi-State Actors in Cybersecurity*. New York: Oxford University Press, 2022.

Eidlin, Fred H. *The Logic of "Normalization": The Soviet Intervention in Czechoslovakia of 21 August 1968 and the Czechoslovak Response*. Boulder, Colorado: Eastern European Monographs, Fred Eidlin, 1980.

"Enercon: Thousands of Wind Turbines Need New Hardware." Energate Messenger, March 2022. https://www.energate-messenger.com/news/220914/enercon-thousands-of-wind-turbines-need-new-hardware.

Erickson, Jon. *Hacking: The Art of Exploitation*. San Francisco: No Starch Press, 2003.

Erlanger, Steven. "Putin, at NATO Meeting, Curbs Combative Rhetoric." *New York Times*, April 5, 2008, sec. Europe. https://www.nytimes.com/2008/04/05/world/europe/05nato.html.

ESET. "Analysis of TeleBots' Cunning Backdoor." *We Live Security* (blog), July 2017. https://www.welivesecurity.com/2017/07/04/analysis-of-telebots-cunning-backdoor/.

ESET. "Bad Rabbit: Not-Petya Is Back with Improved Ransomware." *We Live Security* (blog), October 2017. https://www.welivesecurity.com/2017/10/24/bad-rabbit-not-petya-back/.

ESET. "BlackEnergy by the SSHBearDoor: Attacks against Ukrainian News Media and Electric Industry." *We Live Security* (blog), January 2016. https://www.welivesecurity.com/2016/01/03/blackenergy-sshbeardoor-details-2015-attacks-ukrainian-news-media-electric-industry/.

ESET. "CaddyWiper: New Wiper Malware Discovered in Ukraine." *We Live Security* (blog), March 2022. https://www.welivesecurity.com/2022/03/15/caddywiper-new-wiper-malware-discovered-ukraine/.

ESET. "GREYENERGY." *We Live Security* (blog), October 2018. https://www.welivesecurity.com/wp-content/uploads/2018/10/ESET_GreyEnergy.pdf.

ESET. "Kiev Metro Hit with a New Variant of the Infamous Diskcoder Ransomware." *We Live Security* (blog), October 2017. https://www.welivesecurity.com/2017/10/24/kiev-metro-hit-new-variant-infamous-diskcoder-ransomware/.

BIBLIOGRAPHY 299

ESET. "New TeleBots Backdoor: First Evidence Linking Industroyer to NotPetya." *We Live Security* (blog), October 2018. https://www.welivesecurity.com/2018/10/11/new-telebots-backdoor-linking-industroyer-notpetya/.

ESET. "RansomBoggs: New Ransomware Targeting Ukraine." *We Live Security* (blog), November 2022. https://www.welivesecurity.com/2022/11/28/ransomboggs-new-ransomware-ukraine/.

ESET. "The Rise of TeleBots: Analyzing Disruptive KillDisk Attacks." *We Live Security* (blog), December 2016. https://www.welivesecurity.com/2016/12/13/rise-telebots-analyzing-disruptive-killdisk-attacks/.

ESET. "Sandworm Uses a New Version of ArguePatch to Attack Targets in Ukraine." *We Live Security* (blog), May 2022. https://www.welivesecurity.com/2022/05/20/sandworm-ukraine-new-version-arguepatch-malware-loader/.

ESET. "TeleBots Are Back: Supply-Chain Attacks against Ukraine." *We Live Security* (blog), June 2017. https://www.welivesecurity.com/2017/06/30/telebots-back-supply-chain-attacks-against-ukraine/.

ESET. "Win32/Industroyer." *We Live Security* (blog), 2017. https://www.welivesecurity.com/wp-content/uploads/2017/06/Win32_Industroyer.pdf.

ESET. "XData Ransomware Making Rounds amid Global WannaCryptor Scare." *We Live Security* (blog), May 2017. https://www.welivesecurity.com/2017/05/23/xdata-ransomware-making-rounds-amid-global-wannacryptor-scare/.

ESET Research. "IsaacWiper and HermeticWizard: New Wiper and Worm Targeting Ukraine." *We Live Security* (blog), March 2022. https://www.welivesecurity.com/2022/03/01/isaacwiper-hermeticwizard-wiper-worm-targeting-ukraine/.

ESET Research (@ESETresearch). "CaddyWiper Does Not Share Any Significant Code Similarity with #HermeticWiper, #IsaacWiper or Any Other Malware Known to Us. The Sample We Analyzed Was Not Digitally Signed. 3/7 Https://T.Co/EGp9NnctD9." Twitter, March 2022. https://twitter.com/ESETresearch/status/1503436425676705807.

ESET Research (@ESETresearch). "Interestingly, CaddyWiper Avoids Destroying Data on Domain Controllers. This Is Probably a Way for the Attackers to Keep Their Access inside the Organization While Still Disturbing Operations. 5/7 Https://T.Co/XiXgOMe5wr." Twitter, March 2022. https://twitter.com/ESETresearch/status/1503436433134129158.

ESET Research (@ESETresearch). "Breaking. #ESETResearch discovered a new data wiper malware used in Ukraine today. ESET telemetry shows that it was installed on hundreds of machines in the country. This follows the DDoS attacks against several Ukrainian websites earlier today 1/n", Twitter, February 2022. https://twitter.com/ESETresearch/status/1496581903205511181.

ESET Research (@ESETresearch). "We observed the first sample today around 14h52 UTC / 16h52 local time. The PE compilation timestamp of one of the sample is 2021-12-28, suggesting that the attack might have been in preparation for almost two months. 2/n", Twitter, February 2022. https://twitter.com/ESETresearch/status/1496581904916754435.

ESET Research (@ESETresearch). "This new malware erases user data and partition information from attached drives. #ESET telemetry shows that it was seen on a few dozen systems in a limited number of organizations. 2/7," Twitter, March 2022. https://twitter.com/ESETresearch/status/1503436423818534915.

ESET Research (@ESETresearch). "Similarly to HermeticWiper deployments, we observed CaddyWiper being deployed via GPO, indicating the attackers had prior control of the target's network beforehand. 4/7," Twitter, March 2022. https://twitter.com/ESETresearch/status/1503436428096716800.

Espreso.tv. "Вибухи в Калинівці: Майора, Який Пропустив Сторонніх На Військові Склади, Оштрафували На 2,5 Тисячі." November 2017. https://espreso.tv/news/2017/11/22/vybukhy_v_kalynivci_mayora_yakyy_propustyv_storonnikh_osib_na_viyskovi_sklady_oshtrafuvaly_na_2_5_tysyachi.

Espreso.tv. "У Російських Диверсантів Могли Бути Спільники На Складах у Калинівці,—Генерал Розвідки." September 2017. https://espreso.tv/news/2017/09/27/u_rosiyskykh_dyversantiv_mogly_buty_spilnyky_na_skladakh_u_kalynivci_generalnoyi_rozvidky.

Esterle, Lukas, and Radu Grosu. "Cyber-Physical Systems: Challenge of the 21st Century." *E & i Elektrotechnik Und Informationstechnik* 133, no. 7 (2016): 299–303. https://doi.org/10.1007/s00502-016-0426-6.

"The EU-Ukraine Association Agreement Enters into Force on 1 September 2017." EEAS—European External Action Service, European Commission. Accessed April 16, 2019. https://eeas.europa.eu/delegations/ukraine/30478/eu-ukraine-association-agreement-enters-force-1-september-2017_en.

Euromaidan Press. "30% of Ukrainian SBU Officers Were Russian FSB and GRU Agents." *Euromaidan Press* (blog), April 2014. http://euromaidanpress.com/2014/04/24/30-of-ukrainian-sbu-officers-were-russian-fsb-and-gru-agents/.

Euromaidan Press. "Glazyev Tapes, Continued: New Details of Russian Occupation of Crimea and Attempts to Dismember Ukraine." *Euromaidan Press* (blog), May 2019. http://euromaidanpress.com/2019/05/16/glazyev-tapes-continued-ukraine-presents-new-details-of-russian-takeover-of-crimea-and-financing-of-separatism/.

Euromaidan Press. "Ukraine Publishes Video Proving Kremlin Directed Separatism in Eastern Ukraine and Crimea." *Euromaidan Press* (blog), August 2016. http://euromaidanpress.com/2016/08/23/ukraine-publishes-video-proving-kremlin-directed-separatism-in-ukraine/.

"EuroMaidan Rallies in Ukraine—Nov. 21-23 Coverage." *Kyiv Post*, November 2013. https://www.kyivpost.com/post/7612.

European Council. "EU Imposes the First Ever Sanctions against Cyber-Attacks." July 2020. https://www.consilium.europa.eu/en/press/press-releases/2020/07/30/eu-imposes-the-first-ever-sanctions-against-cyber-attacks/.

Evanson, Robert K. "Political Repression in Czechoslovakia, 1948–1984." *Canadian Slavonic Papers / Revue Canadienne Des Slavistes* 28, no. 1 (1986): 1–21.

Eversden, Andrew, and Jaspreet Gill. "Why Hasn't Russia Used Its 'Full Scope' of Electronic Warfare?" *Breaking Defense* (blog), March 2022. https://breakingdefense.sites.breakingmedia.com/2022/03/why-hasnt-russia-used-its-full-scope-of-electronic-warfare/.

"EXCLUSIVE: Rounding up a Cyber Posse for Ukraine." *The Record by Recorded Future* (blog), November 2022. https://therecord.media/exclusive-rounding-up-a-cyber-posse-for-ukraine/.

Fakty.ua. "Причиной обесточивания части Киева может быть атака хакеров." December 2016. https://fakty.ua/227538-prichinoj-obestochivaniya-chasti-kieva-mozhet-byt-ataka-hakerov.

Farwell, J. P., and R. Rohozinski. "Stuxnet and the Future of Cyber War." *Survival* 53, no. 1 (2011): 23–40. https://doi.org/10.1080/00396338.2011.555586.

Fawn, Rick, and Jiří Hochman. *Historical Dictionary of the Czech State*. Lanham, MD: Scarecrow Press, 2010.

Fearon, James D. "Rationalist Explanations for War." *International Organization* 49, no. 3 (1995): 379–414.
Feiner, Lauren. "Cyberattack Hits Ukrainian Banks and Government Websites." *CNBC*, February 2022. https://www.cnbc.com/2022/02/23/cyberattack-hits-ukrainian-banks-and-government-websites.html.
Filitov, Alexsei. "The USSR, the Federal Republic of Germany, and the Czechoslovak Crisis of 1968." In *The Prague Spring and the Warsaw Pact Invasion of Czechoslovakia in 1968*, Harvard Cold War Studies Book Series, edited by Günter Bischof, Stefan Karner, and Peter Ruggenthaler, 319–340. Lanham, MD: Lexington Books, 2010.
FireEye. "Attackers Deploy New ICS Attack Framework 'TRITON' and Cause Operational Disruption to Critical Infrastructure." *FireEye* (blog), December 2017. https://www.fireeye.com/blog/threat-research/2017/12/attackers-deploy-new-ics-attack-framework-triton.html.
FireEye. "M-Trends." 2020. https://content.fireeye.com/m-trends/rpt-m-trends-2020.
FireEye. "SMB Exploited: WannaCry Use of 'EternalBlue' « SMB Exploited: WannaCry Use of 'EternalBlue.'" May 2017. https://www.fireeye.com/blog/threat-research/2017/05/smb-exploited-wannacry-use-of-eternalblue.html.
Fischerkeller, Michael P., Emily O. Goldman, and Richard J. Harknett. *Cyber Persistence Theory: Redefining National Security in Cyberspace*, Bridging the Gap. New York: Oxford University Press, 2022.
Fischerkeller, Michael P., and Richard J. Harknett. "Deterrence Is Not a Credible Strategy for Cyberspace." *Orbis* 61, no. 3 (January 2017): 381–393. https://doi.org/10.1016/j.orbis.2017.05.003.
Fitton, Oliver. "Cyber Operations and Gray Zones: Challenges for NATO." *Connections* 15, no. 2 (2016): 109–119.
Foreign Broadcast Information Service. "FBIS Special Report on Communist Propaganda—The I. Aleksandrov Article." July 1968.
Franceschi-Bicchierai, Lorenzo. "How Hackers Broke into John Podesta and Colin Powell's Gmail Accounts." *Motherboard*, October 2016. https://motherboard.vice.com/en_us/article/how-hackers-broke-into-john-podesta-and-colin-powells-gmail-accounts.
Frolík, Josef, John Bok, and Přemysl Vachalovský. *Špion vypovídá II· jasná zpráva o konci jednoho světa*. Praha: J. W. Hill, 2000.
Galeotti, Mark. "Controlling Chaos: How Russia Manages Its Political War in Europe." August 2017. http://www.ecfr.eu/publications/summary/controlling_chaos_how_russia_manages_its_political_war_in_europe.
Galeotti, Mark. "The 'Gerasimov Doctrine' and Russian Non-Linear War." *In Moscow's Shadows* (blog), July 2014. https://inmoscowsshadows.wordpress.com/2014/07/06/the-gerasimov-doctrine-and-russian-non-linear-war/.
Galeotti, Mark. "Putin's Hydra: Inside Russia's Intelligence Services." European Council on Foreign Relations, May 2016. http://www.ecfr.eu/page/-/ECFR_169_-_PUTINS_HYDRA_INSIDE_THE_RUSSIAN_INTELLIGENCE_SERVICES_1513.pdf.
Ganssle, Jack. *The Firmware Handbook*. Orlando, FL: Elsevier, 2004.
Gartzke, Erik, and Jon R. Lindsay. "Thermonuclear Cyberwar." *Journal of Cybersecurity* 3, no. 1 (2017): 37–48. https://doi.org/10.1093/cybsec/tyw017.
Gartzke, Erik, and Jon R. Lindsay. "Weaving Tangled Webs: Offense, Defense, and Deception in Cyberspace." *Security Studies* 24, no. 2 (April 2015): 316–348. https://doi.org/10.1080/09636412.2015.1038188.

George, Alexander L., and Andrew Bennett. *Case Studies and Theory Development in the Social Sciences*. Cambridge, MA: MIT Press, 2005.

GfK Ukraine. "Public Opinion Survey in Crimea." March 2014. https://avaazpress.s3.amazonaws.com/558_Crimea.Referendum.Poll.GfK.pdf.

Gibney, Elizabeth. "Where Is Russia's Cyberwar? Researchers Decipher Its Strategy." *Nature* 603, no. 7903 (March 2022): 775–776. https://doi.org/10.1038/d41586-022-00753-9.

Giles, Keir. "Putin Does Not Need to Invade Ukraine to Get His Way." *Chatham House—International Affairs Think Tank* (blog), December 2021. https://www.chathamhouse.org/2021/12/putin-does-not-need-invade-ukraine-get-his-way.

Gill, Jaspreet. "Russia May Be Holding Cyber Capabilities in Reserve, so US Must Keep Its Shields Up: Experts." *Breaking Defense* (blog), March 2022. https://breakingdefense.sites.breakingmedia.com/2022/03/russia-may-be-holding-cyber-capabilities-in-reserve-so-us-must-keep-its-shields-up-experts/.

Gilli, Andrea, and Mauro Gilli. "Why China Has Not Caught Up Yet: Military-Technological Superiority and the Limits of Imitation, Reverse Engineering, and Cyber Espionage." *International Security* 43, no. 3 (February 2019): 141–189. https://doi.org/10.1162/isec_a_00337.

"Global Cyber Attack Could Spur $53 Billion in Losses: Lloyd's Of . . ." Reuters, July 2017. https://www.reuters.com/article/us-cyber-lloyds-report/global-cyber-attack-could-spur-53-billion-in-losses-lloyds-of-london-idUSKBN1A20AB.

Gomez, Miguel Alberto, and Eula Bianca Villar. "Fear, Uncertainty, and Dread: Cognitive Heuristics and Cyber Threats." *Politics and Governance* 6, no. 2 (June 2018): 61–72. https://doi.org/10.17645/pag.v6i2.1279.

Goodin, Dan. "Tuesday's Massive Ransomware Outbreak Was, in Fact, Something Much Worse." *Ars Technica*, June 2017. https://arstechnica.com/information-technology/2017/06/petya-outbreak-was-a-chaos-sowing-wiper-not-profit-seeking-ransomware/.

Google TAG. "Fog of War: How the Ukraine Conflict Transformed the Cyber Threat Landscape." Google, February 2023. https://services.google.com/fh/files/blogs/google_fog_of_war_research_report.pdf.

Gorchinskaya, Katya, and Darina Marchak. "Russia Gives Ukraine Cheap Gas, $15 Billion in Loans." *Kyiv Post*, December 17, 2013. https://www.kyivpost.com/article/content/ukraine-politics/russia-gives-ukraine-cheap-gas-15-billion-in-loans-333852.html.

Gorchinskaya, Katya, Olga Rudenko, and William Schreiber. "Authorities: Hackers Foiled in Bid to Rig Ukraine Presidential Election Results." *Kyiv Post*, May 25, 2014. https://www.kyivpost.com/article/content/may-25-presidential-election/authorities-hackers-foiled-in-bid-to-rig-ukraine-presidential-election-results-349288.html.

Gordiichuk, Dana. "Кібератака за мільйони доларів: за нападом може стояти РФ." *Економічна правда*, February 2022. https://www.epravda.com.ua/news/2022/02/16/682428/.

Gordon, Carol, and Asher Arian. "Threat and Decision Making." *Journal of Conflict Resolution* 45, no. 2 (April 2001): 196–215. https://doi.org/10.1177/0022002701045002003.

Gordon.ua. "СБУ Задержала Российских Агентов, Которые Корректировали Обстрелы Николаевской Области. Ими Оказались Местные Жители / ВОЙНА В УКРАИНЕ / Новости." July 2022. https://gordonua.com/amp/news/war/sbu-zaderzhala-rossiyskih-agentov-kotorye-korrektirovali-obstrely-nikolaevskoy-oblasti-imi-okazalis-mestnye-zhiteli-1617219.html.

Gorst, Isabel. "Russians Invading, Says Ukraine Leader; Tanks Reported Crossing Border." *Latimes.com*, August 2014. https://www.latimes.com/world/europe/la-fg-ukraine-president-russian-forces-20140828-story.html.

Gorwa, Robert, and Max Smeets. "Cyber Conflict in Political Science: A Review of Methods and Literature." Preprint, SocArXiv, July 2019. https://doi.org/10.31235/osf.io/fc6sg.

Götz, Elias. "Russia, the West, and the Ukraine Crisis: Three Contending Perspectives." *Contemporary Politics* 22, no. 3 (2016): 249–266. https://doi.org/10.1080/13569775.2016.1201313.

Grabo, Cynthia R. "Soviet Deception in the Czechoslovak Crisis." *Studies in Intelligence* 45th Anniversary Issue: Special Unclassified Edition, special issue (Fall 2000): 71–86.

Graham, David A. "Rumsfeld's Knowns and Unknowns: The Intellectual History of a Quip." *The Atlantic*, March 2014. http://www.theatlantic.com/politics/archive/2014/03/rumsfelds-knowns-and-unknowns-the-intellectual-history-of-a-quip/359719/.

Greenberg, Andy. "How An Entire Nation Became Russia's Test Lab for Cyberwar." *Wired*, June 2017. https://www.wired.com/story/russian-hackers-attack-ukraine/.

Greenberg, Andy. *Sandworm: A New Era of Cyberwar and the Hunt for the Kremlin's Most Dangerous Hackers*. New York: Doubleday, 2019.

Greenberg, Andy. "The Untold Story of NotPetya, the Most Devastating Cyberattack in History." *Wired*, August 2018. https://www.wired.com/story/notpetya-cyberattack-ukraine-russia-code-crashed-the-world/.

Greenberg, Andy. "The US Sanctions Russians for Potentially 'Fatal' Triton Malware." October 2020. https://www.wired.com/story/russia-sanctions-triton-malware/.

Greig, Ian. *Subversion: Propaganda, Agitation and the Spread of People's War*. London: Tom Stacey, 1973.

Grey, Stephen. *The New Spymasters: Inside the Modern World of Espionage from the Cold War to Global Terror*. New York: St. Martin's Press, 2015.

Groll, Elias. "Did Russia Knock Out Ukraine's Power Grid?" *Foreign Policy* (blog), January 2016. https://foreignpolicy.com/2016/01/08/did-russia-knock-out-ukraines-power-grid/.

Groll, Elias. "In a Hacked Ukrainian App, a Picture of the Future of War." *Foreign Policy* (blog), December 2016. https://foreignpolicy.com/2016/12/22/in-a-hacked-ukrainian-app-a-picture-of-the-future-of-war/.

The Grugq. "Day 2 Keynote: A Short Course in Cyber Warfare." April 2018. https://www.youtube.com/watch?v=gvS4efEakpY.

The Grugq. "Foghorn: Signals through the Fog of War." Substack newsletter. *Info Op* (blog), June 2022. https://grugq.substack.com/p/foghorn-signals-through-the-fog-of?utm_campaign=post_embed.

The Grugq. "Towards an Analysis of Russian Cyber Warfare in Ukraine Feb 2022–Dec 2022." Kings College London, forthcoming.

Grytsenko, Oksana, and Ian Traynor. "Ukraine U-Turn on Europe Pact Was Agreed with Vladimir Putin." *The Guardian*, November 26, 2013, sec. World news. https://www.theguardian.com/world/2013/nov/26/ukraine-u-turn-eu-pact-putin.

Guerrero-Saade, Juan Andrés. "AcidRain: A Modem Wiper Rains Down on Europe." *SentinelOne* (blog), March 2022. https://www.sentinelone.com/labs/acidrain-a-modem-wiper-rains-down-on-europe/.

Guerrero-Saade, Juan Andrés. "HermeticWiper: New Destructive Malware Used in Cyber Attacks on Ukraine." *SentinelOne* (blog). Accessed February 28, 2022. https://www.sentinelone.com/labs/hermetic-wiper-ukraine-under-attack/.

Guerrero-Saade, J. A. (@juanandres_gs). "Ok, Folks, We're Clearly Missing the *MOST* Important Part of All of This. Seeing as Neither @threatintel nor @ESETresearch Have Named This Monster, Let's Call This #HermeticWiper." Twitter, February 2022. https://twitter.com/juanandres_gs/status/1496607141888724997.

Guerrero-Saade, J. A. (@juanandres_gs). "Ok.. This Isn't a Bullshit Wiper like the Last Time. This Thing Is Meant to Be Devastating. Https://T.Co/EvP0g3jjvU." Twitter, February 2022. https://twitter.com/juanandres_gs/status/1496599932966510600.

Guzzini, Stefano. "The Concept of Power: A Constructivist Analysis." *Millennium—Journal of International Studies* 33, no. 3 (June 2005): 495–521.

Habermas, Jürgen. *The Theory of Communicative Action*. Boston: Beacon Press, 1984.

Hafner, Katie, and John Markoff. *Cyberpunk: Outlaws and Hackers on the Computer Frontier*. New York: Simon & Schuster, 1991.

Harding, Luke. "Demoralised Russian Soldiers Tell of Anger at Being 'Duped' into War." *The Guardian*, March 4, 2022, sec. World News. https://www.theguardian.com/world/2022/mar/04/russian-soldiers-ukraine-anger-duped-into-war.

Harding, Luke. "Ukraine Hit by 'Massive' Cyber-Attack on Government Websites." *The Guardian*, January 14, 2022, sec. World News. https://www.theguardian.com/world/2022/jan/14/ukraine-massive-cyber-attack-government-websites-suspected-russian-hackers.

Harknett, Richard J., and Max Smeets. "Cyber Campaigns and Strategic Outcomes." *Journal of Strategic Studies* 45, no. 4 (March 2020): 534–567. https://doi.org/10.1080/01402390.2020.1732354.

Hasherezade. "BadRabbit: A Closer Look at the New Version of Petya/NotPetya." Malwarebytes Labs, October 2017. https://blog.malwarebytes.com/threat-analysis/2017/10/badrabbit-closer-look-new-version-petyanotpetya/.

Haynes, John Earl. *Spies: The Rise and Fall of the KGB in America*. New Haven, CT: Yale University Press, 2009.

"The Head of the Ukrainian Intelligence Service DENIED CULPABILITY! Tried to Transfer Huge Money and Emeralds across the Border, Arrested at the Preševo Crossing!" Republika.rs, Srpski telegraf, June 2022. https://www.republika.rs/top-news/serbia-news/366730/andriy-naumov-arrest-serbia.

Heale, M. J. "Controlling Communist Subversion, 1948–1956." In *McCarthy's Americans: Red Scare Politics in State and Nation, 1935–1965*, American History in Depth, edited by M. J. Heale, 234–253. London: Macmillan Education UK, 1998. https://doi.org/10.1007/978-1-349-14546-1_11.

Healey, Jason. "Preparing for Inevitable Cyber Surprise." *War on the Rocks* (blog), January 2022. https://warontherocks.com/2022/01/preparing-for-inevitable-cyber-surprise/.

Healey, Jason, and Karl Grindal, eds. *A Fierce Domain: Conflict in Cyberspace, 1986 to 2012*. Vienna, VA: Cyber Conflict Studies Association, 2013.

Healey, Jason, and Robert Jervis. "The Escalation Inversion and Other Oddities of Situational Cyber Stability." 2020. https://doi.org/10.26153/tsw/10962.

Herd, Graeme P. "Russia and the 'Orange Revolution': Response, Rhetoric, Reality?" *Connections* 4, no. 2 (2005): 15–28.

Herman, Michael. *Intelligence Power in Peace and War*. Cambridge: Cambridge University Press, 1996.

Hern, Alex. "Hackers Who Targeted Ukraine Clean out Bitcoin Ransom Wallet." *The Guardian*, July 5, 2017, sec. Technology. https://www.theguardian.com/technology/2017/jul/05/notpetya-ransomware-hackers-ukraine-bitcoin-ransom-wallet-motives.

Hern, Alex. "Ukrainian Blackout Caused by Hackers That Attacked Media Company, Researchers Say." *The Guardian*, January 7, 2016, sec. Technology. https://www.theguardian.com/technology/2016/jan/07/ukrainian-blackout-hackers-attacked-media-company.

Herszenhorn, David M., and Andrew E. Kramer. "Ukraine Plans to Withdraw Troops from Russia-Occupied Crimea." *New York Times*, March 20, 2014, sec. World. https://www.nytimes.com/2014/03/20/world/europe/crimea.html.

Hertling, Mark, and Molly K. Mckew. "Putin's Attack on the U.S. Is Our Pearl Harbor." *Politico Magazine*, 2018. https://politi.co/2L1gYOS.

Hill, Patrice. "Monitor Says Ukraine Cease-Fire, Weapons Withdrawal Not Being Honored." Radio Free Europe/Radio Liberty. Accessed August 31, 2020. https://www.rferl.org/a/monitor-osce-says-ukraine-cease-fire-heavy-weapons-withdrawal-not-honored/28324012.html.

Hoffman, Frank G. "The Contemporary Spectrum of Conflict: Protracted, Gray Zone, Ambiguous, and Hybrid Modes of War." 2016. https://www.heritage.org/sites/default/files/2019-08/2016_Index_of_US_Military_Strength_ESSAYS_ALL.pdf.

Holmes, Linda. "The Sports Riot: First We Lose (or Win), Then We Set This Sucker on Fire." *NPR.*, 2011. https://www.npr.org/2011/06/16/137219581/the-sports-riot-first-we-lose-or-win-then-we-set-this-sucker-on-fire.

Holubeva, Olena. "How Much Do Ukrainian Soldiers Earn?" March 2019. https://112.international/opinion/how-much-do-ukrainian-soldiers-earn-38268.html.

Hosaka, Sanshiro. "The Kremlin's 'Active Measures' Failed in 2013: That's When Russia Remembered Its Last Resort-Crimea." *Demokratizatsiya; Washington* 26, no. 3 (Summer 2018): 321–364.

Howard, Philip N. *Lie Machines: How to Save Democracy from Troll Armies, Deceitful Robots, Junk News Operations, and Political Operatives*. New Haven, CT: Yale University Press, 2020.

Howard, Philip N. *Pax Technica: How the Internet of Things May Set Us Free or Lock Us Up*. New Haven, CT: Yale University Press, 2015.

Hromadske.ua. "Terrorism or Negligence? Inside the Investigation into Ukraine's Exploding Military Warehouses." October 2017. https://en.hromadske.ua/posts/terrorism-or-negligence-inside-the-investigation-into-ukraines-exploding-military-warehouses.

Hromadske.ua. "Відключення Електроенергії в Україні Було Хакерською Атакою—Експерти." January 2017. https://hromadske.ua/posts/vidkliuchennia-elektroenerhii-v-ukraini-bulo-khakerskoiu-atakoiu.

Hromadske.ua. "Слідчі розглядають 4 версії вибухів на складі боєприпасів під Вінницею." September 2017. https://hromadske.ua/posts/slidchi-rozhliadaiut-4-versii-vybukhiv-na-skladi-boieprypasiv-pid-vynnytseiu.

Hromadske.ua. "Тероризм чи недбалість: як в Україні розслідуються вибухи на військових складах." October 2018. https://hromadske.ua/posts/iak-v-ukraini-rozsliduiutsia-vybukhy-na-viiskovykh-skladakh.

Hromadske.ua. "У Ніч На 24 Лютого На Україну Була Здійснена Кібератака—Федоров." *Громадське Радіо*, February 2022. https://hromadske.radio/news/2022/02/24/u-nich-na-24-liutoho-na-ukrainu-bula-zdiysnena-kiberataka-fedorov.

Hulcoop, Adam, John Scott-Railton, Peter Tanchak, Matt Brooks, and Ron Deibert. "Tainted Leaks: Disinformation and Phishing with a Russian Nexus." May 2017. https://citizenlab.ca/2017/05/tainted-leaks-disinformation-phish/.

Hulnick, Arthur S. "What's Wrong with the Intelligence Cycle?" In *Strategic Intelligence*, Vol. 2: *The Intelligence Cycle*, edited by Loch K. Johnson, 959–979. Westport, CT: Praeger Security International, 2007.

"Industroyer2: Industroyer Reloaded." *We Live Security* (blog), April 2022. https://www.welivesecurity.com/2022/04/12/industroyer2-industroyer-reloaded/.

Inform Napalm. "FrolovLeaks: Church-Going Kremlin Influence Expert in Ukraine. Episode 1." *Inform Napalm*. (English) (blog), January 2017. https://informnapalm.org/en/frolovleaks-church-going-kremlin-influence-expert-in-ukraine-episode-1/.

Inform Napalm. "Why Surkov Needs Private Army: Union of Donbas Volunteers (UDV) as Reserve of National Guard of Russia." *Inform Napalm*. (English) (blog), April 2017. https://informnapalm.org/en/surkov-needs-private-army-union-donbas-volunteers-reserve-russian-guard/.

"Information on the Possible Provocation." Accessed February 3, 2022. https://cip.gov.ua/en/news/informaciya-shodo-imovirnoyi-provokaciyi.

Interfax. "Kakhovka-Titan Power Transmission Line Feeding Crimea Fixed." Russia Beyond, January 2016. https://www.rbth.com/news/2016/01/02/kakhovka-titan-power-transmission-line-feeding-crimea-fixed_557037.

Interfax-Ukraine. "Kolesnichenko Denies Combining His Parliamentary Work with Advocac." *Kyiv Post*, March 5, 2013. https://www.kyivpost.com/article/content/verkhovna-rada/kolesnichenko-denies-combining-his-parliamentary-work-with-advocacy-321307.html.

Interfax-Ukraine. "Minsk Contact Group Reaches Agreement on Complete Ceasefire in Donbas, Starting from Easter." April 2016. https://en.interfax.com.ua/news/general/340994.html.

International Energy Agency. "Statistics: World—Total Primary Energy Supply (TPES) by Source (Chart)." Accessed May 11, 2019. https://www.iea.org/statistics/?country=WORLD&year=2016&category=Energy%20supply&indicator=TPESbySource&mode=chart&dataTable=BALANCES.

iSight. "ISIGHT Discovers Zero-Day Vulnerability CVE-2014-4114 Used in Russian Cyber-Espionage Campaign." October 2014. https://web.archive.org/web/20141015001101/https://www.isightpartners.com/2014/10/cve-2014-4114/.

Jamieson, Kathleen Hall. *Cyberwar: How Russian Hackers and Trolls Helped Elect a President What We Don't, Can't, and Do Know*. New York: Oxford University Press, 2018.

Jensen, Benjamin, and J. D. Work. "Cyber Civil-Military Relations: Balancing Interests on the Digital Frontier." *War on the Rocks*, September 2018. https://warontherocks.com/2018/09/cyber-civil-military-relations-balancing-interests-on-the-digital-frontier/.

Jervis, Robert. *Perception and Misperception in International Politics: New Edition*. Princeton, NJ: Princeton University Press, 2017. https://doi.org/10.2307/j.ctvc77bx3.

Johnson, Loch K. "On Drawing a Bright Line for Covert Operations." *American Journal of International Law* 86, no. 2 (1992): 284–309. https://doi.org/10.2307/2203235.

Johnson, Loch K., and James J. Wirtz, eds. *Intelligence: The Secret World of Spies: An Anthology*. 4th ed. Oxford: Oxford University Press, 2015.

Jönsson, Christopher. "Diplomacy, Bargaining and Negotiation." In *Handbook of International Relations*, 2nd ed., edited by Walter Carlsnaes, Thomas Risse-Kappen, and Beth A. Simmons, 212–234. Los Angeles: Sage, 2013.

Kalugin, Oleg. *Spymaster: My Thirty-Two Years in Intelligence and Espionage against the West*. New York: Basic Books, 2009.

Kapsamun, Ivan. "СБУ Проти ФСБ." April 2015. https://day.kyiv.ua/uk/article/podrobyci/sbu-proty-fsb.

Kaspersky. "Bad Rabbit Ransomware." October 2017. https://securelist.com/bad-rabbit-ransomware/82851/.

Kaspersky. "BE2 Custom Plugins, Router Abuse, and Target Profiles." November 2014. https://securelist.com/be2-custom-plugins-router-abuse-and-target-profiles/67353/.

Kello, Lucas. "The Meaning of the Cyber Revolution: Perils to Theory and Statecraft." *International Security* 38, no. 2 (2013): 7–40.

Kello, Lucas. *The Virtual Weapon and International Order*. New Haven, CT: Yale University Press, 2017.

KGB Ukrainian SSR. "F.16.Op.01-Spr.0974-0338." July 1968. Archive Department of the Security Service of Ukraine—Former KGB Archive.

KGB Ukrainian SSR. "F.16-Op.01-Spr.0976-0244." July 1968. Archive Department of the Security Service of Ukraine—Former KGB Archive.

KGB Ukrainian SSR. "F.16-Op.01-Spr.0979-0056." October 1968. Archive Department of the Security Service of Ukraine—Former KGB Archive.

KGB Ukrainian SSR. "F.16-Op.01-Spr.0979-0079." September 1968. Archive Department of the Security Service of Ukraine—Former KGB Archive.

KGB Ukrainian SSR. "F.16-Op.01-Spr.0979-0267." October 1968. Archive Department of the Security Service of Ukraine—Former KGB Archive.

KGB Ukrainian SSR. "F.16-Op.01-Spr.0981-0350." December 1968. Archive Department of the Security Service of Ukraine—Former KGB Archive.

KGB Ukrainian SSR. "F.16-Op.01-Spr.0982-0410." January 1969. Archive Department of the Security Service of Ukraine—Former KGB Archive.

Kiepova, Darya. "Потужна Кібератака На Укртелеком Вивела з Ладу Інтернет." Зеркало недели: Дзеркало тижня, *Mirror Weekly*, March 2022. https://zn.ua/ukr/TECHNOLOGIES/potuzhna-kiberataka-na-ukrtelekom-vivela-z-ladu-internet.html.

KIIS. "Press Releases and Reports—Consequences of Ukraine's Accession to Integration Associations." November 2013. http://kiis.com.ua/?lang=eng&cat=reports&id=206&page=31&t=3.

KIIS. "Press Releases and Reports—'The European Union' and 'the Customs Union.'" March 2013. http://kiis.com.ua/?lang=eng&cat=reports&id=186&page=32&t=3.

KIIS. "Press Releases and Reports—Trust in Social Institutions and Parties." December 2020. https://kiis.com.ua/?lang=eng&cat=reports&id=1005.

KIIS. "Press Releases and Reports—Trust in Social Institutions and Social Groups." 2015. https://kiis.com.ua/?lang=eng&cat=reports&id=579.

KIIS. "Press Releases and Reports—Trust to Social Institutes." December 2018. https://www.kiis.com.ua/?lang=eng&cat=reports&id=817&page=2.

KIIS. "Press Releases and Reports—Trust to Social Institutions." 2016. https://www.kiis.com.ua/?lang=eng&cat=reports&id=678.

Kissinger, Henry. *Diplomacy*. New York: Simon & Schuster, 1995.

Kitson, Frank. *Low Intensity Operations: Subversion, Insurgency, Peacekeeping*. London: Faber, 1971.

Klimkovetsky, Markiyan. "СБУ Разоблачила Еще Одного Агента Спецслужб Рф: Планировал Подрывную Деятельность Во Львовской Области." May 2022. https://hromadske.ua/ru/posts/sbu-razoblachila-eshe-odnogo-agenta-specsluzhb-rf-planiroval-podryvnuyu-deyatelnost-vo-lvovskoj-oblasti.

KMU. "Кабінет Міністрів України—Щодо роботи інформаційно-телекомунікаційної системи Казначейства." December 2016. https://www.kmu.gov.ua/ua/news/249559690.

Kofman, Michael, Kltya Migacheva, Brian Nichiporuk, Andrew Radin, Olseya Tkacheva, and Jenny Oberholtzer. *Lessons from Russia's Operations in Crimea and Eastern Ukraine*. Santa Monica, CA: RAND, 2017.

Kofman, Michael, and Matthew Rojansky. "A Closer Look at Russia's 'Hybrid War.'" *Kennan Cable* 7 (2015). https://www.wilsoncenter.org/sites/default/files/media/documents/publication/7-KENNAN%20CABLE-ROJANSKY%20KOFMAN.pdf

Koremenos, Barbara, Charles Lipson, and Duncan Snidal. "The Rational Design of International Institutions." *International Organization* 55, no. 4 (Autumn 2001): 761–799.

Kostyuk, Nadiya, and Yuri M. Zhukov. "Invisible Digital Front: Can Cyber Attacks Shape Battlefield Events?" *Journal of Conflict Resolution* 63, no. 2 (2017): 317–347. https://doi.org/10.1177/0022002717737138.

Kott, Alexander, and Ethan Stump. "Intelligent Autonomous Things on the Battlefield." In *Artificial Intelligence for the Internet of Everything*, edited by William Lawless, Ranjeev Mittu, Donald Sofge, Ira S. Moskowitz, and Stephen Russell, 47–65. London, UK: Academic Press, 2019. https://doi.org/10.1016/B978-0-12-817636-8.00003-X.

Kovacs, Eduard. "Files Encrypted by Bad Rabbit Recoverable without Paying Ransom." Security Week, October 2017. https://www.securityweek.com/files-encrypted-bad-rabbit-recoverable-without-paying-ransom.

Koval, Nikolay. "Revolution Hacking." In *Cyber War in Perspective: Russian Aggression against Ukraine*, edited by Kenneth Geers, 55–58. Tallinn, Estonia: NATO Cooperative Cyber Defence Centre of Excellence, 2015. https://ccdcoe.org/sites/default/files/multimedia/pdf/CyberWarinPerspective_full_book.pdf.

Kovalchuk, Vsevolod. "Цієї Ночі На Підстанції 'Північна' Відбувся Збій . . .—Vsevolod Kovalchuk." December 2016. https://www.facebook.com/permalink.php?story_fbid=1798082313797621&id=100007876094707.

Kramer, Andrew E. "Bomb Kills Pro-Russian Rebel Commander in Eastern Ukraine." *New York Times*, 17 October 2016, sec. World. https://www.nytimes.com/2016/10/18/world/europe/ukraine-rebel-arsen-pavlov-motorola-killed.html.

Krämer, Bernd J. "Evolution of Cyber-Physical Systems: A Brief Review." In *Applied Cyber-Physical Systems*, edited by Sang C. Suh, U. John Tanik, John N. Carbone, and Abdullah Eroglu, 1–4. New York: Springer New York, 2014. https://doi.org/10.1007/978-1-4614-7336-7.

Kraminska, Margarita. "Росія не погоджується укласти договір на постачання електроенергії до Криму через формулювання—М.Джемілєв." *UNN*. Accessed November 24, 2022. https://www.unn.com.ua/uk/news/1537754-rosiya-ne-pogodzhuyetsya-uklasti-dogovir-na-postachannya-elektroenergiyi-do-krimu-cherez-formuluvannya-m-dzhemilyev.

Kraus, Jürgen. "Selbstreproduktion Bei Programmen." Diploma thesis, Universität Dortmund, 1980. http://83.133.184.251/virensimulation.org/lib/mjk00.html.

Kremlin. "Address by President of the Russian Federation." President of Russia, March 2014. http://en.kremlin.ru/events/president/news/20603.

Kremlin. "Подписан Указ о Признании Республики Крым." Президент России, March 2014. http://kremlin.ru/events/president/news/20596.

Kuehl, Daniel T. "From Cyberspace to Cyberpower: Defining the Problem." In *Cyberpower and National Security*, edited by Franklin D. Kramer, Stuart H. Starr, Larry K. Wentz, 24–42. Washington, DC: Potomac Books, 2009.

Kun, Miklós. *Prague Spring, Prague Fall: Blank Spots of 1968*. Budapest: Akadémiai Kiadó, 1999.

Kusin, Vladimir V. *From Dubček to Charter 77: A Study of "Normalization" in Czechoslovakia, 1968–1978*. New York: St. Martin's Press, 1978.

Kuzmenko, Oleksiy. "Think Tank: Cyber Firm at Center of Russian Hacking Charges Misread Data." *VOA*, 2017. https://www.voanews.com/a/crowdstrike-comey-russia-hack-dnc-clinton-trump/3776067.html.

Kuznetsova, Katerina. "'ПриватБанк' Та 'Ощадбанк' Повністю Відновили Роботу Після Другої Потужної Кібератаки." *TCH.Ua*, February 2022. https://tsn.ua/ukrayina/privatbank-ta-oschadbank-povnistyu-vidnovili-robotu-pislya-drugoyi-potuzhnoyi-kiberataki-1979029.html.

Kuznetsova, Kateryna. "Найпотужніша Кібератака За Всю Історію України: Ціль Хакерів, Кого Підозрюють і Які Наслідки Для Держави." *TCH.Ua*, February 2022. https://tsn.ua/ukrayina/naypotuzhnisha-kiberataka-za-vsyu-istoriyu-ukrayini-cil-hakeriv-kogo-pidozryuyut-i-yaki-naslidki-dlya-derzhavi-1979239.html.

Lally, Kathy, Will Englund, and William Booth. "Russian Parliament Approves Use of Troops in Ukraine." *Washington Post*, March 1, 2014, sec. Europe. https://www.washingtonpost.com/world/europe/russian-parliament-approves-use-of-troops-in-crimea/2014/03/01/d1775f70-a151-11e3-a050-dc3322a94fa7_story.html.

Landau, Susan. "Russia's Hybrid Warriors Got the White House. Now They're Coming for America's Town Halls." *Foreign Policy* (blog), 2017. https://foreignpolicy.com/2017/09/26/russias-hybrid-warriors-are-coming-for-american-civil-society-hacking-trump-clinton/.

Langner, Ralph. "To Kill a Centrifuge." November 2013. https://www.langner.com/wp-content/uploads/2017/03/to-kill-a-centrifuge.pdf.

Lanoszka, Alexander. "Russian Hybrid Warfare and Extended Deterrence in Eastern Europe." *International Affairs* 92, no. 1 (January 2016): 175–195. https://doi.org/10.1111/1468-2346.12509.

Lawson, Sean. "Beyond Cyber-Doom: Assessing the Limits of Hypothetical Scenarios in the Framing of Cyber-Threats." *Journal of Information Technology & Politics* 10, no. 1 (2013): 86–103. https://doi.org/10.1080/19331681.2012.759059.

Lawson, Sean, and Michael K. Middleton. "Cyber Pearl Harbor: Analogy, Fear, and the Framing of Cyber Security Threats in the United States, 1991–2016." *First Monday*, March 2019. https://doi.org/10.5210/fm.v24i3.9623.

Lee, Melissa M. *Crippling Leviathan: How Foreign Subversion Weakens the State*. Ithaca, NY: Cornell University Press, 2020.

Lessig, Lawrence. "Code Is Law." January 2000. http://harvardmagazine.com/2000/01/code-is-law-html.

"Lessons from Russia's Cyber-War in Ukraine." *The Economist*, November 30, 2022. https://www.economist.com/science-and-technology/2022/11/30/lessons-from-russias-cyber-war-in-ukraine.

Levin, Dov H. *Meddling in the Ballot Box: The Causes and Effects of Partisan Electoral Interventions*. New York: Oxford University Press, 2020.
Levy, Jack S. "The Causes of War and the Conditions of Peace." *Annual Review of Political Science* 1, no. 1 (1998): 139–165. https://doi.org/10.1146/annurev.polisci.1.1.139.
Leyden, John. "FedEx: TNT NotPetya Infection Blew a $300m Hole in Our Numbers." September 2017. https://www.theregister.co.uk/2017/09/20/fedex_notpetya_damages/.
Leyden, John. "Hop on, Average Rabbit: Latest Extortionware Menace Flopped." October 2017. https://www.theregister.co.uk/2017/10/26/bad_rabbit_post_mortem/.
Libicki, Martin C. *Cyberdeterrence and Cyberwar*. Santa Monica, CA: Rand, 2009.
Libiseller, Chiara. "'Hybrid Warfare' as an Academic Fashion." *Journal of Strategic Studies* 46, no. 4 (February 2023): 858–880. https://doi.org/10.1080/01402390.2023.2177987.
Liff, Adam P. "Cyberwar: A New 'Absolute Weapon'? The Proliferation of Cyberwarfare Capabilities and Interstate War." *Journal of Strategic Studies* 35, no. 3 (June 2012): 401–428. https://doi.org/10.1080/01402390.2012.663252.
Lindsay, Jon R. "The Impact of China on Cybersecurity: Fiction and Friction." *International Security* 39, no. 3 (2014): 7–47.
Lindsay, Jon R. "Restrained by Design: The Political Economy of Cybersecurity." *Digital Policy, Regulation and Governance* 19, no. 6 (July 2017): 493–514. https://doi.org/10.1108/DPRG-05-2017-0023.
Lindsay, Jon R. "Stuxnet and the Limits of Cyber Warfare." *Security Studies* 22, no. 3 (2013): 365–404. https://doi.org/10.1080/09636412.2013.816122.
Lindsay, Jon R., and Erik Gartzke. "Coercion through Cyberspace: The Stability-Instability Paradox Revisited." In *The Power to Hurt: Coercion in Theory and in Practice*, edited by Peter Krause, 179–203. New York: Oxford University Press, 2018.
Lipsky, Andrei. "«Представляется Правильным Инициировать Присоединение Восточных Областей Украины к России»." *Новая Газета—Novayagazeta.Ru*, February 2015. https://www.novayagazeta.ru/articles/2015/02/24/63168-171-predstavlyaetsya-pravilnym-initsiirovat-prisoedinenie-vostochnyh-oblastey-ukrainy-k-rossii-187.
Littell, Robert, ed. *The Czech Black Book*. Westport, CT: Praeger, 1968.
Loiko, Sergei L. "Ukraine Cracks down on Demonstrators; Russia Issues Warning." *Latimes.com*, 2014. https://www.latimes.com/world/worldnow/la-fg-wn-ukraine-raid-russia-supporters-20140408-story.html.
Losh, Jack. "Ukrainian Rebel Leaders Divided by Bitter Purge." *Washington Post*. 3 October 2016. https://www.washingtonpost.com/world/europe/ukrainian-rebel-leaders-divided-by-bitter-purge/2016/10/03/2e0076ac-8429-11e6-b57d-dd49277af02f_story.html.
Low, A. Maurice. "The Vice of Secret Diplomacy." *North American Review* 207, no. 747 (1918): 209–220.
Lukes, Steven. *Power: A Radical View*. 2nd ed. Houndmills, Basingstoke, Hampshire: Palgrave Macmillan, 2004.
Lynn, William J., III. "Defending a New Domain." *Foreign Affairs*, 2010. https://www.foreignaffairs.com/articles/united-states/2010-09-01/defending-new-domain.
Mahoney, James, and Kathleen Ann Thelen, eds. *Explaining Institutional Change: Ambiguity, Agency, and Power*. Cambridge: Cambridge University Press, 2010.
Malwarebytes. "Keeping Up with the Petyas: Demystifying the Malware Family." Malwarebytes Labs, July 2017. https://blog.malwarebytes.com/cybercrime/2017/07/keeping-up-with-the-petyas-demystifying-the-malware-family/.

MalwareHunterTeam (@malwrhunterteam). "XData Is Still Going, Even Closer to Cerber's 24 Hours Numbers . . . Pic.Twitter.Com/Yq0A0Dhoyq." Twitter, May 2017. https://twitter.com/malwrhunterteam/status/865618366412849157.

Mandiant. "UNC1151 Assessed with High Confidence to Have Links to Belarus, Ghostwriter Campaign Aligned with Belarusian Government Interests." November 2021. https://www.mandiant.com/resources/unc1151-linked-to-belarus-government.

March, James G., and Johan P. Olsen. "The Institutional Dynamics of International Political Orders." *International Organization* 52, no. 4 (1998): 943–969.

Marczak, Bill, and John Scott-Railton. "The Million Dollar Dissident: NSO Group's iPhone Zero-Days Used against a UAE Human Rights Defender." *Citizen Lab* (blog), August 2016. https://citizenlab.org/2016/08/million-dollar-dissident-iphone-zero-day-nso-group-uae/.

Mark, Melvin M., Fred B. Bryant, and Darrin R. Lehman. "Perceived Injustice and Sports Violence." In *Sports Violence*, Springer Series in Social Psychology, edited by Jeffrey H. Goldstein, 83–109. New York: Springer New York, 1983. https://doi.org/10.1007/978-1-4612-5530-7_6.

Martin, David. "Russian Hacking Proves Lethal after Ukrainian Military App Hijacked." December 2016. https://www.cbsnews.com/news/russian-hacking-proves-lethal-after-ukrainian-military-app-compromised/.

Martynets, Sergey. "США підозрюють Росію у причетності до кібератак на українські електромережі." Інформаційне агентство Українські Національні Новини (УНН). Всі онлайн новини дня в Україні за сьогодні—найсвіжіші, останні, головні, January 2016. https://www.unn.com.ua/uk/news/1536191-ssha-pidozryuyut-rosiyu-u-prichetnosti-do-kiberatak-na-ukrayinski-elektromerezhi.

Maschmeyer, Lennart. "A New and Better Quiet Option? Strategies of Subversion and Cyber Conflict." *Journal of Strategic Studies* 46, no. 3 (2023): 570–594. https://doi.org/10.1080/01402390.2022.2104253.

Maschmeyer, Lennart. "Subversion, Cyber Operations, and Reverse Structural Power in World Politics." *European Journal of International Relations* 29, no. 1 (March 2023): 79–103. https://doi.org/10.1177/13540661221117051.

Maschmeyer, Lennart. "The Subversive Trilemma: Why Cyber Operations Fall Short of Expectations." *International Security* 46, no. 2 (October 2021): 51–90. https://doi.org/10.1162/isec_a_00418.

Maschmeyer, Lennart. "Subverting Skynet: The Strategic Promise of Lethal Autonomous Weapons and the Perils of Exploitation." In *2022 14th International Conference on Cyber Conflict: Keep Moving! (CyCon)*, vol. 700, 2022, 155–171. https://doi.org/10.23919/CyCon55549.2022.9811008.

Maschmeyer, Lennart, Alexei Abrahams, Peter Pomerantsev, and Volodymyr Yermolenko. "Donetsk Don't Tell—'Hybrid War' in Ukraine and the Limits of Social Media Influence Operations." *Journal of Information Technology and Politics* (2023). https://doi.org/10.1080/19331681.2023.2211969.

Maschmeyer, Lennart, Ronald J. Deibert, and Jon R. Lindsay. "A Tale of Two Cybers—How Threat Reporting by Cybersecurity Firms Systematically Underrepresents Threats to Civil Society." *Journal of Information Technology & Politics* 18, no. 1 (January 2021): 1–20. https://doi.org/10.1080/19331681.2020.1776658.

"Massive Power Outage Hits Crimea." Radio Free Europe/Radio Liberty, 2018. https://www.rferl.org/a/massive-power-outages-hit-crimea-cause-unclear/29288821.html.

Matveeva, Anna. *Through Times of Trouble: Conflict in Southeastern Ukraine Explained from Within*, Russian, Eurasian, and Eastern European Politics. Lanham, MD: Lexington Books, 2018.

Matyash, Tanya. "Зеленський Відсторонив Венедіктову Та Усунув Баканова." LB.ua, July 2022. https://lb.ua/news/2022/07/17/523439_zelenskiy_vidstoroniv_venedikt ovu.html.

Maundrill, Beth. "Why Russia Has Refrained from a Major Cyber-Attack against the West." Cyber Security Hub, June 2022. https://www.cshub.com/attacks/articles/why-russia-has-refrained-from-a-cyber-attack-against-the-west.

Maymí, Fernando, and Scott Lathrop. "AI in Cyberspace: Beyond the Hype." *Cyber Defense Review* 3, no. 3 (2018): 71–82.

Mazarr, Michael J. "Mastering the Gray Zone: Understanding a Changing Era of Conflict." 2015. https://apps.dtic.mil/sti/citations/AD1000186.

McCarthy, Tom, and Alan Yuhas. "Ukraine Crisis: Kiev Launches 'Anti-Terror Operation' in East—Live Updates." *The Guardian*, April 15, 2014. https://www.theguardian.com/world/2014/apr/15/ukraine-military-forces-russia-live-blog.

McClain, Dylan Loeb. "Ludek Pachman, 78, Chess Star Imprisoned after 'Prague Spring.'" *New York Times*, March 13, 2003, sec. World. https://www.nytimes.com/2003/03/13/world/ludek-pachman-78-chess-star-imprisoned-after-prague-spring.html.

McKinsey. "Insider Threat: The Human Element of Cyberrisk." 2019. https://www.mckin sey.com/business-functions/risk/our-insights/insider-threat-the-human-element-of-cyberrisk.

McKune, Sarah, Ronald Deibert, Bill Marczak, Geoffrey Alexander, and John Scott-Railton. "Commercial Spyware: The Multibillion Dollar Industry Built on an Ethical and Legal Quagmire." Citizen Lab, December 2017. https://citizenlab.ca/2017/12/legal-overview-ethiopian-dissidents-targeted-spyware/.

McSherry, J. Patrice. *Predatory States: Operation Condor and Covert War in Latin America*. Lanham, MD: Rowman & Littlefield Publishers, 2012.

Mearsheimer, John J. "The False Promise of International Institutions." *International Security* 19, no. 3 (1994): 5–49. https://doi.org/10.2307/2539078.

Mendel, Iuliia. "In Ukraine, a Huge Ammunition Depot Catches Fire." *New York Times*, 27 September 2017, sec. World. https://www.nytimes.com/2017/09/27/world/europe/ukraine-ammunition-depot-explosion.html.

Menon, Rajan, and Eugene B. Rumer. *Conflict in Ukraine: The Unwinding of the Post-Cold War Order*, Boston Review Originals. Cambridge, MA: MIT Press, 2015.

Michels, Eckard. *Guillaume, Der Spion: Eine Deutsch-Deutsche Karriere*. Berlin: Ch. Links Verlag, 2013.

Microsoft. "Destructive Malware Targeting Ukrainian Organizations." *Microsoft Security Blog* (blog), January 2022. https://www.microsoft.com/security/blog/2022/01/15/dest ructive-malware-targeting-ukrainian-organizations/.

Miller, Greg, and Catherine Belton. "Russia's Spies Misread Ukraine and Misled Kremlin as War Loomed." *Washington Post*, August 2022. https://www.washingtonpost.com/world/interactive/2022/russia-fsb-intelligence-ukraine-war/.

Miller, Maggie. "Russian Invasion of Ukraine Could Redefine Cyber Warfare." Politico, January 2022. https://www.politico.com/news/2022/01/28/russia-cyber-army-ukra ine-00003051.

Min, Byungho, and Vijay Varadharajan. "A Novel Malware for Subversion of Self-Protection in Anti-Virus." *Software: Practice and Experience* 46, no. 3 (2016): 361–379. https://doi.org/10.1002/spe.2317.

Mingas, Melanie. "Ukrtelecom Restores 85% of Services after 'Powerful Cyberattack.'" *Capacity Media* (blog), March 2022. https://www.capacitymedia.com/article/29wch9 71qqy0z3dyifx8g/ukrtelecom-restores-85-of-services-after-powerful-cyberattack.

MKA Cyber. "Maersk Replaces IT Infrastructure After NotPetya Ransomware Infection." *MKACyber, Inc.* (blog), January 2018. https://mkacyber.io/news/maersk-shipping-rein stalled-entire-infrastructure-after-notpetya-ransomware/.

Morgenthau, Hans J. *Politics among Nations: The Struggle for Power and Peace*. New York: Alfred A. Knopf, 1948.

Motyl, Alexander J. "The Weakness of Eastern Ukraine's pro-Russian Separatists." *Al Jazeera*, April 2014. http://america.aljazeera.com/opinions/2014/4/eastern-ukraine-prorussianseparatistsdonetskdonbas.html.

Mueller, Robert S., III. "Report on the Investigation into Russian Interference in the 2016 Presidential Election." March 2019. https://www.justice.gov/storage/report.pdf.

Myers, Philip A. "Subversion: The Neglected Aspect of Computer Security." Master's thesis, Naval Postgraduate School, 1980.

Nakasone, Paul M. "A Cyber Force for Persistent Operations." *Joint Force Quarterly* 92 (2019): 10–14.

"Natanz Enrichment Complex." *Nuclear Threat Initiative* (blog). Accessed January 7, 2022. https://www.nti.org/education-center/facilities/natanz-enrichment-complex/.

National Cyber Security Centre. "Reckless Campaign of Cyber Attacks by Russian Military Intelligence Service Exposed." October 2018. https://www.ncsc.gov.uk/news/reckless-campaign-cyber-attacks-russian-military-intelligence-service-exposed.

NATO. "Closing Press Conference by NATO Secretary General Jens Stoltenberg Following the Meetings of NATO Foreign Ministers in Antalya, Turkey." May 2015. http://www.nato.int/cps/en/natohq/opinions_119432.htm.

NATO. "Keynote Address by NATO Secretary General at the NATO Cyber Defence Pledge Conference." November 2022. https://www.nato.int/cps/en/natohq/opinions_208925.htm.

Navrátil, Jaromír. *The Prague Spring 1968: A National Security Archive Documents Reader*. Budapest: Central European University Press, 1998.

Nechepurenko, Ivan. "Crimea to Face Power Shortages for Months, Officials Say." *New York Times*, 8 January 2016, sec. World. https://www.nytimes.com/2016/01/09/world/europe/crimea-power-ukraine-russia.html.

Nechepurenko, Ivan, and Neil MacFarquhar. "As Sabotage Blacks Out Crimea, Tatars Prevent Repairs." *New York Times*, November 24, 2015, sec. Europe. https://www.nyti mes.com/2015/11/24/world/europe/crimea-tatar-power-lines-ukraine.html.

Nekrasov, Vsevolod. "Украина Проигрывает Кибервойну. Хакеры Наносят Удар По Минфину." Экономическая правда, December 2016. http://www.epravda.com.ua/rus/publications/2016/12/9/613957/.

NetBlocks (@netblocks). Twitter, February 2022. "i Commercial satellite operator Viasat is investigating a suspected cyberattack that caused a partial outage of its KA-SAT network in Europe.

Network data indicate that the incident began on 24 February ~4 a.m. UTC and is currently ongoing ▓", https://twitter.com/netblocks/status/1498365220107997191.

NetBlocks (@netblocks). Twitter, March 2022. "⚠ Confirmed: A major internet disruption has been registered across #Ukraine on national provider #Ukrtelecom; real-time network data show connectivity collapsing to 13% of pre-war levels; the provider reports issues assigning new sessions 📊 Background: https://netblocks.org/reports/

internet-disruptions-registered-as-russia-moves-in-on-ukraine-W80p4k8K," https://twitter.com/netblocks/status/1508453511176065033.

NetBlocks (@netblocks). Twitter, March 2022. "⚠ Update: Ukraine's national internet provider Ukrtelecom has confirmed a cyberattack on its core infrastructure. Real-time network data show an ongoing and intensifying nation-scale disruption to service, which is the most severe registered since the invasion by Russia." https://twitter.com/netblocks/status/1508465391244304389.

New Voice of Ukraine. "Why Zelenskyy Removed the Heads of the SBU and PGO." July 2022. https://english.nv.ua/nation/why-zelenskyy-sacked-the-prosecutor-general-and-sbu-chief-ukraine-news-50257409.html.

NIKCENTER. "Веб-сайти Кабміна не открываются—Минцифры сообщают о массовой DDoS-атаке." February 2022. https://nikcenter.org/newsItem/65950.

NPR. "Ukrainian Servicemen Reported Shot by Masked Soldiers In Crimea." *NPR*, March 2014. https://www.npr.org/sections/thetwo-way/2014/03/18/291148781/ukrainian-servicemen-reported-shot-by-masked-soldiers-in-crimea.

Nye, Joseph S. "Deterrence and Dissuasion in Cyberspace." *International Security* 41, no. 3 (January 2017): 44–71. https://doi.org/10.1162/ISEC_a_00266.

Nye, Joseph S. *The Future of Power*. New York: PublicAffairs, 2011.

Nye, Joseph S. "Soft Power." *Foreign Policy*, no. 80 (Autumn 1990): 153–171. https://doi.org/10.2307/1148580.

Obozrevatel. "Після кібератаки на 'Прикарпаттяобленерго' в США переглянуть захист енергомереж." *Політика*, January 2016. https://www.obozrevatel.com/ukr/news/58420-pislya-kiberataki-na-prikarpattyaoblenergo-v-ssha-pereglyanut-zahist-energomerezh.htm.

Oksamytna, Ksenya. "Ukraine: Russian Attitudes to Ukrainians Can Help to Explain the Atrocities." King's College London, June 2022. https://www.kcl.ac.uk/ukraine-russian-attitudes-to-ukrainians-can-help-to-explain-the-atrocities.

Oliphant, Roland, and Charlotte Krol. "Huge Explosion at Ukraine Ammunition Depot Prompts Mass Evacuation." *The Telegraph*, September 2017. https://www.telegraph.co.uk/news/2017/09/27/fire-ukraine-ammunition-depot-prompts-mass-evacuation/.

Oliveria, Paul. "New 'Prestige' Ransomware Impacts Organizations in Ukraine and Poland." *Microsoft Security Blog* (blog), October 2022. https://www.microsoft.com/en-us/security/blog/2022/10/14/new-prestige-ransomware-impacts-organizations-in-ukraine-and-poland/.

O'Rourke, Lindsey A. *Covert Regime Change: America's Secret Cold War*, Cornell Studies in Security Affairs. Ithaca, NY: Cornell University Press, 2018.

Osborn, Andrew, Polina Nikolskaya, and Polina Nikolskaya. "Russia's Putin Authorises 'Special Military Operation' against Ukraine." Reuters, February 2022, sec. Europe. https://www.reuters.com/world/europe/russias-putin-authorises-military-operations-donbass-domestic-media-2022-02-24/.

OSCE. "International Election Observation Mission." May 2014. https://www.osce.org/odihr/elections/ukraine/119078?download=true.

Office of Strategic Services. "Simple Sabotage Field Manual." 17 January 1944, Washington D.C. https://www.cia.gov/static/5c875f3ec660e092cf893f60b4a288df/SimpleSabotage.pdf

Ouimet, Matthew J. "Reconsidering the Soviet Role." In *The Prague Spring and the Warsaw Pact Invasion of Czechoslovakia, 1968: Forty Years Later*, edited by M. Mark Stolarik, 19–29. Mundelein, IL: Bolchazy-Carducci Publishers, 2010.

Pagliery, Jose. "Scary Questions in Ukraine Energy Grid Hack." *CNNMoney*, January 18, 2016. https://money.cnn.com/2016/01/18/technology/ukraine-hack-russia/index.html.

Pape, Robert A. *Bombing to Win: Air Power and Coercion in War*. Ithaca and London: Cornell University Press, 1996.

Peisakhin, Leonid, and Arturas Rozenas. "Electoral Effects of Biased Media: Russian Television in Ukraine." *American Journal of Political Science* 62, no. 3 (2018): 535–550. https://doi.org/10.1111/ajps.12355.

Perlroth, Nicole, and David E. Sanger. "Cyberattacks Put Russian Fingers on the Switch at Power Plants, U.S. Says." *New York Times*, March 15, 2018, sec. U.S. https://www.nytimes.com/2018/03/15/us/politics/russia-cyberattacks.html.

Peterson, Dale. "Offensive Cyber Weapons: Construction, Development, and Employment." *Journal of Strategic Studies* 36, no. 1 (2013): 120–124. https://doi.org/10.1080/01402390.2012.742014.

Petrov, Nikita. "The KGB and the Czechoslovak Crisis of 1968." In *The Prague Spring and the Warsaw Pact Invasion of Czechoslovakia in 1968*, Harvard Cold War Studies Book Series, edited by Günter Bischof, Stefan Karner, and Peter Ruggenthaler, 145–164. Lanham, MD: Lexington Books, 2010.

Polityuk, Pavel. "EXCLUSIVE: Ukraine Suspects Group Linked to Belarus Intelligence over Cyberattack." Reuters, January 2022, sec. Europe. https://www.reuters.com/world/europe/exclusive-ukraine-suspects-group-linked-belarus-intelligence-over-cyberattack-2022-01-15/.

Polityuk, Pavel. "Massive Cyberattack Hits Ukrainian Government Websites as West Warns on Russia Conflict." Reuters, January 2022, sec. Technology. https://www.reuters.com/technology/massive-cyberattack-hits-ukrainian-government-websites-amid-russia-tensions-2022-01-14/.

Pool, Ithiel De Sola. "Public Opinion in Czechoslovakia." *Public Opinion Quarterly* 34, no. 1 (1970): 10–25.

Poznansky, Michael. "Feigning Compliance: Covert Action and International Law." *International Studies Quarterly* 63, no. 1 (March 2019): 72–84. https://doi.org/10.1093/isq/sqy054.

Poznansky, Michael. *In the Shadow of International Law: Secrecy and Regime Change in the Postwar World*. Oxford: Oxford University Press, 2020.

Prados, John. *Safe for Democracy: The Secret Wars of the CIA*. (Chicago: Ivan R. Dee, 2006).

PResident.gov.ua. "Стратегічні Об'єкти Мають Бути Захищені, а Винні у Вибухах На Військових Складах Притягнуті До Відповідальності—Президент Щодо Ситуації Під Калинівкою." Офіційне інтернет-представництво Президента України, September 2017. https://www.president.gov.ua/news/strategichni-obyekti-mayut-buti-zahisheni-vinni-u-vibuhah-na-43610.

ProofPoint. "What Is Bad Rabbit Ransomware?" *Proofpoint* (blog), February 2021. https://www.proofpoint.com/us/threat-reference/bad-rabbit.

"Pro-Russia Forces Enter Ukraine Naval Base." *Al Jazeera*, March 2014. https://www.aljazeera.com/news/europe/2014/03/pro-russia-forces-enter-ukraine-naval-base-20143198741233396.html.

Prozumenshchikov, Mikhail. "Politburo Decision-Making on the Czechoslovak Crisis in 1968." In *The Prague Spring and the Warsaw Pact Invasion of Czechoslovakia in 1968*, Harvard Cold War Studies Book Series, edited by Günter Bischof, Stefan Karner, and Peter Ruggenthaler, 103–144. Lanham, MD: Lexington Books, 2010.

"Putin Says Crimea Now Free of Reliance on Kiev for Its Power." Reuters, May 2016. https://www.reuters.com/article/us-russia-crimea-power-idUSKCN0Y21K5.

"Putin Says Russia, Ukraine Torn Apart to Prevent Major Rival from Emerging." TASS. Accessed March 1, 2021. https://tass.com/politics/1122727.

Rácz, András. "Russia's Hybrid War in Ukraine." Finnish Institute of International Affairs, June 2015. https://www.fiia.fi/en/publication/russias-hybrid-war-in-ukraine.

Radkovets, Yuriy. "Lessons of Russia's 'Hybrid War' against Ukraine." Accessed March 23, 2020. http://bintel.com.ua/en/article/10-13-lessons/.

Rajivan, Prashanth, and Cleotilde Gonzalez. "Creative Persuasion: A Study on Adversarial Behaviors and Strategies in Phishing Attacks." *Frontiers in Psychology* 9 (February 2018), 1–14. https://doi.org/10.3389/fpsyg.2018.00135.

"Rebels Declare Victory in East Ukraine Vote on Self-Rule." Reuters, May 2014. https://www.reuters.com/article/us-ukraine-crisis-idUSBREA400LI20140511.

Reliaquest. "Threat Advisory: HermeticWiper." *Legacy* (blog), February 2022. https://www.reliaquest.com/i/blog/threat-advisory-hermeticwiper/.

Reuters Staff. "Ukraine, Separatists to Strive for Full Ceasefire from September 1." Reuters, August 2015. https://www.reuters.com/article/us-ukraine-crisis-ceasefire/ukraine-separatists-to-strive-for-full-ceasefire-from-september-1-idUSKCN0QV29A20150826.

ReverseMode. "VIASAT Incident: From Speculation to Technical Details." March 2022. https://www.reversemode.com/2022/03/viasat-incident-from-speculation-to.html.

Řezábek, J. "Let Us Pay Attention." *Mladá Fronta*, July 23, 1968.

Richelson, Jeffrey. *A Century of Spies: Intelligence in the Twentieth Century*. New York: Oxford University Press, 1995.

Rid, Thomas. *Active Measures: The Secret History of Disinformation and Political Warfare*. New York: Farrar, Straus and Giroux, 2020.

Rid, Thomas. *Cyber War Will Not Take Place*. Oxford: Oxford University Press, 2013.

RiskIQ. "Tracking the BadRabbit Ransomware to an Ongoing Campaign of Target Selection." October 2017. https://www.riskiq.com/blog/labs/badrabbit/.

Risse, Thomas. "'Let's Argue!': Communicative Action in World Politics." *International Organization* 54, no. 1 (2000): 1–39.

Romanosky, Sasha, and Benjamin Boudreaux. "Private-Sector Attribution of Cyber Incidents: Benefits and Risks to the U.S. Government." *International Journal of Intelligence and CounterIntelligence* 34, no. 0 (2021): 463–493. https://doi.org/10.1080/08850607.2020.1783877.

Rosen, Kenneth R. "The Man at the Center of the New Cyber World War." Politico, July 2022. https://www.politico.com/news/magazine/2022/07/14/russia-cyberattacks-ukraine-cybersecurity-00045486.

Ross, Stephen A. "The Economic Theory of Agency: The Principal's Problem." *American Economic Review* 63, no. 2 (1973): 134–139.

Roth, Florian, Pasquale Stirparo, David Bizeul, Brian Bell, Ziv Chang, Joel Esler, Kristopher Bleich, et al. "APT Groups and Operations." Accessed July 3, 2022. https://docs.google.com/spreadsheets/d/1H9_xaxQHpWaa4O_Son4Gx0YOIzlcBWMsdvePFX68EKU/edit?usp=embed_facebook.

Rovner, Joshua. "Cyber War as an Intelligence Contest." *War on the Rocks*, September 2019. https://warontherocks.com/2019/09/cyber-war-as-an-intelligence-contest/.

Rovner, Joshua. *Fixing the Facts: National Security and the Politics of Intelligence*. Ithaca and New York: Cornell University Press, 2011.

RSA. "Kingslayer—A Supply Chain Attack." 2017. http://www.rsa.com/en-us/blog/2017-02/kingslayer-a-supply-chain-attack.
Rudenko, Olga. "Separatist Crisis Flares Again Today in Ukraine's Eastern Regions." *Kyiv Post*, April 7, 2014. https://www.kyivpost.com/article/content/war-against-ukraine/separatist-crisis-flares-again-today-in-ukraines-eastern-regions-342351.html.
"Russia Accuses U.S. of Increasing Subversion." *Irish Times*, May 1968.
"Russia Decides to Impose Food Embargo against Ukraine—Minister." TASS, November 2015. http://tass.com/economy/837503.
"Russia Not Seeking Regime Change in Ukraine, People Should Have Freedom of Choice— Lavrov." TASS, April 2022. https://tass.com/politics/1439823.
"Russia Provided 5 Tons of Explosives and Weapons to Yanukovych in January to Disperse the Maidan." *Ukrainian Week*, April 2014. https://ukrainianweek.com/News/106701.
"Russia Says It Wants to End Ukraine's 'Unacceptable Regime.'" AP News, July 2022. https://apnews.com/article/russia-ukraine-zelenskyy-kyiv-black-sea-arab-league-b5c583e8d057897cfdef6b407e113339.
"Russia Takes Control of Chernobyl Nuclear Power Plant." *USA TODAY*, 25 February 2022. https://www.youtube.com/watch?v=lpYoxBTyRec.
"Russia: The FSB Branches Out." *Stratfor* (blog), 2008. https://worldview.stratfor.com/article/russia-fsb-branches-out.
Russia Today. "95.7% of Crimeans in Referendum Voted to Join Russia—Preliminary Results." *RT International*, March 2014. https://www.rt.com/news/crimea-vote-join-russia-210/.
Russia Today. "Bad Rabbit Cryptoware Attack: New Virus Hits Companies in Russia, Turkey, Germany & Ukraine." *RT International*, October 2017. https://www.rt.com/news/407655-bad-rabbit-cryptoware-attack/.
Russia Today. "US Blames Moscow for NotPetya Malware, Which Hit Russia Too." *RT International*, February 2018. https://www.rt.com/news/418955-us-blames-russia-notpetya-cyber-attack/.
"Russians Twice Tried to Storm Zelensky's Compound in Early Hours of War, Aide Says." *Times of Israel*, April 2022. https://www.timesofisrael.com/russians-twice-tried-to-storm-zelensky-compound-in-early-hours-of-war-report/.
"Russophone Identity in Ukraine." Ukraine Center for Independent Political Research, 2017. http://www.ucipr.org.ua/publicdocs/RussophoneIdentity_EN.pdf.
Saito, Mari, and Maria Tsvetkova. "How Russia Spread a Secret Web of Agents across Ukraine." Reuters. Accessed July 29, 2022. https://www.reuters.com/investigates/special-report/ukraine-crisis-russia-saboteurs/.
Salem, Harriet. "Kiev Hits Back at Pro-Russia Rebels as Ukraine Moves towards Civil War." *The Observer*, May 3, 2014, sec. World News. https://www.theguardian.com/world/2014/may/03/ukraine-civil-war-kiev-russia-slavyansk.
Sanger, David. *Confront and Conceal: Obama's Secret Wars and Surprising Use of American Power*. New York: Broadway Paperbacks, 2012.
Sanger, David E. *The Perfect Weapon: War, Sabotage, and Fear in the Cyber Age*. New York: Broadway Books, 2019.
SANS. "Analysis of the Cyber Attack on the Ukrainian Power Grid." March 2016.
"Satellite Outage Knocks out Thousands of Enercon's Wind Turbines." Reuters, February 2022, sec. Energy. https://www.reuters.com/business/energy/satellite-outage-knocks-out-control-enercon-wind-turbines-2022-02-28/.

Viasat Surfbeam 2+ KA-SAT Modem inkl. WLAN Router", Sat_Speed+, accessed January 13, 2023, https://web.archive.org/web/20200921120922/https://www.satspeed.com/internet-via-satellit/satellitemodem-tria-antenna/viasat-surfbeam-2plus-tooway-kasat-modem.html.

Satter, Raphael. "Satellite Outage Caused 'Huge Loss in Communications' at War's Outset—Ukrainian Official." Reuters, March 2022, sec. World. https://www.reuters.com/world/satellite-outage-caused-huge-loss-communications-wars-outset-ukrainian-official-2022-03-15/.

Satter, Raphael, and James Pearson. "Recent Ukraine Outage Caused by Modest Cyberattack, Data Shows." Reuters, February 2022, sec. Technology. https://www.reuters.com/technology/recent-ukraine-outage-caused-by-modest-cyberattack-data-shows-2022-02-17/.

SBU. "СБУ Викрила Агентурну Мережу ГРУ Рф, До Якої Входив Народний Депутат України (Відео)." SSU, June 2022. https://ssu.gov.ua/novyny/sbu-vykryla-ahenturnu-merezhu-hru-rf-do-yakoi-vkhodyv-narodnyi-deputat-ukrainy-video.

SBU. "СБУ Попередила Спробу Російських Спецслужб Вивести з Ладу Об'єкти Енергетики України." December 2015. https://web.archive.org/web/20160103175824/http://www.sbu.gov.ua/sbu/control/uk/publish/article?art_id=170951&cat_id=39574.

SBU. "СБУ Припинила Діяльність Агентурної Мережі Фсб Рф, Яка Діяла в Декількох Областях України (Відео)." SSU, August 2022. https://ssu.gov.ua/novyny/sbu-prypynyla-diialnist-ahenturnoi-merezhi-fsb-rf-yaka-diiala-v-dekilkokh-oblastiakh-ukrainy-video.

Schelling, Thomas C. *Arms and Influence*. New Haven, CT: Yale University Press, 2008.

Schneider, Jacquelyn. "A World without Trust." *Foreign Affairs*, December 2021. https://www.foreignaffairs.com/articles/world/2021-12-14/world-without-trust.

Schwirtz, Michael. "Top Secret Russian Unit Seeks to Destabilize Europe, Security Officials Say." *New York Times*, October 8, 2019, sec. World. https://www.nytimes.com/2019/10/08/world/europe/unit-29155-russia-gru.html.

Sebenius, Alyza. "Will Ukraine Be Hit by Yet Another Holiday Power-Grid Hack?" *The Atlantic*, December 2017. https://www.theatlantic.com/technology/archive/2017/12/ukraine-power-grid-hack/548285/.

Secureworks. "Disruptive HermeticWiper Attacks Targeting Ukrainian Organizations." February 2022. https://www.secureworks.com/blog/disruptive-hermeticwiper-attacks-targeting-ukrainian-organizations.

Secureworks. "WhisperGate: Not NotPetya." January 2022. https://www.secureworks.com/blog/whispergate-not-notpetya.

Segodnya. "В 'Зачистке' Майдана Участвовали Сотрудники ФСБ России—СБУ." April 2014. https://www.segodnya.ua/criminal/v-zachistke-maydana-uchastvovali-sotrudniki-fsb-rossii-sbu-509753.html.

Senko, Ulyana. "Російські Хакери Здійснюють Кібератаки На Логістичні Компанії України Та Польщі." LVIV.MEDIA, December 2022. https://lviv.media/viyna/62344-rosijski-hakeri-zdijsnyuyut-kiberataki-na-logistichni-kompaniyi-ukrayini-ta-polshi/.

Shandler, Ryan, Michael L. Gross, and Daphna Canetti. "Cyberattacks, Psychological Distress, and Military Escalation: An Internal Meta-Analysis," *Journal of Global Security Studies* 8, no. 1 (2023): 1–19.

Shevchenko, Vitaly. "'Little Green Men' or 'Russian Invaders'?" *BBC News*, March 2014, sec. Europe. https://www.bbc.com/news/world-europe-26532154.

Shturba, E., and M. Makhalkina. "Territorial'nyye Anklavy Byvshego SSSR v Kontekste Natsional'noy Bezopasnosti Sovremennoy Rossii." *Istoricheskaya i Sotsial'no-Obrazovatel'naya Mysl* 2, no. 1C (2016): 26–38.

Shultz, Richard H., and Roy Godson. *Dezinformatsia: Active Measures in Soviet Strategy*. Washington, DC: Pergamon-Brassey's, 1984.

Siddique, Haroon, Tom McCarthy, and Alan Yuhas. "Crimean Parliament Seizure Inflames Russian-Ukrainian Tensions—Live." *The Guardian*, February 27, 2014, sec. World News. https://www.theguardian.com/world/2014/feb/27/ukraine-pro-russian-gunmen-seize-crimea-parliament-live-updates.

Silina, Yulia. "Fears of New Flareup in Ukraine as Violence Grows on Frontline." November 2015. http://news.yahoo.com/fears-flareup-ukraine-violence-grows-frontline-080945741.html.

Silina, Yulia. "Ukraine, Pro-Russia Rebels Begin Donetsk Arms Withdrawal." October 2015. http://news.yahoo.com/ukraine-pro-russia-rebels-begin-donetsk-arms-withdrawal-152455026.html.

Simes, Dimitri K. "The Soviet Invasion of Czechoslovakia and the Limits of Kremlinology." *Studies in Comparative Communism* 8, no. 1–2 (1975): 174–180. https://doi.org/10.1016/0039-3592(75)90026-5.

Simons, Jake Wallis. "EXCLUSIVE: Mossad Recruited Top Iranian Scientists to Blow Up Key Nuclear Facility." December 2021. https://www.thejc.com/news/world/exclusive-mossad-recruited-top-iranian-scientists-to-blow-up-key-nuclear-facility-1.523163.

Slayton, Rebecca. "What Is the Cyber Offense-Defense Balance? Conceptions, Causes, and Assessment." *International Security* 41, no. 3 (January 2017): 72–109. https://doi.org/10.1162/ISEC_a_00267.

Slayton, Rebecca, and Brian Clarke. "Trusting Infrastructure: The Emergence of Computer Security Incident Response, 1989–2005." *Technology and Culture* 61, no. 1 (2020): 173–206. https://doi.org/10.1353/tech.2020.0036.

Smale, Alison, and Andrew Roth. "Ukraine Says That Militants Won the East." *New York Times*, 1 May 2015, sec. World. https://www.nytimes.com/2014/05/01/world/europe/ukraine.html.

Smeets, Max. *NO SHORTCUTS: Why States Struggle to Develop a Military Cyber-Force*. S.l.: Hurst & Company, 2022.

Smeets, Max. "The Strategic Promise of Offensive Cyber Operations." *Strategic Studies Quarterly* 12, no. 3 (2018): 90–113.

Smith, Rebecca. "Cyberattacks Raise Alarm for U.S. Power Grid." *Wall Street Journal*, December 2016, sec. US. https://www.wsj.com/articles/cyberattacks-raise-alarms-for-u-s-power-grid-1483120708.

Sohn, Roman. "Opinion: Ukraine: The Empire Strikes Back." *EUobserver* (blog), September 2014. https://euobserver.com/opinion/123339.

"Soldier Killed in E. Ukraine Clashes." *VOA*, November 2015. https://www.voanews.com/a/soldier-killed-in-clashes-in-eastern-ukraine/3058960.html.

Solomon, Erika, Steven Erlanger, and Christopher F. Schuetze. "Scrounging for Tanks for Ukraine, Europe's Armies Come Up Short." *New York Times*, February 28, 2023, sec. World. https://www.nytimes.com/2023/02/28/world/europe/ukraine-tanks.html.

Solonya, Levhen. "Russia's Plan for Ukraine: Purported Leaked Strategy Document Raises Alarm." Radio Free Europe/Radio Liberty, August 2013. https://www.rferl.org/a/russia-ukraine-leaked-strategy-document/25081053.html.

Sonne, Paul, Isabelle Khurshudyan, Serhiy Morgunov, and Kostiantyn Khudov. "Battle for Kyiv: Ukrainian Valor, Russian Blunders Combined to Save the Capital." *Washington Post*. 24 August 2022. https://www.washingtonpost.com/national-security/interactive/2022/kyiv-battle-ukraine-survival/.

Sopova, Alisa, and Neil MacFarquhar. "Russia and Ukraine in a Standoff over Crimea Power Outage." *New York Times* 25 November 2015, sec. World. https://www.nytimes.com/2015/11/26/world/europe/russia-and-ukraine-in-a-standoff-over-crimea-power-outage.html.

Spiegel Staff. "Putin's Gambit: How the EU Lost Ukraine." *Spiegel Online*, November 2013, sec. International. https://www.spiegel.de/international/europe/how-the-eu-lost-to-russia-in-negotiations-over-ukraine-trade-deal-a-935476.html.

SSCIP. "Cyberattack against Ukrtelecom on March 28: The Details." April 2022. https://cip.gov.ua/en/news/kiberataka-na-ukrtelekom-28-bereznya-detali.

SSCIP. "Державна Служба Спеціального Зв'язку Та Захисту Інформації України." January 2022. https://cip.gov.ua/ua/news/informaciya-shodo-imovirnoyi-provokaciyi.

SSSCIP Ukraine (@dsszzi). Twitter, March 2022. "Today, the enemy launched a powerful cyberattack against #Ukrtelecom's IT-infrastructure. According to Yurii Shchyhol, the Chairman of the @dsszzi at the moment massive cyberattack against #Ukrtelecom is neutralized. Resuming services is under way. #Ukraine #CyberAttack #war", https://twitter.com/dsszzi/status/1508528209075257347.

SSU. "СБУ Викрила Спробу Фсб Встановити «жучки» в Кулуарах Верховної Ради (Відео)." SSU, August 2022. https://ssu.gov.ua/novyny/sbu-vykryla-sprobu-fsb-vstanovyty-zhuchky-v-kuluarakh-verkhovnoi-rady-video.

Stokel-Walker, Chris. "Will Russia's Invasion of Ukraine Trigger a Massive Cyberwar?" *New Scientist*, February 2022. https://www.newscientist.com/article/2309369-will-russias-invasion-of-ukraine-trigger-a-massive-cyberwar/.

Stolarik, M. Mark, ed. *The Prague Spring and the Warsaw Pact Invasion of Czechoslovakia, 1968: Forty Years Later*. Mundelein, IL: Bolchazy-Carducci Publishers, 2010.

Strange, Susan. *States and Markets*. 2nd rev. ed. London: Bloomsbury Academic, 1998.

"Stuxnet Malware Is 'Weapon' Out to Destroy . . . Iran's Bushehr Nuclear Plant?" *Christian Science Monitor*, September 2010. https://www.csmonitor.com/USA/2010/0921/Stuxnet-malware-is-weapon-out-to-destroy-Iran-s-Bushehr-nuclear-plant.

Sudduth, Andy. "The Morris Internet Worm." 1988. https://snowplow.org/tom/worm/worm.html.

svv@materik.ru. "Re: Nedeli Opublikovalo Tekst, Pokhozhe Na Utechku." August 2013.

Sych, Oleg. "Zillya! Антивирус провела анализ кибератак на инфраструктурные объекти Украины." February 2016. https://zillya.ua/ru/zillya-antivirus-provela-analiz-kiberatak-na-infrastrukturnye-obekti-ukrainy.

Symantec. "Dragonfly: Western Energy Companies Under Sabotage Threat." *Symantec Security Response* (blog). Accessed August 23, 2017. http://www.symantec.com/connect/blogs/dragonfly-western-energy-companies-under-sabotage-threat.

Symantec. "Stuxnet 0.5: The Missing Link." 2013. McDonald, Geoff, Liam O. Murchu, Stephen Doherty, and Eric Chien. "Stuxnet 0.5: The Missing Link" (Symantec, February 2013). https://web.archive.org/web/20150112172930/http://www.symantec.com/content/en/us/enterprise/media/security_response/whitepapers/stuxnet_0_5_the_missing_link.pdf.

Symantec. "W32.Stuxnet Dossier." 2011. Falliere, Nicolas, Liam O. Murchu, and Eric Chien. "W32.Stuxnet Dossier" (Symantec, 2011). http://www.symantec.com/security_response/writeup.jsp?docid=2010-071400-3123-99.

Tantzscher, Monika. "Maßnahme »Donau« und Einsatz »Genesung«. Die Niederschlagung Des Prager Frühlings 1968/69 Im Spiegel Der MfS-Akten." Analysen Und Berichte, Reihe B (BStU, 1998). https://d-nb.info/103633225X/34.

Technopedia. "Source Code Definition." n.d. Accessed July 20, 2017.

Thomson, Iain. "So You've Got a Zero-Day—Do You Sell to Black, Grey or White Markets?" April 2018. https://www.theregister.co.uk/2018/04/15/mature_bug_bounty_market_bsidessf/.

Thornton, Mary. "'Hackers' Ignore Consequences of Their High-Tech Joy Rides." *Washington Post*, May 21, 1984. https://www.washingtonpost.com/archive/politics/1984/05/21/hackers-ignore-consequences-of-their-high-tech-joy-rides/6ab0d2fa-68dd-44af-89fe-7dd30927133b/.

Thornton, Rod. "The Changing Nature of Modern Warfare." *RUSI Journal* 160, no. 4 (July 2015): 40–48. https://doi.org/10.1080/03071847.2015.1079047.

Tigrid, Pavel. *Why Dubcek Fell*. London: Macdonald and Co, 1971.

"Timing and Performance | Nmap Network Scanning." Accessed March 29, 2023. https://nmap.org/book/man-performance.html.

Townsend, Sean. "FrolovLeaks VI: Tomorrow Was the War." *Inform Napalm* (English) (blog), November 2018. https://informnapalm.org/en/frolovleaks-vi-tomorrow-was-the-war/.

Traynor, Ian. "Ukraine Protests: End Nears for Viktor Yanukovych despite Concessions." *The Guardian*, February 21, 2014, sec. World News. https://www.theguardian.com/world/2014/feb/21/ukraine-protests-viktor-yanukovych-election.

TrendMicro. "Sandworm to Blacken: The SCADA Connection." *TrendLabs Security Intelligence* (blog), October 2014. https://blog.trendmicro.com/trendlabs-security-intelligence/sandworm-to-blacken-the-scada-connection/.

Trenin, Dmitri. "The Putin Doctrine." Carnegie Moscow Center, February 2013. https://carnegie.ru/2013/02/01/putin-doctrine-pub-51085.

Treverton, Gregory F. *Covert Action: The Limits of Intervention in the Postwar World*. New York, NY: Basic Books, 1987. https://doi.org/10.5040/9780755612529.

Trifonov, Denis. "Russian Intelligence Presence in the CIS." *CACI Analyst*, December 2003. http://www.cacianalyst.org/publications/analytical-articles/item/8615-analytical-articles-caci-analyst-2003-12-17-art-8615.html.

Tsagourias, Nicholas. "Cyber Attacks, Self-Defence and the Problem of Attribution." *Journal of Conflict and Security Law* 17, no. 2 (2012), 229–244.

Tsarev, Oleg. "О Комплексе Мер По Вовлечению Украины в Евразийский Интеграционный Процесс." *LB.Ua* (blog). Accessed August 16, 2021. https://lb.ua/blog/oleg_tsarev/220762_komplekse_mer_vovlecheniyu_ukraini.html.

TSN. "Очільник СБУ Розповів Про Мотив Хакерів, Які Атакували Україну Вірусом Petya." TCH.ua, July 2017. https://tsn.ua/ukrayina/ochilnik-sbu-rozpoviv-pro-motiv-hakeriv-yaki-atakuvali-ukrayinu-virusom-petya-955817.html.

Tucker, Maxim. "Coal Cutoff Escalates Russia-Ukraine Tensions." Politico, November 2015. https://www.politico.eu/article/coal-russia-ukraine-crimea-sanctions-putin-turkey/.

Tucker, Patrick. "DNC Hackers Linked to Russian Activity against Ukraine Two Years Ago." *Defense One* (blog), December 2016. https://www.defenseone.com/technology/2016/12/dnc-hackers-linked-russian-hacks-ukraine-two-years-ago/134098/.

Tuma, Oldrich, Mikhail Prozumenshchikov, John Soares, and Mark Kramer. "The (Inter-Communist) Cold War on Ice: Soviet-Czechoslovak Ice Hockey Politics, 1967–1969." CWIHP Working Paper #69 12, February 2014.

Tversky, Amos, and Daniel Kahneman. "The Framing of Decisions and the Psychology of Choice." *Science* 211 (1981): 453.

"Two Servicemen Killed in Past 24 Hours in East Ukraine: Kiev Military." Reuters, April 2015. https://www.reuters.com/article/us-ukraine-crisis-casualties/two-servicemen-killed-in-past-24-hours-in-east-ukraine-kiev-military-idUSKBN0MZ0UN20150408.

Tyson, Laura, and Susan Lund. "The Promise of Digital Finance." *European Financial Review*, 2017. http://www.europeanfinancialreview.com/?p=16598.

UK Foreign Office. "Kremlin Plan to Install Pro-Russian Leadership in Ukraine Exposed." January 2022. https://www.gov.uk/government/news/kremlin-plan-to-install-pro-russian-leadership-in-ukraine-exposed.

UK NCSC. "Russia behind Cyber Attack with Europe-Wide Impact an Hour before Ukraine Invasion." May 2022. https://www.ncsc.gov.uk/news/russia-behind-cyber-attack-with-europe-wide-impact-hour-before-ukraine-invasion.

"Ukraine Cyber Police Chief Says Ukraine Hit by 'Badrabbit' Malware." Reuters, October 2017. https://www.reuters.com/article/us-ukraine-cyber-police-idUSKBN1CT27G.

"Ukraine Power Company Says It Was Hit by a Second Cyber Attack." *Fortune*, June 30, 2017. http://fortune.com/2017/06/30/ukraine-power-station-cyber-attack/.

"Ukraine Provides Evidence of Russian Military in Civil Unrest." *New York Times*, April 20, 2014, sec. World. https://www.nytimes.com/interactive/2014/04/20/world/europe/ukraine-provides-evidence-of-russian-military-in-civil-unrest.html, https://www.nytimes.com/interactive/2014/04/20/world/europe/ukraine-provides-evidence-of-russian-military-in-civil-unrest.html.

"Ukraine Resumes Power Supply to Crimea." December 2015. https://www.euractiv.com/section/energy/news/ukraine-resumes-power-supply-to-crimea/.

"Ukraine Says Ammo Depot Explosions Huge Blow to Combat Capability." Reuters, September 2017. https://www.reuters.com/article/us-ukraine-explosions-idUSKCN1C316Z.

"Ukraine Sees First Direct Combat in Two Months Before EU Meeting." November 2015. https://www.bloomberg.com/news/articles/2015-11-09/ukraine-sees-first-direct-combat-in-two-months-before-eu-meeting.

"Ukraine Tensions: US Sources Say Russia 70% Ready to Invade." *BBC News*, February 2022, BBC https://www.bbc.com/news/world-europe-60276342.

"Ukraine War: Putin Signs Ukraine Annexation Laws amid Military Setbacks." *BBC News*, October 2022, sec. Europe. https://www.bbc.com/news/world-europe-63149156.

"Ukraine's Party of Regions Expels Presidential Hopefuls Tigipko, Tsariov and Boiko." Interfax-Ukraine. 7 April 2014. https://en.interfax.com.ua/news/general/199490.html.

"Ukrainian Clashes with Pro-Russian Separatists Turn Deadly." *Denver Post*, April 13, 2014. https://www.denverpost.com/2014/04/13/ukrainian-clashes-with-pro-russian-separatists-turn-deadly/.

"Ukrainian Leaders Blame 'Sabotage' for Huge Blast at Munitions Depot." Radio Free Europe/Radio Liberty, September 2017. https://www.rferl.org/a/artillery-warehouses-explode-evacuations-ordered-around-vinnitsa-ukraine-kalinovka-evacuated/28759382.html.

Ukrinform. "Українські Урядові Сайти Знову Зазнали Кібератаки." February 2022. https://www.ukrinform.ua/rubric-technology/3410832-ukrainski-uradovi-sajti-znovu-zaznali-kiberataki.html.

Ukrop News. "In the Kherson Region. the Military Stole and Tried to Sell Anti-Tank Mines with TNT." *Ukrop News 24* (blog), February 2017. https://ukropnews24.com/in-the-kherson-region-the-military-stole-and-tried-to-sell-anti-tank-mines-with-tnt/.

"Uncorrected Design Flaws, Cyber-Vulnerabilities, and Unreliability Plague the F-35 Program." Project on Government Oversight. Accessed October 10, 2021. https://www.pogo.org/analysis/2020/03/uncorrected-design-flaws-cyber-vulnerabilities-and-unreliability-plague-the-f-35-program/.

UNIAN. "Novaya Gazeta's 'Kremlin Papers' Article: Full Text in English." February 2015. https://www.unian.info/politics/1048525-novaya-gazetas-kremlin-papers-article-full-text-in-english.html.

UNN. "В 'Укренерго' не виключають кібератаку на підстанцію 'Північна', через яку частину Києву було знеструмлено." Інформаційне агентство Українські Національні Новини (УНН). Всі онлайн новини дня в Україні за сьогодні—найсвіжіші, останні, головні, December 2016. https://www.unn.com.ua/uk/news/1628435-v-ukrenergo-ne-viklyuchayut-kiberataku-na-pidstantsiyu-pivnichna-cherez-yaku-chastinu-kiyevu-bulo-znestrumleno.

"Unsubstantiated Reports." *Zemědělské Noviny*, July 1968.

US CYBERCOM. "Achieve and Maintain Cyberspace Superiority—Command Vision for US Cyber Command." April 2018. https://www.cybercom.mil/Portals/56/Documents/USCYBERCOM%20Vision%20April%202018.pdf?ver=2018-06-14-152556-010.

US Department of State. "Soviet 'Active Measures' Report No. 88 Forgery, Disinformation, Political Operations." 1981. https://www.cia.gov/library/readingroom/docs/CIA-RDP84B00049R001303150031-0.pdf.

US Treasury. "Treasury Sanctions Russian Cyber Actors for Interference with the 2016 U.S. Elections and Malicious Cyber-Attacks." US Department of the Treasury, March 2018. https://home.treasury.gov/news/press-releases/sm0312.

Vaas, Lisa. "How Hackers Broke into John Podesta, DNC Gmail Accounts." *Naked Security* (blog), October 2016. https://nakedsecurity.sophos.com/2016/10/25/how-hackers-broke-into-john-podesta-dnc-gmail-accounts/.

Valenta, Jiri. "The Bureaucratic Politics Paradigm and the Soviet Invasion of Czechoslovakia." *Political Science Quarterly* 94, no. 1 (1979): 55–76. https://doi.org/10.2307/2150156.

Valenta, Jiri. *Soviet Intervention in Czechoslovakia, 1968: Anatomy of a Decision*. 2nd rev. and expanded ed. Baltimore, MD: Johns Hopkins University Press, 1991.

Valeriano, Brandon, Benjamin Jensen, and Ryan C. Maness. *Cyber Strategy: The Evolving Character of Power and Coercion*. New York: Oxford University Press, 2018.

Valeriano, Brandon, Ryan C. Maness, and Benjamin Jensen. "Analysis: Cyberwarfare Has Taken a New Turn. Yes, It's Time to Worry." *Washington Post*, July 13, 2017. https://www.washingtonpost.com/news/monkey-cage/wp/2017/07/13/cyber-warfare-has-taken-a-new-turn-yes-its-time-to-worry/.

Vandiver, John. "SACEUR: Allies Must Prepare for Russia 'Hybrid War.'" *Stars and Stripes*. Accessed December 14, 2020. https://www.stripes.com/news/saceur-allies-must-prepare-for-russia-hybrid-war-1.301464.

Vasovic, Alexander. "Ukraine Rebels Speak of Heavy Losses in Battle against Government Troops." Reuters, June 2014. https://www.reuters.com/article/us-ukraine-crisis-fight

ing/ukraine-rebels-speak-of-heavy-losses-in-battle-against-government-troops-idUSKBN0EU0K320140619.
Verbyany, Volodymyr, Elena Mazneva, and Eduard Gismatullin. "Twin Ukraine Power Cable Blasts Leave Crimeans in the Dark." November 2015. https://www.bloomberg.com/news/articles/2015-11-22/crimea-declares-emergency-as-1-9-million-people-lose-electricity.
Viasat. "KA-SAT Network Cyber Attack Overview." March 2022. https://news.viasat.com/blog/corporate/ka-sat-network-cyber-attack-overview.
Victor Zhora (@VZhora). "@lukasmaeder @LenMaschmeyer @lukOlejnik Huge Loss in Communications!= Huge Loss in Coordination. The Impact Was Direct, but the Goal Wasn't Reached." Twitter, June 2022. https://twitter.com/VZhora/status/1534279624347230208.
Volz, Dustin. "Russian Hackers Tracked Ukrainian Artillery Units Using Android Implant: Report." Reuters, December 2016. https://www.reuters.com/article/us-cyber-ukraine-idUKKBN14B0CU.
Voo, Julia, Irfan Hemani, Simon Jones, Winnona DeSombre, Dan Cassidy, and Annina Schwarzenbach. "National Cyber Power Index." Belfer Center of International Affairs, 2020. https://www.belfercenter.org/publication/national-cyber-power-index-2020.
V. V. Shtol. "Geopoliticheskiye Zadachi Rossii Na Postsovetskom Prostranstve." *Vestnik Moskovskogo Gosudarstvennogo Oblastnogo Universiteta*, no. 3S (2014): 171–180.
Walker, Shaun. "Ukraine's EU Trade Deal Will Be Catastrophic, Says Russia." *The Guardian*, September 22, 2013, sec. World News. https://www.theguardian.com/world/2013/sep/22/ukraine-european-union-trade-russia.
Walker, Shaun, and Ian Traynor. "Ukraine Crisis: Crimea Now Part of Russia, Local Parliament Declares." *The Guardian*, March 6, 2014, sec. World News. https://www.theguardian.com/world/2014/mar/06/ukraine-crisis-crimea-part-of-russia-local-parliament-declares.
Waltz, Kenneth N. *Theory of International Politics*. Reissue ed. Long Grove, IL: Waveland Press, 2010.
Warner, Michael. "A Matter of Trust: Covert Action Reconsidered." *Studies in Intelligence* 63, no. 4 (2019), 33–41. https://web.archive.org/web/20201016162622/https://www.cia.gov/library/center-for-the-study-of-intelligence/csi-publications/csi-studies/studies/vol-63-no-4/pdfs/Covert-Action-Reconsidered.pdf.
Warner, Michael. "Wanted: A Definition of "Intelligence." *Studies in Intelligence* 46, no. 3 (2002). https://web.archive.org/web/20080611153835/https://www.cia.gov/library/center-for-the-study-of-intelligence/csi-publications/csi-studies/studies/vol46no3/article02.html.
Watling, Jack, and Nick Reynolds. "Ukraine at War: Paving the Road from Survival to Victory." RUSI, July 2022. https://www.rusi.org/explore-our-research/publications/special-resources/ukraine-war-paving-road-survival-victory.
Watson, Adrienne. Twitter, @NSC_Spox, "The U.S. has technical information linking Russian GRU to this week's distributed denial of service attacks in Ukraine. Known GRU infrastructure has been noted transmitting high volumes of communications to Ukraine-based IP addresses and associated banking-related domains." February 2022. https://twitter.com/NSC_Spox/status/1494796573959725057.
Weber, Max. *Max Weber: The Theory of Social and Economic Organization*. Edited by A. M Henderson and Talcott Parsons. New York; London: Free Press; Collier Macmillan, 1964.

Wesolowsky, Tony. "Ukraine's Exploding Munition Depots Give Ammunition to Security Concerns." Radio Free Europe/Radio Liberty, 6 October 2017. https://www.rferl.org/a/ukraine-exploding-munitions-security-concerns-russia/28777991.html.

"The West Is Struggling to Forge a New Arsenal of Democracy." *The Economist*. 19 February 2023. https://www.economist.com/briefing/2023/02/19/the-west-is-struggling-to-forge-a-new-arsenal-of-democracy.

"WhisperGate Malware Corrupts Computers in Ukraine." *Recorded Future* (blog), January 2022. https://www.recfut.com/whispergate-malware-corrupts-computers-ukraine/.

Wiener, Norbert. *Cybernetics or Control and Communication in the Animal and the Machine*. 2nd ed. Cambridge, MA: MIT Press, 2000.

Wilde, Gavin. "Cyber Operations in Ukraine: Russia's Unmet Expectations." *Carnegie Endowment for International Peace*. 12 December 2022. https://carnegieendowment.org/files/202212-Wilde_RussiaHypotheses-v2.pdf.

Williams, Brad D. "How Russia Adapted KGB 'Active Measures' to Cyber Operations, Part I." Fifth Domain: Cyber, March 2017. http://fifthdomain.com/2017/03/19/how-russia-adapted-kgb-active-measures-to-cyber-operations-part-i/.

Williams, Holly. "Russian Hacks into Ukraine Power Grids a Sign of Things to Come for U.S.?" December 2016. https://www.cbsnews.com/news/russian-hacks-into-ukraine-power-grids-may-be-a-sign-of-things-to-come/.

Williams, Kieran. "New Sources on Soviet Decision Making during the 1968 Czechoslovak Crisis." *Europe-Asia Studies* 48, no. 3 (May 1996): 457.

Williams, Kieran. *Prague Spring and Its Aftermath: Czechoslovak Politics, 1968–1970*. Cambridge: Cambridge University Press, 2011. http://public.eblib.com/choice/publicfullrecord.aspx?p=4641036.

Windsor, Philip, and Adam Roberts. *Czechoslovakia, 1968: Reform, Repression, and Resistance*. London: Columbia University Press, for the Institute for Strategic Studies, 1969.

Winner, Langdon. *The Whale and the Reactor*. Chicago: University of Chicago Press, 1986.

Withnall, Adam. "Ukraine Crisis: Donetsk 'Declares Independence from Kiev' and Sets Date for Referendum on Joining Russia." *The Independent*, April 2014. https://www.independent.co.uk/news/world/europe/ukraine-crisis-officials-in-eastern-city-of-donetsk-proclaim-independence-from-kiev-and-set-date-for-9243750.html.

Wohlforth, William C. "Realism and Great Power Subversion." *International Relations* 34, no. 4 (December 2020): 459–481. https://doi.org/10.1177/0047117820968858.

Womack, Helen, ed. *Undercover Lives: Soviet Spies in the Cities of the World*. London: Weidenfeld & Nicolson, 1998.

Work, J. D. "Burned and Blinded: Escalation Risks of Intelligence Loss from Countercyber Operations in Crisis," *International Journal of Intelligence and CounterIntelligence* 35, no. 4 (2 October 2022): 806–833. https://doi.org/10.1080/08850607.2022.2081904

Work, J. D. "Evaluating Commercial Cyber Intelligence Activity," *International Journal of Intelligence and CounterIntelligence* 33, no. 2 (2 April 2020): 278–308. https://doi.org/10.1080/08850607.2019.1690877.

World Bank. "GDP (Current US$)—Ukraine: Data." 2023. https://data.worldbank.org/indicator/NY.GDP.MKTP.CD?locations=UA.

Wylie, J. C., and John B. Hattendorf. *Military Strategy: A General Theory of Power Control*, Classics of Sea Power. Annapolis, MA: Navel Institute Press, 2014.

Yagofarov, Timur. "Кібератака на енергосектор розвивалася півтора місяці." *Computernoe Obozrenie*, April 2022. https://ko.com.ua/kiberataka_na_energosektor_rozvivalasya_pivtora_misyaci_140789.

Yana. "Opinion: 'We Were Trapped': Eyewitness to the Massacre in Kiev." *CNN*. Accessed August 18, 2021. https://edition.cnn.com/2014/02/24/opinion/yana-ukraine-eyewitness/index.html.

Yasinskiy, Aleksey. "BlackEnergy Phase 2: From Media and Electric Companies to Darknet and TTPs." *SOC Prime* (blog), January 2016. https://socprime.com/en/blog/blackenergy-phase-2-from-media-and-electric-companies-to-darknet-and-ttps/.

Yasinskiy, Aleksey. "DISMANTLING BLACKENERGY, PART 2—'THE MARK.'" *SOC Prime* (blog), March 2016. https://socprime.com/en/blog/dismantling-blackenergy-part2-the-mark/.

Yasinskiy, Aleksey. "DISMANTLING BLACKENERGY, PART 3—ALL ABOARD!" *SOC Prime* (blog), March 2016. https://socprime.com/blog/dismantling-blackenergy-part-3-all-aboard/.

Yasinskiy, Aleksey. "Dismantling KillDisk: Reverse of the BlackEnergy Destructive Component." *SOC Prime* (blog), February 2016. https://socprime.com/en/blog/dismantling-killdisk-reverse-of-the-blackenergy-destructive-component/.

Young, Susan, and Dave Aitel. *The Hacker's Handbook: The Strategy behind Breaking into and Defending Networks*. Boca Raton, FL: CRC Press, 2004.

ZA, Sekretariat des Ministers (SdM) 1469. "Information Nr. 942/69 Der ZAIG Über Die Ereignisse in Der CSSR Anläßlich Des Ersten Jahrestages Der Militärischen Hilfsaktion Der Sozialistischen Länder." n.d. BStU.

Žáček, Pavel. "The KGB and the Czechoslovak State Security Apparatus in August 1968." *Journal of Slavic Military Studies* 29, no. 4 (2016): 626–657. https://doi.org/10.1080/13518046.2016.1232561.

Zarudnia, Natalia. "Російська Програма-Вимагач RansomBoggs Націлилася На Кілька Українських Організацій." November 2022. https://cybercalm.org/novyny/rosijska-programa-vymagach-ransomboggs-natsilylasya-na-kilka-ukrayinskyh-organizatsij/.

"Zelensky Says Two Generals Stripped of Their Rank Due to Treason." *Kyiv Independent*, March 2022. https://kyivindependent.com/uncategorized/zelensky-says-two-generals-stripped-of-their-rank-due-to-treason.

Zeman, Z. A. B. *Prague Spring*. New York: Hill and Wang, 1969.

Zetter, Kim. "Everything We Know about Ukraine's Power Plant Hack." *Wired*, January 2016. https://www.wired.com/2016/01/everything-we-know-about-ukraines-power-plant-hack/.

Zetter, Kim. "Inside the Cunning, Unprecedented Hack of Ukraine's Power Grid." *Wired*, March 2016. https://www.wired.com/2016/03/inside-cunning-unprecedented-hack-ukraines-power-grid/.

Zetter, Kim. "Second Wiper Attack Strikes Systems in Ukraine and Two Neighboring Countries." Substack newsletter. *Zero Day* (blog), February 2022. https://zetter.substack.com/p/second-wiper-attack-strikes-systems.

Zetter, Kim. "So What This Means Is That Now They Have to Send a Farmer out to Look at the Turbines and Report Back: 'Yep, They're Still Working.'" Twitter, @KimZetter. March 2022. https://twitter.com/KimZetter/status/1507389719411236871.

Zetter, Kim. "An Unprecedented Look at Stuxnet, the World's First Digital Weapon." *Wired*, March 2014. http://www.wired.com/2014/11/countdown-to-zero-day-stuxnet/.

Zetter, Kim. "Viasat Hack 'Did Not' Have Huge Impact on Ukrainian Military Communications, Official Says." Substack newsletter. *Zero Day* (blog), September 2022. https://zetter.substack.com/p/viasat-hack-did-not-have-huge-impact.

Zetter, Kim. "What We Know and Don't Know about the Cyberattacks Against Ukraine (Updated)." Substack newsletter. *Zero Day* (blog), January 2022. https://zetter.substack.com/p/what-we-know-and-dont-know-about.

Zetter, Kim. *Twitter*, April 2022. https://twitter.com/KimZetter/status/1514508733908348930.

Zhong, Ray Y., Xun Xu, Eberhard Klotz, and Stephen T. Newman. "Intelligent Manufacturing in the Context of Industry 4.0: A Review." *Engineering* 3, no. 5 (October 2017): 616–630. https://doi.org/10.1016/J.ENG.2017.05.015.

"О Комплексе Мер По Вовлечению Украины в Евразийский Интеграционный Процесс." *ZN.Ua*, 16 August 2013. https://zn.ua/internal/o-komplekse-mer-po-vovlecheniyu-ukrainy-v-evraziyskiy-integracionnyy-process-_.html.

"Бывший Офицер КГБ Попов: Агентов в Украине Россия Выращивала. Это 'Парничок'. Завербовать Человека, Когда Он Уже На Самом Верху, Намного Сложнее / ПОЛИТИКА / Новости." 25 November 2022. https://gordonua.com/amp/news/politics/byvshij-ofitser-kgb-popov-agentov-v-ukraine-rossija-vyrashchivala-eto-parnichok-zaverbovat-cheloveka-kogda-on-uzhe-na-samom-verhu-namnogo-slozhnee-1637706.html.

Єгошина, Валерія. "Таємний Кадр СБУ: Alter Ego Головного «контролера Порядності» Спецслужби Андрія Наумова (Розслідування)." *Радіо Свобода*, 29 October 2020, sec. Політика. https://www.radiosvoboda.org/a/schemes/30919292.html.

"Из-За Кибератаки Минфин и Госказначейство Потеряли 3 Терабайта Информации." Accessed October 13, 2021. https://biz.nv.ua/economics/iz-za-kiberataki-minfin-i-goskaznachejstvo-poterjali-3-terabajta-informatsii-330784.html.

Красномовець, Павло. "Російські Хакери Із ГРУ Спробували Залишити Без Світла Вінницьку Область, Як у 2017 Київ. Чому Їм Не Вдалося—Forbes.Ua." 12 April 2022. https://forbes.ua/innovations/rosiyski-khakeri-namagalis-zalishiti-bez-svitla-vinnitsku-oblast-atatsi-vdalos-zapobigti-12042022-5409.

ОЛЕНА БУРКАЛО. "На Сумщине Мэра Бурыни и Его Пособников Задержали За Коллаборационизм—Korrespondent.Net." 1 May 2022. https://korrespondent.net/amp/4473984-na-sumschyne-mera-buryny-y-eho-posobnykov-zaderzhaly-za-kollaboratsyonyzm.

"СБУ підозрює старосту села Сумського району в колабораціонізмі." 28 June 2022. https://debaty.sumy.ua/news/sbu-pidozryuye-starostu-sela-sumskogo-rajonu-v-kolaboratsionizmi.

Свобода, Радіо. "Ексначальник з СБУ Наумов Міг Передавати Спецслужбам РФ Секретні Дані Щодо Чорнобильської АЕС—«Схеми»." *Радіо Свобода*, 17 June 2022, sec. Новини | Політика. https://www.radiosvoboda.org/a/news-skhemy-sbu-naumov-chaes/31902729.html.

Свобода, Радіо. "У Сербії Офіційно Підтвердили Затримання Ексначальника в СБУ, Який Фігурував у Розслідуванні «Схем»." *Радіо Свобода*, 11 June 2022, sec. Новини: Суспільство. https://www.radiosvoboda.org/a/nws-serbia-zatrymannia-naumova/31893820.html.

Станіславович, Шабловський Владислав. "Отношения России и Нато в Контексте Кризиса На Украине." *Постсоветские Исследования* 2, no. 2 (2019): 1032–1041.

СУМСЬКА ОБЛАСТЬ. "Хотів 'Здати' Місто Росіянам: Голова Громади в Сумській Області Піде Під Суд." РБК-Украина. 26 August 2022 https://www.rbc.ua/ukr/news/hotel-sdat-selo-rossiyanam-glava-obshchiny-1661518671.html.

"У Донецьку Ідеї Сепаратизму Несподівано Виявилися Непопулярними." *Українська Правда*, 9 April 2014. https://www.pravda.com.ua/news/2014/04/9/7021883/.

"Хакери Атакували Транспортні Та Логістичні Компанії в Україні й Польщі, Microsoft—Delo.Ua." 15 October 2022. https://delo.ua/telecom/xakeri-atakuvali-transportni-ta-logisticni-kompaniyi-v-ukrayini-i-polshhi-microsoft-405412/.

Юрій Щиголь.*Як Вдалося Зберегти Зв`язок, Кібератаки На Україну,Відключені Військові Супутники*. 2022. https://www.youtube.com/watch?v=-K9OyhGWDRI.

Index

For the benefit of digital users, indexed terms that span two pages (e.g., 52–53) may, on occasion, appear on only one of those pages.

Tables and figures are indicated by *t* and *f* following the page number

AcidRain malware, 191
AES-NI cybercrime tool, 161
Aksyonov, Sergey, 127
ALLA, illegal agent, 102–3
Andropov, Yuri, 66, 67–68, 82, 85, 87, 91
Arbuzov, Serhiy, 187–88
ARTYMOVA, illegal agent, 102–3
Azarov, Mykola, 187–88

BadRabbit ransomware, 164–67
 balancing trilemma, 164–67
 effects, 165–66
 strategic role, 165
 targets, 165
Bakanov, Ivan, 194–95, 196
Bilak, Vasil, 65–66, 84–85
BlackEnergy malware, 134, 135
2015 Blackout (Ukraine), 136–41
 development time, 137
 GE CIMPLICITY HMI (Human Machine Interface) systems, 138
 role of luck 137, 138–39
 trilemma trade-offs 139–40
 Effects 139–41
 SCADA systems, 138
Bogdan, Vasily, 151–52
BootPatch malware, 179–80
Borzov, Gennadi, 71
botnet, 181–82
Brandt, Willy, 26
'Brezhnev Doctrine,' 63, 69
Brezhnev, Leonid, 64, 65–67, 68, 78–79, 81, 84–86, 89, 91, 92, 94–95, 104, 111
Brusov, Georgiy, 128–29

CaddyWiper malware, 185–86, 200
Cerny, Vaclav, 72–73, 74
Chaliy, Aleksei, 125–26
"Charter 77," 113
Chernovtsoblenergo, 137
 from Cold War to hybrid war, 208–11
"Complex of Measures" document, 119–20, 122, 125, 188
computer code, 44
contingency planning, failure and fallback to, 86–92
control, in subversive trilemma, 4, 12, 13*f*, 13–14, 35–38, 40–41, 42–43, 55, 56, 57–58
 BadRabbit operation, 172, 180–81
 in cyber conflicts, 57–58
 in fulfilling strategic promise, 99–100
 HermeticWiper, 183–84
 as key determinant of strategic value, 36–37
 KHODOKI operations, 61, 114
 NotPetya and the limits of control, 157–64
 power grid sabotage attempt in April 2022, 202
 in PROGRESS operations, 61
 Soviet Union over Czechoslovakia, 92–93
 speed and intensity and, inverse correlation between, 36, 76–77, 95, 100–1, 179, 224–25
 when intensity increases, 55
control over targets, 34–38
covert operations, 68, 117
 definition 7–8
 advantages of, 29–30

covert operations (*cont.*)
  assassination plots, 74–75
  clandestine mode versus, 7–8
  covert warfare
    secrecy lowering escalation risks in, 3–4, 29
  cyber operations as, 2–3
  cyber operations versus, 9, 13–14, 45, 48–50, 51–52
  effects, 9, 10, 13–14, 24, 27, 48–49, 51–52, 72, 117
  'escalation ladder' for, 72
  as independent tools of statecraft, 8
  information technology aiding, 10
  strategic value of, 9
  subversive operations versus, 22–23
  traditional subversion and, 24
  use of force, 214 –15
Crimea Blackout (2015), 137, 141–44
Crimean power grid sabotage, 137, 141–44
critical infrastructure sabotage, 115–16, 175–76, 196–201
  CaddyWiper malware, 200
  Crimea Blackout (2015), 137, 141–44
  enabled by territorial conquest, 197–98
  INDUSTROYER and energy sector sabotage, 150, 200
  Kyiv Blackout (2016), 144–50
  operations in Ukraine, 196–201
    attempt to disrupt the power grid, 196–97
    disrupting Ukrtelecom, 196–97
  Russia against Ukraine, 118
  Sandworm hacking group strikes back, 196–201
  Sandworm I (2015 Blackout), 136–41 (*see also* 2015 Blackout [Ukraine])
  Sandworm II (2016 Kyiv Blackout), 144–50 (*see also* Kyiv Blackout, 2016)
  Sandworm strikes back in Ukraine, 196–201
  through cyber means, 119
CyberBerkut hacker group, 132–33
cyber-enabled subversion, 117–73. *See also* "hybrid war," Russia against Ukraine (2013–2018)

cyber operations, 42–43
  "attack surface" for, 49
  comparison to traditional subversion, 42–43, 55–56
  in degrading material capabilities, 51
  in disrupting the economy, 51
  effects, 47–48
    scope and scale of, 48, 53
  challenges, 42–43, 49–50
  for long-term "erosion" strategies, 50 (*see also* erosion strategies)
  manipulating government policy, 51
  in manipulating public opinion, 50–51
  relative advantages, 42–43, 48–50
  strategic role and promise of, 48–52
  subversive nature, 3–4
  scalability, 48–49
cyber power, subversive nature of, 43–48
  phishing, 44
  social vulnerabilities targeted, 43–44
  technical vulnerabilities targeted, 43–44
"Cyberpunk" hacker group, 43–44
Czechoslovakia, 15
  Andropov's strategy on, 68, 87
  anti-Soviet nationalism" in, 116
  armed force, 67–68
  KGB's illegals in, 14–15, 61, 111, 192 (*see also* KHODOKI campaign; PROGRESS campaign)
  Kremlin perception and strategic goals, 63–70
  Prague Spring and, 60 (*see also* Prague Spring (1968–1973), crushing the)
  Soviet strategic goals at, 98–99, 101, 102
  Soviets' subversion failure in, 61, 176–77, 208
  as a "testing ground" for subversion use, 14–15

Danyliuk, Oleksandr, 160–61
Derkach, Andriy, 193
diplomacy
  definition, 19
  interaction with use of force, 19, 25, 117
  interaction with subversion, 1–2, 64, 70, 92–93, 121–22
  interaction with warfare, 1–2, 17–18, 19, 21

INDEX 331

distributed denial of service (DDoS), 178–87, 201
Dobrynin, Anatolii, 69–70
Donbass failure and escalation, 129–31
Dubček, Alexander, 60, 62, 64, 65, 66–67, 81, 84–87, 91, 92–93, 104, 105, 106–7, 109, 110, 114
Dubov, Dmitry, 128–29, 155

economic and psychological (cyber) warfare, 178–88
erosion strategies, 28, 30–31, 50
  causing collateral cognitive damage, 223–24
  cyber operations as, 50, 56–57
  effects of, 28
  long-term campaigns effects on the balance of power, 219–20, 223
  by Russia in Ukraine, 118–19
    2014, 118–19
    2022, 174, 178
  strategic role, 57
  strategic value of, 39–40
  in subversive campaigns, 42–43
  to undermine trust, 223–24
  to weaken the adversary, 28
escalation, 56–57
  in Czechoslovakia, role of subversion, 90–91, 93–94, 113–14, 216–17
  in the Donbass region, 129–31
  'escalation ladder' for covert operations, 72, 74–75, 76, 95, 117–18, 136–37, 143, 146, 151, 194, 198–99
  KHODOKI campaign in, 62–63
  Kremlin decision to invade Czechoslovakia, 176–77, 208
  lowered risks in covert warfare, 3–4, 7–8, 29
  military escalation, 10, 213, 214–15, 218
  subversion lowering the risk of, 29–30, 37–39
  time pressure as the cause, 213
  in Ukraine, 174, 210–11
exploitation
  analysis of the mechanism of, 75, 111–12, 224–25
  challenges in the process of, 40–41

of computer systems, 46, 48
as distinguishing feature of subversion, 23–24
failure of, 203
force use to facilitate, 23–24
immaterial means of, 46–47
indirect and secret nature of, 25
by IsaacWiper, 184–85
prevention of, 226–27
of psychological and sociological vulnerabilities, 7, 21
secret mode of operation, 22–23, 30, 31, 38
spies using the technique of, 26, 103–4
by subversion, in practice, 17–18
subversion speed limited by, 31–32, 35, 37
subversion's reliance on, 3–4, 7, 11–12, 21, 23–24, 207
as subversive nature of cyber power, 43
traditional subversion and, 51–52, 55, 57
of Ukrtelecom's network, 197
using unpatched VPN device, 191, 199
of vulnerabilities in ICTs, 43–44, 45, 48, 57

Fedorov, Mykhailo, 182
firmware, 44, 190, 191
force, 24–25, 69
  and diplomacy, 19–20
  military force, 67–68, 75, 84–85, 105, 116, 126–27
  spies using, 23–24
  subjugation by, 69–70
  subversion in the service of, 188–96
  subversion versus, 7, 17–18, 25, 28–31, 38–39, 174–75
Frolov, Kirill, 14, 120–21, 122–23, 126–27, 130
FYODOROV illegal agent, 102–3, 111–12

GE CIMPLICITY HMI (Human Machine Interface) systems, 138
German Stasi Records Agency, 14
Glazyev, Sergey Yuryevich, 122–23, 126, 127
government policy, subversion influencing, 26

Granovski, Vladimir, 123
Grechko, Marshal, 109
GreenPetya ransomware, 159, 160
GreyEnergy group, 141
Groysman, Volodymyr, 151–52
Guillaume, Günther, 26

hacking, 11–12, 134
  APT28, 132
  cyber operations as, 43–44
  CyberBerkut, 132
  "Cyberpunk" hacker group, 43–44
  hack-and-leak operations, 50–51
  KillDisk module, 137, 156–57
  over industrial control systems, 53, 139
  Russian sponsored, in Ukraine, 118, 120–21, 131–32
  Sean Townsend, 160
  stealth in, 45
  subversive nature of, 45, 46
  target systems for, 55, 138
  Ukrainian hacktivists, 127
  Viasat hack, 189–90, 191, 211, 217
  vulnerabilities targeted, 43–44
"HermeticWiper" malware, 183–85
Husak, Gustav, 62–63, 110
"hybrid war," Russian strategy against Ukraine (2013–2018), 117–73. *See also* Russia's invasion of Ukraine
  "Complex of Measures" document, 119–20, 122
  Donbass failure and escalation, 129–31
  economic warfare, Sandworm's pivot to scale, 153–67
  Euromaidan movement, 122
  Kremlin perception and strategic goals, 119–22
  new technology, old limitations, 169–73
  public trust in the government, 170, 171f
  Russia turning to subversion, 118
  sabotage, cyber versus traditional subversion, 135–53
    GE CIMPLICITY HMI systems, 138
    KillDisk module, 137
    learning requirement, 139
    Sandworm I: The 2015 Blackout, 136–41
    SCADA systems, 138
    Sandworm II, The 2016 Kyiv Blackout, 144–50
    Sandworm III, The 2016 compromise of the Ministry of Finance 154–57
    Sandworm IV, NotPetya and the limits of control, 157–64
    Sandworm V, BadRabbit, 164–67
    (*see also* BadRabbit ransomware)
  shadow forces take Crimea, 124–29
    Euromaidan crisis, 127
    "pro-Russian demonstrators," 126
  subversion falters for Russia, 122–24
    constraints posed by the trilemma, 124
    Ukraine Cyber Alliance, 123
  subversive election interference, 2014–2015, 131–35
  traditional sabotage I, 2015 Crimea Blackout, 141–44
    operation and cyber sabotage, difference between, 143
  traditional sabotage II, arms depot explosion in Kalynivka, 150–53
  Ukrainian D-30 artillery and the tactical sabotage, 167–69

illegal agents, 15, 67–68.
  See also KHODOKI campaign; PROGRESS campaign
  advantage of, 80–81
  Aleksandr Alekseev, 71
  ALLA, 102–3
  ARTYMOVA, 102–3
  in Czechoslovakia, sent by Andropov, 67–68
  during Prague Spring, 71
  FYODOROV, 102–3, 111–12
  Gennadi Borzov, 71
  Georgii Fedyashin, 71
  of KGB, infiltrating Western societies, 23, 61
  KRAVCHENKO, 110
  Mikhail Sagatelyan, 84
  near the West German border, 76, 80–81
  Vladimir Surzhaninov, 71
  V. Umnov, 71

Indra, Alois, 84–85
industrial control system (ICS), 48, 55, 138, 139, 145–46, 149–50
  GE CIMPLICITY HMI (Human Machine Interface) systems, 138
  SCADA (Supervisory Control and Data Acquisition) systems, 138
  TRITON malware, 53
INDUSTROYER, 145, 146–48, 149, 150, 200
information communications and technologies (ICTs), 43–44
information technology and subversion, 42–59. *See also* cyber operations
insider threats, 197–98, 199
  in cybersecurity, 220
intelligence, 5–6, 7
  artificial intelligence, 226–27
  collection activity, 65, 71, 82–84, 192–93
    by KSC, 84, 86
    by Ukrainian KGB, 85
  CyberBerkut, 132
  Israel's intelligence service, 219
  by KGB agent(s) in Czechoslovakia, 72–73, 74, 76–77, 108
  open-source intelligence, 4–5, 14
  operations, 7–8
    in Greece, 27–28
  Russian intelligence services in Ukraine, 151–52, 162
  GRU, 163, 181–82
  Russian intelligence services to Chernobyl, 195–96
  slanted intelligence, 82, 91, 176–77, 187–88
  theory, 1–2
  "threat intelligence" providers, 54
  Ukrainian intelligence services, 141–44, 193
  WhisperGate, 179–80
intensity, in subversive trilemma, 4, 12, 13*f*, 13–14, 35–38, 40–41, 42–43, 55, 56, 57–58
  BadRabbit operation, 172, 180–81
  control and speed and, inverse correlation between, 36, 76–77, 95, 100–1, 179, 224–25
  in cyber conflicts, 57–58

as determinant of strategic value, 36–37
  in fulfilling strategic promise, 99–100
  HermeticWiper, 183–84
  KHODOKI operations, 61, 114
  NotPetya and the limits of control, 157–64
  power grid sabotage attempt in April 2022, 202
  in PROGRESS operations, 61
  Soviet Union over Czechoslovakia, 92–93
international relations theory, 7
IsaacWiper, 184–85

Kalugin, Oleg, 91
Kalynivka, arms depot explosion in, 150–53
Katana malware, 182
KHODOKI campaign, 61, 62–63, 70–92, 208
  major subversive operations, 72
    exploitation mechanism, 75
    fake arms caches influence, 77, 79
    KGB, errors by, 76–77
    kidnapping leading intellectuals, 72
    planting false flag "evidence," 76
    using GROMOV, 73, 74
    using GURYEV, 73, 74
    weakening the liberalization movement, 72
KHODOKI Redux, 104–10
  "Aeroflot Incident," 104–10
  Dubcek's "conspiracy theory" flaws, 107
  Vltava radio station, 104–5
  Zpravy magazine, 104–5
Kievoblenergors, 137
KillDisk malware, 139, 154, 156–57
Kluyev, Andriy, 187–88
Kolder, Drahomir, 84–85
Kolesnichenko, Vadim, 124
Kovalchuk, Vsevolod, 146
Koval, Nikolay, 133, 148–49, 163–64
KRAVCHENKO illegal agent, 110
Kremlin
  Brezhnev doctrine and, 69
  "Complex of Measures" document, 119–20, 122

Kremlin (*cont.*)
  cyber-enabled subversion against Ukraine by, 119–22
  Euromaidan movement, 122
  leaked documents and emails, 4–5
  "loss" of Czechoslovakia, prevention plans, 67, 98–99, 109
  Prague Spring and, 60, 63–70
  Prozumenshchikov's analysis of, 68, 116
  reliance on diplomacy, force, and subversion, 64
  subversive activities by, 101–2, 117–18
  taking Crimea, contingency plan, 124–29
  in Ukraine invasion, 2022, 176–78
    economic and psychological (cyber) warfare, 178, 187–88
    subversion in the service of force, 188–96
Krivosheev, Vladlen, 78
Kryvoruchko, Serhiy, 194–95
Kyiv Blackout, 2016 (Ukraine), 144–50
  destructive potential of malware, 146
  development time, 145–46
  effects and strategic value, 150
  failure of malware, 148–50
  INDUSTROYER developed, 145, 146–48, 149, 150
  Severyana power substation de-energized, 145
  signaling interpretations and problems, 146–49

Lappi, Leo, 102–3, 111–12
Lavrov, Sergej, 177
Lenin, Vladimir, 8

Makhalkina, M., 121
Malofeev, Konstantin, 123
Markovets, Sergiy, 163–64
Medvedchuk, Viktor, 196
Medvedev, Dmitry, 142
military escalation, 10, 213, 214–15, 218
Ministry of Finance compromise, 2016, 154–57
  development time, 154–55
  effects and strategic value, 155
  KillDisk malware, 154

  vulnerabilities exploited, 156–57
Mirai malware, 182
Moonraker worm, 159
Morris, Robert Tappan, 54–55
"Morris worm," 54–55

Naftogaz, 197–98
Nalivaychenko, Valentin, 127–28
Narozhnyy, Pavlo, 168–69
Naumov, Andriy, 195–96
nonintervention principle, 29–30
NotPetya malware, 157–64
  AES-NI cybercrime tool, 161
  collateral damage and loss of control, 157–64
  data and computers, disabled, 157–58
  development time, 159
  disk wiping functionality 158–59
  effects and strategic value, 153, 160–61, 163, 172
  supply-chain mechanism, 159–60, 162
  XData., 159, 161
Novikov, Andrey, 126–27, 130
Novotny, Antonin, 64
Nye, Joseph, 20, 140–41

October CMS exploited, 178–79, 180–81
Ohryzko, Volodymyr, 120–21

Pachman, Ludek, 110
Parubiy, Andriy, 151–52
persistent engagement, 6
  and erosion, 219–20
  limitations, 50
phishing, 47–48, 137
  exploitation by, 44
  to exploit software vulnerabilities, 46
  by Sandworm, 134, 154–55
Podesta, John, 44
Poroshenko, Petro, 158
power
  as an essential contested concept, 18
  diplomacy as an instrument of, 19
  force as an instrument of, 19–20
  and subversion, 17–41
  in world politics, 18–20
power grid sabotage operation, 154, 157, 159, 172

Prague Spring (1968–1973),
crushing the, 60–116.
See also KHODOKI Redux
"armed counterrevolution," 62
contingency planning, failure and
fallback to, 86–92
KHODOKI failure, 90–91
PROGRESS failure, 90–91
failed coup and tanks in Prague, 92–99
ambitious operational design, 98–99
constraints posed by the trilemma, 95
Czechoslovak radio stations
continued operation, 96
lack of adequate preparation, 97
military invasion, 93
public resistance, 98
regime change failure, 93, 94–95
subversive actors influence, 93–94
"illegal" spying activities, 67–68
intelligence collection activity, 65
KHODOKI campaign, 61, 62–63, 70–92
Kremlin perception and strategic
goals, 63–70
"normalization" and permanent
occupation, 99–113
illegal agents role deepened, 102–3
KHODOKI operations, scaled
down, 100–1
"massive interference," 101–2
PROGRESS, lack of impact
from, 103–4
PROGRESS and a normalization
incomplete, 110–13
disillusionment with the reformist
leaders, 112–13
economic recovery from
1972, 112–13
PROGRESS campaign, 61, 62–63,
70–92
"Silent Invasion," commencing, 70–92
operational timelines, 71
training, 71
subversion and military force, 67
Prochizka, Jan, 72–73, 74
PROGRESS campaign, 61, 62–63, 70–92,
208
and a normalization
incomplete, 110–13

subverting government and civil
society, 81–86
established network of spies and
informers, 82–83
GROMOV agent, 81–82
GURYEV agent, 81–82
HUMINT collection, 84
KGB records on Czechoslovakia, 83*f*
SADKO agent, 81–82
YEFRAT agent, 81–82
YEVDOKIMOV agent, 81–82
Prykarpattyaoblenergo, 137
psychological vulnerability, 7, 21
public opinion, subversion influencing, 26
Putin, Vladimir, 121, 146–47, 177, 196
Python/TeleBot.A malware, 159

quality of subversion, 38–41, 57–59
continuity over change in, 57–59
independent and a complementary
strategic role, 57
secret exploitation and
manipulation, 57
subversive trilemma
persisting, 57–58
defining, 38–41
operational trilemma, 39
significant strategic value, 38–39
quantity over quality, 207–27

regime change, subversion in, 27
Russia's invasion of Ukraine, 2022, 174–
206. *See also* "hybrid war," Russia
against Ukraine (2013–2018)
BootPatch malware, 179–80
botched coup, 187–88
botnet operation, 181–82
CaddyWiper malware, 185–86
critical infrastructure sabotage,
196–201
attack enabled by territorial
conquest, 197–98
defacements, 178–87
distributed denial of service
(DDoS), 178–87
DNSs targeted, 182
economic and psychological (cyber)
warfare, 178–87

336 INDEX

Russia's invasion of Ukraine, 2022 (cont.)
  "HermeticWiper" malware, 183–84
  IsaacWiper, 184–85
  Katana malware, 182
  Kremlin perception and goals, 176–78
  October CMS exploited, 178–79, 180–81
  subversion in the service of force, 188–96
    AcidRain malware, 191
    KA-SAT disruption, 190, 191–92
  WhisperGate malware, 179, 180, 181
  WhisperKill malware, 179
  WhiteBlackCrypt, 179–80
  wipers, 178–87

sabotage. *See also* critical infrastructure sabotage
  curious case of the artillery, 167–69
  cyber operations best suited for, 46
  cyber versus traditional subversion, 135–53, 136*t*, 209–10, 219
  Kalynivka, arms depot explosion in, 150–53
  KGB operation in Greece, 27–28
  of a power substation in Germany, by a KGB agent, 23
  Russian-sponsored cyber operations against Ukraine in, 118
  Stuxnet operation, 10
  as subversive operations goal, 8, 26
  Ukraine's Ministry of Finance compromise (2016), 154–57
  Ukraine's power grid, 2–3
  Ukrtelecom disruption, 201
  "unknown unknowns" risk in, 34
  Viasat compromise, 201
Sagatelyan, Mikhail, 84–86, 87
Sandworm hacking group, 133–34
  economic warfare, Sandworm's pivot to scale, 153–67
  Sandworm I (2015 Blackout), 136–41 (*see also* 2015 Blackout)
  Sandworm II (2016 Kyiv Blackout), 144–50 (*see also* Kyiv Blackout, 2016)
  Sandworm III, (Ministry of Finance compromise, 2016), 154–57 (*see also* Ministry of Finance compromise, 2016)
  Sandworm IV (NotPetya and the limits of control), 157–64 (*see also* NotPetya malware)
  Sandworm V (BadRabbit), 164–67 (*see also* BadRabbit ransomware)
SCADA (Supervisory Control and Data Acquisition) systems, 138. *See also* industrial control system (ICS)
  GE CIMPLICITY HMI (Human Machine Interface) systems, 138
Sivkovich, Vladimir, 187–88
Smrkovsky, Josef, 84–86, 104–5
"social engineering," 44
social vulnerabilities, 7, 11–12, 21, 44, 52–53, 134, 137
speed, in subversive trilemma, 4, 12, 13*f*, 13–14, 35–38, 40–41, 42–43, 55, 56, 57–58
  BadRabbit operation, 172, 180–81
  control and intensity and, inverse correlation between, 36, 76–77, 95, 100–1, 179, 224–25
  in cyber conflicts, 57–58
  in fulfilling strategic promise, 99–100
  HermeticWiper, 183–84
  as key determinant of strategic value, 36–37
  KHODOKI operations, 61, 114
  NotPetya and the limits of control, 157–64
  power grid sabotage attempt in April 2022, 202
  in PROGRESS operations, 61
  Soviet Union over Czechoslovakia, 92–93
spies, 53
  advantages, 17–18
  cautions to follow, 33
  exploiting flawed security rules and practices, 23
  exploiting individual-level vulnerabilities, 23
  force and coercion use by, 23–24, 33
  illegals, definition, 67–68
  in PROGRESS, 102–4
  risks, 37
  as subversion key tool, 17–18, 23
  traditional subversion using, 11–12
  undercover spies, 26–28, 225

INDEX 337

stability and subversion, 207, 213
Stoltenberg, Jens, 190
Stuxnet, 10–11, 47–48, 52–53, 56, 146–47, 219
subversion. *See also* quality of subversion
   alternate explanations and limitations, 221–27
   basic conditions of, 31–34
      available target with suitable vulnerabilities, 31–32
      exploiting vulnerability without being discovered, 34–36
      subversive agent with suitable abilities, 32–33
   falters for Russia, 122–24
   force and warfare versus, 7
   influencing government policy, 26
   influencing public opinion, 26
   influencing target state's material capabilities, 26
   as an instrument of power, 5, 7
   limits of, 113–16
      constraints and trade-offs predicted by trilemma, 114
      dependence on vulnerabilities in societies, 116
      reliance on illegal agents, 113–14
      use of force, 114
   new possibilities and new perils, 207
   nonmilitary options as, 7–8
   offering strategic potential, 29
   and power, 17–41
   power through exploitation and manipulation, 21–25
   reduces cost of escalation, 29
   reduces follow-on costs, 30
   in regime change, 27
   in the service of force, 188–96
   speed, intensity, and control variables and, 35–37
   spies as key tools of, 23
   strategic potential in scholarship and strategy, 5–6
   strategic role and promise of, 25–31
   targeting systems, 22
   technological change changing, 5
   trilemma and strategic value, 31–38
   types of effects, 50
   undermining institutional effectiveness, 26–27
   use in invasion, 211
   in war, 174–206 (*see also* Russia's invasion of Ukraine)
subversive election interference, 2014–2015, 131–35
subversive trilemma, 11, 12–13, 13*f*, 16, 52–58
   limiting strategic value, 31–38, 90
   control over effects, 34, 104
   intensity of effects, 32–33
   in speed, 31–32
Surkov, Vladislav, 14, 123, 126
Surzhaninov, Vladimir, 71
Svoboda, Ludvik, 93–94, 105

tactical sabotage, 167–69
   Ukrainian D-30 artillery, 168
tactics, techniques, and procedures (TTPs), 54
technical vulnerability, 43, 44, 45, 52–53
TeleBots group, 141
Townsend, Sean, 148–49, 168
traditional sabotage I, 2015 Crimea Blackout, 141–44
traditional subversion, 3–4, 5–6, 8, 24, 55–56, 60–116. *See also* Prague Spring (1968–1973), crushing the
   vis-a-vis cyber-enabled subversion, 4–5
traditional versus cyber sabotage, 135–53, 136*t*
TRITON malware, 53, 55
Turchynov, Oleksandr, 152–53

Ukraine Cyber Alliance, 123
Ukraine's Ministry of Finance compromise (2016), 154–57
   power grid sabotage operation
      2015, 157, 159, 172
      2022, 202
Ukraine's State Service of Special Communications and Information Protection (SSSCIP), 179–80, 186, 189, 197–99
Ukrainian D-30 artillery and the tactical sabotage, 168
Ukrenergo, 143–44

Ukrtelecom disruption, 201
Umnov, V., 71

Vaculík, Ludvík, 81–82
Venediktova, Irina, 194–95
Viasat compromise, 201
Vltava radio station, 104–5
vulnerability
  in adversary systems, 41
  agents using, 24
  cyber operations exploiting, 43–44
  identifying, 12, 21, 31–32, 52–53, 80–81
  in information communications and technologies (ICTs), 43–44, 48, 49
  individual-level vulnerabilities, 23
  INDUSTROYER exploiting, 149
  NotPetya malware exploiting, 157–58
  in October CMS, 178–79
  psychological, 7, 21
  social, 44, 52–53, 134, 137
  sociological, 7, 11–12, 21
  software vulnerabilities, 46
  spies exploiting, 23–24
  subversion depends on, 31, 116, 129–30, 210, 226
  subversive operations using, 26, 39, 42
  technical, 43, 44, 45, 52–53
  of Ukraine, 140–41, 146, 156
  of VPN devices, 191
  zero-day, 138

warfare and diplomacy, 1–2, 19, 21
website defacements (Ukraine), 178–87

WhisperGate malware, 179, 180, 181
WhisperKill malware, 179
WhiteBlackCrypt, 179–80
world politics, power in, 18–20
world politics, subversion implications for, 211–21
  balance of power remains unaffected, 212–13
  destabilizing mass effects and systemic disruption risk, 215–16
  increases the risk of unintended/inadvertent escalation, 216–19
  stabilizes world politics, 213
  state–society and states–nonstate actors relations impacted, 221
  traditional subversion still more relevant in, 219–20

XData malware, 159, 161

Yakovlev, Aleksandr, 96
Yanukovych, Viktor, 117–18, 121–22, 124–26, 130
Yuryevich, Sergey, 123

Zatulin, Konstantin, 126
Zelenskiy, Volodymyr, 187, 194–95
zero-day vulnerability, 138
Zhivkov, 84–85
Zhora, Victor, 132, 133, 134, 148–49, 180, 186, 189, 202–205
Zpravy magazine, 104–5

The manufacturer's authorised representative in the EU for product safety is Oxford University Press España S.A. of El Parque Empresarial San Fernando de Henares, Avenida de Castilla, 2 – 28830 Madrid (www.oup.es/en or product.safety@oup.com). OUP España S.A. also acts as importer into Spain of products made by the manufacturer.

Printed in the USA/Agawam, MA
March 28, 2025

885041.012